*Caribbean Reasonings*

*Rupert Lewis and the Black
Intellectual Tradition*

**Other Titles in the Caribbean Reasonings Series**

*After Man, Towards the Human: Critical Essays on Sylvia Wynter*

*Culture, Politics, Race and Diaspora: The Thought of Stuart Hall*

*George Padmore: Pan-African Revolutionary*

*The Thought of New World: The Quest for Decolonisation*

*The George Lamming Reader: The Aesthetics of Decolonisation*

*M. G. Smith: Social Theory and Anthropology in the Caribbean and Beyond*

*Caribbean Political Activism: Essays in Honour of Richard Hart*

*Freedom, Power and Sovereignty: The Thought of Gordon K. Lewis*

Caribbean Reasonings
*Series Editors*
**Anthony Bogues
Rupert Lewis
Brian Meeks**

# *Caribbean Reasonings*

Rupert Lewis and the Black Intellectual Tradition

*edited by*
**Clinton A. Hutton, Maziki Thame
and Jermaine McCalpin**

IAN RANDLE PUBLISHERS
*Kingston • Miami*

First published in Jamaica, 2018 by
Ian Randle Publishers
16 Herb McKenley Drive
Box 686
Kingston 6
www.ianrandlepublishers.com

Introduction and editorial material
© Centre for Caribbean Thought, University of the West Indies

ISBN 978-976-637-950-6 (pbk)

**National Library of Jamaica Cataloguing-In-Publication Data**

Caribbean reasonings : Rupert Lewis and the Black intellectual tradition /
  edited by Clinton A. Hutton, Maziki Thame and Jermaine McCalpin.

  p. ; cm  - (Caribbean reasonings)
Bibliography : p. – Includes index
ISBN 978-976-637-950-6 (pbk)

1. Lewis, Rupert – Intellectual life
2. Lewis, Rupert – Political and social views
3. Black Nationalism   4.   Intellectual life
I. Hutton, Clinton A., editor.   II. Thame, Maziki, editor.
III. McCalpin, Jermaine, editor.

320.5    dc 23

All rights reserved. While copyright in the selection and editorial material is vested in the Centre for Caribbean Thought, University of the West Indies, copyright in individual chapters belongs to their respective authors and no part of this publication may be reproduced, stored in a retrieval system or transmitted in any form or by any means electronic, photocopying, recording or otherwise, without the prior express permission of the author and publisher.

Cover and book design by Ian Randle Publishers
Printed and bound in the United States of America

# Contents

Introduction   /**vii**
  *Maziki Thame*

Acronyms and Abbreviations   /**xiii**

1. UWI Mona and the Government of Jamaica, 1967–69   /**1**
   *Ken Post*

2. Jamaican Black Power in the 1960s   /**39**
   *Rupert Lewis*

3. Reflections on the Caribbean Radical Tradition:
   A Conversation with Professor Rupert Lewis   /**64**
   *Rupert Lewis interviewed by Jermaine McCalpin*

4. Radical Caribbean Thought:
   Rupert Lewis and the Politics of an 'Internal Dread'   /**83**
   *Anthony Bogues*

5. Edward Seaga and the Question of Levelling:
   Seeing Manley from the Other Side   /**97**
   *F.S.J. Ledgister*

6. Characteristics of the Grenadian Revolution and the
   Caribbean Situation   /**116**
   *Maurice Bishop interviewed by Rupert Lewis*

7. Blowing the Abeng:
   Rupert Lewis and the Rebuilding of Caribbean
   Socialism   /**137**
   *Paget Henry*

8. Echoes of the Bandung Movement in the Caribbean and
   China's Presence in the Region Today   /**162**
   *Rupert Lewis*

9. Quobna Ottobah Cugoano: Black Radical Heretic
   or Black Radical Liberal? /**172**
   *Charles W. Mills*

10. Jean-Jacques Dessalines and the Haitian Revolution:
    Global Agency of Universal Modernity /**191**
    *Clinton A. Hutton*

11. The Sett Girls and the Pedagogy of the Streets:
    An Aural Black Counterpublic /**207**
    *Linda Sturtz*

12. 'Sankofa':
    Garvey's Pan Africanism, Negritude, and
    Decolonising Narratives /**239**
    *Mawuena Logan*

13. Arthur Lewis: Mild Afro-Saxon or Militant Anti-Racist?
    Lessons from His Struggles and His Disparagement by
    Other Black Power Advocates /**250**
    *Mark Figueroa*

14. Memory Gems of Revolution:
    The Lived Experiences of Elean Rosalyn Thomas /**280**
    *Linnette Vassell*

15. Pedagogy and Leroy Clarke's Philosophy of Being,
    Freedom and Sovereignty /**297**
    *Clinton A. Hutton*

16. The Radical Aesthetic of Sistren Theatre Collective,
    Jamaica /**311**
    *Nicosia Shakes*

Contributors /**337**

Index /**341**

# *Introduction*

Maziki Thame

When asked by Jermaine McCalpin how he would define the Caribbean Radical Tradition, Rupert Lewis responded that it is about liberation, that the tradition

> is framed as an answer to the existential question of what it means to be human. This is above and beyond the ruminations of the liberation of the European person. What it means to be a human for peoples who have been defined as anything other than human requires more than philosophy; it involves praxis.[1]

The idea for the production of this volume came from Clinton Hutton, who posed in a Department of Government meeting at the University of the West Indies, Mona, the need for the Department to honour Professor Rupert Lewis with a conference on the occasion of his retirement and to publish a selection of essays from the conference presentations. The Department immediately embraced the idea and a core of its members – Christine Cummings, Clinton Hutton, Jermaine McCalpin, Dhanaraj Thakur and myself, almost all of whom were taught by Rupert Lewis, were in the vanguard of the organisation of a successful conference.

This volume began with the effort of colleagues at the University of the West Indies (UWI) and within the Caribbean diaspora (many of whom were also his students) to recognise the contributions of Rupert Lewis in the pursuit of Caribbean and human liberation. The idea of Caribbean liberation is not static and, while beginning with the enslavement of Africans racialised in the wake of European capitalist expansion, those who peopled the Caribbean have been faced with multiple types of dehumanisation in the process of becoming Caribbean that required them to imagine liberation in different ways. Lewis has been steadfast in working in the spirit of Marcus Garvey's idea that the emancipation of the body could be externally bestowed but that mental emancipation depended on black people's own agency.

Indeed, the two types of emancipation that Garvey spoke to were connected in ways that he did not imagine, and is a part of the struggle for liberation in the Caribbean present. We might think, for instance, of the ways women of the Caribbean have been perpetually required to face down attempts to reduce them to being bodies without agency or the politics around sexual agency in the contemporary Caribbean.

In his philosophy and practice of politics, Lewis has been centrally preoccupied with the trouble with blackness and with those at the bottom and faced with 'downpression'. The praxis of Rupert Lewis was seeking to radically transform Caribbean reality. Disappointment about the meaning of independence mobilised his generation, who believed they had the opportunity to remake the Caribbean, to reposition it in relation to its colonial and oppressive past. His ideas were shaped as part of the ferment of his time, coming of age and to activism as a student at Mona in the 1960s, he became part of the struggle for Black Power centred around Abeng and Rastafari. Lewis has remained rooted in Black Nationalism and his academic and life's work reflect that anchoring, influenced by his time with fellow travellers, spanning generation, including the second wife of Marcus Garvey, Amy Jacques Garvey, and Walter Rodney. His work on Marcus Garvey, Walter Rodney and the African-Caribbean experience are important sources for anyone wanting to understand how people of African descent have or might contend with the psychic and material challenges they faced in their past and present. Lewis is also a thinker on the political Left. His involvement in the politics of the Left that matured in the 1970s and 1980s can be seen as part of the alternatives created by the global Left during the Cold War, the African liberation struggles and in the aftermath of the Cuban revolution in the Caribbean.

This volume addresses those issues that Lewis has grappled with as a radical intellectual and activist. It does so by including not only academic papers but also personal reflections, which are acts of memorialisation that locate Rupert Lewis and his contemporaries in relationships cemented in the process of struggle and in making life in serious times. The first chapter is one such effort by Ken Post to record the memories of his two years in Jamaica in a time of protest at Mona and across Kingston, which brought him into activism alongside his students and colleagues. Post assesses the larger national context and his contradictory place as a white Marxist in the midst of 'Jamaican Black Power in the 1960s' (Rupert Lewis advances Post's telling in chapter 2). Linnette Vassell is also engaged in an effort to memorialise in chapter 14, 'Memory Gems of Revolution: The Lived Experiences of Elean Rosalyn Thomas.' She reflects on the life and meaning of Elean Thomas, who, with Lewis, was among the leaders of the Marxist-Leninist Workers Party of Jamaica. Vassell's telling of Thomas's journey introduces us to some of the leading women of the radical Left who sought to centre ordinary people in the politics of the 1970s and 1980s and who were mobilised around what it meant to be women in that struggle. Vassell declares her intention to make known those women who stood up for progress and on whose backs men's achievements have been made.

Politics on the Left is also explored by Rupert Lewis, Fragano Ledgister and Paget Henry. We saw it fitting to reproduce in this volume an interview Lewis conducted with Maurice Bishop in the period of the Grenada Revolution. The interview is a primary source which speaks to how the Left and vanguard politics of the Grenadian Revolution were being defined, what were seen as its challenges and how Bishop located the revolution in its time and place. We see through Bishop, the ever-present consideration of American interests in the region and how governments of the day and their opposition were responding to Reaganomics at the cusp of the neoliberal turn. Ledgister's 'Edward Seaga and the Question of Levelling: Seeing Manley from the Other Side' (chapter 5) examines the views of the leader of one such government, Edward Seaga, regarding the 1970s and specifically, Michael Manley, the leader of that process. In chapter 7, 'Blowing the Abeng: Rupert Lewis and the Rebuilding of Caribbean Socialism', Henry discusses Lewis's contributions as a figure who is both involved in the politics of Black Nationalism and the political Left and as an academic studying the conjunctures of race and class in the Caribbean. Paget Henry is also concerned to address the question of the future of black socialist transformation emerging out of the collapses within it, what he sees as Lewis's and others' retreat from it, and the crisis within global capitalism. Lewis himself considers this new juncture in chapter 8, 'Echoes of the Bandung Movement in the Caribbean and China's Presence in the Region Today', republished from *Inter-Asia Cultural Studies* (2016). He is keen to raise the race question at a defining moment of China's rise in the Caribbean and the world.

Anthony Bogues's (chapter 4) 'Radical Caribbean Thought and the Politics of an "Internal Dread"' advances the position that Lewis 'intervened', as it was the work of a radical intellectual to so do, through centering radical ideas in journalistic work – in *Impact*, *Bongo Man*, *Abeng*, *Struggle* and *Socialism* – newspapers and journals that served as an 'archive of Caribbean political thought'. Bogues draws mainly on the ideas of Sylvia Wynter to explore the meaning of Lewis's radical blackness, how it shapes his engagement with 'politics as practice' around the black experience and decolonisation. As a thinker on racial matters, as an 'internal Dread', Lewis dedicated much academic space to studying Garvey's philosophies and activism, making them available to Jamaican and global publics. It is therefore important that Mawuena Logan's '"Sankofa": Garvey's Pan-Africanism, Negritude, and Decolonising Narratives' (chapter 12) ties Garvey's idea of return to Africa to the Akan concept of Sankofa and to Negritude as ways of connecting the continent and its diaspora, its past and its decolonising future. Still on the matter of race politics and its discontents, Mark Figueroa seeks to repair the memory of W.A. Lewis, one of the Caribbean's foremost economists in 'Arthur Lewis: Mild Afro-Saxon or Militant Anti-Racist? Lessons from His Struggles and His Disparagement by Other Black Power Advocates' (chapter 13). Figueroa challenges the views on Arthur Lewis held by Black Power advocates of the 1960s within the Abeng Group (Rupert Lewis included). Rather than being the stooge of white imperialism they saw him as, Figueroa places W.A. Lewis in an anti-racist struggle, achieved through the example of his personal achievements in the positions he took in his own experiences with racism and in his engagement with the British Empire.

The chapters in this volume build on the tradition of Caribbean Thought, both in the study of thought expressed in written form, as well as through art. With respect to written traditions, in chapter 9, 'Quobna Ottobah Cugoano: Black Heretic or Black Liberal?', Charles Mills reviews Anthony Bogues's conceptualisation of black anti-slavery thinker Cugoano as a heretic and argues that Cugoano is instead a liberal, using the masters' tools to destroy his house. His essay speaks to the ways black thinkers have radicalised and emancipated white or Western political thought. Meanwhile, in chapter 10, 'Jean-Jacques

Dessalines and the Haitian Revolution: Global Agency of Universal Modernity', Clinton Hutton notes that Dessalines

> was, objectively, a central defining figure of modernity, despite the rituals of obscurity and marginality to which he was, and continues to be subjected, in the narratives of certitude spun in the epistemic and intellectual culture of occidental empireism, the assumed unimpeachable source of thinking, knowing and constructing meaning and certifying the nature of things.

Hutton further notes that narratives of the Haitian Revolution were, for the most part, 'constructed within an occidental epistemic culture which denied the existence of an indigenous/autonomous cognitive and intellectual agency in blackness and its pioneering role in raising a category of humanist values in modernity that would mark the genesis of the epistemology and culture of equality, justice and freedom as universal categories'.

Chapters by Clinton Hutton, Linda Sturtz and Nicosia Shakes advance ideas about how thought is embedded in art and how through these forms, we might appreciate the breadth and depth of a praxis of resistance existent in African diasporic life, including among women, the less studied subject of Caribbean thought. In chapter 15, Hutton looks at the 'Pedagogy and the Philosophy of Being, Freedom and Sovereignty in LeRoy Clarke's Art'. Specifically, he examines the anti-colonial and Africanist thrust of Clarke's art and its relationship to issues of self-identity. He categorises Clarke's work as being engaged in a project of decolonising the mind. Hutton is in the process of exposing the possible readings of Clarke's works and doing what he implores others to do, teach LeRoy Clarke. Sturtz's chapter 11, 'The Sett Girls and the Pedagogy of the Streets: An Aural Black Counterpublic' focuses on how Sett girl bands 'functioned as an aural counterpublic' and created a 'trickle-up, de facto Pan-Africanism' during the period of plantation slavery in Jamaica. Sturtz argues that the Sett girls' practices of dance and song critiqued their social context and those in authority and were acts of agency where women decided how they ought to be represented in spite of the limitations of their world. Nicosia Shakes considers the relationship between art and women's political activism in chapter 16, 'The Radical Aesthetic of Sistren Theatre Collective, Jamaica'. She conceives of Sistren's theatre as a transgressive feminist force but also as engaged in a creative process that emerged from and was community forming for its women. Its use of collectivism, orality and 'subversive movement', she argues, forms part of the development of a distinctly Jamaican theatre aesthetic that is also importantly, political.

The chapters of this book were, for the most part, papers first presented at a conference held in honour of Rupert Lewis in October 2013 at the Mona Campus of the UWI. The publication is in recognition of Lewis for his work in guiding and building the Department of Government at Mona, the Institute of Jamaica and its African-Caribbean Institute of Jamaica and the Jamaica Memory Bank division, and the making and institutionalising of Liberty Hall, the Museum of Marcus Garvey, as well as his contribution to Caribbean public life. Rupert Lewis served as faculty in the Department of Government from 1972 to 2012 and was a key figure in defining its character and its engagement with the Caribbean public. His scholarship advanced theoretical understandings of the Caribbean and moved many undergraduate students in his courses in Caribbean Political Thought and Garveyism to go deeper. His effort to better understand the region was also importantly pursued with former members of the Department – Anthony Bogues and Brian Meeks – in establishing the Centre for Caribbean Thought. The Centre's Caribbean Reasonings Conferences led to the series of Caribbean Reasonings publications of which this volume has become a part. To honour Lewis through the conference and this volume is part of the effort to see to our liberation.

**Note**

1. Jermaine McCalpin, 'Reflections on the Caribbean Radical Tradition: A Conversation with Rupert Lewis.'

# *Acronyms and Abbreviations*

| | |
|---|---|
| AES | American Economic Association |
| AIB | Asian Infrastructural Bank |
| API | Agency for Public Information |
| AWOJA | Association of Women's Organizations of Jamaica |
| BBC | British Broadcasting Corporation |
| BPO | Business Processing Outsourcing |
| BITU | Bustamante Industrial Trade Union |
| CAF | Central African Federation |
| CAFRA | Caribbean Association for Feminist Research and Action |
| CARICOM | Caribbean Community |
| CARIFTA | Caribbean Free Trade Association |
| CBI | Caribbean Basin Initiative |
| CDB | Caribbean Development Bank |
| CDC | Colonial Development Corporation |
| CEAC | Colonial Economic Advisory Committee |
| CEDC | Colonial Economic and Development Council |
| CIA | Central Intelligence Agency |
| CSJP | Citizens Security and Justice Programme |
| CTC | Cultural Training Centre |
| CWC | Central Water Commission |
| CWP | Committee of Women for Progress |
| DAWN | Development Alternatives for Women of a New Era, Caribbean |
| EEC | European Economic Community |
| FCB | Fabian Colonial Bureau |
| FCBAC | Fabian Colonial Bureau Advisory Committee |
| GDP | Gross Domestic Product |
| GDR | German Democratic Republic |
| GNP | Gross National Product |
| GRC | Grenada Resorts Corporation |
| HTCG | Hannah Town Cultural Group |
| IAFE | International African Friends of Ethiopia |
| IASB | International African Service Bureau |
| IMF | International Monetary Fund |
| ISER | Institute of Social and Economic Research |
| ITU | In-service Training Unit |
| ITUAC | Independent Trade Union Action Committee |
| JAMAL | Jamaica Movement for the Advancement of Literacy |
| JDF | Jamaica Defence Force |

| | |
|---|---|
| JIS | Jamaica Information Service |
| JLP | Jamaica Labour Party |
| JPC | Joint Policy Committee |
| JSD | Jamaica School of Drama |
| JUS | Jewish Union Society |
| LCP | League of Coloured Peoples |
| LPAC | Labour Party Advisory Committee |
| LSE | London School of Economics |
| MNIB | Marketing and National Importing Board |
| NAACP | National Association for the Advancement of Coloured People |
| NGO | Non-governmental Organisation |
| NCB | National Commercial Bank |
| NDTC | National Dance Theatre Company |
| NIEO | New International Economic Order |
| NITEP | National In-service Teacher Education Programme |
| NJM | New Jewel Movement |
| NWA | Negro Welfare Association |
| NWU | National Workers Union |
| OPEC | Organization of the Petroleum Exporting Countries |
| OWP | Organisation of Women for Progress |
| OWTU | Oilfield Workers Trade Union |
| PAJ | Press Association of Jamaica |
| PNM | People's National Movement |
| PNP | People's National Party |
| PPP | People's Progressive Party |
| PRG | People's Revolutionary Government |
| RCG | Rockfort Cultural Group |
| SCM | Student Christian Movement |
| SOAS | School of Oriental and African Studies |
| STC | Sistren Theatre Collective |
| TURL | Trade Union Recognition Law |
| UCWI | University College of the West Indies |
| UKNA | United Kingdom National Archives |
| UN | United Nations |
| UNIA | Universal Negro Improvement Association |
| UNDP | United Nations Development Programme |
| UWI | University of the West Indies |
| WAND | Women and Development |
| WBRAP | World Bank Research Advisory Panel |
| WC | Women's Committee |
| WIGUT | West Indies Guild of University Teachers |
| WLL | Workers' Liberation League |
| WMR | World Marxist Review |
| WMWJA | Women's Media Watch of Jamaica |
| WPJ | Workers Party of Jamaica |
| WTO | World Trade Order |

# 1 | UWI Mona and the Government of Jamaica, 1967–69

Ken Post

Readers of this chapter expecting the kind of academic piece usually presented at conferences may be disturbed by the personal nature of what follows.[1] The point is that it is based on my own experiences during the period in question, during which Rupert Lewis was a student at Mona, indeed, one of mine. We shared the experience, therefore, of that most unusual event, the direct confrontation of the University and the Jamaican government, into which I hope to give some insights.

The basic proposition to be examined is that the period in question was one in which Jamaicans at the lower social levels were politically mobilised to a greater extent than ever before, even during the major labour disturbances in 1938, and that UWI managed to get itself caught in the reaction of the government of the day to this phenomenon. This was because the student body itself had become radicalised by the same forces affecting the masses.

I went to the Mona branch of UWI, which then numbered around 2,000 students, in time for the beginning of the academic year 1967–68. I was scheduled to spend three years in all as a Lecturer in Political Science, on secondment from the University of Manchester, ironically, as it happened, as part of the British government's aid assistance to Jamaica.

**Mona in Context: Jamaica in the Late 1960s**

One basic determinant of the society within which this story must be set is expressed in an essential set of statistics. Whereas in Nigeria, where I had lived for a total of four years and done my first research, the key population statistic was the tribal breakdown, in Jamaica it was the racial one. The 1960 census had recorded 76.8 per cent as 'African' and 14.6 per cent as 'Afro-European', with the rest divided among various ethnic categories, most importantly East Indians, Chinese and Europeans.

Both of the two main categories, together over 90 per cent, were direct descendants of the slaves captured in Africa and shipped across the Atlantic under appalling conditions.[2] The presence on the university campus of a ruined aqueduct which had once supplied the Mona plantation served as a reminder of this past. Hopefully, in this day and age, it is unnecessary to dwell on the enormities of the slave trade and of slave production on plantations, a sort of mega-crime perpetrated by Europeans and white Americans from the mid-sixteenth to the mid-nineteenth centuries.[3] The point for my story is that this experience had shaped the society and mentality of the vast majority of Jamaicans alive when I arrived, and would continue to do so. I was thus inserting myself as, at least on the surface, a white descendant of the slavers.

As for relations among Jamaicans, the historical background of white masters' sex with African slave women and the relative statuses of whites and blacks had produced a set of magic markers which were used to establish social status. To put it simply, even in the mid-twentieth century the more Caucasian physical features you displayed the higher up you were likely to be in the class system. This meant that, especially at the middle and upper levels, there was an almost obsessive concern with skin colour, hair texture, facial features and even the characteristics of fingernails. Claims to be white were judged by these, and usually the verdict was that it was only a case of 'pass for white'. Conversely, blackness, tightly curled hair, 'African' features and some kind of fingernails (I was never sure which) marked you immediately as peasant or working class. Most of my Jamaican (and other West Indian) colleagues were light brown, although by the time I lived in Jamaica the class bounds had to some extent overridden the markers. There were 'African' businessmen, senior civil servants and lawyers, for example, but in no way proportionate to their census numbers.

In terms of the Jamaican economy, after slavery came to an end by Act of Parliament in August 1838, former slaves either went off to become independent peasants, who above all developed the original basis for the banana trade (before the plantations), or were forced to work as cheap wage labour in sugar. This kept the economy going, at a fairly low colonial level, until the Second World War, with many Jamaicans going off to work abroad, particularly on building the

Panama Canal in the early twentieth century and on Cuban sugar plantations up to the early 1930s. Others went to the US, but to Britain in large numbers only from the early 1950s. By then, some light industry was being established in Jamaica, but sugar and bananas were still important in the late 1960s. However, Jamaica had also become the world's largest producer of bauxite, the basis for aluminium, with the mines owned by US and Canadian capitalists. Another important development since the Second World War was tourism, with 345,300 visitors in 1966.[4]

I will come to the crucial link between the Jamaican economy, the issue of race and class and the radicalisation of politics in the mid-1960s. Here, I should set in place my work at Mona, which brought me into contact with students like Rupert. I was teaching two undergraduate courses and leading a postgraduate seminar. One of those for the bachelor's degree was in African politics and government, the other was in 'Modern Political Thought'. My seminar was on theories of political analysis. At Mona, I attempted to do what I always did as a university teacher, make it clear from the beginning that students should always keep it in mind that, as a convinced Marxist, I had my own positions, which would become clear, and they should therefore pay special attention to the literature presenting other standpoints.

The Political Thought course was the one which basically linked me to the wider political world in Jamaica, because I brought in writers like Frantz Fanon and the Black Power intellectuals in the US, such as Stokely Carmichael. Books by the latter group were in fact banned in Jamaica, so I had to tell my students that this part of the course was optional and would not be examined. I never noted any falloff in attendance for those lectures. Incidentally, I later heard that my course booklist was the first item in my police security file, compilation of which, as I shall later explain, was part of the reason that I never in fact got my third year at Mona.

I remember two of my undergraduate students who were to be especially involved in the events at Mona to which I am moving. Rupert Lewis was a black Jamaican and very bright but rather intense, highly political. Ralph Gonsalves was a light-skinned man (actually of Portuguese descent) from the eastern Caribbean island of Saint Vincent and in 1968–69 President of the Mona Guild of Undergraduates, the students' union.[5]

At this point, it needs to be noted that female students were few and far between in those days. I do not have actual figures, but there would have been only a couple of hundred in the whole university. I did have some in my undergraduate classes, like Rosina Wiltshire from Trinidad, who was later to become the head of the United Nations Development Programme in the Caribbean.

During my two years at Mona, I was blessed with a very good group of students in my postgraduate seminar, hoping to get a master's degree and then (most of them) go abroad to do a doctorate. Some of them later told me that I came over as a rather too demanding figure at our first group meeting, but we soon settled into friendly interchanges. Here, I must single out Robert 'Bobby' Hill, with whom I was to become close in terms of political activities. Light-skinned, he was from an elite Jamaican family, although two of his uncles had been leaders of the pro-Communist activists in politics and union affairs in the late 1940s and early 1950s. The family tradition of radicalism had continued in him.

Some comments are needed on my staff colleagues, especially those who were to play roles of one kind or another in the events of October 1968 and thereafter. Professor Gladstone Mills (who in those days preferred to be called Charles), was the Head of the Department of Government, to which I was attached. In the all-pervading racial terms, he was the son of a policeman, but that fairly low social level was balanced by a genetic inheritance of a quite light skin. Then in his late 40s, Charles had been a senior civil servant until 1960, when he moved over to his university chair. Logically, he taught public administration. I have a problem in commenting on him. He was in effect my boss at Mona, and this was to lead in time to a mutual wariness. In his 1994 memoirs, he described me as 'larger than life', which is fine, but in his account of the events with which I am concerned paints me as a villain, responsible for one of the three worst experiences of his life.[6]

In the same department was Archie Singham, who was the most colourful of my Mona colleagues. He was a Tamil from Sri Lanka, so with a relatively dark skin, but his other magic markers did not fit into the Jamaican scale. Lower class Jamaicans sometimes located him as a 'coolie man', a descendant of the nineteenth century Indian immigrant indentured labourers. Highly intellectual, dynamic and witty, it was not surprising that he was influential in circles beyond the

Department, beyond the Faculty, even beyond the University. He had not finished his doctorate, but instead turned his extensive research on Grenada into a thick book, *The Hero and the Crowd in a Colonial Polity*, published in 1968.

As for other colleagues, in either the Faculty or attached to the Institute of Social and Economic Research (ISER), I especially remember three economists, all from Jamaica, George Beckford, Norman Girvan and Owen Jefferson. Jefferson later left academic life to become a prominent public servant, eventually Chairman of the Export-Import Bank. Norman, an expert on the bauxite industry, was very bright, energetic, a thoroughly agreeable man. 'G Beck' was a more complex figure. Darker than the others on the marker scale, and from a lower class background, his concern was with the historical origin and subsequent development of what he termed 'plantation societies'. I always got on well with him, but had the feeling that, deep down, he did not really like white people. I once saw him, when rather drunk, having to be restrained from physically attacking a white lecturer whose latent racism had emerged as he also imbibed. Sadly, Beckford died, aged only 54, in 1990.

In October 1968 began the events which were to affect students and staff at Mona, catching us all unawares. I had returned from long vacation leave early in that month and resumed normal teaching, which was soon to be dramatically interrupted. Some understanding of how Jamaican politics worked, and of general sociocultural developments, is necessary here to complete the scene for this paper's focus.

**The Political and Social Context**

Out of the 1938 Labour Rebellion had emerged the major leaders and the linked trade union federations and parties which still dominated in the late 1960s. Alexander Bustamante had led the Bustamante Industrial Trade Union (BITU) and the Jamaica Labour Party (JLP), Norman Manley the National Workers Union (NWU) and the People's National Party (PNP). 'Busta', although 'pass for white', had based himself in the black working class, aided by his remarkable ability to tune into the thinking and idiom of the lower levels. It was typical of his self-projection that the union bore his name. By 1967 he was out of active politics. Manley, a light brown eminent lawyer and actually distantly related to his opponent, was still active. Originally, and still in some of its rhetoric, the PNP had been more 'socialist' in its approach than the labourist JLP, but neither had considered any real break with capitalism, and by 1967 were in no sense radical, although the PNP still, uneasily, retained on its left the Young Socialists, now purged of its most radical members.

The political system of Jamaica, which became independent on August 6, 1962, had remained (and still remains) closer to the British 'Westminster' model than the Nigerian one which I had studied and written on, which broke down already five years after independence. This was above all manifested in the alternation of the two main parties in power won through elections. You might say that, given the British 'first-past-the-post' system, in which total votes cast do not necessarily match up with total seats won, the Jamaican electorate has occasionally been wise – or fickle – enough to shift allegiances in sufficient numbers to give the current opposition a majority. Where the governing party won again, 'gerrymandered' constituency boundaries were sometimes a factor. Interestingly, in its reports back to Washington the US embassy noted this, and the general deviation from the Westminster model, including an absence of true freedom of the press.[7]

Another important element in Jamaican politics was the use of governmental power to pass out benefits to supporters in key areas, basically through job-schemes for the unemployed and access to new housing projects. A major factor here was the concentration of the population in the Kingston area, in the late 1960s around 380,000 people, nearly a fifth of the Jamaican total and increasing each year by migration from the rural areas.

That phenomenon of urban concentration brings us to the fact that, precisely in the years I lived in Jamaica, the system was facing its greatest challenge since 1938. The basic reason can be summed up in some statistics. In 1967, it was estimated that 90 per cent of Jamaican households were trying to live on less than £300 a year. Unskilled and semi-skilled workers might be making around £4 10s. a week and casual labourers and domestic servants getting £3 if they were lucky. A quarter of a million members of the workforce earned less than £1 a week.[8] Some 81 per cent of National Income went to 40 per cent of the population. The mass upsurge of discontent based on the sad condition of most people, above all in Kingston, which got under way in 1966 and peaked in 1969, really shook and worried the ruling elite which split its control between the two parties. The unrest was what Marxists would see as class struggle, but importantly was expressed in discontent based on a feeling of a profound disadvantage experienced by black people. Of course, the two identities very closely overlapped, but it was the one based on race which was dominant in people's minds.

Old-style Marxists would have seen this as a case of 'false consciousness', which meant that workers and peasants failed to develop a 'true' class awareness and act accordingly. I would suggest that it was more complicated than that. If we take it that every person carries around a bundle of identities – gender, race, class, religious, national and generational – which are varyingly brought into play in different situations (sometimes in combination, like 'black woman'), then in Jamaica in the late 1960s class consciousness was present but, from a more sophisticated Marxist point of view, was being displaced onto race, religion and generation.[9] In the next discussion, therefore, it must be kept firmly in mind that, in identity terms, I am an elderly, white, reluctantly British, atheist, middle-class male. I will do what I can to present the upsurge of the above all black Jamaican masses, but this must necessarily be limited by my own 'markers'.

Let us begin with the class aspect, which I am best equipped to handle. By 1967, economists estimated that up to 20 per cent of the potential workforce was unemployed, making control of access to jobs by the BITU and NWU, often through deals with employers, very important vehicles of party patronage, but alienating those who remained workless. Made more complex by the activities of a third union central, the Trade Union Congress, whose leadership stood somewhat to the left of the PNP, industrial strife had peaked in April–June 1966, involving, among others, dock workers, postal workers, construction workers, hotel staff and teachers. A particularly ominous aspect was the frequent violent clashes between rival union/party gangs and them and the police. As the campaign got under way for the February 1967 election, the political side of the street-fighting became predominant.[10]

Although the strikes and disturbances affected Montego Bay, the sugar plantations and other areas, it was developments in Kingston which were the key to the peak events in October 1968, and moreover involving generational and racial issues rather than class ones directly. It was in West Kingston that things were in fact brewing. Beyond the city centre new housing developments like Tivoli Gardens (controlled by the JLP) petered out into a mishmash of streets and compounds in various stages of decay and squatters' areas dotted with shacks, with water supplies and sanitation what you would expect from this. Similar conditions on a smaller scale existed to the east of the city. Those newly moving in could do little but pile up in these areas, places like Trenchtown, Back O'Wall and the Foreshore Road, which was forcibly cleared in June 1966 to make way for an extension of the docks. With about one in five of the potential workforce unemployed at any one time, an official report in 1969 was to recognise that most people living there could reckon on never being regularly employed. They 'scuffled', doing anything, legal or illegal, to live from day to day. In the case of the regularly employed in Kingston, it was difficult to organise them, since this was not a 'proletariat' working in large units like plantations and mines; the biggest single employer in the city was in fact the University, with 927 non-academic staff.

Among the intermittently employed and unemployed, two groups in particular are important to the story, the 'rude boys' and the Rastafarians. The former was a self-identification by young men in the age range roughly 15–25 who saw themselves as rebellious and confrontational. They were also macho with regards to women, although in this, reflecting general Jamaican male attitudes. To them, girls were 'ting [thing]' or 'beef'.[11] Many of them belonged to gangs with names like the Blue Gang, the Vikings and the Roughest and the Toughest, which were often involved in various kinds of crime and also provided strong-arm groups for the politicians. However, the violence they wreaked with 'ratchet' knives and sometimes guns was most often random and on one another. In the popular song by the Slickers, 'Johnny Too Bad', the hero was depicted as 'Walking down the road with a ratchet in his waist/Robbing and stabbing and looting and shooting.'[12]

Of course, not all the rude boys were violent. Moreover, by 1968, they were beginning to become politically aware. As one of them put it, 'We no longer going to hold our brothers and sisters up because they haven't got what we want. What we want is this, equal rights and justice.' Joining violence and politics, the ska number 'Dreader Than Dread' called for revolution, urging 'Stand fast together and unite'.[13]

The rude boys and Rastafarians overlapped sociologically but, at least originally, not ideologically. The latter were a much older phenomenon, beginning in the early 1930s as a movement emphasising African origins and, centrally, the importance of Ethiopia.[14] Their name, in fact, was derived from that of the Emperor Haile Selassie of Ethiopia before he was crowned in November 1930, and the central tenet of the faith was that he was the Living God. It followed that the basic need was to return to Africa, the ancestral continent and the divine seat, while in the meantime rejecting the values and way of life of Jamaican society as 'Babylon'.

Over time, the Rastafarian movement, originally basically peasant, tended to move with the migrants into the towns, above all Kingston, and, with expansion to include tens of thousands of believers, it differentiated internally. The most devout lived in their own communities, such as the Disciples of the Great King and the Sons of Negus Churchical Hosts, and the men did not shave and grew their hair long enough to make into the now well-known 'dreadlocks'. The devout had strict rules on diet and behaviour and developed their own form of Jamaican English (already evolved beyond the colonial language), marked by such usages as 'I and I' for 'we', with doctrinal justifications, sometimes complex, for these. Rasta doctrine was in general impressively elaborate.[15] They also used 'ganja', the local term for marijuana, as the 'Wisdom Weed', capable of producing enlightenment. Some at least of these basics were shared by a much wider range of the poor, including those who regarded themselves as Rastas but shaved and cut their hair in order to get jobs.

The Rastafarian movement's influence therefore became extended over many more people than were actual members. For example, the growing, selling and possession of ganja were in fact illegal, and with increased penalties since November 1964, but its use was also extensive among the rude boys. The linkages were reinforced by the sharing of popular music forms, in the '60s marked by a move from 'mento' to 'ska' to 'rock steady' and then 'reggae', changing in rhythm and tempo. Numbers like 'Beardman Ska' and 'Babylon's Burning' directly reflected Rasta doctrine.

Yet another body of ideas became widely generalised from the mid-60s and fused with rude boy rebelliousness and Rasta concern with Africa and the fate of black people, namely the teachings of Marcus

Garvey (1887–1940). A black Jamaican, in 1914 he had founded the Universal Negro Improvement Association (UNIA), which, however, really got under way after he migrated to the US. At its peak, its branches among descendants of African slaves may have numbered eight million members, subscribing to the message of racial pride, African unity and black separatism. It is scarcely surprising that the white US Establishment moved against Garvey, and his poor business sense in running the UNIA's Black Star shipping line, which was meant to bind African people together, gave an excuse to jail him for fraud from 1923 to 1927. Returning to Jamaica on his release, he was not successful in getting a political party off the ground and moved to London, where he died in 1940.[16]

There can be no doubt that Garvey was the key figure in launching what became the Black Consciousness Movement, the US version of which had, crucially, moved over into Jamaica by the late 1960s. Above all for the Rastas, but having wider reverberations because of the general revival of black consciousness, a great impetus was given by the state visit to Jamaica of none other than Haile Selassie in April 1966 as part of a wider Caribbean tour. An estimated 10,000 Rastafarians greeted their God on the runway as he stepped from the plane at Palisadoes airport, among other things terrifying its staff, as one of them later told me, with the thought that the dedicated smoking by many of the ganja 'spliff' raised the chance of a fuel explosion. In a speech to the Jamaican legislators the emperor repeated the Garveyite message of the unity of all people of African descent.[17]

The political implications of the visit became apparent as the light-skinned politicians vied to be presented to him and having almost literally to rub shoulders with black Rastafarians like Mortimo Planno, a leader important to the story because he was one of a minority of his faith who advocated engagement in local politics. This became for some the idea of 'building Africa in Jamaica' rather than returning.

The majority of Rastas were now in a sense caught in a contradiction, which one can see in a broadsheet issued in April 1968 by Ras Dizzy, a self-described 'journalist and poet' who was in fact in contact with UWI circles. On the one hand, he wrote that 'I am too continuous to turn I back on I Fathers continent...Too proud in dignity to walk and beg, too wise to gaze in the sky for God and too true to accept Babylon Blue eyed God.' On the other, he demanded his Human Rights and asked 'How long must I continue before the head of Government stop treating I with psychological victimization and spite and ignore I.'[18] Short of a massive migration back to Africa, the redemption of the Rastafarians, and of the poor in general, seemed to be in the hands of a government which was in no way sympathetic to demands from them for rights or major policy changes. That was confirmed when in April 1967 the JLP was again returned to power with an increased majority.

When in power earlier, the PNP had actually considered sponsoring repatriation of those who wished to leave, appointing three academics from UWI in 1960 to write a report on the Rastafarian movement, with that possibility in mind. These were M.G. Smith, whose work on the plural society was basic for sociological analysis of the West Indies, Rex Nettleford, a leading figure in UWI's extra-mural programme, and Roy Augier, professor in Caribbean history. Given their mandate, there is a certain irony in the fact that Mike Smith could be described as 'pass-for-white', Rex was light brown [ed. note: black, actually], and Roy, a short jolly man, was from St Lucia, characteristics which seem to remove them from the world which they were now called on to investigate. Their report advocated better integration of the Rastafarians into Jamaican society, but also a mission to Africa to investigate the chances of repatriation for those who wished to leave. In fact, neither of these things was seriously pursued by successive governments.

The immediate reason for appointing the UWI commission was the repatriation movement led by the Reverend Claudius Henry, not a Rastafarian but self-styled 'Repairer of the Breach', who had sold tickets to thousands of people which he said would entitle them to leave for Africa on October 5, 1959. Nothing happened, but six months later he ended up in prison, charged with storing arms for a rebellion; he was said to have written to Fidel Castro, who had just taken power in Cuba, asking for help. While he awaited trial, Henry's son Ronald and a group of Black Power militants came in from the US and, armed with automatic weapons, tried to take over some Rastafarian rural camps, presumably as a base for armed insurrection. In June 1960, the police and military (still British troops) attacked their camp, but some of the rebels escaped, killing two soldiers on the way, and were only captured six days later.[19] Ronald and two others were later hanged and Rev. Henry was sentenced to ten years in jail.

The point about this affair is that, already before independence, it raised the spectre of armed rebellion for the business and political elite, and this was sustained in April 1963 by the Coral Gardens incident, in which armed Rastas attacked a petrol station and then fought with the pursuing posse of civilians and police, two of whom were among the total of eight dead.

There were no more major incidents, but police harassment of people in Kingston continued through the time of my coming to UWI, including of well-known figures like Prince Buster, owner of a record shop and recording studio. As Mohammed Ali, he had become a follower of the Black American Nation of Islam and was raided in May 1968.[20] Less prominent black people could expect to be beaten by the police, (who cynically called their batons 'rock steady', after the popular music, because they made victims dance), or even shot without warning. It is scarcely surprising that the celebration of 1968 as the international Human Rights Year attracted attention, as in the cited statement by Ras Dizzy. A rally on August 4 at the Marcus Garvey Shrine in downtown Kingston called for 'full freedom of expression for the Black Man' and the lifting of the ban on US Black Power literature.

All of the above was the background to the events on October 16, 1968 which were centred on the University. As a whole, UWI was not integrated into Kingston life; the five miles between campus and city were a major breach. The Guild of Undergraduates had tried to organise discussions downtown under the title 'University Students Speak', but this was very limited. On the other hand, on the campus itself the US radicals had adherents grouped as the Black Power Movement, with aims including 'To reject white cultural imperialism' and 'To seek to ensure the rule of Blacks in a black society'. My students Edwin Jones, Rupert Lewis and Richard Jacobs were among its activists.[21] Another was Garth White, a student specialising in sociology and cultivating contacts in the Kingston slums among the rude boys. It is worth noting here that the basic external influence on UWI students was the movement in the US. The May 1968 events in Paris, spearheaded by Sorbonne students, did not affect them as they did others in Europe.

As far as I know, no students were Rastafarians, at least to the point of outer distinguishing features, but there were sympathisers. One university link with that world was Ras Dizzy, who I have already mentioned. On one occasion a Rastafarian group was invited to give a performance at the Senior Common Room on their ritual drums, which were made of wooden staves covered with goatskin. The event went well, but the evening turned ugly, actually after the performance finished, when a rather drunken white faculty member insisted on trying to play a drum, offensive enough to our guests, but then actually broke it! Jamaican staff eventually calmed them down.

The main UWI link with downtown in 1968, especially with the more political Rastas and rude boys, was an individual, Walter Rodney, a young Guyanese. After gaining a first-class degree in history at Mona he went to do postgraduate work at London University. I had met him there at a seminar in May 1966, where he presented a paper arguing that slavery had not existed in West Africa before the coming of the Europeans. (Editor's note: Rodney's University of London PhD thesis (1966) does discuss domestic slavery in the Upper Guinea Coast, 1545–1800.) After getting his doctorate shortly thereafter, he had gone to teach at the University of Dar-es-Salaam, in Tanzania, but was persuaded to come to UWI in January 1968 to launch a new course in African history. Very soon, he began to teach off-campus as well, to groups of the more politically-aware youth, on black consciousness and the history of black people.[22] I remember once meeting him as he hurried to another of these 'groundings' and saying, jokingly, 'Ah Walter, off to denounce me again?' He asked me what I meant, so I pointed out that I was white, and he assured me that not all whites were bad. I always found him serious but likeable.

Inevitably, the security police took note of Walter and the government decided that he was a real threat, involved in a seditious conspiracy based among Rastafarians, Kingston youth gangs and the followers of the Reverend Claudius Henry who, released from prison, had reorganised.[23] On October 15, 1968, when he arrived back at Palisadoes airport after attending a Black Writers' Congress in Montreal, where he read a paper on 'African History in the Service of Black Revolution' he was detained and sent back, in effect deported.[24] The news had an instant impact on the Mona campus, where he had been popular beyond the Black Power activists, although I was not the only one surprised by the extent of the reaction.

**Mona in Ferment**

At about nine o'clock on the morning of Wednesday October 16, I was woken up by a banging on my ground floor bedroom shutters and a female voice (I never knew whose) crying 'Ken, Ken, the Revolution has started!' I had, unusually, been at the Bamboo Club, my favourite downtown haunt, on the Tuesday evening (as opposed to Saturday), and, having no morning classes scheduled, had allowed myself to sleep late. When I emerged, somewhat hung-over, from the flat, it was to find that a group of students had taken over the main administrative building, while a larger one had left at seven o'clock on a march into Kingston to demonstrate about Walter's banning. Some staff had joined them, notably George Beckford and Norman Girvan, but I had not heard about the plan. All other staff could do was wait to see what happened to the marchers.

Beginning in the early afternoon, groups of them started to straggle back, often shocked by what had happened to them and some injured. Sympathetic staff tried to calm them down and patch up minor wounds, while sending the worse cases to the University Hospital.

I never did know how many of the students marched, but it must have been several hundreds. Ralph Gonsalves and the other Guild of Undergraduate leaders had moved fast overnight to organise them, appointing marshals and emphasising the need for 'discipline and order,' especially since 'Other Brothers and Sisters sympathetic to Dr Rodney's cause are expected to be present.' To mark themselves off, the marchers were instructed to wear their academic gowns, while at the same time wetting strips of these to use as masks was part of the advice given in case tear gas was used.[25] It was this part of the instructions which proved most relevant.

Already when beginning to march along Aqueduct Road, which ran through the campus, the column came up against the Jamaica Constabulary, suggesting that the authorities had been tipped off by telephone. There was even a machine gun mounted on the aqueduct which spanned the road. However, the police were apparently unsure what to do and allowed many marchers through, while others slipped round the roadblock and joined them. Not much further along the planned route the first tear gas was used, and then more tear gas and batons came into play as part of the now split-up column moved on down Hope Road, passing the Governor-General's residence. By then sympathisers were offering water for impromptu face masks, and by the time the marchers reached downtown Duke Street, members of the general public, notably poor youths, were joining them. At the Ministry of Home Affairs, Ralph Gonsalves and George Beckford were admitted to see the minister, who agreed to meet university representatives on Friday.

With some success thus gained, the marchers then moved off to rally at the East Race Course, but it was at this stage that things began really to go wrong. At the Bustamante Industrial Trade Union (BITU) headquarters, an attack with stones was launched on the column from inside the building. The culminating rally was in fact in King George VI Memorial Park, at which George Beckford urged against replying to such actions with return violence. However, the police really stepped in, with tear gas and baton charges. It was then that marchers were injured and the students dispersed.[26]

While they straggled back, a full-scale riot got under way downtown, beginning with youth groups chanting 'Black Power' and attacking buildings, vehicles and the police. Foreign-owned businesses like Barclay's Bank and Pan-American Airways, and local enterprises like Marzoucas Stores (Lebanese-Jamaican), Uncle's Inn (Chinese-Jamaican) and Jamaica Mutual were targets. Extensive looting, some organised, took place, focused on places like Woolworth's and the Bata Shoe Store. They had of course been closed, but an ingenious method was found of breaking them open, by commandeering municipal buses and backing them into the plate glass windows. Fighting between rioters and police continued and Jamaica Defence Force (JDF) armoured cars were deployed to overawe the former. Two men were killed during the day, one shot, presumably by the security forces, and another electrocuted by a severed power line.[27] A curfew and further deployments of security forces kept incidents to a very few next day, although Uncle's Inn, a popular restaurant, was now burned down, and they finally petered out.

On the evening of the 16th the trancelike state which had settled on the campus was dispelled by a mass meeting, which I of course attended. I don't remember who spoke, but I am sure Ralph Gonsalves and George Beckford would have been prominent. As was to be expected, speech after speech attacked the authorities, and then we, typically for academics, passed a motion. I don't directly remember, but it looks as if I may have proposed it, since, scribbled in the inside cover of my pocket diary of the time, I find a three-part draft text condemning the exclusion of Walter, the police attack on the students, and the 'threat to the continuing functioning of the University'. The last part was to be made complete during the night. The meeting broke up late in the evening and we dispersed to our beds (or perhaps other peoples') in a cathartic state. When we awoke next morning it was to find that the continuing functioning of the University had now been radically affected, since the campus was surrounded by soldiers of the Jamaica Defence Force.

We stayed shut in for the next five days, and during that period the university community was in effect divided in two. Quite a number of students who wished to go home were allowed to leave the campus. I have no figures or numbers, but it must have been a fair proportion, and my impression was that it was often those from wealthier families, who would not have been sympathetic to the movement. Those who remained were open to pressures from the government on one side and the student militants on the other, and it is relevant here that the university authorities had in the past been against student marches, for instance forbidding one in late 1965 to protest the white takeover in Southern Rhodesia.

On the one side, therefore, we had the staff who wanted to manoeuvre the University out of the siege. Unsurprisingly, this included the Vice-Chancellor, Sir Philip Sherlock, and the Finance and General Purposes Committee (F&GPC), and senior staff members like Douglas Hall, the leading professor of history, Charles Mills and, perhaps rather ambivalently, Rex Nettleford. I had not actually met the Vice-Chancellor. Now 66, he was a very light-skinned Jamaican with long experience in education, who had taken an interest in popular culture. He had been at the Cabinet meeting on October 14 which had decided to exclude Walter, but was now in a tricky position, caught between the government and the radical students.[28] On the afternoon of October 16 the F&GPC had suspended all teaching, which in effect ratified what had already happened, and the next day Sherlock announced that further marches were forbidden, but lawful means to make the University position clear to the public were permitted. A Joint Policy Committee (JPC) of senior university officials and representatives of the campus branch of the West Indies Guild of University Teachers (WIGUT) and the Guild of Undergraduates was set up to manage the situation.

In fact, another march would have been impossible, because outside the gates there were soldiers with rifles and submachine guns and even armoured cars with manned machine guns. To call this a 'siege' would be somewhat misleading; food and drink were allowed in, and individual students and academic and non-academic staff (but not other individuals) were permitted to go in and out. A major concern in the next days was controlling activity on the campus side of the gates, which were major assembly points for the other pressure point of the campus situation, the militant 'Black Power' students. They had originally built barricades on the campus side, and even when these were cleared groups would assemble and shout insults at the soldiers. Each gate had been placed by the JPC under the control of a Faculty, and Social Sciences actually had the main one, on Aqueduct Road. I took my turn at supervising what was going on there, which often meant persuading the radicals not to abuse the soldiers. I was on their side, but had the vision of some young nervous soldier being pushed into waving his gun and accidentally – even purposely – pulling the trigger, with tragic consequences.

During those days, tension was mounting, not helped by the Prime Minister, Hugh Shearer, who in a broadcast on October 18 noted, among other things, that 'over the past few months the University Campus at Mona has developed into a hot-bed of anti-Jamaican organization.' Walter Rodney, he stated, and other non-Jamaicans, allied with local individuals, some from outside the University, had given the lead to this.[29] The press, which in effect meant the right-wing *Daily Gleaner*, was also pushing this kind of line. Attempts to put the University point of view were therefore very necessary. The JPC attempted this through a broadsheet printed at the University Press called *Comment At Mona*. Contributions from the public were invited, but the problem was to spread copies.

That was also the case with the publications being produced by the radicals, on commandeered university mimeograph machines amid a haze of ganja smoke! (I seem to remember Rupert being one of those involved.) One example of the products was entitled 'Subversion in High Places' and focused on increasing US control of Jamaican resources and training of the security forces, and on ministers' self-enrichment. Using popular dialect, it attacked politicians who 'talk bout black dignity, but yet unoo piss pon it every day. Unoo call Bredder Garvey, hero, yet unoo a trample upon Black man so!' Garvey was duly quoted, in an attack upon 'traitors of their own race' who oppressed the poor. Although sympathetic staff, and some of their wives, smuggled such literature out in their car boots, it is extremely unlikely that many copies actually circulated downtown.

Amid all this, faculty members had to take sides. Above all, the 'New World' group, to which I will come later, which includes people like Norman Girvan and G Beck, was working with the radicals, among whom were numbered many of my own students and myself. Other whites kept their heads down, most of them, I am sure, were not sympathetic with the radicals.

In the end we lost. Vice-Chancellor Sherlock made a deal with Shearer, presumably undertaking to keep better control if the troops were withdrawn. Significantly, in a speech to the University on the afternoon of Monday, October 21, he distinguished between freedom of expression and subversion. He ordered the staff and students back to work, and although the radical students, supported by some staff, including myself, tried to call a strike, this lasted only another day. The JDF moved out, and it was clear that the majority of students were tired of the stress, and most staff had simply kept their heads down and waited for the crisis to pass.

Of course, the campus was never going to be the same again. For one thing, the University now became a major target for the politicians and their press outlets. As in 1938, the people in power never really lost overall control; in Marxist terms there was no revolutionary, or even pre-revolutionary, or even pre-pre-revolutionary situation. Nevertheless, the ruling elite were badly shaken and focused their ire on the University. Edward Seaga, Minister of Finance and Planning, questioned the role of the University as a centre for the whole English-speaking Caribbean (except Guyana, which had had its own university since 1963). According to him, it was 'sapping some of the nationalism that Jamaican Youth required and needed to take them towards a development of their country.' In the face of continual denunciation in the *Daily Gleaner* and its companion, the *Star*, the radical students, for example a group calling itself Africa Youth Move, kept up the publication of broadsheets, which were also passed downtown.

Seaga, who was to have an influence on my own activities although I never met him, was a trained anthropologist and regarded as an authority on Jamaican music. He had been one of the first commercial record producers. As Minister of Development and Welfare in the 1962–67 government he pushed for the expression of Jamaican culture, including ska music, and started the annual Jamaica Festival.[30] Representing a constituency based in Tivoli Gardens, he pushed a populist and nationalist line, reflected in his new speech. Now he was denounced by the university radicals for his partly Syrian descent and hypocrisy in selling out to 'the rising flood of U.S. domination' while presenting himself as spokesman for Jamaican nationalism.[31]

In December a new 'journal of African Youth', *Bongo-Man*, appeared, edited by my student Rupert Lewis and deliberately taking its title from the elite's disparaging term for the black person. The contents of its first issue give a good idea of the student radicals' thinking. It reproduced the paper presented at the Montreal conference by Walter Rodney and a talk on the implications of his banning given by C.L.R. James, the veteran Trinidadian Trotskyist who, after a brief participation in Caribbean left-wing politics in the late 1950s, had returned to his self-imposed exile in Britain, his main base since 1932.

'Bongo Rupert' contributed an article on 'Marcus Garvey and the Damned', linking Walter's ideas to that basic figure (on whom later, as an academic, Rupert was to become an authority) and other radical writers like George Padmore and Frantz Fanon (who he would have encountered in my lectures). As the unifying theme he took Walter's comment on the role of post-colonial politicians as 'the representatives of metropolitan-imperialist interests' which were 'white-racist oriented'. In another piece 'Bongo Peter' revealed the division among students. He denounced 'certain members of the Academic staff and well-established student leaders' as causing the main body of students to abandon the struggle in October and 'white informers' as working to keep the campus struggle separate from the popular one. 'The students', he wrote, 'called a mint of meetings and agreed upon as many resolutions', but these were all ineffective. The University, in fact, had always been elitist and cut off from the people, as in its refusal to rent its unused land to workers to raise food.[32]

This was one of the few class references in these discussions, and Marxist ideas were notably absent; black consciousness was the basic theme. The Rastafarians were represented but on a rather low level, as when Bongo Peter unconnectedly ended his article with 'Give thanks to God, Jah Rastafari.' A piece by Ras Dizzy, who was about to be gaoled for nine months for assault, was reproduced. By the standards of nowadays, women's special struggles were markedly absent, although one female student did call on her sisters to abandon the straightening of their hair.[33]

The radicals' statements also did not come to terms with the form of future action. Bongo Rupert had spoken of 'confrontation' and Bongo Peter in his conclusion denounced those 'who just want to sit on their fat bombos and live good life' as 'blood-clates' and quoted Bob Marley and the Wailing Wailers – 'who you gonna turn to? Babylon burning ....' An article in *The Truth* I have just cited saw 'the logic' of the oppression of the poor as the necessity to fight back.

Clearly, given the nature of the Jamaican social system and its government, the issues of the necessary form for struggle and its organisation were now on the agenda in UWI radical circles, and how this came to express itself will be the major focus from now on. However, personally, through December 1968 and into January, I was absorbed with immediate problems which took my mind off long-term political organisation.

On Thursday, December 12, *Scope*, the Guild of Undergraduates journal, carried the headline 'Yet Another Crisis Ken Post May Be Deported'. At the beginning of the month, the news had been passed to the university authorities that I was scheduled to be the first case under a new deportation law, which would replace the old colonial one, which could not be applied to actual British citizens. It was a time for divided emotions – of course, given that Jamaica was now independent, they should no longer be privileged, but why me first? Of course, deportation was in no way comparable to imprisonment, but it would be really inconvenient and also return me to Manchester, where I had problems with my head of department.

The question that still interests me is, why was I picked out as the second dangerous university staff member after Walter? Clearly, I was an unlikely candidate for preacher of the Black Power line (although in fact I broadly supported it). Presumably, my course reading list had a lot to do with it. Interestingly, during one of his attacks on the University as a hive of subversion the political commentator in the *Daily Gleaner* had referred to an unnamed lecturer who had recommended banned books. In addition, I was also a comparatively easy target, since the JLP government, which had flirted with the black consciousness position, could portray me as a white man and citizen of the country which had been the colonial oppressor.

The deportation move had another dimension, involving no less than the Ministry of Overseas Development in London. The key here is that my job was financed by them. Anyway, the Jamaican security people sent a copy of my file to the Ministry, I presume through MI5, their British counterparts. The civil servants then contacted the Department in Manchester, and also the University's Vice-Chancellor, with the message, in effect, 'get that bum out of there!' So, in early December, my Manchester colleague, Bill Tordoff, turned up to take me home. At least, that is how I read Manchester's preference, although the Vice-Chancellor's message through Bill was that it was entirely up to me to decide and there would be no negative repercussions if I stayed, which was very decent of him. On the other hand, there was a certain ambiguity about the position relayed by Bill, since it was promised that Manchester would provide a suitable replacement if I was actually deported. In other words, the action would have been taken as in effect correct.

Bill was a nice man and clearly found his mission embarrassing, and I'm afraid I treated him rather badly, in effect casting him in the villain's role. This was especially notable at a meeting of Social Science Faculty staff and students at which I was at my posturing best/worst and Bill had to sit and listen and then present the Manchester position. Mine was that I wasn't leaving voluntarily. As *Scope* reported it, I announced that I would remain at my job 'and face whatever consequences may be coming'. At the same time, and here I think my better side came out, 'Mr. Post warned the students against doing anything rash about his case but, instead, to treat it as a further educative illustration.' I asked that there should be no demonstrations on my behalf, since that would have brought in the police. Of course, there was another reason which I did not make public, namely to avoid a split among the radical students, assuming that a demonstration was actually proposed, with the harder Black Power militants unwilling to back a white man.

So I stayed, and Bill went back to Manchester with my answer. In fact, after quite a brief period, the news was passed to me that, although the Jamaican law would be changed, my immediate deportation would not follow. Apparently, the Prime Minister, Hugh Shearer, had been persuaded that the ejection of a British citizen would be a bad idea when he was scheduled to go to London in January to attend a meeting of Commonwealth leaders. Notably, the argument had been made by none other than Edward Seaga, who was considerably smarter than Shearer, a former BITU leader who always struck me as not the brightest wolf in the pack. Seaga, who as an intellectual liked to keep a line open to the University, then informally relayed the news to the university authorities and so to me.

However, it was not long before an even gloomier future opened up before me. The news reached some Faculty members that seven people were about to be arrested and charged with seditious conspiracy. I was never sure of the exact list, but it seems that six were in fact from the University: I believe it was Norman Girvan, George Beckford, Clive Thomas (a radical Guyanese economist) and myself from the staff and my students Bobby Hill and Rupert Lewis. The seventh, from outside, was I think Hugh Small, a young lawyer who had been active in the human rights movement. The way in which we heard of the government's planned action was through none other than Norman Manley, founder of the PNP and former Prime Minister. Apparently, the senior, currently opposition, politician had been asked by Hugh Shearer whether he would make a political issue of the planned trial, and had said no, not if the accused had been plotting against his country. However, he then passed on the news to those of the suspects who had been active in the PNP.

Let me make it quite clear that such a conspiracy did not exist, and what bound us together was dislike of the system from various points of view. It looked as if the security police cobbled together a list of known radicals. The supposed seditious group never even got together for mutual support, partly because that would have given the security people further grist for the plotting mill. (This is why I am not entirely sure who my supposed co-conspirators were.) Doubtless, each of us had at times remarked to one or more of the others that things needed to change radically, but getting together had not happened. I had never even met Small (and never did). Notably, I was the sole white (although Clive was a non-Jamaican), and I can only suppose that I was cast as the link person to 'international Communism'. By the way, in case it is not entirely clear, I would certainly have supported a popularly-based movement to overthrow the Shearer government!

I cannot recommend the experience of waiting to be arrested and put on trial for something which in theory could have earned us long prison terms. One of the things you can expect, if you have friends like mine, is bad jokes, such as 'Don't worry Ken, you'll probably get sent to a prison farm, which will be healthier.' Another tip would be to keep a bag permanently packed with things like toothpaste and toothbrush and a change of underclothes, so you can grab it immediately as they take you away. In my experience, the single most unpleasant aspect is the effect it has on your sleep. Expecting the police will come for you at the traditional early hour, you wake up every time a car pulls in close to where you live. The fact that my flat was on the ground floor, with an open space next to my bedroom where I and other residents parked, did not help here.

Christmas 1968 remains an almost total blank in my memory. I can only suppose that copious Red Stripe flushed me through the toilet bowl of trepidation. Shortly after it, to adapt a remark by Friedrich Hegel, my personal history shifted from potential tragedy to farce. The news was leaked to us that the government had decided not to go through with the trial. Looking back, it may well be that they were never truly serious. After all, what real case for an actual conspiracy could they have made, given that Jamaican courts were still not directly politically controlled and we would have had good lawyers? In addition, there would inevitably have been international attention and some bad publicity. The idea may just have been to scare us, which at least in my case worked.

Once recovered from that, my reaction to the government's threats was 'If those fuckers want to make my life difficult, I'll try to do something bad to them.' The key issues, it seemed to me, were organisation and appropriate action in late 1960s Jamaica. Already earlier in 1968 I had got off my fat bombo and begun to involve myself in leftist activity, and what is more, outside the University, working with a group which stemmed from the Unemployed Workers' Council, the most radical Jamaican working class organisation, with a leadership heavily influenced by Marxist ideas. That, however, is not relevant to this paper, which is concerned with the radicalisation of the campus and what it did to its relations with the Jamaican government (and always remembering that we are looking at the background to Rupert's university career). Here, my own contribution was the work I did with the new radical weekly newspaper, *Abeng*, launched in February 1969 and based at Mona.

The basic impetus for this came from people who had been part of the group which ran the quarterly *New World*, an important focus of radical intellectual discussion for the West Indies as a whole and, unusually, taking an interest also in developments in Puerto Rico and the Spanish-, French- and Dutch-speaking parts. The group was of course interested in developments in Fidel Castro's Cuba, and in 1965 the Jamaican government had withdrawn the passport of George Beckford for visiting it. G Beck was a very important member of the *New World* group and other active participants at Mona included Norman Girvan, Owen Jefferson, Steve de Castro and Wilfred Beckles.

The journal had begun to appear in mid-1963, then based in Guyana, but a political crisis there caused suspension of further publication until late 1964, and was now based at Mona. A rather heterogeneous range of contents did not permit a consistent ideological position, and some activists, including former members of the Jamaican Young Socialists, tried to push the journal into a more openly left position. Others, notably Lloyd Best, a lecturer in economics at the Saint Augustine campus in Trinidad, opposed the 'activists' and criticised 'the populist obsession of the Mona contingent'. He believed in the on-going effect of critical discussion within existing institutions.[34]

It seems fair to say that, although it continued to appear, by late 1968 *New World Quarterly* had passed its peak. Moreover, the level of discussion in it had usually been highly intellectual, even abstruse. For both reasons, and because of its spread of connections through the Caribbean, it was not suited to give any lead to a Jamaican popular movement, which is where *Abeng*, the new weekly newspaper, came in.

As was explained in the first issue, on February 1, 1969, the new paper's name came from that of the horn historically used for communication by people in the interior, especially the Maroons, the escaped slaves who had fought several wars with the British colonial forces and eventually were recognised as a self-governing community. It was promised that, while examining what was wrong with Jamaican society, 'the newspaper will invite the views of everyone'. The second issue gave it what was to remain the basic slant, by adopting the front page slogan 'We want our people to think for themselves,' a quotation from Marcus Garvey. In fact, the first issue had already set the tone by attacking the Prime Minister for subservience to Britain, revealing the harmful effects of government area redevelopments, and attacking police actions against youths and their treatment in the courts.[35]

The first issue also carried an article on the situation in Southern Rhodesia by 'Omo Ogun', first of a regular column on African affairs. The writer was in fact me, using the name of the Nigerian Yoruba war god as a pseudonym. The first piece called for armed struggle against the Smith government, and the tone of my contributions remained radical. I was even later told that some middle class readers found my comments too radical, even too 'Black', which, given my own racial identity, I found especially pleasurable. I was in fact the only white person working on the paper.[36]

I was not part of the central planning group, composed of academics and others from the city. By early March there was a formal Editorial Committee, composed of G Beck, Bobby Hill, Rupert Lewis and Horace Levy, a lecturer in sociology who was later to become an expert on the Kingston slums. My role was as a foreign sympathiser and so properly peripheral to policy decisions. I wrote for the paper and, like others, contributed money now and again to keep it going.

Duly registered under the Companies Law, *Abeng* appeared on Saturdays and was priced at six pence, actually rather expensive for its target audience. Printed on very cheap paper, despite the group's ambitions it never managed to exceed four pages. Since contributors were not paid, the biggest single cost was for printing, done by a small downtown firm whose owner actually made it clear that he was not really in sympathy with the paper's aims, but felt that all views had a right to be heard. Some commercial sympathisers did pay for advertisements, like Herbie's Snack Counter, offering curry goat among other delights, and notably Prince Buster, the recording studio and record shop owner.

Distribution was not a major cost, since the core group undertook this themselves. Late on Friday evenings they would load bundles of the week's issue into their cars and set off to all points of the island to deliver them or else leave early next morning, in any case devoting much time and petrol to the effort. I only got involved in this once, since it would have been bad public relations to have a white man seen delivering a Black Power paper. I also only had to deliver downtown, to Prince Buster's Record Shack, which distributed to the actual vendors. Another such Kingston centre was the bar owned by Bongo Neville, who earned police harassment as a result.

Elsewhere, distribution had to be based on whatever local sympathisers could be found. The first editorial promised that local committees, 'independent of existing political parties and commercial interests' would be set up to provide a basis for investigations and reports, which would also have greatly facilitated distribution and sales. These did come into existence in some places, but there was never a full supporting organisation.

Some idea of the difficulties of distribution and sales can be gained from a report by one of the central group from off-campus, Dennis Sloly, a young lawyer active in the human rights movement who was responsible for raising money for the paper. (Shortly after writing it, he was tragically killed in a car accident.) He had taken 400 copies of the March 21 issue to Montego Bay, but managed to distribute only 222. He had tried to make contact with individuals suggested as distributors by others, offering 25 per cent commission. Some already established distributors had not been very successful; one had received 200 copies each of the first and second issues and sold only 88 and 98 respectively. The hostility Sloly encountered from youths wearing Black Power insignia was doubtless due to his status as a 'pass for white' individual, since he reported that they became friendly when they learned he was from the paper.[37]

Despite such difficulties, the success of *Abeng* must be emphasised. In its first March issue it announced that the print run had now reached 10,000 and appealed for financial support to enable an expansion to eight pages, giving room for more adverts. As already noted, this never occurred, but by the paper's last months the print run was up to 15,000 and for one issue 20,000. The point here is that, not only was this remarkable for a radical paper managed, as it were, on the hoof, but each copy would almost certainly have been read by more than one person, and even by a literate to a group of illiterates, multiplying its influence. The paper's sounding of the horn would also have been increased by the local Abeng Assemblies which were held in towns across the island. It was in effect a tribute to the paper's impact that already in mid-March reports began to come in of police harassment of its street-vendors.

All this was achieved by a great deal of work by a few people, who of course were at the same time doing full-time jobs, but it was a problem for *Abeng* that its activists were divided among various ideological positions. There was a group like George Beckford, Norman Girvan and Dennis Sloly who might be described as Jamaican nationalists inclined to the Black Power stance, who were socially radical. Then there were fellow intellectuals, but also others on the distribution side, all the way down the social scale, who were in essence Black Power advocates, which in Jamaican conditions also necessarily made them radicals. Linked to this position, but made distinct by doctrine and way of life, were the politicised Rastafarians like Mortimo Planno.

Then there were the Marxists, sympathetic to the black consciousness position but concerned above all with the class struggle, which in Jamaican conditions was of course integrally linked to the racial one. In fact, the Marxists were represented at the paper's centre by just one person, Bobby Hill, of course with my support and occasional advice, so little influence could be exerted on content. This was in spite of the fact that it was Bobby, aided by the paper's one paid employee, Norma Hamilton, who had the onerous task of putting together each issue. In that sense they were the actual editors.[38] The replacement of Horace Levy in early March on the Editorial Committee by Trevor Munroe, a committed Marxist who had just returned from Oxford, where he was working on his doctorate, did not shift the balance. In fact, as Bobby once despairingly explained to me, the contents of each issue and the relative prominence given to articles often became a struggle between factions. The Rastas were not above appearing at the printer's workshop and demanding a change favourable to their standpoint as the actual production was in progress!

In practice, class struggle was not ignored and sometimes featured prominently, as in articles supporting various strikes. Emphasis was placed on the control of great stretches of land by the sugar producers at the expense of poor peasants and other negative aspects of the industry. The Bauxite Company profits were revealed, with a demand for the establishment of a state processing plant, as in Guinea, which meant more proceeds would remain in the country, and the industry's downside was further featured.[39] Also relevant to the contemporary class struggle were references which were quite often made to the events of mid-1938.

Understandably, considerable attention was paid to persecution of Rastafarians, as happened, for example, during a police sweep in mid-March in West Kingston, when one target was the camp of the well-known figure Prince Edwards. Sacred drums were destroyed, dreadlocks forcibly cut off and individuals beaten with the 'rock steady'.[40] Periodically, Rasta leaders contributed articles and letters, as in mid-April by the well-known Ras Negus.

Support for student struggles was given, as at the Jamaica School of Agriculture. This was also extended to West Indian students abroad, like those at the Sir George Williams University in Montreal in their dispute with the authorities in February–March 1969. Conversely, women's issues got little attention. There were only stray items, like a picture of a female student with an Afro hairdo in the March 1 issue, with a promise of a series entitled 'Black is Beautiful', which did not in fact materialise. However, two weeks later a manifesto did appear, calling for full rights for women, including control of their own bodies, for performance of domestic tasks by men, and for special women's organisations. In Jamaica's male chauvinist society this was revolutionary. However, when the women's issue was raised again, two months later, it was in a different way, by 'Sister Gate', who urged that the 'black Mother' should 'return from the sea of Mini, Wigs, false pride' and turn to Jah Rastafari.

Of course, *Abeng* rejected the Jamaican political system and its parties. It headlined its report on the contest for successor to Norman Manley as the PNP leader in April, which his son, Michael, won, as between 'Black Dog' and 'Monkey', borrowing metaphors from a proverb to mean 'the same'. The political system was correctly depicted as expressing a basic economy controlled by foreign interests. A particularly vivid depiction of this came in my favourite photograph, reproduced from a tourist trade publication, which showed a big, fat, white woman, fortunately dressed in a frock, not a bathing suit, *standing on the shoulders* of a small black man, each smiling broadly although one can safely assume with different degrees of sincerity.

Nevertheless, in my view there was a weakness in the paper's political stance, in that no line was taken – indeed, one could not be taken because of internal divisions – on alternative political organisation and action. In fact, I would dare to say that the most consistent line was taken in my 'Omo Ogun' column, revolution and armed struggle. That was of course in the context of African affairs, but with heavy hints that it should be generalised. In terms of Jamaica, the *Abeng* position was, in retrospect, more realistic, namely, that the task was to make the voice of the poor consistently heard, and it must be recognised that in less than a year, the paper certainly did that. Each issue contained, for example, a 'Sufferer's Diary' recounting someone's personal experiences, and the readers' letters column, 'Blow the Horn Tell the People', served the same purpose.

Reviewing the full span of issues, it can be seen that the Black Power position increased in strength in the paper's columns. From the beginning, passages from Garvey's writings had been reproduced each week, and pieces by Walter Rodney were periodically reprinted. On March 28, the first appeared of what became regular columns by Minister Cecil X, the leader of the Nation of Islam, a Jamaican offshoot of the US's radical Black Power organisation. At the end of May a very significant letter was published, from Bongo Jere, a well-known young Rasta, in which he reproached the paper for not specially celebrating the recent Africa Day and focusing on Labour Day, 'which disenchants black people'. No other 'collegiate' could match up to Walter Rodney, he wrote, and the intellectuals must appreciate that 'the Black Mass is ideologically, culturally and organised-wise ahead of the theoreticians', who needed to catch up.

Although the next issue continued to feature the struggle of sugar workers, it also devoted a full page, a quarter of the total, to reprinting an article by Huey Newton, leader of the US Black Panthers. Significantly, the editorial called for a worldwide revolutionary struggle, but not in Marxist class terms; the aim was unity of black people everywhere and 'a complete breakup of the white power structure'. On June 14, the inside pages reflected the opposition of tendencies, with one basically devoted to an article on '100 Years of Workers Struggle' and the other to one by Marcus Garvey Jr., the founder's son, who lived in Jamaica. The next issue continued the same mixture, but swung the balance to

Black Power with a reprint from the Panthers' Eldridge Cleaver and an article entitled 'Black Man Time Come Beware Black Traitors!'

On May 3 and 10 my column did not appear, but resumed on the 17th. It was missing again on the 24th, but that issue featured the first of two articles marking the anniversary of the labour uprising in 1938 by 'Historian', who was in fact me. Bobby got them in, to give the leftists a voice, and they were among the longest which ever appeared. The articles were based on a paper I had given at the Department of Government's annual rural weekend outing some time before. Rereading them, I think I should have done more to make the analysis readable by a non-academic audience and more political, in the sense of relevance to the present.

My undoubtedly relevant Africa column was now finally dropped. I do not know why, but it must have been linked in some way to the paper's increasing 'black' content. Looking back, I think that Trevor Munroe may have been involved here, since he was the university core group member to whom I was less close; indeed, he didn't know me at all and I had no real contact with him. I have mentioned him as a Marxist. However, on his arrival at the beginning of 1969, having to his great chagrin missed the events of October 16 and after, he established himself at the centre of things by putting himself forward, not as a Marxist, but a Black Power adherent.

Early in February he gave an open lecture at the University, which I did not attend but later could read the reprint in *Bongo-Man*, which had strongly backed *Abeng* from its launching. Rejecting a 'sterile terminological dispute as to what Black Power means exactly', Trevor defined it as 'the ability of black sufferers to control their environment in the interests of their own humanization.' In an unashamedly academic presentation, he took the materialist line that the economy was the key. However, his central theme was to distinguish between authority, which black individuals might have through the political system but wield on behalf of outside – by implication white – interests, and Black Power, true control of one's own life. The task, he concluded (and not ruling out violence), was to begin to organise, to be ready 'when the means of arriving at consciousness are suppressed, as they inevitably will be'.[41]

Where this links up with me is his remarks on 'the white revolutionary', who might sympathise with the Black struggle. Trevor's position, emphasized in the printed text, was that such a person must 'KEEP OUT'; 'his business is not to hang around black people as if they were exotic curios or to enter the dungle to do good works', rather, he must 'be our fifth columnist in the cocktail party circuit'. Frankly, I found these remarks unrealistic and even offensive, but the position obviously touched a chord in the audience. A note to the *Bongo-Man* text recorded that in the later discussion one audience member 'mentioned that the cardinal function of the white revolutionary was to make revolution in his own country.' So, although I later got to know Trevor and had great respect for him because, on into the middle 1980s, he worked tirelessly to maintain a Marxist, not Black Power, position in the union movement and the Workers' Party of Jamaica he founded, he seems well-cast as the influence to get me out of *Abeng* and into cocktail party – or at least Red Stripe drinking – white circles. In later encounters with him I always found him friendly but seemingly holding something back.

Maybe I am being paranoid. In any event, I was in effect out of *Abeng* from mid-May. Pressures were now beginning to take their toll on the production group. Part of these must have been sheer exhaustion, which would be one reason for devoting much space to reprints rather than original analyses. There was also the perennial problem of funds. A new appeal for financial contributions was now appearing, and in the final week of June a major blow was struck at the paper when, a few days before it was due to go to press, the print shop was completely burned out. This was the owner's reward for his liberal views! When you factor in the delay in the arrival of the fire service, a reasonable assumption might be that this was a case of arson by government supporters. The *Abeng* directorate scurried round and found another printer, and the week's issue did appear, but the need to continue paying a commercial printer made such costs central.

On August 2 (after I had left the country) an editorial statement on the front page, 'Our Present Position', declared that the paper 'has reached a crossroads' and was unable to continue without an immediate injection of £500. Each issue was costing roughly £180, mostly printing costs since the work on contents was done free of charge, and the great weakness was lack of its own press. Setting up one would cost much money, and in the meantime donations, even small ones, were called for, and an appeal was also made for distributors and vendors to pay what they owed. Of course, in Jamaican conditions these solutions were impossible. No wealthy person would put capital into such an enterprise, the black poor could never provide enough even to meet weekly costs, and the necessities of scuffling explained why even vendors spent all the sixpences they took, without remitting the paper's cut.

Disarray and competing ideological tendencies may have accounted for the comparative lack of attention which the paper paid to the incident when, early in September, the government repeated its exclusion technique with another Guyanese teacher at Mona, Clive Thomas. This was met with student protests, but this time about 20 demonstrating at a cocktail party on the lawn of Seaga's house, not by a mass march. Clive, a Marxist, had contributed very little to the paper, by my count only one short piece, and had not been part of the nuclear group.[42]

*Abeng* finally died with its 34th issue on September 27, having failed to appear in the previous week. As it explained, that issue had already been printed when it was discovered that its reprint of an article by a black American Maoist, Robert F. Williams, was forbidden by the laws inherited from the colonial period, under which his magazine, *The Crusader*, had been banned. It was decided not to risk having *Abeng* shut down in consequence. In any case, it had now shot its radicalising bolt.

In the two last issues in August 'Blackman,' who was now a prominent contributor (and may have been Trevor Munroe), called for 'the politics of movement', turning away from the JLP and PNP, but rejected the idea of forming an actual party to compete with the others. Of course, the JLP as a party and the current government was interested in what *Abeng* had been saying, and I have already noted harassment of various kinds, although not of the key activists at the University. They were indeed convinced that they were followed when they drove off campus, and may well have been. I never noticed this myself, but should record, if only for comparative purposes, that the Jamaican security police, unlike their Nigerian counterparts whose attention I had earned during my time there, seemed to have learned the basic trick of using two cars and randomly rotating these as the direct follower, so that the subject is less likely to notice what is happening. Again, I don't know if Mona phones were actually being tapped, but they might well have been, and in any case confidential matters were discussed outside, although that severely limited range of contact! I remember attending a meeting at which the possible role of a police informant on *Abeng* matters, someone outside the campus, was discussed, and one option seriously put forward was killing him. Being soft intellectuals, our final consensus was to give him a warning to stop.

The general political situation on campus continued to be volatile, with the radical students, like those who ran *Bongo-Man*, primed for new action. Some individuals were also active off-campus, serving as DJs at downtown dances and even as far off as the Clarendon sugar-country, of course playing records which would foster black consciousness. On at least one occasion students did take politics downtown, and I was central to this.

In March 1969 a crisis in the small island of Anguilla, in the Eastern Caribbean, outraged radical students. For administrative convenience, the British government had grouped it with two others, St Nevis and St Kitts, but a majority of the 5,000 or so inhabitants wanted a separate status, and their political movement took control of the island. The answer of the British Labour Party government when negotiations failed was to send parachute units! (Incidentally, they were not resisted.) With some of the Mona campus activists, naturally predominantly from the Eastern Caribbean, I planned a demonstration at the British High Commission. An extra personal dimension, of course, was that, as a British citizen, this was my own diplomatic representative and would have been required to intervene had I been arrested in the previous December. That's called biting the hand that might have fed you....

In fact, the Rodney demonstration experience had taught us that if you just made a noise in the street the police would attack you, so I planned an occupation of the High Commission's offices. This was to be only for a few hours, with the knowledge that the police would gather outside but, for diplomatic reasons, only enter if invited. My plan was to have the students withdraw through the police cordon, with just myself and a few others willing to risk arrest staying until they had been allowed to get away, with the threat that we would trash the offices if the police moved in on them. In fact, one of the farcical aspects of the actual event was that the 30 or so students and I assembled outside the Commission, having travelled from Mona in small groups so as not to attract attention, carried out the occupation and left unmolested *without the police even appearing*.

The true farce was my grave defects as a protest organiser. Previously visiting the High Commission to scout the layout, I had surveyed the reception hall and adjacent offices, which were on the building's first floor, but had not realised that the Commissioner's own office suite, the most important part to seize if you wanted to have an effect, was on the floor above! So we took over the first floor, upsetting the unfortunate lady receptionist and other junior staff (incidentally, there was no evidence of security guards), writing political slogans and scurrilous comments in the visitors' book (perhaps not the most revolutionary act ...), but not noticing that there was no really impressive office and assuming that an unusually modest High Commissioner was unfortunately somewhere else. In fact, he was probably upstairs talking to the police on the phone and assuring them there was no real danger. We ended up leaving on an anti-imperialist high but without even getting publicity in next day's *Gleaner*, as my planning had also not extended to tipping it off anonymously.

This mismanaged affair was my last act in campus politics, and, as noted above, in May my work for *Abeng* ended. My activities in collaboration with the left wing radicals in Kingston had also greatly diminished as a need for them to avoid police attention had arisen. In terms of academic work, plans for the 1969–70 teaching had to be made. Manchester, perhaps as an apology for the attempt to bring me home, had promoted me to Senior Lecturer. I had also got the Manchester Government Department's approval of taking my three years secondment to Mona in a continuous bloc, rather than the original plan of returning to my base for the fourth year and then coming back to UWI for the last in my five-year contract. I therefore participated in the planning of the next year's syllabus, in particular trying to make the one for Political Thought more relevant to the West Indies.

However, I was never to implement it, since the government had come up with a simple solution to the problem of my undesirable presence. They informed the University that they would not renew my annual work permit, due to expire at the end of July, which meant that I could not stay in the island except, I suppose, as a tourist. If, as Charles/Gladstone Mills says, the deal which the Mona authorities had made was that I would not be expelled but could complete my originally-planned stay, from their point of view the non-renewal was logical, since I had originally been due to go back to Manchester in July. Not knowing this, I had gone to the trouble of working out the new syllabus for my course, assuming I would teach it. It is scarcely surprising that my request for a third year, when duly made to Professor Mills, caused him consternation.[43]

Late July at Mona was filled with packing and shipping possessions, taking leave of students and friends (often identical categories) and drinking my last Red Stripes. Now, when I try to sum up my Jamaican experience, I cannot adequately do so. I think it not exaggerated to say that in long-distance retrospect these were the best two years of my life. For me, of course as a privileged white outsider, Jamaica in the late 1960s was a magical place, where I found so many good friends, Jamaican and others, and had really good students like Rupert. Above all, the island was full of fascinating people, basically descendants of slaves who had kept their ancient African culture hidden in their heads and were now building new ideas and actions on its basis. It was a privilege, as a white man, to get some chance to look at these and even give faulty support.[44]

## Notes

1. I have to confess that what follows is adapted from my unpublished autobiography.
2. From a wide literature on the slave period in Jamaica I would select Orlando Patterson, *The Sociology of Slavery* (London: MacGibbon and Kee, 1967), Edward Brathwaite, *Creole Society in Jamaica 1770–1820* (Oxford: Clarendon Press, 1971) and Robin Blackburn, *The Making of New World Slavery* (London: Verso, 1997).
3. Datum from Owen Jefferson, *The Post-War Economic Development of Jamaica* (Kingston: Institute of Social and Economic Research, UWI, 1972), 174, and for the bauxite ownership structure see 151–52. For the changes up till the end of the Second World War, see Ken Post, *Arise Ye Starvelings* (The Hague: Martinus Nijhoff, 1978), chapters ii, iv and v, and *Strike the Iron* (New Jersey: Humanities Press, 1981), Chapters i, ii, xii and xiv. Jefferson should be read for the post-War period.
4. Ibid.
5. In time, of course, he was to go on to be elected as a progressive Prime Minister of St Vincent in 2001 and to be re-elected in 2005 and 2010.
6. *Grist to the Mills* (Kingston: Ian Randle Publishers), 119 and 121. Perhaps it is also significant that I do not appear in the index! Even more important, his memory was incorrect on several points in what he says about my role in the 1968–69 events, but I will not get into this, since he died in September 2004 and cannot reply.

7. See Michael O. West, 'Walter Rodney and Black Power: Jamaican Intelligence and US Diplomacy,' *African Journal of Criminology and Justice Studies* 1, no. 2 (November 2005): 35–36. This article is an important piece based on US files opened through the Access to Information Act and other means.
8. Estimates based on Terry Lacey, *Violence and Politics in Jamaica 1960-70* (Manchester: Manchester University Press, 1977), 31 and 32. The Jamaican pound, replaced by the dollar in 1969, was worth the same as the British one.
9. For a full discussion of this phenomenon in general, see Ken Post, *Regaining Marxism* (Houndmills, Basingstoke: Macmillan 1996), 305–30.
10. For details, see Terry Lacey, *Violence and Politics in Jamaica, 1960–70: Internal Security in a Developing Country* (Totowa, New Jersey: F. Cass, 1977), 87–94.
11. On this see Maureen Rowe, 'Gender and Family Relations in Rastafari: A Personal Perspective', in *Chanting Down Babylon*, ed. Nathaniel Samuel Murrell, William David Spencer and Adrian Anthony McFarlane, 78–79 (Kingston: Ian Randle Publishers, 1998). For a picture focused on a later period, see Imani Tafari-Ama, *Blood, Bullets and Bodies* (Multimedia Communications, 2006), 151.
12. Stephen Davis, *Bob Marley* (Arnold Barker 1983), 47. Pages 23 and 46–47 are useful on the West Kingston slums and the rude boys, but, of course, basic texts are Rupert Lewis's, 'Learning to Blow the Abeng,' *Small Axe* 1, 1997 and 'Political and Cultural Context of Rasta and Rudeboy in the 1960s,' in *Marley – The Man and his Music*, ed. Eleanor Wint and Carolyn J. Cooper (Kingston: Arawak Publications, 2003).
13. Quoted in Rex Nettleford, *Mirror Mirror* (Kingston: Collins and Sangster, 1977), 96, and Davis, *Bob Marley*, 47.
14. For the early history of the movement see Post, *Arise Ye Starvelings*, 163–67.
15. Here, I should make my attitude to the Rastas clear. I was, and am, really fond of them as people who truly sought/seek to emancipate themselves from the colonial inheritance and capitalism. I sympathise with their rejection of white people as inherently tainted. However, Haile Selassie as God is out of my universe.
16. The eccentric spelling is his. I am now completely in Rupert's territory. See here especially his 'Marcus Garvey and the Early Rastafarians: Continuity and Discontinuity,' in *Chanting Down Babylon*, ed. Nathaniel S. Murrell, William D. Spencer and Adrian A. McFarlane (Kingston: Ian Randle Publishers, 1998). Interestingly, another of my students, Bobby Hill, as a professor at UCLA, also became a well-known specialist on Garvey.
17. On the impact of the visit from different Jamaican points of view see Nettleford, *Mirror Mirror*, 62–64 (sympathetic intellectual) and I JabulaniTafari, *A Rastafari View of Marcus Mosiah Garvey* (Great Company, 1996), 1–5 (believer).
18. Ras Dizzy I, 'From Heaven to Hell and Back,' mimeographed, 4 and 5. Copy in my possession.
19. This is based on Nettleford, *Mirror Mirror*, 82–83.
20. *The Black Man Speaks* (mimeographed bulletin) 1, no. 2, May 1968, 1.
21. Undated mimeographed leaflet in my possession.
22. For texts see Walter Rodney, *The Groundings with My Brothers* (Bogle-L'Ouverture Publications, 1969). For analysis, see Rupert Lewis, Walter Rodney's *Intellectual and Political Thought* (Detroit, MI: Wayne State University Press, 1998) and

*Walter Rodney Revisited* (Cave Hill: Canoe Press, 1998). The security police were keeping a special eye on Bobby Hill at this time, seeing him as a close associate of Walter who was both a Black Power advocate and a Marxist. See West (2005, 22–23).

23. It is important to note that Jamaican intelligence had been watching Walter since his student days: For the intelligence assessment on the supposed conspiracy, see West 2005, 19–20.
24. The text may be found in *The Groundings*. Walter went back to teach in Dar-es-Salaam, then in 1974 was appointed to a chair at the University of Guyana, but the Burnham government refused to allow him to take it up. He published a major work, *How Europe Underdeveloped Africa*, and turned to full-time political activity as a leader of the Guyanese left opposition to the increasingly authoritarian regime, which in July 1979 arrested him on a charge of arson. In June 1980, he was murdered by a planted bomb.
25. Details from unsigned mimeographed instructions, copy in author's possession. Unless otherwise stated, documents quoted in this section are all from this collection.
26. Account based on 'Diary of Events – 16th October,' in 'Scope' (mimeographed, no date, no pagination). West (2005, 28–33) gives a detailed account which seems rather confused, perhaps because it is based on various intelligence reports. See further Norman Girvan, 'After Rodney: The Politics of Student Protest in Jamaica,' *New World Quarterly* 4, no. 3, 1968; Ralph Gonsalves, 'The Rodney Affair and Its Aftermath,' *Caribbean Quarterly* 25, no. 3, 1979; and Anthony Payne, 'The Rodney Riots in Jamaica: The Background and Significance of the Events of October 1968,' *Journal of Commonwealth and Comparative Politics* 21, no. 2, 1983.
27. West 2005 speaks of six deaths in all (33).
28. On the Cabinet meeting, see West 2005, 25–26.
29. Cited in *Comment*, November 1, 1968, 3 (unnumbered). The Shearer government saw the UWI reaction as a serious threat; the US embassy in Kingston was less perturbed. See West 2005, 39–41.
30. See Verena Reckord, 'From Burru Drums to Reggae Ridims: The Evolution of Rasta Music,' in *Chanting Down Babylon*, ed. Nathaniel Samuel Murrell, William David Spencer and Adrian Anthony McFarlane (Kingston: Ian Randle Publishers 1998), 237–38.
31. 'New Ideas or Plain Crap,' *The Truth*, mimeographed, no date.
32. Bongo Peter, 'Who You Gonna Turn To,' *Bongo-Man*, no. 1, December 1968, 37–41.
33. Bunny Cunningham, 'Go Afro,' 30–31.
34. See Lloyd Best, 'Whither New World,' *New World Quarterly*, Vol. IV, No. 1, Dead Season 1967. He went on to play a role in the politics of his own country, on the 'progressive' side, and died in March 2007.
35. Although my academic background should demand it, I will not give references for every citation from *Abeng* in the present discussion. It should be noted that I have a complete file of the paper in my own archives, which may be rare.
36. Some years later, this earned me the single most pleasurable compliment I have ever received. I met the wife of a Jamaican lecturer I had known at

Mona, who had herself been away studying while I was there. She looked at me and remarked with surprise, 'Oh, you're white!' 'Yes,' I answered, 'I always have been.' 'But no one ever said you were,' was her response. In other words, when my name was used after leaving Mona no one found it relevant to mention my colour.

37. 'His Last Route Report,' *Abeng* 1, no. 10, April 5, 1969. The whole issue, with the exception of a short piece by Clive Thomas, was devoted to tributes to Sloly, who I never met but was clearly regarded with great affection by his friends.
38. In line with the comment by Tafari-Ama (op. cit., 151), I have to admit sharing the *Abeng* group's 'gender blindness'. I did not know of the work of Farika Birhan, to use her later preferred Rastafarian name, until I read the cited work. For Mama Birhan's valuable comments on the group's workings, see op. cit., 151–52.
39. See the March 8 lead story, 'Plan for Bauxite: Work for Thousands More End Foreign Exploitation.'
40. See the March 14 lead story, 'New Police Violence Launched against the People Crime Only an Excuse.'
41. I am basing this on the text in *Bongo-Man*, mimeographed, June 1969.
42. Back in his own country, he joined the staff of the University of Guyana and worked with Walter Rodney to establish the Working People's Alliance. In 2005, he was given the title of Distinguished Professor of Economics and continues to be a critical voice.
43. *Grist for the Mills*, 121.
44. I did get back later for three more visits, although the first, in March 1971, was very short, since I was detained at Palisadoes airport on arrival, allowed in for 24 hours, and then deported. With the change of government to the PNP, the ban was in principle kept, but I was allowed in for six weeks in October–November 1972 to complete my research, and again in May 1978 when UWI stood surety for my good behaviour while attending a conference. The ban was, incidentally, generally circulated in the Caribbean, and I later had difficulty in entering Trinidad; one of my former students had to stand surety that I would leave after the limited stay which was granted.

# 2 | *Jamaican Black Power in the 1960s*

Rupert Lewis

This essay traces the particular manifestations of Black Power in the Jamaican context during the 1960s – the first decade of independence. In this analysis, the origins of Black Power can be traced to the ongoing legacies of the transatlantic slave trade and the plantation system which gave birth to specific manifestations of racism and inequality as well as specific forms of anti-colonial black mobilisation. Thus while the Black Power movement in Jamaica is linked to the student and youth demonstrations in Kingston on October 16, 1968, the protests had far deeper roots. As Walter Rodney proposed, the slogan of Black Power was new but it was 'really an ideology and a movement of historical depth.'[1] In Jamaica this historical depth was rooted in social movements especially among the urban poor, working class and lower middle class that drew heavily on the ideas of the Garvey movement and the world-views of Rastafari. I explore how these currents fed into the Black Power movement of the 1960s, the nature of Black Power mobilisation in the period, and the response of the Jamaican state, before reflecting on its repercussions and relevance in the present day.

**The Jamaican Context**

Black Power activists engaged a Jamaican state marked by colonial legacies that included a head of state, the Governor-General, who represented the Queen; a Prime Minister who functioned with a constitution that had been arranged between the British government and the leaders of the two main parties without the input of the people; and a judiciary, civil service and police system engineered in the era of colonial rule to serve British and sugar plantation interests. By the 1960s, these institutions were being taken over by brown (mulatto) and black Jamaicans. The Jamaica Labour Party (JLP), whose leader Alexander Bustamante emerged as a hero of the 1938 labour revolt, led Jamaica to independence in 1962. Bustamante's successor and protégé, Hugh Shearer, was Prime Minister when the Black Power protests broke out in 1968.

In Rodney's analysis, the main beneficiaries of the 1938 labour revolts were 'a narrow, middle-class sector whose composition was primarily brown, augmented by significant elements of white and other groupings, such as Syrians, Jews and Chinese'. In a statement issued after the Shearer government had banned him from re-entering Jamaica on October 15, 1968, Rodney noted that,

> Of late, that local ruling elite has incorporated a number of blacks in positions of prominence. However, irrespective of its racial or colour composition, this power-group is merely acting as representatives of metropolitan-imperialist interests. Historically white and racist-oriented, these interests continue to stop attempts at creative social expression on the part of the black oppressed masses.[2]

Rodney was also highly critical of the administration of justice, particularly police violence against citizens. Between August 1967 and April 1968, 31 people were shot by the police, 16 of them killed.[3] Social and economic inequalities and deeply held racial prejudices against the black majority persisted in post-independence Jamaica.

The independent Jamaican state, like the colonial state before it, saw black nationalism as culturally and politically subversive. Between 1955 and 1962, when the People's National Party (PNP) were in government, 128 people were banned from Jamaica; a further 91 were banned by the subsequent JLP government in the years 1962 to 1968.[4] Not all of these bans were on political radicals, but the latter became targets especially in the Cold War climate from the late 1940s. In this climate, publications as well as people were targeted for exclusion from the Jamaican state. In a letter to Amy Jacques Garvey, the Jamaican socialist W.A. Domingo noted that a 'formidable list of publications' had been banned from entry into Jamaica. By this act, he wrote,

> ...the government simply reveals its fears. Colonial peoples have a double problem. They have to fight their own reactionaries as well as the naturally reactionary government of the controlling power. The situation is worse when the two elements fuse and work against the masses, one openly as the agent of an alien over-lord and the other concealed as the friends of the people of whom they are a part. The question that the people should ask: of what are the rulers afraid?[5]

The JLP government, however, did not only respond to black mobilisation by recourse to repressive methods. The repatriation of Marcus Garvey's body from London to Kingston in 1964, the official visit of Emperor Haile Selassie to Jamaica in 1966, and the award of the Marcus Garvey Prize for Human Rights to Martin Luther King Jr, received by his widow, Coretta Scott King, show that the JLP government was also concerned to promote its own version of moderate Black Power.

Jamaican Black Power, however, had multiple streams of resistance to British colonial legacies and to the neocolonial rule of the independence era. These streams drew on Garveyism, Rastafarianism, aspirations for social and economic mobility, and strong identification and solidarity with Africa. As Rex Nettleford has shown, Jamaican Black Power was a vigorous effort to correct the prejudices against black Jamaicans, the negative stereotyping of Africa and the internalisation of self-hate.[6] Thus, the struggle was not only against a white Jamaican elite or propertied racial minorities, nor was it only against a black political elite that protected the interests of the propertied class, but was also a struggle against the thinking of black Jamaicans who felt themselves inferior to their white and light-skinned compatriots. Black Power also struggled to change the material conditions that held black Jamaicans in poverty. Issues of race and class were thus inseparable in Black Power discourse of the 1960s.

## Influences and Antecedents

### Garveyism

For the early twentieth century, Marcus Garvey represented the foremost thinker and mass leader of people of African descent. His Universal Negro Improvement and Conservation Association (UNIA) was organised in over 40 countries through approximately 1,200 divisions in Africa, Australia, Europe and the Americas. Garvey's core ideas of racial self-determination and Black Nationalism were set out in the Declaration of Rights of the Negro Peoples of the World, adopted at the 1920 UNIA Convention. Unlike ideas of white supremacy, Garveyites did not preach the subjection of whites or of any other peoples.

Just as Garvey's original vision encompassed multiple locations across the black world, so too his influence was felt across Africa, the Caribbean and the United States. His impact on the rise of African nationalism has been documented in two volumes of Robert Hill's compilation of Garvey papers, which illustrate the activities of the UNIA and African Communities League (ACL) on the African continent.[7] Among the pioneering group of African independence leaders, Kwame Nkrumah was Garvey's staunchest disciple and became a powerful symbol of Pan-Africanism from the 1940s until the early 1970s.[8] In the US, the civil rights and Black Power movements can be traced of course not only to Garveyism but also to other movements such as the National Association for the Advancement of Colored People (NAACP), intellectuals such as Dr W.E.B. DuBois and a wider canvas of Pan-Africanists that includes George Padmore and Malcolm X. As the recent biography of Malcolm X by the late Manning Marable shows, Malcolm's parents, Earl and Louise Little, were organisers for the Garvey movement in Omaha, Nebraska, as well as in Milwaukee, Wisconsin.[9] In turn, US Black Power and the civil rights movement were to have a considerable impact on the Caribbean, especially among the youth. Caribbean Black Power, however, was not an imitation of its Northern equivalent. Daily engagement with white racism did not exist in the same way as it was experienced by the African American minority; there was also a greater sense that black Jamaicans belonged in the Jamaican environment and could shape it, notwithstanding the repatriation to Africa trend in Jamaican Black Nationalism.

The return of Garvey's body to Jamaica in 1964 and his subsequent designation as an official national hero was an important moment in the discussions about Jamaica's national identity, prompting debates over Garvey's significance and the role of majority and minority groups within concepts of Jamaican nationhood.[10] Rodney's comment that they had 'brought Garvey's bones but not his philosophy' resonated with many people.[11] Thousands turned out to witness his interment in what became known as National Heroes Park. Many veteran Garveyites were still a part of the political landscape, some active in the trade union movement, political parties and community organisations, and others who tried to revive the UNIA. Most prominent was Garvey's widow, Amy Jacques Garvey, who assumed a greater public presence in the 1960s, and became a strong critic of the JLP government. Jacques Garvey spoke at Black Power meetings on the University of the West Indies (UWI) campus, contributed articles to Black Power publications, and spoke out publicly against the ban on Walter Rodney in October 1968.

Marcus Garvey Jr was also involved in establishing his own organisation, the African Nationalist Union (ANU) in 1969. The ANU publication, *The Blackman*, which described itself as the 'authentic voice of Garveyism in Jamaica' emphasised a version of Black Power described as 'African National Socialism', an attempt to merge the African Nationalism of his father and the African Socialism of Kwame Nkrumah and Julius Nyerere. Garvey Jr argued that Black Power consisted of four concepts: first, black awareness or pride in African heritage; second, pride in being black; third, that 'the only salvation for the black man lies in black institutions under black leadership'; and fourth, the forging of national and international black unity. He contended that the 'fifth concept of Garveyism, which the modern black power advocates have not so far stressed…is the concept of the United States of Africa.'[12] This fifth point is a distinguishing feature in that some interpretations of Black Power focused on the struggle for equality in a national context without reference to Africa. For Garveyites and Rastafarians, for whom Africa was the motherland, the focus on a free and united Africa was cardinal. Repatriation to Africa therefore became the clarion call.

## Rastafarianism

Garvey is seen as the prophet of the emergence of Ethiopian leader Ras Tafari as Emperor Haile Selassie in November 1930. A group of Jamaicans came to identify Ras Tafari as their King and God, articulating a philosophy that was not only critical of the British monarchy but also switched allegiance to the Ethiopian King and gave him godly status. They also asserted the right of repatriation to Ethiopia. These subversive ideas were never accepted by the majority of the African-Jamaican population, most of whom were loyal to the British monarchy. Rastafari was therefore a profound act of alienation from colonial Jamaica with its slave and colonial legacies. Gaining many new recruits after Italy invaded Ethiopia in 1935, Rastafari became part of a wider anti-colonial movement against European colonialism.[13] Perceived by the authorities and by large sections of the middle class as a dangerous sect, Rastafarians were subject to stringent measures of repression and humiliation, including prison sentences for minor offences such as the smoking of marijuana, placement in the lunatic asylum for public utterances deemed seditious, the cutting of sacred hair locks, and whipping with the cat o' nine tails.[14] We owe a debt of gratitude to Deborah Thomas and her team for work done on the film *Bad Friday*. It is an important documentary highlighting the harassment after the 1963 Coral Gardens repression.

One of the leading figures in the early Ras Tafari movement was Leonard Howell, who attracted hundreds of supporters from the 1930s to the 1950s. In the 1950s and 1960s, adherents of Ras Tafari grew 'locks' or matted hair in the style of the Kenyan Mau Mau fighters. By the 1960s, Ras Planno in West Kingston and Ras Negus in East Kingston were among the most influential leaders. They were to play important roles in the awakening of black consciousness among youth, and particularly among musicians and singers: Ras Planno for example had a significant influence on Bob Marley's Rastafarian outlook, and consequently, on his music.

Part of the appeal of Rastafari was its delegitimising of the colonial system and critique of the continuation of that system in the period after political independence. In designating the colonial system and modern capitalism as 'Babylon', Rastafari offered an anti-systemic critique of modern capitalism and developed its own type of postcolonial thought. It delegitimised the Christian God, deified 'I and I' (the self), and provided an alternative 'livity' or way of living. Being among the people in their daily life, especially within the poorest rural and urban communities, Rastafarians have been able to challenge fundamental premises of human existence derived from the colonial period such as the innate inferiority and sub-human status of people of African descent. They have also engaged their fellow citizens in dialogues about what they eat and drink, how they dress, who they worship and how they live. Rastafari therefore became an existential and epistemic type of Black Power embedded in and arguing from within the mass of the population. Rastafari also challenged the hegemony of the church which they argued was based on the theology of the Church of England and the Pope of Rome, instead purveying a different hermeneutic of the Bible that highlighted the importance of Ethiopia in early Christianity. However, while Rastafari developed this new type of spirituality, there was some reluctance to engage in politics.

Debates on political activism frequently took place, with some Rastafari withdrawing from all aspects of political life while others emerged as political activists, especially during the turbulent months of 1968.

The decade of the 1960s saw the growth of Rastafarianism as an important social force. Their contribution was a vision away from Jamaica, like Garvey looking to Africa, but simultaneously creating an indigenous black consciousness movement that would reshape Jamaican spirituality, language, aesthetics and music.

## *The Reverend Claudius Henry*

Fear of Rastafari subversion was strong, as exemplified by the severity of the state response to the killing in 1963 of a gas station owner, allegedly by Rastafarians, in the community of Coral Gardens just outside Montego Bay. The state responded with ferocity killing three Rastafarians and detaining hundreds in neighbouring parishes. Jamaican political and business elites, along with the middle class, feared that the Rastafarian movement, if politicised, could pose a serious threat to the state. Revd Claudius Henry posed just such a threat, and as such was a marked person throughout the 1960s. A spiritual leader in the heretical and prophetic tradition of black radicalism, Henry established contacts with the Rastafari, came to believe that Haile Selassie was 'earth's returned Messiah', and advocated repatriation to Africa.[15] In 1960, Claudius Henry and his son Ronald were involved in an attempt to challenge the Jamaican state by force of arms. Naively, they had appealed to Fidel Castro, writing him a letter which was found in the subsequent police raid on Henry's headquarters. The letter read in part:

> We wish to draw your attention to the conditions which confront us today as poor, underprivileged people which were brought from Africa by the British slave traders over 400 years ago to serve as slaves. We now desire to return home in peace, to live under our own vine and fig tree, otherwise a government like yours that gives justice to the poor. All our efforts to have a peaceful repatriation has [sic] proven a total failure. Hence we must fight a war for what is our rights [sic].[16]

Ronald Henry and a group, including African Americans, launched a guerrilla campaign in the hills of St Catherine and were captured by the police. Ronald was sentenced to hang for murdering one of his supporters and his father sentenced to ten years. On his way to the gallows, Ronald was said to have declared his commitment to the ideas of Marcus Garvey.

In 1966, Claudius Henry organised the International Peacemakers Association which established headquarters in the district of Green Bottom in the parish of Clarendon. The economic mainstay of this enterprise was the entrepreneurial fish vendor, Edna Fisher, who became Henry's wife. She developed the business activities of the commune which included a bakery, church, school, vehicles, farm and shop, block and tile-making works and an electrical plant. Through her work the idea of self-reliance became a central part of Henry's evangelical Black Power.[17] When I travelled with Walter Rodney in the summer of 1968 to visit Revd Henry, the church was packed. Sabbath was marked on a Saturday, the congregation was disciplined, and nyabinghi drumming of the Rastafarian brethren punctuated the singing. The rituals and the centrality of biblical hermeneutics were Christian but Henry's Afro-centric message, Rastafarian following and prison record meant that he was seen as subversive by the Jamaican state. Soon after Rodney was barred from re-entering Jamaica, *Bongo Man* reported that Henry had spoken to a large crowd on the second anniversary of his release from prison. The description of this meeting hints at the encounter between the various currents of black radicalism in the Jamaican context:

> Conscious Conscious! Marcus Garvey hymns. Pictures of Black Christ. Black Mary. Emperor Haile Selassie. Drums! Original chants & Black Christmas. [Henry] spoke of Dr. Rodney's lectures on African History and Marcus Garvey and of his son Trevor whom they hanged.[18]

Rodney's presence at Henry's church in rural Jamaica was ill regarded by Special Branch, and was later used by Shearer as evidence that Rodney was planning subversion.

### *Plantation Legacies: Rural Poverty and Urban Realities*

While Black Power has primarily been understood as an urban phenomenon, it is crucial to grasp the importance of rural poverty and its impact on the movement. The Jamaican economist George Beckford insisted on this point in his classic work, *Persistent Poverty– Underdevelopment in Plantation Economies of the Third World* (1972). Beckford's work points to the rural dimensions of Black Power in its focus on the plantation economies of the world and observation that the 'greatest concentration of plantation economies is to be found in the Caribbean'. More importantly, he contended that some 130 years since Emancipation, the Jamaican peasantry had still not managed to secure much of the country's agricultural land and other resources. Beckford also identified the racial structure of the plantation system as laying the foundations for ongoing racism, so that persistent poverty and persistent racism were different sides of the same coin. In this vein, he noted that

> the predominant social characteristic of all plantation areas of the world is the existence of a class-caste system based on differences in the racial origins of plantation workers on the one hand and owners on the other.... In every instance, the system was introduced by white Europeans who had to rely on non-white labour for working the plantations. Race, therefore, was a convenient means of controlling the labour supply.[19]

What Beckford calls the class-caste system, I prefer to refer to as the socio-racial structure of Jamaican society.

Rural impoverishment led to rural-urban migration and the consequent development of slums. By 1951 there were four large squatter settlements in West Kingston, in Trench Town, Dung Hill and Kingston Pen, otherwise known as Back O'Wall.[20] These locations in the 1960s, especially Trench Town, became the source of Jamaican popular music as well as contested areas between rival gangs connected to political parties, with housing schemes built by the two main parties being allocated to their respective supporters. This laid the economic foundation for 'garrison politics' where party support is guaranteed and where violence is used to enforce political control of an area.[21] Impoverishment impacted both on the nature of party politics, and on the appeal of Black Power. As Jamaican political scientist Carl Stone observed,

> ...evidence of strong feelings of black solidarity within the black working and lower classes in urban Jamaica is not surprising in a society which has given birth to the Garvey and Rastafari movements. The ideological thrust of these movements have [sic.] attempted, with some manifest success, to counter the history of black denigration that is rooted in the plantation slave history of the Caribbean, in spite of the fact that residues of these historical forces persist. The

fundamental obstacle to the elimination of these residues ... is not the absence of appropriate black racial ideologies but black poverty and white affluence.[22]

## Black Power Activism and the State Response

In 1967, a Black Power group was formed at the Mona campus of the University of the West Indies, loosely structured around the four Halls of Residence that formed the core of campus life. Its aims, as outlined in an early pamphlet, were: '1. To create an awareness of what it means to be black; 2. To mobilize and unify Black people to act in their own interest; 3. To reject white cultural imperialism; 4. To seek to ensure the rule of Blacks in a black society.'[23] Among those associated with this group were students from across the Anglophone Caribbean, including Peter Phillips, Garth White, Keith Noel (based at Irvine Hall), Bernard Marshall, Arnold Bertram, Edwin Jones (Chancellor Hall), Jackie Vernon, Maureen Stephenson, (Mary Seacole Hall), Wyck Williams, Marva Henry and John Dowie (Taylor Hall). A subset of this group which included Peter Phillips, Jerry Small, Garth White and Minion Phillips connected the UWI campus with inner city Afro-centric cultural and political activism.[24] This network facilitated lecturer Walter Rodney's 'reasonings',[25] especially in the communities of the poor in Kingston. No single grouping, however, can claim the movement, which was broad and amorphous, not coalescing around any group or individual.

Jerry Small and a group of young men, who had been secondary school students at Jamaica College, were some of the most active Rastafarian-influenced Black Power activists in Kingston, and were among the most articulate and politically aware youth groups with whom Walter Rodney worked. Small was one of the organisers of a strike at Jamaica College in 1964, called in solidarity with a strike at the newly developed Jamaica Broadcasting Corporation (JBC). A product of the black middle class, Small broke with the tradition of higher education and professional advancement to become a Rastafarian and engage in the risky activities surrounding Black Power activism. Among the Jamaica College group were Garth White, Peter Phillips, John Davis and Poco Morgan, all of whom went on to study at the University of the West Indies. Moving in the wider circles of the Rasta movement in the city, the group had a passion for reading about the history and contemporary realities of Africa. Rodney's expertise in this field made him sought after by many groups as his reputation spread by word of mouth.

Rodney knew Jamaica well from his days as a student from 1960 to 1963. When he returned in 1968 with a PhD in African History from the School of Oriental and African Studies, with the willingness to speak in schools, churches, communities of the poor and Rastafarian gatherings, he developed a following. His return to UWI followed a period of teaching and political activism at the University of Dar es Salaam between 1965 and 1966, where he had taken part in discussions about Julius Nyerere's radical agrarian reform and established links with Southern African liberation movements. Moreover, he had also been to Cuba, placing him firmly on the watch list of the Special Branch, who feared his '[charisma] at the grass-roots level and...following among young intellectuals.'[26] Soon after his arrival in Jamaica in January 1968, Rodney offered his services to the newly formed African Studies Association of the West Indies (ASAWI) and was elected its Treasurer. The President of ASAWI was the Trinidadian linguist, Mervyn Alleyne, and on the Executive Council were Amy Jacques Garvey and the young Jamaican sociologist Orlando Patterson, whose 1964 novel *Children of Sisyphus* depicted the ethos of hopelessness of the urban poor and captured the growth of Rastafarian influence among them. This was also the period when poet-historian Edward Kamau Brathwaite joined the history department at Mona and the appearance of his trilogy *Rights of Passage* (1967), *Masks* (1968), and *Islands* (1969) bore testimony to the awakening of a Pan-African consciousness.

It was not easy, however, to transfer this level of growing black consciousness into an organisation. For instance, Small cites the Rastafarian fear of forming organisations, arguing that 'Rastaman always wary of organisations; and...because of the history of Marcus Garvey, plenty people feel that organisation is a readymade way for a betrayal to formalize itself.'[27] Nevertheless, in January 1968 the group decided to publish a magazine, *Blackman Speaks*, with articles on Africa, speeches by Haile Selassie and sections of the UN Human Rights Charter. Small recalls how he met Walter Rodney:

> I remember Peter Phillips...told me that there was this young history teacher just come from Africa who...had a lot of personal contact

with the liberation struggle in Africa...who would like to help us in the work that we were doing...[and could get us] in personal contact with the OAU...They arranged for me to meet him...I was struck you know, the smallness of his size and the pleasantness of his features, almost a kind of little boy look, not looking really hard and tough and aloof...[28]

Rodney put Jerry Small in touch with the OAU Liberation Committee based in Dar es Salaam. Observing Rodney's revolutionary outlook, Small recalls:

> I remember coming down to McGregor Gully and Walter kind of want to revolutionize things more, you know...because you know Rasta more deal with repatriation, human rights on a local level, but him did really want [to] get the man them to address the problem of the political situation in Jamaica, and to...confront the system here and now. I remember him suggested to the man them one time that the paper [*Blackman Speaks*] should be edited from week to week by [different groups of us]...It wasn't really a practical way of editing a publication, but in that time of revolutionary experimenting and wanting to democratize, we approve, we say alright go on...I remember [one] edition [edited by Rodney, Ruddy and Ras ID] did cause some commotion...on the back page them put a picture of Fidel Castro, and a quotation by Castro which is very powerful and relevant...'The exploitation of man by man must be dug out by the roots'. But now I remember one of the main man who used to take the most amount of them was Prince Buster... When [he] saw the picture of Fidel Castro he asked 'what this man a do on *Blackman Speaks*' and he dumped the entire consignment.[29]

Small's interpretation of Prince Buster's rejection of the image is that the singer feared being targeted by the authorities for subversive activities. Another possibility is that Buster did not approve of a white person, revolutionary or not, being featured in the magazine.

Among those Rodney met through Small's group were Ras Single (McGregor Gully), Frank Hasfal (Bull Bay), Ras Negus (Dunkirk, East Kingston), Count Ossie (Wareika Hills), Ras Planno (West Kingston) and Ras Dizzy, Ras ID and Ras Historian (Laws St). Other connections were Neville Howell who was close to elements in the Young Socialist League attached to the PNP in Trench Town, and persons in Ghost Town, a PNP garrison community known as Concrete Jungle. What did Rodney see in Rastafari? In Small's view, it was the African sentiment, high element of fearlessness and resistance, articulateness and ability to communicate with the rest of the population: 'although Rasta is a minority...like many articulate minorities, they can speak for the rest of the population and both interpret things for the rest of the population when the rest of the population don't feel to really examine things too closely for themselves'.[30] Rodney, however, did not accept Selassie's divinity, a view he articulated in some circles but not in others where it would not have been politic to do so.

Rodney's talks at the University, schools, and in poor communities took place in a climate of state intimidation, with intense police surveillance and repressive measures against Black Power activists brutally enforced by the police. Rodney himself was under constant surveillance. As Small recalls,

> Walter's car would be tailed day and night by more than one car of the special branch. They [activists] would borrow cars from family members, especially the mothers and rotate their use to dodge special branch detection...more than one car would have to leave town in different directions...and at some point later on you would pick up the person and proceed to where you going, but you would have to use some tactics to get them off your tail.[31]

One of the places in rural Jamaica Rodney visited regularly was the home of Dr D.K. Duncan, a young dentist recently returned from studying in Montreal and very active in the Black Power movement. Duncan lived in Brown's Town some two hours' drive from Kingston. Small recalls that one night the police sealed off all exits leaving the town. 'We was down at Duncan yard and some of us leave to go buy some herb [marijuana], when we coming back through them block off every road and search the whole place...them take away all literature from us...and them all want to frame we with herb and gun.'[32] This was the climate when Rodney left the island in 1968 to attend a Black Writers Conference in Montreal along with Robert Hill.

**The Riots**

On October 15, 1968, the Shearer government banned Rodney from re-entering Jamaica. On hearing the news, students at the University of the West Indies campus gathered at a meeting organised by Ralph Gonsalves, then President of the UWI Students' Guild. His description of the events is worth recounting:

The aircraft which brought Rodney back from Montreal where he was attending a Congress of Black Writers landed at 2:20 p.m. on Tuesday 15th October. However, it was not until 9:00 p.m. that the students learnt that he was refused re-entry and confined to the aircraft. Immediately, the Guild President contacted the Vice-Chancellor for his reaction but the latter declined to comment until he knew the facts. Soon thereafter a meeting of students on the campus was advertised for 11:00 p.m. in Mary Seacole Hall. The meeting of some 900 students unanimously accepted a resolution to march the following day on the offices of the Minister of Home Affairs and the Prime Minister to deliver two petitions. To this end Messrs McCauley were contacted to provide the necessary transportation but when they failed to turn up at the agreed time (7:00 a.m.) on Wednesday 16th, the students decided to proceed on foot.[33]

That evening Arnold Bertram and the present author went to neighbouring August Town to discuss how to respond. We supported the student mobilisation and the word was spread through the grounding networks of the student march. In Small's assessment, prior to the ban on Rodney 'most of the people on campus at the time' had been 'antagonistic' towards Rodney and the Black Power grouping, but were outraged by the ban and decided to show solidarity.[34] Soon after the march started from the campus the students were met by armed policemen with guns and tear gas and broken up, but the students regrouped. 'At Jamaica House, a tear gas canister was thrown at the feet of Pat Rodney, pregnant wife of the banned lecturer', further enraging the demonstrators. Marching in their scarlet gowns to distinguish themselves from others, the students' protest 'gathered support on the streets as they marched to the offices of the Minister of Home Affairs.' By this time 'the crowd...had grown to over 2000 – a number of unemployed youths, workers and Rastafarians having joined the protest.'[35] Black Power activists from the student body issued leaflets protesting the ban and many non-campus people joined the march, but the vast majority had their own agendas and the demonstration provided a pretext for their actions against the state, especially the police.

On their way to the Prime Minister's office the demonstrators had to pass the headquarters of the Bustamante Industrial Trade Union (BITU), the union affiliated with the ruling JLP. '[A] clash ensued in which stones, bottles and miscellaneous missiles were flung...A detachment of the police intervened with batons and tear gas to disperse the crowd. A few people were injured in the process including a policeman. Several cars were destroyed.'[36] According to Gonsalves, the violence outside the BITU headquarters was not instigated by the students but by workers belonging to a rival union associated with the opposition People's National Party. Thus the student protest was the match that lit the fire for wider protests in downtown Kingston. In the evening, commercial Kingston was shut down by rioters who emerged to loot business places and smash cars. The students made their way to George VI Memorial Park where George Beckford urged non-violence; however, the police continued to use their batons and throw tear-gas. The student march was thrown into disarray as they found their way back to the campus. Meanwhile, the University of the West Indies was surrounded by the military and access to it its compounds was highly restricted.

While the conservative *Gleaner* emphasised the 'widespread vandalism' caused by 'hooligan gangs [taking] charge of many areas of the city',[37] Gonsalves's account focuses instead on the social causes:

> ...unemployed youth and workers gave the events a new turn. For them the protest was not so much about a lecturer who was banned – however influential he might have been – but about the inequalities stemming from the class and racial oppression in the country. More than likely criminal elements also took advantage of the commotion to loot and plunder...Big businesses, both foreign and local, were attacked. They included Canadian Imperial Bank of Commerce, Bank of London and Montreal, Pan American, Air Jamaica, Kingston Ice and Commodity Service, Woolworth, North American Life and Bata Shoe Store. On Orange Street Marzouca's Building was damaged; Royal Bank of Canada's Manchester Square Branch was stoned and so was the Jamaica Public Service Station at Gold Street. Significantly, 53 JOS [Jamaica Omnibus Service] buses were burnt or otherwise damaged and this was clearly related to the fact that the fare had been increased recently...Looting continued at many stores in the city and on Spanish Town Road throughout the night of October 16th ...Three persons were reported killed in incidents related to these disturbances.[38]

From the perspective of the Jamaican government, Prime Minister Shearer sought to justify his actions on the grounds that Rodney was a threat to national security. Shearer claimed that the exclusion order was prepared without the knowledge that Rodney had left the country, but when it was discovered that he had, and was due to return on October 15, they decided to ban him from re-entering. Defending this action to the Jamaican Parliament, Shearer stated that Rodney was banned not for his attendance at the Black Writers Conference, but for his 'destructive anti-Jamaican activities in Kingston, St Andrew, Clarendon and St James.'[39] In this, the Prime Minister was relying on Special Branch reports identifying locations where Rodney had visited or given talks. His visit to Claudius Henry's compound in Clarendon, for example, was taken as evidence that he was planning a violent overthrow of the government. Shearer therefore argued that the government had 'acted to save the nation from a Castro plot' – citing Rodney's attendance at a students' congress in Leningrad and two visits to Cuba in 1962 as evidence of his extreme communist views and association. Shearer claimed that when Rodney returned to Jamaica to take up an appointment as Lecturer in the Department of History, he 'lost little time in engaging in subversive activities on his return':

> He quickly announced his intention of organizing revolutionary groups for what he termed…'the struggle ahead' and then closely associated himself with groups of people who claimed to be part of the Rastafarian Movement and also with Claudius Henry who was convicted in 1960 of Treason Felony as a result of activities which required the use of armed force…He openly declared his belief that as Jamaica was predominantly a black country all brown-skinned mulatto people and their assets should be destroyed. He consistently told the groups with whom he associated that this could only be achieved by revolution and that no revolution had ever taken place without armed struggle and bloodshed. This resort to violence was the recurrent theme of all his discussions with these groups as was his condemnation of the democratic system of government in Jamaica.[40]

The Prime Minister and the island's leading newspaper, the *Daily Gleaner*, also blamed non-Jamaicans for the events of October 16, pointing to the fact that Rodney was from Guyana and that several of the leaders of the UWI Students Guild were not Jamaicans, including the Guild President, Ralph Gonsalves, from St Vincent; the first Vice-President from Trinidad; and the second Vice-President from England; leaving only the Treasurer as a Jamaican.[41]

However, the assessment of the US Embassy in Kingston provides an interesting divergence in opinion as to the reasons for the protests.

The Embassy reports assessed that the protests were 'spontaneously generated' and no evidence was found of involvement by the Rastafarians, Revd Henry's group or the Nation of Islam, nor did the Americans find 'any real connections between the Jamaicans who rioted and UWI students and teachers,' despite the presence at the university of a 'core of radical intellectuals...working to incite the Jamaican masses.'[42] This assessment is closer to the truth as the core of students and academics at UWI did not have the capacity to stage these protests.

**The Jamaican Aftermath**

On October 17, Maxwell Carey, Member of Parliament representing the PNP in the South Eastern Westmoreland 'seized the Mace, the symbol of authority of Parliament...and walked with it towards the door of the chamber' in protest at the banning of Rodney without the opportunity of seeing his wife and child. The same day, Roy McNeil, the Minister of Home Affairs, imposed an order banning all marches and meetings in the Corporate Area, which includes downtown Kingston and suburban St Andrew. This was symptomatic of the increasingly repressive measures taken by the state in the immediate aftermath of the Rodney demonstrations. UWI students were confined to campus and 'units of the Jamaica Defence Force and the police took up positions at the entrances to the University, allowing students to enter but not to leave.'[43] While Shearer did not have much evidence to indict the Black Power core and students on campus, a leaflet entitled 'Tactics! Tactics! Tactics!' produced on the morning of the demonstration, played into the hands of the government as it called on demonstrators to 'provoke the police don't argue with them! Insult them, ridicule them, goad them, let them attack you! And reveal the true nature of the system.' It also encouraged the making of Molotov cocktails, called on students to close the University, to advocate for student representation on university committees and for solidarity with workers, ending with the invocation 'Burn UWI...Burn UWI... Burn UWI'.[44]

The *Gleaner* went on the offensive, determined to secure more intelligence about radical groups and to urge the use of more force to quell protests: 'As the party in office, the party in opposition, the professors, the politicians and the public settle down in the next few days and weeks, clearly they all must come to the cold and chilling conclusion that there has been a change in the national climate. There has now come to live with us a fearsome shadow – a new stark dimension – the imminence of instability, awaiting which are ready-made agents of evil, gulled and trained to throw fuel on the flame of national calamity.' The editorial called for 'more and more money to buy information for the state's protection...more and more money to recruit, train and arm the brave and patriotic personnel who guard the ramparts of secret information...so as to forewarn the country of hostile plans of iniquity and revolt.'[45]

After the ban on Rodney, a respondent in Small's group recalls that he stayed on the campus for four days before going to his home in August Town. On the night of his return,

> 'bout 60 soldiers and police in about 8 vehicles come down the August Town Road and them stop in front of the University playing field... The yard where them stop in front of is my brethren yard, a bredder name Dippy....So him tek a short cut behind and run come down and tell we say, bwoy, a whole heap of soldier and police up the road deh and them a come fe we. So when we hear them coming we just finish smoking what we ah smoke, and sweep out all like little herb and little herb seed what was in the house and sit down there and wait on them. And after about 10 minutes we hear the brakes, you know them big Bedford truck, you always hear the brakes a squeal a come down the road. We sit tight man, everybody nervous but we clean still....

The group had put up Jamaican flags and images of the Prime Minister and when the police entered with guns and ordered 'Don't move a rass...' the soldiers and police rushed through the front door and 'when him see Shearer picture and see Jamaica flag...the Commanding officer said:

> The Prime Minister wrong to rass, man.....Anyway them search, them tear open the ceiling, search up and down and turn over the bed, and mash up everything in the place, and them a look for prohibited literature and them find some little book by Martin Luther King and special branch man them a tek down name of book.

Not finding any herb, the police sent someone to buy a quarter ounce, and when the man returned with the herb they were charged with it. Four males and two females, high school youths who were drawn to Rastafari, were put in the police truck and beaten.⁴⁶ Later on, among the prominent activists harassed was Marcus Garvey Jr who was arrested while participating in a demonstration on May 24, 1970 in solidarity with the liberation movements in Africa. Members of his organisation were beaten by the police. About his arrest he wrote:

> When I was arrested I was first taken to Hunt's Bay Police Station and then afterwards spirited off to Matilda's Corner Station. The intention was to keep me incommunicado for as long as possible so that a good period of solitary confinement would dampen my revolutionary ardor. The police lied to my mother and other relatives when they came to bail me.... They pretended that they did not know where I was.... On orders from their white superior officers – the pigs – you can be sure. I have seen white power at work in Jamaica. I have seen at first hand the brutality of Shearer's bully boys from Harmon Barracks. I know now where the sufferers go, every day, every week...Black power for black people! Down with the pigs!⁴⁷

## Political and Cultural Repercussions

While the demonstrations met with state repression they also helped to catalyse the growing political and cultural consciousness around Black Power. In the wake of Rodney's expulsion a number of new radical publications appeared across the Anglophone Caribbean. Jamaica's *Abeng* newspaper, founded in 1969, was part of a regional awakening that included new publications such as *Moko, Pivot* and *East Dry River Speaks* (Trinidad), *Black Star* (Barbados), *Outlet* (Antigua) and *YULIMO* (St Vincent), that appeared alongside existing publications such as Jamaica's *Impact* (1967–68) and *Bongo-Man* (1968–72), Trinidad's *Tapia* and Guyana's *Ratoon*.⁴⁸ Like other periodicals of the period, its name was chosen for its local significance, the 'abeng' being the horn used by the Maroons for communication in the mountains of Jamaica. The Abeng Group was a political matrix for the Black Power movement, socialists, the independent trade union movement, Rastafarians, supporters of the opposition People's National Party and others disaffected with the two main political parties. The *Abeng* newspaper, whose editors included Robert Hill (a graduate student at the University of the West Indies), George Beckford (UWI lecturer), Rupert Lewis (UWI graduate student) and Trevor Munroe (UWI lecturer), became a focal point of critique and activism against the ruling Jamaica Labour Party and a harbinger of the radicalism in Jamaica of the 1970s. Almost every issue included articles taken from Marcus Garvey's Jamaican newspapers *The Blackman* (1929–31) and the *New Jamaican* (1932–33), which were reprinted alongside articles on Jamaican history.[49] Other manifestations of the vibrant political-cultural consciousness that flowered in Jamaica in the era of Black Power can be traced in the development of more West Indian-focused curricula at the University of the West Indies, the Afro-centric re-orientation of performance poetry and dance, and, mostly obviously, in the black-conscious messages of the popular music of the day.

The radical journalism represented by *Abeng*, the mobilisation of young people, the linkages between middle-class and community activists, between elements on the campus and the urban population of 'sufferers', and the development of connections with the working class that bore fruit in the formation of the University and Allied Workers Union in 1971, were to contribute to strengthening the electoral prospects of Michael Manley as Prime Minister of Jamaica. As leader of the PNP since 1969, Manley had actively campaigned to win over activists from the University of the West Indies and the wider Black Power movement. In 1969, Manley visited Ghana where he received a plaque from Dr Busia, the Ghanaian Prime Minister. Such public acknowledgement of Jamaica's African heritage – indicative of the impact of the Black Power movement on the mainstream political parties – played a part in gaining Manley support from within the movement. Claudius Henry, for example, chose to support Michael Manley after he embraced some of the tenets of Black Power, such as support for African Liberation movements and re-orienting the educational system to valorise the African heritage of the Jamaican people. Key activists of the Black Power group of the UWI campus also opted to support Manley, including Arnold Bertram and Dr D.K. Duncan, the latter subsequently becoming the General Secretary of the PNP and the leading figure on the left wing of that party. The Black Power movement was therefore the prelude to the most radical period in twentieth century Jamaican political history with the electoral victory of Michael Manley in 1972 and his party's adoption of 'democratic socialism' from 1974 to 1980. It was also the harbinger of the broader Caribbean regional left-wing movement that culminated in the Grenada Revolution of 1979 to 1983.

Some proponents of Black Power, however, rejected the political system as a whole. Marcus Garvey Jr, for example, was implacably opposed to the two main political parties and their leaders. Responding to his arrest in 1970, Garvey Jr. noted that '[the] experience makes me more determined than ever to fight against Shearer, Seaga, Michael Manley, McNeil, Coore and all the other puppets and jokers of the two party system who work to keep the whites, Chinese and Mulattoes in power in their black, African country of Jamaica.'[50] The Rastafarian movement also remained outside of party politics, with one new group, the Twelve Tribes, continuing a strong focus on repatriation to Africa.

## Conclusion

The political agenda articulated through Black Power in the 1960s and 1970s has been only partially accomplished. The Black Power demonstrations and activism had a profound impact on the political climate in Jamaica, brought intense pressure to bear on the Shearer administration and helped to shift political support to Michael Manley's PNP, which systematically recruited many activists into the party after Manley's huge electoral victory in 1972. The Black Power movement therefore acted as yeast to assist in the realignment of relations between the state and the people in a particular historical moment. However, the need to address socio-economic deprivation – a key demand of the popular movement – remains an ongoing issue. Economic challenges still exist as Afro-Caribbean participation in corporate life continues to be restricted, although this is being challenged by a younger generation of entrepreneurs. The black middle classes have been the main beneficiary of a less racialised society with wider opportunities, particularly in education and politics. The grandchildren of the rudeboys of the 1960s, however, have had their social base considerably expanded with the growth of the black lumpen-proletariat and the emergence of transnational gangs. While structural racism has been eroded in the traditional plantation sense, the world economy has re-invented itself, and capitalism remains globally dominant. In today's global economy, migrants to the industrially developed countries from Africa and the Caribbean, locked into low-wage jobs and new ghettoes, encounter twenty-first century racism. However, while the legacies are mixed, the themes of Black Power deserve to be revisited to understand the role it played in the formidable task of remaking the colonial and post-colonial world.

## Notes

1. Walter Rodney, *Groundings with my Brothers* (London: Bogle-L'Overture Press, 1969), 21.
2. Ibid., 12.
3. Ibid., 14.
4. Editorial, *Bongo Man*, No.1, (1968) 2.
5. 'Historical Letters of Marcus Garvey, W.A. Domingo and George Padmore,' *Bongo Man*, no.1 (1968), 22.
6. See Rex Nettleford, *Mirror, Mirror: Identity, Race and Protest in Jamaica* (Kingston: W. Collins and Sangster, 1970).
7. Robert Hill, *The Marcus Garvey Papers*, Vol. 9 (1995) and Vol. 10 (2006).
8. See Jacques Garvey, *Garvey and Garveyism* (New York: Collier Books, 1963), 168.
9. Manning Marable, *Malcolm X: A Life of Reinvention* (New York: Viking, 2011) 20–23, 27, 28.
10. Nettleford, *Mirror, Mirror,* 19–37.
11. Walter Rodney, 'Message to Afro-Jamaica Associations,' *Bongo-Man*, no.2, 15.
12. Garvey Jnr., 'The American Scene: An Interview with Marcus Garvey,' *The Blackman* 2, no. 6 (1970): 13–17.
13. Rupert Lewis, 'Marcus Garvey and the Early Rastafarians,' 145–58.
14. George Eaton Simpson, *Religious Cults of the Caribbean: Trinidad, Jamaica, Haiti* (Puerto Rico: Rio Piedras, Institute of Caribbean Studies, University of Puerto Rico, 1970), 219.
15. Anthony Bogues, *Black Heretics, Black Prophets: Radical Political Intellectuals* (New York: Routledge, 2003), 12–13, 166–74.
16. Barry Chevannes, 'The Repairer of the Breach,' (1976): 277.
17. M. Bignall, 'The Construction of a Self-Reliant Community in Jamaica,' (2012): 8.
18. Editorial, *Bongo-Man*, no.1 (1968): 3.
19. George Beckford, *Persistent Poverty: Underdevelopment in Plantation Economies of the Third World* (New York: Oxford University Press, 1972), 15, 23, 67.
20. C. Clarke, *Kingston, Jamaica: Urban Development and Social Change, 1692-2002* (2006) 139.
21. See Gray (2004), Sives (2010) and Hutton (2010).
22. Carl Stone, *Class, Race and Political Behaviour in Urban Jamaica* (Mona: Institute of Social and Economic Research, University of the West Indies, 1973), 112.
23. Mimeographed leaflet in Rupert Lewis's 'Black Power in the 1960s', personal collection.
24. Peter Phillips became general secretary of the People's National Party, served as Minister in the administrations of Michael Manley, P.J. Patterson and Portia Simpson Miller and as of 2017 is PNP President. Garth White is a noted authority and writer on Jamaican popular music. Keith Noel is an educator and former Principal of St Jago High School. Trinidadian by birth, he has lived in Jamaica since the late 1960s. Bernard Marshall hailed from St Vincent and was a historian and lawyer. Arnold Bertram is a prominent historian and former Minister in the administrations of Michael Manley and P.J. Patterson. Edwin Jones is a distinguished academician in Public

Administration. Wyck Williams is Guyanese and published a novel. Jerry Small was a public intellectual long before the term was known, with a unique narrative style drawing on Rastafarian argot and his own native intelligence. He now has his own radio talk show.
25. 'Reasonings', known in the Rastafarian language as 'groundings', were informal gatherings where discussions took place. The location might be a gully bank where squatters lived, a camp of Rastafarians, a school, a church, a trade union hall or any place where ordinary people could meet and discuss issues of interest. In many instances Rodney listened and at other times he gave talks.
26. Frank Davis, Interview with Rupert Lewis (June 3, 1991). Davis worked in Special Branch.
27. Small, Interview with Rupert Lewis. Typescript, (1989), 16.
28. Ibid., 18.
29. Ibid., 32.
30. Ibid., 59.
31. Ibid., 33–34.
32. Ibid., 35.
33. Ralph Gonsalves, 'The Rodney Affair and its Aftermath', *Caribbean Quarterly* 25, no. 3 (1979) 1–24. Dr Ralph Gonsalves is presently Prime Minister of St Vincent and the Grenadines.
34. Small, Interview with Rupert Lewis. Typescript (1989), 40.
35. Gonsalves, 'The Rodney Affair and its Aftermath,' 6–7.
36. 'Campus row brings out vandals', The *Daily Gleaner*, October 17, 1968.
37. Ibid.
38. Gonsalves, 'The Rodney Affair and its Aftermath,' 9.
39. 'Shearer tells House Details of Guyanese's 'Castro plot,' The *Daily Gleaner*, October 18, 1968.
40. Ibid.
41. West, 'Walter Rodney and Black Power,' 2005, 34–35.
42. 'Shearer tells House Details of Guyanese's 'Castro plot,' The *Daily Gleaner*, October 18, 1968).
43. 'Shearer tells House of Details of Guyanese's 'Castro plot,' The *Daily Gleaner*, October 18, 1968).
44. Ibid.
45. 'Chilling but real,' The *Daily Gleaner*, October 18, 1968.
46. Small, Interview, 44–45.
47. Garvey Jr., 'Mwalimu Marcus Garvey Speaks,' *The Blackman* 2, no.5 (1970): 1.
48. This period is dealt with at length in Rupert Lewis, *Walter Rodney's Intellectual and Political Thought*, 1998, chapter v.
49. See Bogues's chapter in this volume.
50. Garvey Jr., 'Mwalimu Marcus Garvey Speaks', 1. Published in *Black Power in the Caribbean*. ed. Kate Quinn, 53–75 (Miami: University of Florida Press, 2014).

## References

Beckford, G. 1972. *Persistent Poverty: Underdevelopment in Plantation Economies of the Third World*, New York: Oxford University Press.

Bignall, M. 2012. The Construction of a Self-Reliant Community in Jamaica: Claudius Henry's Peacemakers Association. Research report, Masters in Social Work, Faculty of Social Sciences, University of the West Indies, Mona.

Bogues, A. 2003. *Black Heretics, Black Prophets: Radical Political Intellectuals*, New York and London: Routledge.

*Bongo-Man*.1968. Editorial, No.1.

Chevannes, B.1976. The Repairer of the Breach: Reverend Claudius Henry and Jamaican Society in *Ethnicity in the Americas*, ed. Frances Henry, 263–290. The Hague: Mouton.

Clarke, C. 2006. *Kingston, Jamaica: Urban Development and Social Change, 1692-2002*. Kingston: Ian Randle Publishers.

Davis, F. 1991. Interview with Rupert Lewis, June 3.

Domingo, W.A. and George Padmore. 1968. Historical Letters of Marcus Garvey. In *Bongo-Man*, No.1.

Garvey, Marcus, Jnr. 1970. The American Scene: An Interview with Marcus Garvey. In *The Blackman*, 2:1.

———. 1970. Mwalimu Marcus Garvey Speaks. In *The Blackman*, 2:5.

*Gleaner*. 1968. Campus Row brings out vandals, marches, fires, thugs on rampage menace capital. October 17.

*Gleaner*. 1968. Shearer tells House of Guyanese's 'Castro plot'. October 18.

Gonsalves, R. 1979. The Rodney Affair and its Aftermath. *Caribbean Quarterly*, 25: 3, 1-24.

Gray, Obika. 2004. *Demeaned but Empowered: The Social Power of the Urban Poor in Jamaica*. Mona: University of the West Indies Press.

Hill, R. 1983. 1995. 2006. *The Marcus Garvey and Universal Negro Improvement Association Papers*, Berkeley and Los Angeles: University of California Press, Volume 1, Volume 2, Volume 9, Volume 10.

Hutton, C. 2010. Oh Rudie: Jamaican Popular Music and the Narrative of Urban Badness in the Making of Post-colonial Society. In *Caribbean Quarterly*, 56: 4, 22-64.

Jacques Garvey, A. 1963. *Garvey and Garveyism*. New York: Macmillan.

Lewis, R. Mimeographed leaflet in 1998. Marcus Garvey and the Early Rastafarians: Continuity and Discontinuity. In *Chanting Down Babylon: A Rastafari Reader*, ed. Nathaniel Samuel Murrell et al, 145-158. Philadelphia: Temple University Press.

———. 1998. *Walter Rodney's Intellectual and Political Thought*. Kingston and Detroit: University of the West Indies Press and Wayne State University Press.

Marable, M. 2011. *Malcolm X: A Life of Reinvention*. New York: Viking.

Rupert Lewis. 'Black Power in the 1960s' personal collection.

Nettleford, R. 1970. *Mirror, Mirror: Identity, Race and Protest in Jamaica*. Kingston: William Collins and Sangster Ltd.

Rodney, W. 1969. Message to Afro-Jamaica Associations. In *Bongo-Man*, No.2.

———. 1996. *The Groundings with My Brothers*. [1969]. London: Bogle L'Ouverture.

Simpson, G. E. 1970. *Religious Cults of the Caribbean: Trinidad, Jamaica, and Haiti*. Rio Piedras: University of Puerto Rico.

Sives, A. 2010. *Elections, Violence, and the Democratic Process in Jamaica, 1944-2007*. Kingston: Ian Randle Publishers.

Small, J. 1989. Interview with Rupert Lewis. Typescript.

Stone, C. 1973. *Class, Race and Political Behaviour in Urban Jamaica*. Mona: Institute of Social and Economic Research, University of the West Indies.

West, M. 2005. Walter Rodney and Black Power: Jamaican Intelligence and U.S. Diplomacy. In *African Journal of Criminology and Justice Studies*, 1: 2, 1-50.

# 3 | *Reflections on the Caribbean Radical Tradition*
## *A Conversation with Professor Rupert Lewis**

Rupert Lewis interviewed by Jermaine McCalpin

JM: This is a conversation with Rupert Lewis, Caribbean political thinker, activist, humanist and scholar. We will be talking about the Caribbean Radical Tradition. I want to start off by asking, how do you theorise/define the Caribbean Radical Tradition?

RL: Well, the Caribbean Radical Tradition centres on the ideas around liberation. In the Caribbean we have had mostly to theorise about the radical tradition of freedom within the contradictory framework of European enslavement and its adjunct plantation systems, colonial rule and white minority rule throughout the entire Caribbean. For me, the Radical Caribbean Tradition transcends linguistic and geographic barriers so that it represents the collective efforts to gain freedom and to develop the nations that emerged in the period of decolonisation. In essence, this tradition is framed as an answer to the existential question of what it means to be human. This is above and beyond the ruminations of the liberation of the European person. What it means to be a human for peoples who have been defined as anything other than human requires more than philosophy, it involves praxis.

JM: Who are persons and movements that you would include within this tradition?

RL: Certainly one would have to start with the Haitian Revolution, and Toussaint L'Ouverture and Jean-Jacques Dessalines come to mind immediately. Of course, in the Jamaican context you have Nanny and Tacky, and Sam Sharpe and Paul Bogle in the post-slavery period. The Morant Bay Rebellion and also the intersection between Jamaica and the American Civil War have to be included. The nineteenth century saw the beginning of the modern expression of Pan-Africanism and that coincided with the back to Africa movement. People like Edward Blyden and others who returned to West Africa to develop missionary kinds of programmes were practical proponents of this tradition. Then you come to the twentieth century and you are dealing with the big movements that affected change, migration being a central one. The two important movements were that of American capital to the region and West Indian migrant labour that built the Panama Canal as well as the involvement of millions of Africans, West Indians and Asian colonials in European armies and support systems in the First World War. The cumulative impact of these experiences contributed to the emergence of anti-colonial movements especially the Garvey movement.

In 2016 there was the centenary celebration of the 1916 Irish uprising and the destruction by the English of Liberty Hall in Dublin, Ireland. Garvey then takes this symbol (Liberty Hall) and develops many more Liberty Halls than the Irish had conceived of for their struggles, in different parts of the world.

The Russian Revolution, and hence, the arrival in the region of Marxist ideas and the Marxist tradition throughout the twentieth century and the social democratic tradition, which preceded it, became a part of the Caribbean Radical Tradition. This Marxist tradition would jockey for political space and viability with the Garvey movement, or more explicitly, Black Nationalism. The post-Second World War era and the emergence of the Cold War [from] 1989 to '90, as well as national liberation movements, are critical to understanding the viscosity of the tradition.

The West embarked on a kind of exultant response to the collapse of communism in the late 1980s and beyond. This has now been replaced by a more sober examination of capitalism, particularly after the global financial recession of 2008. I would argue that we are in a new period now where people are more open to ideas that are critical of neoliberalism, so the Caribbean tradition feeds on all of this.

It would, however, be an incomplete assessment if I neglected the Christian tradition, both the traditional African syncretic religious expressions such as Revivalism, as well as the native

Baptist tradition represented by that whole series of deacons from Sam Sharpe through to Paul Bogle. The Christian tradition is a central part of Caribbean radicalism, because of the role Christians have played in the respective social movements in the region.

JM: I want to go back to something you said concerning the Radical Tradition. You provided an assessment of several different streams within the Radical Tradition. You spoke of Black Nationalism, particularly Garveyism, you spoke of liberation theology, and you spoke of Marxism. Which of these have been the primary and most significant traditions in terms of shaping the intellectual thought of the Caribbean?

RL: I think the essential issue in the Caribbean Radical Tradition really revolves around freedom and sometimes the Marxist gets it, sometimes the Black Nationalists get it, sometimes neither gets it, so these are the sets of values around which people are prepared to make sacrifices and around which they gather to have collective actions. Ironically, freedom posed many challenges; Marxism has within it a certain authoritarian tradition and this comes into conflict frequently with people's sense of freedom. At the same time, capitalism itself, because of the power of money, the power of capital denies basic rights and freedom to many people in terms of work, in terms of hunger and in terms of money being the measure of one's social prospects or possibilities. So both Marxism and capitalism have within them obstacles to the realisation of freedom, so I am open to looking at alternative ways whereby people can construct the systems around which their values relating to freedom can be realised.

JM: I want to turn your attention to a watershed period within the Caribbean. It has been nearly 50 years since the Rodney riots and the Black Power Revolution in Jamaica and Trinidad, respectively. How would you assess their contribution, those two events and series of events to radicalism in the Caribbean?

RL: The Black Power Revolution and the Rodney riots centred on the same idea and that was the incompleteness of political independence for the masses of people of African and Indian descent. The 1970 Trinidad Black Power demonstrations almost led to the demise of Eric Williams's regime in Trinidad. The essential contribution of the Black Power movement was to pose the racial question. The independence cohort of Caribbean political leaders had neglected the racial question for a number of reasons; one is that the transition to political independence in the Caribbean was not marked by any fundamental change in the economic relations of the society. The change was primarily functional, symbolic and personnel change. Independence was a negotiation of the fledgling native political elites and the British ruling class. Louis Lindsay's 'Myth of Independence'[1] was very accurate. It points to something Walter Rodney used to say, that the transition to political independence was not real. He didn't see why we should use the word 'neocolonialism' because not much had changed. So that, in that context, what the Black Power revolt in the Caribbean meant was: it challenged the kind of transition that benefited the British because the British could, after 300 years of profit-making in the Caribbean, abandon it and say, 'We now have given you your sovereignty, it's up to you to make something of it.'

Lost in that 'bequeathing of power' was any recognition that a debt had been incurred by the British, hence the issue of reparation for slavery was hardly raised, not by the Marxist left, or even by the socialists. It was being raised by the Rastafari (who were often seen as a problem: first as a colonial problem, then as a post-colonial problem). This was the group that took up the radical cause of reparations from the 1930s right through as a consistent aspect of its advocacy. To that extent we cannot talk about Black Power without including the Rastafari ethos. It was they who embodied that historical memory of loss of homeland, thus advocating for cultural, ideational and physical repatriation. Second, they constantly reminded us of the debt (reparation) that Britain had escaped from with the illusion of granting power to the middle-class tier of political leadership, who, in exchange for the 'keys to the political kingdom' would not raise such destabilising issues such as reparations.

The Black Power movement posed the racial question and the racial question has several other aspects to it. I've raised the economic aspect but there is also the mental aspect, in that much of the Caribbean political elite at the time of independence was British-trained and British-oriented. They looked up to Britain and those who were educated in England came back with English accents, and they came back with English wives. They were totally consumed with being like the coloniser. The contradiction is not lost on me that this educated elite, through language and education, sought to mimic the colonial class but would never be accepted as its equal. This is what is discussed by, first, Frantz Fanon in *Black Skin, White Masks*, and later by Walter Rodney in *How Europe Underdeveloped Africa*.[2] That was the situation that faced us in the 1960s and the younger generation decided we would have no more discrimination, discrimination in the banking system, in employment and the recruitment of light-skinned people for most of the frontline jobs, discrimination in the hotels and tourist industry, and general discrimination in all areas of social life. I can recall there being a time as recent as the 1960s and '70s when there were benches in some churches that were reserved for the privileged, propertied, moneyed or lettered. The front row was not for the ordinary congregant. This is the social situation against which Black Power emerged in all of the islands. Although the US situation had its own internal dynamics, it also impacted on Black Power in the Caribbean; this was due in no small part to the influence and impact of Stokely Carmichael and others of Caribbean ancestry during the 1960s Black Power developments.

JM: I want to go to a discussion about the Grenadian Revolution and whether or not you believe the demise of the revolution in 1983 meant the setting of the sun on Caribbean radicalism and how would you assess the Grenadian Revolution in this regard?

RL: The Grenadian Revolution was led by Marxists, but they all came out of the Black Power movement. I would argue that the quest of the Grenadian Revolution was to find a way to gain political power by mobilising the people and then to consolidate this political power into people power. The Cuban Revolution had the biggest impact on my generation. However, the Cubans always told us that 'you (the Anglophone Caribbean) have a different political history. It is different from what we faced with the Batista dictatorship' so we were not likely to be able to transition into the kind of system that existed in Cuba. They argued that their political system needed to be like it was not only because of the dictatorship that was overthrown but because of the threat of invasion from the United States; you therefore had to consolidate rather than diffuse power. The multiparty system within the Anglophone Caribbean and the political culture of the mass of people required that we work within it in order to effect change.

The Grenadian Revolution ended primarily because of internal party leadership feuds, the abuse of vanguardism and the American invasion. As I stated earlier, vanguard parties, while they may win power, can only consolidate power by non-democratic means if they do not open up to competition. The demands of participatory democracy did not always fit well with a vanguard party.

JM: So the Grenadian Revolution was an attempt to superimpose this kind of radical tradition on the structure of the Westminster democracy?

RL: Yes. In other words, the Cuban argument continued that we in the Anglophone Caribbean have more flexibility along the lines of democratic competition than they did. Therefore, the model that they developed out of historical necessity should not be imitated in other places where the political traditions were different. That was the kind of discussion that we had. But in the context of the Cold War and, in the context of the grave American involvement in places like Argentina and Chile where they actually supported military coups and in 1973, helped to overthrow the democratically elected Socialist leader Salvador Allende, you realise that, while it is true we had the democratic competitive system, the threat of destabilisation was always imminent. It was in full play in the 1980 elections in Jamaica.

So we recognise that you had to have a strong organisation and strong mass mobilisation to prevent that kind of destabilisation from taking place. It was this kind of development in the Cold War that led to the development of ideas around very strong vanguard parties such as the New Jewel Movement in Grenada.

The problem with the vanguard party is that the internal processes of democracy could be frustrated and could lead to a certain kind of elitism that ran contrary to the political declarations about mass involvement and mass participation. You get a big contradiction between what you hear PM Bishop saying in the interview I did with him, and what was really happening inside the party in difficult situations.[3]

JM: So did the internal feuds you spoke of earlier show up these contradictions concerning vanguard parties and mass participation?

RL: I would say that more attention needs to be paid in the literature on the Grenadian Revolution to the relationship between American intelligence and the inner party feuds at the top. We have a good grasp of what the inner party feuds were about, but not a good grasp of the relationship between that and US intelligence in terms of infiltration and manipulation of actors and political situations. Again, all the things that Louis Lindsay had theorised concerning the psychology of political manipulation are critically important.[4] Vanguardism was important in the overthrow of the Grenada Gary dictatorship, but between 1979 and 1983 it was being utilised in the context where you have the fear of US intervention.

I think the People's Revolutionary Government (PRG) needed some more openness in communicating honestly with the population rather than interpreting questions or objections as the opinion of 'enemies of the Revolution'. A year or so before the demise of the Revolution not many Grenadians, or others elsewhere, were aware of the split between those who were in support of Maurice Bishop, and those who were in support of Bernard Coard in matters concerning joint leadership of the party.

The demise of the Grenadian Revolution, in my view, meant that a certain stage of Caribbean radicalism came to an end. It was the stage that coincided with the emergence of global neoliberalism collapse of the Soviet Union and communist systems in Eastern Europe leading to the end of the Cold War. This 'end of history' global neoliberalism forced all the Caribbean states into a common economic system with the neoliberal rules that now govern our society. The 2008 global recession saw the emergence of strong critiques within the United States, Europe and elsewhere. Despite the negative fallout on regional economies, this recession has however spawned something positive: it has resulted in the emergence of social movements around the world, and their spokespersons are asking questions of global capitalism. Politically, in the United States, the emerging critique on the Left led to the rise of Bernie Sanders' 2016 presidential campaign. Whether or not he got the democratic nomination, for me, is not as important as what he represents: a groundswell of radical democratic opinion among young Americans. Imagine having a democratic socialist candidate with millions of people supporting him in the United States, that hasn't happened since the first 30 years of the twentieth century when American socialism and movements around that, the labour movement and so on, emerged. Caribbean societies are at a kind of crossroads of Western capitalism. We have been one of the centres which have enabled capitalism to grow and emerge and, because of our migratory movement, we are part of the Western labour markets, whether it is in North America or Europe. It is natural that developments in the Western world will have a direct and immediate impact on the Caribbean. What shape, what form this impact will take is another matter, but I think we are at the start of another round of Caribbean radicalism that is responding to global capitalism.

JM: Going back to your first remarks concerning Caribbean Radical Tradition, is it the case that Caribbean radicalism can only be theorised as an inherent response to some kind of external threat but never as a native intellectual political development? How would you assess this reading?

RL: Well, that is a complex formulation, because I don't believe that the external exists in the way that you have posed it. How we think about the world is a function of an existential situation which is not entirely external; it has to do not only with the way in which we are positioned in relationship to the emergence of global capitalism. But there is another tradition – the cultural and intellectual resources that we brought with us across the Atlantic from Africa and Asia and which we have remoulded into the religious and cultural practices that we have. These resources have made us partially but not fully autonomous, because they have to respond and strengthen our capacity to survive and go beyond survival. So it is a dialectic of forces that have shaped our existential thought, our philosophical principles and how we make our way in difficult circumstances.

JM: So in light of that, how would you best describe the intellectual and political climate of the Caribbean today?

RL: I would describe it as emerging from a low ebb. I wouldn't describe it at the moment as strong. I think that the orthodoxy of neoliberal thinking is not being sufficiently challenged. It is being challenged externally, but I see a lot of conformity in the Caribbean. So this is why I say we are at a low ebb. There are, however, some autonomous expressions of non-conformism, the Rastafari would be one example of this, but even Rastafari itself, I would argue, is in a quandary in terms of the newer generations that have embraced it but who have more of a commercial response rather than the intellectual, philosophical one of earlier generations. So there is a crisis of reproduction, because the younger generation is not going to simply repeat what the older generations did. So they themselves are working through what it means to be a Rastafari in this twenty-first century, bearing in mind the global networks around which Rastafari are flung.

JM: What other group, in your estimation, is upholding the Caribbean Radical Tradition?

RL: I believe there is a search among young people that is beginning to emerge and you see some evidence of this in the music. The arts are always an area where we see people taking risks, rethinking, and I think some of the younger musicians and singers and so on, like Chronixx, are doing this. So my belief is that this generation of youths will have to formulate their own responses in this twenty-first century. This response may add new elements to the radical tradition. There are a lot of possibilities that can't be predetermined, bearing in mind that a strictly materialist radicalism, given our trajectory, won't be adequate in dealing with the spiritual yearnings of the population. So we cannot shelve the spiritual component of the Caribbean Radical Tradition. The West has demonstrated for me that a purely materialist political philosophy can't cope with human yearnings and therein lies a whole arena of struggle. There is a level of honest inadequacy even within, say, Fidel Castro and the Cuban context. Cuba, which has been the most radical Caribbean revolution since the Haitian Revolution, is not adequate. The overthrow of Batista did not, for example, address the ways in which the Afro-Cuban felt undervalued or underrepresented in post-revolution Cuba. This is what I mean by a critique of the materialist philosophy which underlay Marxism. This philosophy is inadequate because the human needs for freedom, for expression, for realisation of self have deeper requirements than a political programme and an economic programme can provide.

JM: How would you assess Cuba's role in the Caribbean Radical Tradition?

RL: I think that both José Martí and Antonio Maceo are critical to Cuba and the Caribbean. I link them both because, very often, people talk of Martí and neglect Maceo. They represent the beginnings of Cuba's modern contribution to the radical tradition. The July 26 movement led by Fidel Castro was an expression of Cuban radical nationalism and anti-imperialism. I would say that Cuba demonstrated that you can make a break with imperialism. However, Cuba succeeded in doing that only because there was an alternate system that they could trade with. When that system collapsed you had to go back to capitalism and they traded with all the countries except the United States, and the United States is just coming on board.

Even radicalism requires pragmatism and this is what China has shown since they embarked on opening their economy under Deng Xiaoping in 1979. China has demonstrated that both the market and the state are important. This balance is at the heart of China's expansionist policies into Africa and the Caribbean.

The world has changed significantly since the end of the Cold War. It is no longer where one part of the world was socialist and one part is capitalist; the whole world is capitalist and you have to navigate state capacity within global markets.

I think that in terms of Caribbean radicalism then, I would say that Cuba, particularly in the military involvement in Angola, provided moral, ideological and physical support to the cause of freedom. This was a key military achievement of the twentieth century. To stay under the eye of United States and to send thousands of soldiers to fight in Africa is akin to Toussaint L'Ouverture's nineteenth century dream of stopping the slave trade had he gained state power after the Haitian Revolution.

I have been told by P.J. Patterson that when Zimbabwe got independence in 1980, he was on a plane (Prime Minister [Michael] Manley couldn't go because of the electoral campaign in Jamaica) with Bob Marley and Forbes Burnham and when they landed in Harare there was this huge crowd. Burnham said to him, 'I have never been met by so many people in all my life.' It was soon apparent that it wasn't him; it was Bob Marley. They had to reschedule the formal ceremony for the handing over of power in Zimbabwe because of Bob Marley's concert. So we had a symbolic and cultural Pan-African impact, whereas Cuba was able to effectively do the military and political side.

The final thing I would say on Cuban Caribbean radicalism is that it gave the region a sense that we were capable of doing things differently from the colonial tradition; that we could actually initiate something and follow it through even in the context of harsh opposition and a greater physical military force. So it gave encouragement, and those states in 1972 which gave Cuba diplomatic recognition – Jamaica, Trinidad and Tobago, Barbados, and Grenada – they have reaped more benefits from Cuba from the education of thousands of young people through scholarships and in the availability of Cuban medical personnel.

When Fidel first visited Jamaica, they made sure that they had a black presence high up in their delegations, because there was the recognition that Jamaica is a black country and if Cuba had had a revolution, Jamaicans would ask where are the black people? So Cuba impacted Jamaica and the rest of the Caribbean, but they were also impacted by Jamaica and the rise of the status of the black majority, especially in the politics of the 1970s.

JM: Now, you did the interview we referred to earlier with Prime Minister Bishop 34 years ago concerning, specifically, the Grenadian Revolution, but also his own assessment of Caribbean radicalism. In what ways have your own views changed, if any at all, concerning the Grenadian Revolution and its meaning for the Caribbean?

RL: Let me say the way in which the idea has not changed, and it is this: we continue to underestimate the capacity of our population to transform their environment. In Grenada, we tried to find a way of enabling the transformation of the people. However, our methods were problematic. The Gairy dictatorship had been overthrown but in its wake the masses were not incorporated into charting the political direction of the country. They were not consulted on key political questions, although they were consulted on the budget and matters to do with the policies of the state; but they were only told what had been decided on politically essential matters. The 'they' I refer to are the general population. I think that that was the weakness, but I also feel that the Caribbean had to go towards multiparty regimes and therefore, part of the challenge of the Grenada period was that a one-party de facto regime was politically disabling and the PRG had postponed having an election. They needed to have an election earlier on; they were preparing for it but it was taking too long. And the final thing is, you had to be prepared to lose power. I do not believe the

PRG had thought this through. Further, the Cuban Revolution was not a model in this regard. Their one-party regime may be thought of as a historical necessity but it is not a model of politics of the future. Revolutions must not be taken to mean that only one party should rule in perpetuity.

JM: How would you assess your own contribution to the Caribbean Radical Tradition?

RL: It is a modest contribution. I have sought to study Garveyism in particular because of how it represented in the early twentieth century the rise of black internationalism. I have also done work on Walter Rodney who was geared towards understanding Caribbean political, economic, and cultural transformation in the era of decolonisation. I have been involved in political party activism, especially the Workers' Party of Jamaica, from the beginning in the 1970s and even in the pre-party organisations such as the Workers' Liberation League right down until the end of the 1980s.

I could not be a member of the Jamaica Labour Party or the People's National Party because I have never shared their orientation. I might have been more sympathetic to Manley's democratic socialism, but from the outside. So I am committed to developing alternative vehicles. There is a long 80-year stretch ahead of the oncoming generations to develop their own vehicles. You don't have to drive the vehicles created in the 1930s and '40s. This is the twenty-first century so my mind is oriented towards thinking about more effective vehicles for change and, of course, we live in a different world now where civic organisations, non-government organisations (NGOs), individual churches, community organisations as well as Caribbean diasporas need to play a bigger role in the day-to-day life of the country. The political parties continue to play a game with the electorate. You cannot solve the problem unless more of the people are involved more of the time with the issues that face us, because the parties in and of themselves do not have the answer. So, we are at a kind of twilight zone in the Caribbean at the moment, and I think new forms of Caribbean thinking and new solutions to the problems that beset us need to be forged. I don't believe that they can or need to be forged entirely within the Caribbean; they can be wider than the Caribbean. I mean the older generation was not so concerned with the physical environment; yet the environment is a critical issue. We in the Caribbean cannot just deal with it in a parochial sense as a collection of small island states. The environment is complex, it is important not just for the environmentalist but for all of us. All of the islands from Cuba in the north right down to Trinidad are affected by tourism. Tourism impacts on the environment, receding beach lines and so on. So, even in the environmental area you will see the importance of the international factor. What's important for me is that the Caribbean can play a leadership role on many of these issues that go beyond their actual physical size as small states.

JM: Well, now a very critical and vexing issue that is often glossed over or ignored is the question of women within the Caribbean Radical Tradition. Do you believe that women have been properly included, not just in the theorising about, but also the praxis of the Caribbean Radical Tradition?

RL: I would have to say women were marginalised in the Caribbean Radical Tradition, certainly in my generation. There is still considerable patriarchal resistance in terms of giving just credit to the role of women in Caribbean freedom. This resistance will decrease, especially because more women are going to be playing roles that will enable the society to move ahead. What I have in mind again, not so much in Jamaica, but, if you look at Trinidad and the education of women of East Indian descent, that has broken down the patriarchal barriers that I was familiar with in the '60s and '70s. So, I think that I am optimistic on that score of gender equality. I think more men are in support of it and see the wisdom and necessity of recognising the equality of women.

JM: So, if we look at it historically, is it the case that women were not significant contributors to the Caribbean Radical Tradition, or they were just excluded from being given proper and honest roles in the Caribbean intellectual tradition?

RL: Well, they made important contributions and certainly the work of Rhoda Reddock documented the struggles of women. She brought to life many of these female figures on the left who were in the movements of the anti-colonial period.[5] Many of these women were, before now, only marginally referenced as footnotes to a history of radicalism in which they were critical players. So there is need for historic excavation and rectification. There were thousands of female activists in the Garvey movement in 40 countries and work is being done on some of them. In recent years outstanding books have been published on Una Marson, Claudia Jones and Sylvia Wynter.[6] And yet there are many women thinkers and activists in the black radical tradition still to be recovered. I also believe that women will play a bigger role in re-defining and re-shaping the Caribbean Radical Tradition and diminishing its patriarchal aspects.

JM: How do you think the advocacy for reparations for slavery fits within the Caribbean Radical Tradition and historically was this a part of the intellectual thought of the Caribbean Radical Tradition?

RL: Reparation has always been a part of the tradition primarily in terms of the philosophy of return to and reclamation of Africa. However, the intellectuals paid too little attention to the debt that had been incurred by the colonial metropoles. Eric Williams in *Capitalism and Slavery* made a very strong case, but when Eric Williams became prime minister this was never on the political agenda of his regime. The writings of Hilary Beckles and Verene Shepherd have done much to refocus our attention on reparations. So, this is part of the correction that is needed. We need to look at development within the region, but we must also examine the historical effects of slavery on the Caribbean. The CARICOM Reparations Commission Ten Point Plan has been crafted and needs to be followed up.[7] We must use popular education to inform the people that reparation is not asking for assistance or loans; it is about compensation for both the historic injustice and the effects of slavery. It is not only about monetary compensation but about how we understand our history and the new beginnings we must make in framing sense of self and our future.

The global indifference and ignorance concerning the need for reparations for slavery is not just among whites. In my conversations with friends from across the African continent, they indicated that many Africans are not aware that the Caribbean had slavery and where these slaves came from and why they came. I think we underestimate the need for the education of our population this side of the Atlantic as well as the other side of the Atlantic. Personally, the importance of memorialising these islands that were slave colonies ensures that the memory doesn't die. As Caribbean people, this is an important part of our sense of self: that we were not destined to be slaves, we were enslaved and robbed of our humanity and resources. The resilience of the Caribbean and its people indicates that we have the capacity to transform ourselves.

JM: In your own intellectual thought, what are your views on the expediency and the moral necessity of reparations?

RL: Well, the expediency/moral necessity – I make a distinction between the two; I will start with the moral necessity for information, for understanding the factors that have shaped us. I think the expedient part is that reparation was paid to the planters and therefore it is not that you are starting from a baseline of no action being taken; actions were taken on behalf and in favour of the planters, no actions were taken in favour of the enslaved. That is the expediency that is the business part of the reparations agenda. It is long overdue, the time is now.

JM: In terms of the role of The University of the West Indies as a ground on which much of this intellectual thought developed, what do you consider the role of the university, not just the UWI but the university as a model, in sustaining and expanding this Caribbean Radical Tradition?

RL: Well, that's a very deep question, deeper than you may even think, because I don't think the university was conceived with the Caribbean Radical Tradition in mind. The UWI was conceived within the context of a colonial tutelage relationship with Britain. It was to prepare the elite of the Caribbean to assume positions of authority in the state, in the economy and so on. It is the academics employed in the university who have the time and the space to choose subjects, to choose topics, to research areas; that tradition can only be enhanced by them. The survival and thriving of the tradition cannot be enhanced by bureaucratic edict. There is academic freedom to pursue one's agenda. It is what you want to do, it is what you choose to do; you have that freedom. I believe that UWI can be a model of what a twenty-first century university looks like. Populations of especially Africans and Indians were drawn into an oppressive, conflictual environment of slavery and indentureship but have assimilated and made the Caribbean their own. We as a region have mastery in survival and creativity especially in the cultural sphere. This is the Caribbean tradition that the UWI can foster. We have to combine that resilience and creativity with problem-solving. Then, the university will be a nursery of and for transformation. Students of the UWI of today have to see themselves more than just potential graduates with a degree. They must engage and change the space they inhabit. Students in South Africa have formed movements for curriculum change, for better representation of African scholars and greater participation in the governance of institutions of higher learning. We have been through that in the '60s and '70s and the thing was that we went through what is called a 'West Indianisation' phase where you were training your people in the best places, and bringing them back and they were transforming the curricula and making headway with their research. We have to get back to that, where the economic luxury of the colonial metropoles does not remove a natal obligation to develop the place that developed you.

I am aware that the economic vicissitudes of our times necessitate that Caribbean people have to leave the region. The university, through its administration and academic staff, must affirm and reignite the creativity of our people, encouraging innovation and excellence. This is the only bulwark against the university becoming simply another place where you churn out degrees. Producing degrees is good but what is required is cutting-edge research and innovation for transformation. The university must provide solutions to the problems that we face. We are as relevant as the solutions we produce. To paraphrase Lloyd Best, the job of the intellectual worker is to produce thought, thought is action for us. However, let us not think that the academic is just a thinker, he is a doer; that is the essence of Caribbean freedom; that we can think through our countries' and region's problems and provide solutions. It is in independent thought, a world of our own making, that Caribbean freedom is best captured.[8]

*The above conversation that Jermaine McCalpin had with Rupert Lewis took place on March 30, 2016 in Kingston, Jamaica.

## Notes

1. 'The Myth of Independence: Middle Class Politics and Non-Mobilization in Jamaica,' The University of the West Indies, Sir Arthur Lewis Institute for Social and Economic Studies, 1975, reprinted 1981 with new Introduction 2005.
2. *Black Skin, White Masks* was originally published in 1952 (in English 1957) and was an assessment of the dehumanising nature of colonial domination. It typified colonialism as a total institution, impacting all aspects of the native's existence and future. Rodney's magnum opus was originally published in 1973.
3. The interview referenced was conducted by Rupert Lewis in May 1982 and was entitled 'Maurice Bishop: Grenada is Building a New Life.' It was later published in *Grenada: History, Revolution and US Intervention* (Moscow: USSR Academy of Sciences, Arbat, Moscow and Latin America: Studies by Soviet Scholars, 1984), 108–124.
4. Louis Lindsay, *Myth of a Civilizing Mission: British Colonialism and the Politics of Symbolic Manipulation* (Kingston: Institute for Social and Economic Research, University of the West Indies, 1981).
5. Rhoda Reddock, *Women, Labour and Politics in Trinidad and Tobago: A History* (Atlantic Highlands, New Jersey: Zed Books, 1994).
6. For Marcus Garvey's two wives who were Pan-Africanists see Tony Martin, *Amy Ashwood, Pan-Africanist, Feminist and Mrs Marcus Garvey No. 1 (Or, A Tale of Two Amies)* (Dover, MA. The Majority Press, 2007); Ula Yvette Taylor, *The Veiled Garvey, The Life & Times of Amy Jacques Garvey* (Chapel Hill: The University of North Carolina Press, 2002). For Una Marson, see Delia Jarrett-Macauley, *The life of Una Marson 1905–1965* (Kingston: Ian Randle Publishers, 1998); Alison Donnell, *Una Marson, Selected Poems*, Leeds: Peepal Tree Press, 2011; and Una Marson, Pocomania and London Calling (Kingston: Blouse and Skirt Books and National Library of Jamaica, 2016). For Claudia Jones see Marika Sherwood, *Claudia Jones – A Life in Exile* (London: Lawrence & Wishart, 1999); Carol Boyce Davies, *Left of Karl Marx: The Political Life of Black*

*Communist* (Durham: Duke University Press, 2008). For Sylvia Wynter see Anthony Bogues ed., *After Man Towards the Human: Critical Essays on Sylvia Wynter* (Kingston: Ian Randle Publishers, 2006); Katherine McKittrick, ed., *Sylvia Wynter: On Being Human as Praxis* (Durham: Duke University, 2015). CARICOM Reparations Ten Point Plan, 2013, accessed at http://ibw21.org/commentary/caricom-reparations-ten-point-plan/, April 8, 2016.

7. Selwyn Ryan, ed., *Independent Thought and Caribbean Freedom: Essays in honour of Lloyd Best*, Sir Arthur Lewis Institute of Social and Economic Studies, 2003.

# 4 | *Radical Caribbean Thought:*
*Rupert Lewis and the Politics of an 'Internal Dread'*

Anthony Bogues

**Introduction**

I would like to begin by thanking the organisers for asking me to be one of the keynote speakers at this conference to honour Professor Rupert Lewis. Much honour is due to this scholar and intellectual whose life and work have been a central thread of mid-twentieth century Caribbean radicalism, particularly in the phase of the post-independence moment – the historic moment of grappling with decolonisation. I wish to begin my talk with a few opening remarks. One cannot think of radical politics during the 1970s without referencing the work and intellectual practice of Rupert Lewis. And here, I am not only thinking specifically about his work on Marcus Garvey,[1] which has been a consistent thread in his political and intellectual life, but rather his work as a radical political journalist/intellectual, and therefore, his editorship of the journals and newspapers like *Impact, Bongo Man* and his editorial work on the editorial committee of that remarkable newspaper of the late 1960s, *Abeng*, as well as his editorship of the newspaper of the Workers Party of Jamaica, *Struggle*, and the party's theoretical journal, *Socialism*.[2] These small newspapers/journals were one of the cores of radical political and intellectual life at the time. Rupert Lewis was deeply involved in these because, for him, radical ideas mattered, but more importantly – it was how he understood the role of the radical intellectual. For Lewis, the work of the radical intellectual was to intervene; to create possible terrains of new thinking which would augment the organising of change. Thus, his journalistic practices were not literary in the narrow sense, but necessary radical intellectual activity. In engaging in this practice, he extended the Jamaican and Caribbean tradition of radical journalism.[3]

This work of the small radical journal/newspaper in the Caribbean and its centrality to radical practice/political thought is a deeply understudied area in Caribbean radical political thought. In this lacuna, we miss a contemporary archive of Caribbean political thought.

My second point is about Rupert's relationship to Walter Rodney. Professor Lewis's book on Walter Rodney[4] is not just an extraordinary work of radical political intellectual history and detailed scholarship. It is a remarkable text because, in it, Rupert Lewis attempts to work out some of the conundrums of post-independence Caribbean radicalism; Marxism; Black Nationalism; the relationship of Africa to the Caribbean; Rastafari and the Caribbean Revolution; and centrally, the problematic role of the relationship of the radical intellectual to the ordinary Caribbean person. All these matters he works through while thinking about Walter Rodney's life. In a profound sense, Rupert's relationship to Rodney is one which is mediated by some of the similar concerns of Walter Rodney, in particular, those about Africa, questions of democracy and the role of individual political leadership. But I go one step further. If Walter Rodney was moved by a passion, as he puts it in *Groundings with My Brothers*, for 'history in the service of the African Revolution', Rupert Lewis is moved by a profound passion to understand politics as a practice. His work is not framed by the conventional protocols of political science, rather, at its core he tries to grapple with the complex meanings of the *experience of politics*.

Now, much has been said and will be said about Rupert Lewis's quality of humanness, one, in my view, which is rooted in his profound belief in a democratic ethos. We will hear of the many ways he has motivated students and his deep personal concern for others. In this regard, I want to publicly thank him for three things.

Firstly, in the early 1970s while still in high school in sixth form, I joined the Abeng group where I met Rupert Lewis. He then lived at 12 Mona Road in a flat located on the compound of Mrs Amy Jacques Garvey. At that time he was working on Garvey and I asked if I could help organise some of the papers. He said yes, and I and Honor Ford-Smith, a founder of Sistren, the theatre collective, visited him a few times to organise papers. It was in his flat that I first encountered African Literature and borrowed two books which for many years I constantly read. The books were a small collected volume of Marx/Engels on Art and Literature, and a book on Marxism and African Literature.

Years later, when I wrote one of my undergraduate honours theses on African Literature and the writings of Ngugi wa Thiong'o, supervised by Professor Maureen Lewis, I was working through the ideas I first picked up both in discussions with him and reading these two books.

My second thanks relates to both him and the late Professor Rex Nettleford. After years of political activism, I decided to apply to the University of the West Indies (UWI) to do a PhD. The late Professor Nettleford did all the necessary administrative negotiations, since UWI at the time felt that my past activism, some of it on the Mona campus, had not been congenial. Rupert Lewis was asked to work with me and this two-person committee of himself and Nettleford, along with the external reviewer, philosopher Charles Mills, made it possible for me to work on C.L.R. James. I want to publicly thank Rupert for all his efforts as one of the supervisors of this thesis. In this sense, I am one of his students.

My third thanks relate to something he did when he was the head of the Department of Government. After completing my PhD in the field of political thought/theory, I went to Howard University as a postdoctorial fellow and when I returned to UWI, Professor Lewis gently 'commanded' me to teach the two African politics courses in the department. I was reluctant but agreed and began an intellectual journey in which the study of Africa is now critical to my own reframing of the history of political thought. So, I want to thank Rupert for this gentle 'command'.

I relate these thanks publicly both as a public tribute but also to indicate some of the reasons why I would end up here this morning talking about radical political thought and the Caribbean Intellectual Tradition.

**The Radical Caribbean Tradition**

As I said, Rupert Lewis's intellectual sensibility is one in which politics is a practice, and I often recall his discussions with me on the Oxford political theorist and intellectual historian, Isaiah Berlin's essay 'Political Judgment'.[5] This essay by Berlin raises a number of questions on the relationship between knowledge and good judgment in politics. Interestingly, both Nettleford and Lewis made constant references to this essay in conversations but without footnotes in their work. For both of them, I suggest that politics was a form of lived experience.

If I am allowed here a personal note. It is the many conversations over years with these two Caribbean figures that created one ground of my own transition from normative political philosophy to political thought/theory and intellectual history. What we have neglected to reflect upon in examining the history of the social sciences at UWI is how both Nettleford and Lewis practised a form of interpretive social science which helped to reconfigure and reposition Caribbean thought. Such practices placed them in the forefront of what we now call interdisciplinary work.[6] What this means is that in any review of their work it would be productive to draw upon Caribbean intellectuals who themselves operated outside of the field of social science but who practised what I have called elsewhere a 'worldly hermeneutics'.[7]

Rupert Lewis consciously works within a black radical Caribbean tradition and to better understand his work I want to turn to two figures in that tradition – Sylvia Wynter and Wilfredo Lam. I take this detour as a way of illumination, to make the case for a tradition which I think we have not yet grasped in its world historical significance. This is not a matter of nationalism; rather, it is understanding how radical thinkers from the Caribbean have postulated a series of questions about human life in the twentieth century. In following this procedure, I am thinking about a moment in twentieth century Caribbean Radical Thought and a network of ideas which were deeply interconnected through individuals in the region while arguing that this network and the individuals within it are central to any twentieth century history of thought.[8]

It is the year 2000 in San Fernando, Trinidad and the Oilfield Workers Trade Union (OWTU) has invited me to deliver the annual C.L.R. James Lecture. At that time, I was still collecting material on James with the intention of writing an intellectual/political biography. After the lecture, I decided to stay on for a week to go through the boxes/archives of the James material housed where he had lived in a residence given to him by the OWTU. C.L.R. James had lived in this place for a short spell and then returned to London where he died in 1989. In the third box of ten boxes, I came upon two articles written by Wynter – one I had already read some time ago, the 1971 review of Audvil King's book, *One Love*, published by Bogle L'Ouverture Publications in London.[9]

King's text was an important critical intervention around the issue of blackness in Jamaica. He writes, '[inside] agencies are most times, more influential on our behaviour, conditions of living, enjoyment of life, than we ourselves'. We should here recall that King was writing this in the midst of the upsurge of Black Power in the region and three to four years after the Walter Rodney 1968 riots in Jamaica.

In the James archive at the OWTU, both papers bear the stamp on their covers of the Caribbean Unity Conference, Washington, DC.[10] The essay of Wynter which reviews *One Love* was published by the Institute of the Caribbean Studies in Puerto Rico.[11] I mention this because, in thinking about the Caribbean today, I want to suggest that the boundaries which have been created – the borders which separate us – island-from-island – that these borders were historically porous. Just think about it: An essay on a Jamaican writer, published in Puerto Rico and then read and circulated by a group of Caribbean individuals in Washington, DC, and in 2000 it lays in a box in San Fernando, Trinidad. What does such a circulation mean? I want to propose to you that this travelling of ideas and networks which it created are a critical element in any thinking about radical Caribbean thought in the twentieth century. For Wynter, King's book represents what she calls 'Afro-Jamaicanism'. She writes that 'Afro-Jamaicanism is a part of a new wave of writers'. She then argues that the 'old wave of writers were national...and provided the catalyst for the birth of national consciousness...This new wave born in the 1940s living in a neo-colonial moment now find that they need to engage with revindication of blackness, which is, in a sense, the revindication of the native, the revindication of the humanness of Man.'[12]

I suggest to you here that 'Afro-Jamaicanism' becomes a moment in which the questions of blackness puncture the neocolonial settlement of Jamaica's constitutional independence. It draws from a long genealogy of Afro-Caribbean religious forms and Black Nationalism and a preoccupation with Africa as a central node in an alternative symbolic order. Wynter writes that at that moment of 'Afro-Jamaicanism', 'the certainty is gone. The name of the game is changed. The stage was only a stage...in a neo-colonial situation; in a world dominated by a handful of metropolitan mega-corporations...This experience of alienation...links the new wave of writers to the earlier Caribbean movements of Negritude – the literary counterpart of the political and social movement of Garveyism.'[13]

This is a critical observation since Lewis's work intervenes into this stream of 'Afro-Jamaicanism'. His work within this stream is explicitly political, making an attempt to think about the lived experiences of blackness in Jamaica within the political domain. In doing this, blackness would become a radical force in his work and would remain one of his central preoccupations. Just think of some of the titles of his writings: 'Claude McKay's Jamaica (1977); 'Black Nationalism in Recent Years' (1977); 'Love and Bedward in Jamaica' (1987). This is not a blackness of phenotype; rather, it is how the lived experiences of being black in a racist colour-coded society produces a set of political ideas. It is, as I have argued elsewhere about a 'radical blackness'.[14]

## A Lacuna in Caribbean Radical Thought

The second paper in the James archive is in File 10/Box 3. On the cover of this paper James writes: 'the best mind in the Caribbean'. I pause, simply stunned. I had read most of James's letters, all of his published works and many of his unpublished writings. I had done so travelling to libraries in Detroit, London, New York and the Caribbean. One of James's colleagues, the late Martin Glaberman, had opened his library and papers to me, yet I had never read anything that James had written about Wynter, nor was there any reference I could recall.

So I stopped going through the box and read her essay titled 'We Know Where We are from – The Politics of Black Culture from Mayalism to Marley', a paper delivered at a conference in Houston, Texas, November 1977.

For some time and still today, I wonder about this absence of the references to Wynter, not so much in James's work but more importantly – Wynter's absence in the discussion of radical ideas in the 1970s, since it is now clear that she was one of the essential figures working through a 'praxis of decolonization'. I think three reasons offer themselves for her absence:

1. Her gender. In this regard I think it is safe to say that radical Caribbean thought was organised around what the African American scholar Geri Augusto has called the 'West Indian Manhood project'.[15] In other words, the intellectual tradition was very masculine.
2. The fact that her late brother, Hector Wynter, was deeply connected to the conservative Jamaica Labour Party and the

ways in which 'political tribalism' works to marginalise people sometimes by mere association.
3. The fact that within radical Caribbean intellectual practice in the 1970s there were the following radical dominant schools of thought:
    - The Theory of Creole society developed by Kamau Brathwaite.
    - The Theory of Plantation Society in which the political economy work of Lloyd Best, George Beckford, Norman Girvan and Kari Levitt dominated.
    - The emergence of Marxism, particularly in a version of Stalinism which then came to dominate the political left within the region.

Within such a discursive political context Wynter, although having an extensive cluster of writings with numerous essays in journals like *Jamaica Journal*, *Savacou*, and *New World*, along with her plays as well as her work on the National Heroes Committee, then chaired by Frank Hill, where she wrote the document which became the platform for the Order of National Hero, continued until recently to live on the margins of Caribbean radical thought. Today, it is safe to say that there is now a revival of Wynter, although this revival focuses on her later and more recent work.[16]

This is not the place to explicate the work of Wynter; however, I wish to draw your attention to two elements of her work before she leaves Jamaica, which I would argue frames her 'praxis of decolonization' and then suggest to you that Rupert Lewis, in his work, operated along similar lines and within the same field of thought. I am not suggesting here that Lewis follows Wynter. There is a conventional practice within the academy in which individuals grappling with similar problems are linked together and then a neologism is developed to describe a complex process and relationship of ideas. Instead, what I am trying to point to is how individuals working in specific historical moments, face questions and that when they do they reach for ideas which come out of a tradition. In this reaching, they expand and rework the tradition which they work through. In Wynter's case, she does this by developing theories of Caribbean social life and in Lewis's case he attempts to formulate a series of understandings about politics from the same ground. For Wynter, one of these two theories is a theory of indigenization followed by notions of a praxis of decolonial history.

Let us take her theory of indigenisation. In 1970, Kamau Brathwaite published his path-breaking historical work *The Development of Creole Society in Jamaica 1770–1870*. When the book was published it transformed the word 'creole' from a descriptive to an interpretive one of Caribbean societies. We are aware that there is another genealogy of creole that we should be attentive to and that is the way in which the British writer Anthony Trollope uses it in his 1859 book *The West Indies and the Spanish Main*, where he makes a set of distinctions between Africans living in Africa and those living in the Caribbean. Trollope notes that the latter were 'creole Negroes' and therefore capable of being civilised by British colonial power, while for Africans living on continental Africa this was a more daunting task. However, to return to Brathwaite, he posits the notion of creolisation which he further elaborates in that 1974 remarkable essay 'Contradictory Omens, Cultural Diversity and Integration in the Caribbean'. This concept of creole as a framework for Caribbean society was in contradiction to M.G. Smith's frame of a plural society. In this talk, I am not able to deal with the afterlife of the concept of creole, nor do we have the space and time to review how creoleness/creolisation emerges in the French Caribbean in the work of Édouard Glissant. Briefly though, I would draw your attention to the writings of Patrick Chamoiseau and Raphael Confiant and their 1989 Manifesto *In Praise of Creoleness*. In this manifesto, they argue that they want to replace Negritude, which they stated replaced the 'illusion of Europe with the illusion of Africa… and that with Glissant we defuse the trap of Negritude and spelled out Caribbean'.

I mention this because I want to argue that Wynter's theory of indigenisation works through Aimé Césaire's and Léopold Sédar Senghor's conception of Negritude. Secondly, she does what theories of creolity/creoleness do not do – she thinks about Haiti as a Caribbean space. Working through the 1928 seminal book of the Haitian thinker, Jean Price Mars, *And So Spoke Uncle* while reading Frantz Fanon on National Culture and working with Césaire particularly his writings on Haiti, Wynter develops a theory of indigenisation. This is how she describes the theory in her remarkable article, 'Jonkonnu in Jamaica'. The history of the Caribbean islands is, in large part, the history of the *indigenisation* of the black man. What this means is that rather than the process of creolisation, Wynter wants to point to us how the ex-slave became a 'native' in the New World.[17] In this historical process she notes further that this history of indigenisation is a 'cultural history – not in writing but of those *'homunculi'* who humanize the landscape by peopling it with gods and spirits, with demons and duppies, with all the rich panoply of man's imagination.'[18] For Wynter the enslaved African created a set of cultural practices not in a model of a creole matrix but rather one in which in which African cultural forms were re-organised and adapted to a new space. Wynter's theoretical insight here is an important one because she is sensing that the twentieth century emergence of creole nationalism as a form of cultural/political ideology would subordinate the subaltern classes. This is critical to the thought and work of Rupert Lewis. His attachment to blackness and Africa meant that he would be convinced that forms of radicalism which did not draw from nor recognised these African adapted forms were not sustainable. Thus, in an interview with David Scott, he responds this way to a question posed to him about the relationship between culture and radical politics of the WPJ, 'There was a sense that there was a tradition, but there was a sense that the revolution about which the WPJ was speaking was different from these traditions…therefore, in a naïve way, it was necessary to help create this revolutionary proletarian culture.'[19]

I sense in Lewis and his work a disquiet about the way in which forms of Leninism were adapted in Jamaica and the Caribbean since he was very aware of the troubled history of the relationship between Marxism as practised by the then Soviet Union and black radicalism.[20] If Wynter is an anti-colonial thinker operating at the moment of political independence, then Lewis is a radical decolonial thinker operating in the inauguration of the neocolonial moment in Jamaica. It is not only a matter of generation, but it is also about the questions posed. For Wynter, coming of age in colonial Jamaica and studying in London as part of the Caribbean anti-colonial generation of the 1950s, the central question was political independence. On the other hand, Lewis goes to UWI in the 1960s as part of the creation of a native elite that was now trained to rule the de jure independent nation. That he rejects this role and quickly attaches himself on to the growing current in which blackness would become a rallying cry to posit radical politics as an attempt to decolonise the nation, is a mark of what Wynter calls the 'new wave' pushing the boundaries of political independence.

**The Praxis of Decolonisation**

The other theoretical insight of Wynter which emerges from her work at this time is that of decolonial history. Here, Wynter posits a series of arguments about reframing Jamaica's history noting in particular that one needed to understand the period of Spanish colonialism and the relationship between the early Maroons and the indigenous population.

I submit that in thinking about the intellectual history of the Caribbean and general practices of the history of thought that this idea of a praxis of decolonisation is critical not only for historical scholarship and thought but for all forms of human activity within the post-colony. It is from this frame that I wish to briefly turn to the Afro-Cuban artist Wilfredo Lam.

In the history of art and modernism, Lam is considered a central figure. The San Francisco Museum features him and the Mexican painter and muralist Diego Rivera as figures of modernism. In art history, his name appears alongside Picasso and Matisse and then with the founding figure of surrealism – Andre Breton. In her history of Caribbean art Veerle Poupeye considers Lam a key figure in a category she calls 'Caribbean modernism'.[21]

Space does not permit any profound discussion of the emergence of 'modernism' and its relationship to particularly French colonialism in Africa. In part, the story is about how sacred African masks circulated in European capitals and then their emergence as a fetishism. One needs only to recall Picasso and Henri Matisse's finding these masks in the markets of Paris and then how these masks reshaped their own 'figurative' paintings, producing in Pablo Picasso paintings an art form now seen as part of Cubism.[22]

It is the moment of the 1940s that Lam is in Paris after fighting in the Spanish Civil War against Franco's fascism. In Paris, he becomes acquainted with the surrealist artists, Picasso and left political debates. However, it is a visit to Martinique, Haiti and his return to Cuba which becomes the grounds for him to produce his most startling works, including *The Jungle*.[23]

Lam painted *The Jungle,* his masterpiece, in 1943 after returning to his native Cuba. The work was 'intended to communicate a psychic state,' Lam said. It depicts a group of figures with 'crescent shaped faces that recall African/Pacific Islander Masks on vertical background suggesting Cuban sugarcane fields thereby addressing the issue of slavery in colonial Cuba.'[24] What is important for this talk is Lam's comment that his art was about 'acts of decolonization'. So here we have a cluster of thinkers and artists within the Caribbean radical intellectual tradition whose works are explicit acts of decolonisation. If Wynter today in her work seeks to elaborate a theory of the human and the necessities of epistemic rupture, she does so because, as an anti-colonial thinker, rupture was the only possible route for full decolonisation. For Lam, decolonisation was only possible within the domain of art by reconfiguring the figurative through an engagement with Afro-Cuban culture. Placing Lewis within this cluster, I want to suggest that, for him, a politics of radical blackness was necessary to develop forms of democratic political practice. It explains, I think, his consistent preoccupation with the life and work of Marcus Garvey and his remarkable, successful effort of rebuilding Liberty Hall.

**Not an Ending but a Beginning**

The issue of decolonisation in the Caribbean 50-odd years after political independence is still a knotty one, in part, because colonial power was also about creating subjects, and thus, subjectivities. That Wynter, Lam and Rupert Lewis wrestled with this question is something we should pay attention to. That Rupert Lewis's life's work has also been about fashioning a possible frame for decolonial-political history for a passage of new histories and therefore possibilities of futures for the Afro-Caribbean subaltern person is what I wish to end with. But, it is an ending which gestures towards the possibilities of new thinking.

In the 2001 interview with David Scott published in the journal, *Small Axe,* Rupert, in response to a question about Rastafari says, 'I am more an internal Dread in the sense of trying to appropriate some of the ideas of Rastafarism but not believing in its religiosity.' I have thought about this for some time. What does it mean to be an 'internal dread'? In the end, I have come to the conclusion that, for Lewis, it means the following things:

- A firm commitment to blackness and Africa as central to the symbolic order of Afro-Jamaicans and Afro-Caribbeans.
- A commitment to practising a democratic politics which is both rooted in and routed through this understanding, alongside a commitment to understand and theorise politics as experience.
- Raising of the critical question about the relationship between thought and practice.

All of the above I suggest can be discerned from a reading of his 2010 essay 'Notes on the West Kingston Crisis and Party Politics' in which he argues that politics is separate from our contemporary notions of governance. For Lewis, politics is prior to governance and he writes, 'Politics undergirds activities in the state and influences notions of freedom and the way political life is conducted...I give politics an autonomy as a sphere of activity that cannot be fully explained with reference to the economic....'[25]

After many years in political life and studying politics, Lewis sums up how he sees politics. It is a view of political life as a practice and therefore as lived experience.

We leave the final words to Rupert. He writes in 1997 in an article in *Small Axe:*

> Learning to Blow the Abeng means confronting and overcoming the ignorance that parades behind academic titles and elegant political rhetoric...and even if one has a proficiency in blowing the Abeng the complexity of peoples' experience and frame of reference calls for a more genuinely democratic approach to social change.[26]

Rupert Lewis has kept on blowing the Abeng and for that we should give thanks and praises.

## Notes

1. Rupert Lewis's work on Garvey is extensive, including edited volumes. His single-authored book, *Marcus Garvey, Anti-Colonial Champion* (Trenton, New Jersey: Africa World Press, 1988) was an important addition to the scholarship on Garvey and still stands as one of the most important texts on Garvey.
2. There is a story to be told about these small journals and newspapers as essential to radical political thought and practice in Jamaica. Indeed, there is a longer history dating from the early twentieth century which includes the publications of the Garvey movement like the *Negro World* and *The Black Man*. In the 1930s, the journal *Plain Talk* was an important anti-colonial newspaper. Rupert Lewis's journalistic work is squarely within this tradition.

3. In discussions with Lewis himself, he revealed that, after leaving Calabar High School one of his main ambitions was to be a sports journalist. This ambition I would suggest represented a broad outlook which I would argue influenced his political work and his preoccupation with questions of democracy.
4. Rupert Lewis, *Walter Rodney's Intellectual and Political Thought* (Detroit: Wayne State University Press, 1998).
5. Isaiah Berlin, 'Political Judgment,' *New York Review of Books*, October 3, 1996. It is of interest to note that the late Rex Nettleford was a student of Berlin at Oxford. We spent many hours discussing Berlin's work. Again, there is a story here waiting to be told of one tendency in Caribbean political thought where the idea of politics, experience and practice are closely linked. Nettleford, in my view, was the key figure in such a current.
6. Here, I am thinking specifically of Rupert Lewis teaching the work of the novelist and poet Claude Mckay in the course, 'Modern Political Thought', in the Department of Government.
7. For a discussion of this phrase and its meaning, see Anthony Bogues, *The Humanities and the Social Sciences: Knowledge, Change and the Human Today* (Providence: Watson Institute, Brown University, 2013 ).
8. Rupert Lewis, 'Learning to Blow the Abeng: A Critical Look at Anti-Establishment Movements in the 1960s and 1970s', *Small Axe* (March 1998): 5–17.
9. This was one of the most important radical publishing houses of the period and was formed by Eric and Jessica Huntley. Jessica recently passed. It is safe to say that perhaps the most important publication of this publishing house was Walter Rodney, *How Europe Underdeveloped Africa* (1972).
10. The Caribbean Unity Conference was an organisation in which Caribbean intellectuals and artists met regularly in Washington, DC to discuss the future of the region. In 1972, Walter Rodney presented at a conference hosted by the group at Howard University, a seminal paper on twentieth-century Caribbean political thought. The title of the paper was 'Some Thoughts on the Political Economy of the Caribbean'.
11. Institute of Caribbean Studies was established in 1958 at the University of Puerto Rico. Its journal *Caribbean Studies* remains one of the oldest academic journals in the region.
12. Sylvia Wynter, 'One Love: Rhetoric or Reality? Aspects of Afro-Jamaicanism,' *Caribbean Studies* 12, No.3 (October 1972).
13. p. 72.
14. See Anthony Bogues, 'The *Abeng* Newspaper and the Radical Politics of Post-Colonial Blackness,' in *Black Power in the Caribbean*, ed. Kate Quinn (Gainesville: University of Florida Press, 2014), 76–97. In the essay, I make the point that radical blackness specifically means that there is a black radical tradition which is central to any form radical black politics. I would argue that Lewis's work on Garvey, Robert Love and Claude Mckay was an attempt to develop a political history which foregrounded this tradition in Jamaica.
15. Conversations with Prof Geri Augusto.
16. See for example the following works: Paget Henry, *Caliban's Reason* (2000); David Scott, 'The Re-Enchantment of Humanism: An Interview,' *Small Axe*, no. 8 (September 2000): 119–209. In 2003, the Centre for Caribbean Thought

held a conference examining her work. Papers from the conference were published in 2006.
17. I would argue that this preoccupation about how the African slave became a 'native' dominates Wynter's work right up until the 1970s and is best seen in her unpublished three volume work, *Black Metamorphosis*, initially written for the Institute of the Black World.
18. Sylvia Wynter, 'Jonkonnu in Jamaica: Towards the Interpretation of Folk Dance and Cultural Process,' *Jamaica Journal* 4, no. 2:3.
19. "The Dialectic of Defeat: An Interview with Rupert Lewis" in *Small Axe* 5, no. 2 (2001): 45.
20. It was from Rupert Lewis that I was given an important issue of the journal *Radical America* 5, no 3, in which there were major essays on Black radicalism and Marxism in the US. He had marked sections of the journal, particularly those that dealt with the disquiet of black Marxists with Soviet policy. This essay does not address Lewis's Marxism and there needs to be a discussion about this, but for this writer it requires an in-depth interview with Lewis. In interviews with Lewis when he addresses this period of his political life he speaks with a distant tone and one does not get any feel for his grappling with the politics of Marxism which he practised for a number of years. I am hopeful that his diaries when published might reveal insights into his grappling with Marxism. See for extensive discussion of the relationship between communism and black radicalism, H. Adi, *Pan-Africanism and Communism: The Communist International, Africa and the Diaspora* (2013).
21. See Veerle Poupeye, *Caribbean Art* ( London: Thames & Hudson, 1998).
22. For a brief discussion of this and how 'modernism' then produced its opposite 'primitive' art, see Simon Gikandi, 'Picasso, Africa and the Schemata of Difference,' in *Beautiful Ugly: African and Diaspora Aesthetics*, ed. Sarah Nuttall (Durham: Duke University Press, 2006), 6–29.
23. There was profound friendship and exchange of ideas between Lam and Césaire.
24. For discussion on Lam's work, see Lowery Stokes Sims, *Wifredo Lam and the International Avant-Garde, 1923–1982* (Austin: University of Texas Press at Austin, 2002) For a very recent assessment which focuses on his work in Cuba, see Elizabeth T. Goizueta, ed., *Wifredo Lam: Imagining New Worlds* (Chicago: University of Chicago Press, 2014).
25. Unpublished paper, 'Notes on the West Kingston Crisis and Party Politics,' author's copy.
26. Rupert Lewis, 'Learning to Blow the Abeng: A Critical Look at Anti-establishment Movements in the 1960s and 1970s,' *Small Axe* (March 1998): 5–17.

# 5 | Edward Seaga and the Question of Levelling:
Seeing Manley from the Other Side

F.S.J. Ledgister

> *Deliverance!*
> *Deliverance!*
> *Is so de message say,*
> *Hear de word!*
> *Hear de word!*
> *Evil gone away.*[1]

To understand Jamaica in the 1970s, it is necessary to look at the political process from more than one side. From the side of the government of Michael Manley's People's National Party (PNP), between 1972 and 1980 Jamaica was engaged in a struggle for greater democracy, greater equality, true social justice, and assuring ordinary, black Jamaicans a real stake in their country. Other Jamaicans saw this as threatening to stability, good order, tradition, their sense of identity, and even as an alien threat. Manley presented his reforms under the name 'democratic socialism', and both noun and adjective were given equal weight. His opponents publicly feared that this was a mask for something more sinister. Yet, Manley had undoubted appeal, and his position had to be challenged. His opponents in the Jamaica Labour Party (JLP) presented that challenge, ultimately, as civilisational. Manley represented a threat to all that was good, honest, and Jamaican. To do that, Jamaican values had to be interpreted as entrepreneurial and capitalistic, while Manley had to be dismissed as a soft-headed idealist who understood neither Jamaican reality nor Jamaican values. Edward Seaga, his rival, had to project himself both as more pragmatic than Manley, but also as, and this was the difficult part, more authentically Jamaican.

I have a vivid memory of alighting from a Jamaica Omnibus Service bus in downtown Kingston on December 14, 1976, on my way home to St Elizabeth to vote in the election on the next day, and seeing that the sides of the bus had been plastered with posters for the member of parliament for the Western Kingston constituency, Edward Seaga. 'Closer than a Brother', they proclaimed. I was amused by the slightly blasphemous tone of the advertisement, as the phrase comes from a popular hymn which declares 'Closer than a brother my Jesus is to me'. On maturer reflection, I am also amused by the fact that the black Jamaica Labour Party (JLP) supporters who had pasted those posters on buses and walls appeared to be advocating with enthusiasm that their candidate, a man who appears to be white and is a member of the Levantine Arab minority in Jamaica, was closer to them than a black man would be.

Edward Philip George Seaga was not only the member of Parliament for Western Kingston, he had been the leader of the JLP for two years and would continue to lead the party until 2005, serving as leader of the parliamentary opposition from 1974 through 1980 and from 1989 through 2005. He served as Prime Minister from 1980 to 1989. Having been appointed to the Legislative Council in 1959 (before independence), when he retired from parliament in 2005 he did so as 'father of the House', the longest serving member. Indeed, he was almost the last public figure in Jamaican politics to have entered public life before independence who was serving in an office of state in the twenty-first century.[2] He is an extraordinarily paradoxical person, a man generally seen as white who, from 1962 to 2005, represented a black, urban constituency and gave every evidence of being adored by his constituents. To gain his initial political foothold, furthermore, he had to overcome challengers who emphasised their black credentials, something that he could hardly do.

Yet, 14 years after seeing off a man – Dudley Thompson – who called himself 'Mr Black' and 'Mr Africa' (with very good reason, he had been one of the lawyers who defended Jomo Kenyatta when he was tried for treason by the British, and who was a globally recognised Pan Africanist), and yet other men: Millard Johnson – who had wrapped himself in the mantle of Marcus Garvey, and a Rastafarian activist, Ras Sam Brown, Seaga was 'closer than a brother'. That was an achievement in which he clearly took pride.

In the election of 1976, Seaga's party was to go down to defeat. Four years later, he was to achieve a smashing victory – the Jamaica Labour Party won 51 of the 60 seats in the House of Representatives, leaving only nine to the PNP – and take charge of the Jamaican state.

He held office as prime minister for almost nine years. I am not interested here in what he did and said in his time in office, but in his reaction to Michael Manley's government in the 1970s. He was, not surprisingly, the foremost critic of Manley. His critique, it turns out, is even today couched in the language of the Cold War. It is also presented in the terms of an astonishingly narrow, indeed parochial, Jamaican nationalism.

Where Manley's nationalism was nested as one layer of a world view that broadened into Caribbean regionalism and Third-World internationalism, Seaga's world view seems always to have been much more suspicious and distrustful of the world. Yet he could, and did retain the support of his constituents for over four decades, and the leadership of his party for three. Those are not easy achievements; they are particularly noteworthy when, for a large part of his career, he faced a rival, Michael Manley, whose style, charm, and charisma he could not hope to match, and whose vision of Jamaica's future was radically different from his.

Like Manley, Seaga's political career began in the 1950s. Unlike Manley, his entry did not come via the labour movement but as a result of his initial desire to turn his bachelor's degree in social sciences into a more advanced academic degree. This had led to his engaging in anthropological research on Revival cults in Buxton Town in the parish of St Catherine and in Salt Lane in downtown Kingston between 1953 and 1955.[3]

Boredom with study at the University of London, where he had gone at the urging of M.G. Smith to follow up on his research, led to his returning to Jamaica and entering into politics.[4] Though, in fact, he took a detour into record producing on the basis, initially, of folk material he had collected during his research.[5]

Seaga's political activity began in the late 1950s when he campaigned for the JLP (actually for the West Indies Democratic Labour Party) during the Federal election campaign of 1958 and the Jamaican general election the following year.[6] Although he states that his work was 'in the backroom', it was significant enough for party chief Sir Alexander Bustamante to nominate him to the Legislative Council, the upper house of the late colonial legislature, in the aftermath of the latter election, launching him on the career in public life that was to end 46 years later.[7]

## Of Haves and Have-Nots

Seaga's name was to be made by a speech he gave in the Legislative Council in 1961, during the State of the Nation Debate (the debate in response to the throne speech by the Governor laying out the government's policy proposals). I focus on it briefly here because it was so important to Seaga's own sense of his political identity that he returned to it in his farewell speech to Parliament in 2005.

This was the 'Haves and Have-Nots' speech of April 21, 1961, which was, declared Seaga, 'a by-product of my years of exposure and experience, living in the poor conditions of a rural village and an inner-city depressed area'.[8] His direct connection to the lives of poor Jamaicans had led him to want to understand the pattern of income distribution.

However, data on that matter was not easily available so he resorted to using income tax data, *which was*. What Seaga found, and announced in the Legislative Council Chamber was that income tax payers, who constituted seven per cent of the population were better off by 172 per cent, while non-taxpayers, the remaining 93 per cent, were worse off by 72 per cent.[9] It is particularly noteworthy that at the time it required an annual income of £300 to become liable to income tax.

Seaga, looking at the speech from the perspective of half a century later, considered that it was politically devastating for the government of Norman Manley.[10] He states that the Legislative Councillors were 'visibly shaken' by his presentation, and that the media 'gave great prominence' to what was, essentially, a claim that Manley's government was 'enriching the rich at the expense of the poor'.[11] He had also provided a challenge to the PNP's claim to be the party of social justice.

In his farewell speech to the Jamaican Parliament on January 18, 2005, Seaga returned to the theme he had touched on 44 years earlier. His understanding of Jamaican society had been formed in discussions about his research with M.G. Smith which had led to the conclusion that there were two Jamaicas, one of which was a modern, Western society, the 'haves', and the other a traditional, Afro-centric, non-modernised society, the 'have-nots'.[12] The boundary between these two societies at the moment Jamaica entered independence was, it seems, an income of £300 a year.[13]

Four decades of independence had produced little real improvement for the 93 per cent who constituted the have-nots. A government, said Seaga, should provide three basic services to its people: a criminal justice system, education, and economic opportunity.[14] On all three scores, Jamaica's governments since independence, including, presumably his own, have fallen short.

Four decades after independence, the system of criminal justice had deteriorated 'to world record levels of crime and alarming levels of abuses of rights', with the poor bearing the brunt of both.[15] Reforms to the education system over the decades had not succeeded in improving the educational experience of the poor.[16] As for the economy, it had experienced 'both rapid advance and rapid decline' and undergone both recovery and stagnation, with the net result that the country was only a little better off than before independence, and those who had benefited were not the poor.[17]

Indeed, said Seaga in 2005, 'It's an embarrassment to all of us that more than 40 years have passed and this problem is still with us, when in fact some of these problems can be solved if they are treated as priorities and with will and determination.'[18] It is worth noting that he is pointing the finger at himself, having served eight and a quarter years as prime minister in the 1980s; apparently he did not then see them as priorities, or else lacked the will and determination.

It is the have-nots, the people who come from the traditional, Afrocentric part of Jamaican society, whom Seaga sees as the creators of what is truly valuable and lasting in Jamaica:

> There is a tendency in the country to ignore what happens in the traditional society. To ignore injustice if the outcry is from the inner city and the rural poor; to ignore the plight of the uneducated, if the uneducated are from that underprivileged segment of the society; to ignore the inability to move upward and to earn more and have better career opportunities if those who are unable to do so are the 'have-nots' of the society. But let me say this. It is that segment of the society that has put Jamaica on the map internationally. It is the young people from poor households, humble households that gave us worldwide recognition and success in the last and previous Olympics, establishing by their outstanding performances a better ratio of success than any other country, taking into account the medals won and the size of the population. Those young people come from humble households. They are part of the 'have-nots'; they are part of

the society that is the traditional folk culture of the country. It is the young people from that segment of society too who have blazed the trail that made Jamaica an internationally recognised centre in the world of popular music. They are the ones who are leading the way to take us forward globally while our industry and agriculture flounder.[19]

This is undoubtedly true. But it is easy to praise the 'humble' when you do not have to share their lot.

**Seaga as Critic of Michael Manley**

Following the JLP's electoral victory in April 1962, Seaga served as Minister of Development and Welfare under Bustamante and Donald Sangster, and after 1967 as Minister of Finance and Planning under Hugh Shearer. The electoral victory of the PNP at the end of February 1972 upset him, he said, and led to him withdrawing from significant political activity for the next two years.[20] In the wake of the JLP's defeat in the local government elections of February 1974, Seaga claims, there was discontent with Hugh Shearer's continued leadership of the party and he was approached by some of his colleagues, 'young stars of the future', about taking the helm. After receiving the blessing of Bustamante, he decided to go for the job.[21] It is noteworthy that he recalls advising his wife that he thought that becoming party leader and leader of the opposition would be dangerous 'because Michael Manley was vindictive.'[22]

It is interesting that his first self-appointed task on deciding to lead the JLP was 'more intense reading on socialism' and discussion with others in order to be able to evaluate it. He believed that it could not work in Jamaica, although he believed it might have value in some cases, because Jamaicans were too individualistic and lacked the necessary discipline and self-denial: 'Faced with failure there would be the grave possibility that it would be enforced by a dictatorship or persecution and terror tactics.'[23]

While he shared some of the objectives of socialism, he saw it as flawed because it 'was built on the premise that people would forgo their own desire to excel motivated by the incentive for reward.'[24] The only thing that could suppress this would be force, and this, he feared, would be where Manley's experiment in socialism would end up.

Now, what is curious about this is that his decision to become party leader took place before the PNP's announcement of its recommitment to democratic socialism. Manley's public pronouncements, and Manley's monograph *The Politics of Change*, published in 1973, had avoided the term.[25] However, by the time he took charge of the party, the PNP had made that commitment and Seaga was rising to challenge it. His inaugural speech as leader of the JLP contained a direct attack on socialism as both meaningless and as 'a philosophy of something for nothing'.[26]

Michael Manley's socialism, Seaga notes, was presented as a continuation of his father's Fabian socialism, though he adds that:

> both Manleys were committed to the belief in the right of every Jamaican to own private property; both rejected the traditional capitalist model of individualism as the system upon which to base the future of Jamaica; and both accepted the commitment to work towards the building of an egalitarian society.[27]

So, from Seaga's perspective, Michael Manley's democratic socialism built upon Norman Manley's Fabian socialism or, as Seaga had it, the Fabian socialism he 'purported'.[28] But while Norman Manley's approach was gradual, Michael's, in Seaga's eyes, was radical and not necessarily democratic. The younger Manley presented socialism, in his initial announcement, as 'love' in order to rally support for it because, said Seaga, he realised 'that he could not sell the concepts and principles of democratic socialism to the broad, unsophisticated and poorly educated masses' but the projects identified as socialist, such as the literacy programme JAMAL, were merely populist. The really socialist parts of the scheme such as public ownership came after.[29] Furthermore, Manley's use of the phrase 'the word is love' was, from long before his initial entry into conventional politics, his expression of commitment to a vision of egalitarian democracy and nationhood.[30]

Support for public ownership, in Seaga's view, appealed to the urban working class and the peasantry but frightened the middle class 'and other elites'.[31] But Manley was not interested in elite support, he wanted to build mass support for state control of the economy, with the masses enthusiastically denouncing racism, classism, and imperialism as the trammels on their hopes and development:

> It was the economy, controlled by capitalists and imperialists in Manley's view that created the race, colour and class oppression. He considered that an egalitarian society required elements of dignity

and equality and these were denied to the people by an economy operated by capitalists and imperialists. These were the two target groups of oppressors.[32]

Seaga goes on to make the point that this puts Manley in line with Claudius Henry and with Walter Rodney. His own view is presented as 'an alternative argument'. This is that government had failed to create the proper environment to stimulate economic growth and ensure that Jamaicans had 'employable skills'. On this view 'race and colour were collateral links'. Had there been a proper debate between these two viewpoints, Seaga contends, the 1970s would have been a truly transformational period.[33]

Seaga then raises the question of whether Manley actually intended to pursue a socialist path, suggesting that there is evidence that he might not have initially intended to do so.[34] But he then goes on to cite countervailing evidence before declaring that Manley's intentions were inconsequential as, no matter what, radical reform would have resulted in elite groups' 'protective pre-emptive responses'.[35] It is rather interesting, by the bye, that while he speaks of the working class, the peasantry, and the middle class, in precisely those terms he refers to the upper classes not as the bourgeoisie, plantocracy, or aristocracy, but as 'elite groups'. That is a rather odd reticence.

His fear was that socialism would, because it stifled capitalist individualism, only be able to survive if it relied on force to engage in such suppression. Not merely of the abstract quality of individualism, but of civil society as a whole by becoming completely autocratic. He, therefore, had to adopt a strategy that would secure Jamaican democracy 'so that there would be room for an alternative when the socialist ideology destroyed itself'.[36]

That strategy was to put Manley on the defensive by exploiting the similarities between socialism and communism and engaging in a 'proactive anti-communist campaign'.[37] The JLP used Manley's public statements as a basis to stigmatise socialism as an alien ideology.[38]

Seaga reiterates that the programmes of which he approves had little to do with socialism, but were populist projects, but then goes on to say that 'there was a need to strengthen the social fabric of the society' and praises 'a number of mostly worthwhile projects' that did just that in the first three years of the PNP government.[39] He also evaluates the programmes he identifies as the main projects of Manley's administration. We should pay particular attention to the grounds on which he assesses those programmes that were central to the egalitarian and economic democracy elements of Manley's overall project.

Thus, he notes that worker cooperatives were established to run the sugar estates taken over by the government as 'an extension of the policy of worker participation in the means of production' but adds that they were a disaster because the workers in charge lacked management knowledge and 'the respect of the workforce'. The result was that the estates became uneconomic and unmanageable.[40] The National Home Guard, which he states was modelled on the Cuban People's Militia (although it was an auxiliary to the police, and not the army), was 'infiltrated by partisan political activists who were attracted by the power of arrest given to a member for each group who would also have a gun.'[41] Making the National Youth Service compulsory was seen as senseless because there was never enough funding to maintain the programme – enrolling all high school graduates – at full strength. He defines the purpose, oddly, as 'to improve the work ethics of the country's young workforce, as well as facilitate social and cultural exchange programmes', although Manley clearly intended it to promote egalitarianism.[42]

Seaga, writing from the perspective of more than a quarter century later, declares that Manley's social legislation was most successful and has endured. It is worth noting that one item that he fits in this category is the Employee Stock Ownership Plan Act, which encouraged worker participation in private companies by providing tax advantages for doing so. He states that this promotion of economic democracy 'failed to attract significant support because of unpopularity with employers and lack of full appreciation from employees'.[43]

Seaga contends that many of the social programmes were to collapse because of conceptual weakness, excessive ambition, or lack of proper financing.[44] But, while the social reforms and the plans for economic transformation of the 1970s did not sink any roots, the social legislation of the period, except for the Employee Stock Ownership Plan did, in Seaga's estimation, because they 'went directly to the correction of social alienation and deprivation of the rights of women and children,' settlement of employment disputes, and other social problems experienced in daily life by a considerable number of people'.[45]

Seaga makes an extraordinary judgment about Manley's impact on Jamaican society:

> It was the rhetoric of Michael Manley that raised the bar of self-esteem and racial pride among people of African origin, in continuation of Garvey's mission. This was not the result of any single effort. It was a consequence of Manley's repeated references to the injustices of being poor and black, and the perception that these barriers were being removed by the collective impact of reform programmes that created a significant shift in social awareness.[46]

For this reason, Manley was the right man at the right time for 'the many who were anxious for beneficial change and patronage' but the exact opposite for those who 'were determined not to walk with him on any adventure to the mountain top, as he had promised to do with Fidel Castro'.[47]

Thus, Seaga sketches out the boundaries of his understanding of Manley: His social programmes had value, his rhetoric was inspiring when it raised the consciousness of the Jamaican people, and he was a dangerous radical who was far too close to that even more dangerous fellow 90 miles across the water.

Indeed, after passages discussing relations with Cuba,[48] and purported resemblances between the PNP and the Workers Party of Jamaica (WPJ),[49] Seaga comes to the point: Both Michael Manley and his father were impractical dreamers with internationalist visions. Norman Manley had crashed into the reef of Federation, and Michael, who thought he could cast a spell over the minds of the people, nonetheless 'was too much of an intense political ideologue to change course' when the people demonstrated that they rejected the course on which he was set.[50] The PNP–WPJ resemblance was one that Seaga emphasised at the time, notably in an interview with CBS News shortly after taking office in 1980.[51]

Manley's mistake, domestically, was to completely misunderstand the structure of Jamaican society:

> Manley misread the interdigitation of the classes in the social structure, which was an organic whole unable to be separated into class layers and pulled apart, section by section, without damaging interaction. The social model of egalitarianism collapsed on this mistaken strategy of 'pulling down' the class layer above instead of 'pulling up' the layer below. The damage was the withdrawal of

support for the economy by the holders of wealth, because of the creation of an unsure future with seemingly overwhelming risks.[52]

Given Seaga's analysis of the society as divided into 'Two Jamaicas', to claim that the two were at the same time one that could not be pulled apart is disingenuous to say the least. Seaga seems to recognise this, since he follows this statement by asserting that if Manley had followed what he believed to be Marcus Garvey's policy of promoting a combination of racial pride and economic upliftment this would have had the best results. This conveniently omits the fact that as leader of the party opposing Manley it would have been his bounden duty to oppose just such a policy even as, decades later, he praises Manley for promoting cultural empowerment and strengthening racial awareness among the mass of black Jamaicans. But then, given that he is perceived in Jamaica as a member of a white ethnic minority, the Lebanese, although actually multiracial, he has to tread much more carefully than the mixed-race Manley whose black ancestry is well-known, unlike Seaga's.[53]

**The Problem in Black and White**

Seaga, thus, is stuck with a problem; he was Manley's foremost critic and, by virtue of the fact that he followed his ambition to the leadership of his party, his chief rival. That meant, *a fortiori*, having to oppose his policies. It is obviously difficult, when you are visibly a member of a privileged racial minority, to come out against a government that has committed itself to the promotion of racial consciousness, the valorisation of the African heritage, the praise of African elements in the national culture, that adds to the National Heroes a rebellious slave and a female Maroon chieftain, and that praises the products of popular culture just at the moment that they are acquiring worldwide acclaim. Seaga, as a member of a government that had, during its decade of tenure, a mixed record on the subject of black cultural identity – it had repatriated the embalmed body of Marcus Garvey, invited Haile Selassie to Jamaica to the joy of Rastafarians and the horror of many upper and middle class Jamaicans who were shocked when the emperor did not, as expected, deny his divinity when he was acclaimed by the dreadlocked brethren, but it had also banned the writings of Elijah Muhammad, H. Rap Brown, Stokely Carmichael, and other black radicals, prevented Walter Rodney from returning to the island after he had left to attend a conference, and shown considerable hostility to the Rastafarian brethren among other things. Seaga was caught on the horns of a dilemma.

We see how he resolves it: Manley is attacked on personal grounds (his 'vindictiveness'), on ideological grounds, and on grounds of competence. But at the same time, Seaga has no choice but to praise him for having done something to improve the condition of the mass of Jamaicans and for having raised their consciousness. Marcus Garvey provides him with a means of doing the latter.

Garvey allows Seaga to cover himself with a borrowed shroud of blackness, since he was responsible for the repatriation of Garvey's remains, which had been buried in London from 1940 to 1965. Seaga advocated in cabinet for the repatriation and entombment of Garvey's body in what was to become National Heroes Park 'as the greatest Jamaican in history' and obtained Bustamante's approval for this, rather to his surprise.[54]

This permits him to use Garvey as the means to critique contemporary radicals such as Walter Rodney, and Michael Manley whose own embrace of Black Nationalism as an element of democratic egalitarianism derived from Rodney. The reflected aura of Garvey could provide protective cover for his whiteness.

Thus, Seaga can unproblematically point out that Jamaica's history has been one of white dominance, and that issues of colour, class, and race have been problematic within the country's culture because of the history of white racial supremacy.[55] Marcus Garvey was one of the 'social engineers' who worked to change this.[56] Garvey's approach, said Seaga, was to promote black enterprise; that is, Seaga sees Garvey not only as a black nationalist, but also as an advocate for black capitalism.[57] Since Garvey's time, Jamaica, along with the rest of the Western world, has been caught up by a 'new spirit' which has produced more liberal attitudes towards race accompanied by the emergence of trade unions and universal suffrage. This has permitted black people to rise to positions of power and authority, and racial prejudice is being uprooted in Jamaica.[58] This does rather seem to reverse cause and effect; the new spirit, after all, was the product of the emergence of labour organising and universal suffrage, both of which ensured that black people, being the bulk of the population, acquired opportunities previously denied to them. Garvey, nonetheless, was the crucial figure for Seaga. It was he who 'broke the mental prison of racism' making possible what came after.[59]

Seaga notes that the founder of Rastafari, Leonard Howell, was contemporary with Garvey.[60] Rastafari, which reveres Garvey as a prophet, became 'a symbol of defiance of the white man and his style of living'.[61] Their profession of black pride and dignity made them the vanguard of the black consciousness movement in Jamaica; the government in the 1960s, of which Seaga had been part, responded by inviting the Ethiopian emperor Haile Selassie, the divinity worshipped by the Rastafari, to Jamaica.[62]

The Claudius Henry Affair of 1959–60, which had led to a brief armed revolt in 1960, had raised fears within the establishment of serious insurrection.[63] Walter Rodney, like Claudius Henry, saw racism as the result of economic oppression. The solution to that oppression was to oppose racism and the power of white people and their fellow members of the establishment.[64] Rodney, during his time as a lecturer at the university, had taken his message beyond the bounds of the campus and attracted police attention. The Special Branch reported to Prime Minister Shearer that he had gone to Montego Bay and spoken there: 'The police was alarmed that this could lead to death and destruction among tourists and attacks on hotels as was the case with the Chinese riots of 1965 in which there was both death and destruction.'[65] As a result, Shearer decided to take action and have Rodney excluded from the country when he returned from the Black Writers' Congress in Montreal in October 1968. The suppression of Rodney's opinions was justified, Seaga contended, because

> Expressing racialist views was one matter. It was free to anyone to express such feelings in a democratic society. But the fear was that such passionate views expressed in volatile communities of the poor could provoke incitement against perceived target groups as a means of dealing with economic oppression as the message was interpreted as portraying.[66]

Free speech is a right, but not if poor people might hear you.

The government, he added, feared that unrest might imperil foreign investment. Jamaica at that time was in 'a fragile state' and Hugh Shearer's government didn't want to spook potential investors.[67] In noting the student protest at the ban on Rodney, and the subsequent riot, Seaga contended that these proved the wisdom of the government's decision:

> The violence displayed vindicated Shearer's pre-emptive action to prevent worse which could have happened, if allowed. But the episode only pointed to the soft under-belly of government which was not identifying itself overtly with racial causes, allowing the natural progression of improving racial harmony to take place at its own effective but slower pace and promoting the cause with the visit of iconic leaders in the racial struggle.[68]

The idea that visits by such figures as Haile Selassie and Martin Luther King improved race relations in Jamaica seems rather ludicrous, especially given King's well-known dictum that time itself is neutral.[69]

Michael Manley's attempt to create an egalitarian state involved linking wealth and colour to class. This put him in the same line as Claudius Henry (with whom he had discussions) and Walter Rodney. Seaga, in classically conservative terms, sees this as a pulling-down approach that will produce social disintegration, as opposed to a pulling-up approach, which will not.[70]

Manley, at least, had a plan that contained some positive elements, for which Seaga applauded him; at a point, however, when he could not receive the plaudits:

> Among those who, like Samson, who would pull down the temple, only Michael Manley recognized that positive solutions must be put in place. His ideological commitment to socialism was his replacement, his new temple, but that did not work; it self-destructed, as he himself admitted in 1990. But his search for replacement by a new dynamic, led him to a fervent commitment to social justice which resulted in the introduction of a far-reaching package of social legislation to alter the unjust framework which circumscribed the helpless poor: tackling illiteracy, repudiating bastardy, adjudicating workers grievances and providing maternity leave. These were heralded as welcome social prescriptions to change the life of the poor. In this Manley succeeded.[71]

So Manley's social policy, at least, represents a gain for poor, black Jamaicans. But Seaga cannot quite deal with the crucial issue, which is that the mass of Jamaicans long perceived their society to be a racial hierarchy in which people of Seaga's complexion possessed both the political and economic power. Michael Manley sought to redress that by promoting a broader and deeper conception of democracy that drew directly from Walter Rodney's valorisation of Africa and African history. Manley was able to cross the lines of race and class in a way that Seaga could not. Manley could point to his roots in a manner not available to the white-appearing Seaga. Seaga's only options were to brandish the symbol of Marcus Garvey and to emphasise his knowledge of and connection to black folk culture, and the latter was of little help in dealing with the changing society of the 1970s.

## Conclusion

Seaga's approach was to confront and challenge Manley. That is not surprising since he was, like Manley, operating within the constraints of the Westminster parliamentary system and that institutional framework presupposes that party leaders will see each other as rivals for the affections of the electorate. As both Seaga and Manley were to find out, it is far easier to woo the voters with criticisms of the incumbent government and promises of better days than it is to govern.

Both Seaga and Manley, perhaps to each other's astonishment, were staunch democrats and nationalists. Seaga had the grace to note, at Manley's death, that 'As unyielding adversaries we knew where we stood with each other as neither of us had the gift of hiding our feelings and reaction.'[72] Yet Seaga, for all his eagerness to commend, since Manley's death, his rival's commitment to the mass of poor Jamaicans, misses the nature of Manley's democratic ethos.

This comes out clearly in the way in which Seaga describes the Employee Stock Ownership Plan as a social programme. For it was one way in which Manley sought to give workers 'a voice at the workplace' and ensure that worker and employer stood at an equal gate, to use a phrase of Seaga and Manley's mutual friend M.G. Smith. It was a step towards not merely social inclusion but economic democracy, moving democracy from the political sphere through the space of social equality and into the economic realm. This broadening of the scope and meaning of democracy was central to Manley's political project. That is to say, it was a central part of both his political theory and of his political action. Seaga's mischaracterisation of it is a grave category error. It is, indeed, a serious misunderstanding of Manley's overall project.

Similarly, Seaga faces a major dilemma in dealing with the intertwining of race and class. Manley, in responding to the obvious ferment that the Henry and Rodney Affairs had exposed, declared that the solution to Jamaica's national crisis of self-confidence was the assertion of pride in its core black identity. Minorities had to adjust to that fact, and the majority should rejoice in its history, not feel ashamed of it. As a visible member of a minority who, nonetheless, had a deep and intimate knowledge of black folk culture, and who had made his living promoting popular culture, Seaga was caught in the middle. Manley was too, as a man of mixed race; but his marriage to a definitely black woman, as well as his two decades of labour activism, provided an inoculation. Seaga's visible whiteness, and the concomitant invisibility of his non-white heritage, was problematic and meant that he had constantly to provide his bona fides on the subject. As a result, he had to resort to appealing to the symbolic figure of Marcus Garvey in support of the trite conservative claim that the solution to problems of social injustice should be 'levelling up not levelling down', as he insists more than once.

But Manley is not talking about bringing the wealthy and powerful down. He is, quite consistently, asserting that Jamaicans all belong to an equal community and, except in regard to the administration of enterprises, the exercise of scientific and technical expertise, and the functions of office, in which cases particular expertise or electoral will are what matter and those who lack that expert knowledge or do not possess the relevant elected authority should defer to those who do *in those particular areas*, all are equal and have equal voice. It is thus not a matter of downward or upward levelling but of securing that equal voice through the proper, equal democratic institutional structures that is at issue.

We need to take note that Manley's vision of democracy was broader and deeper than social democracy but was still firmly rooted in Westminster parliamentary democracy. Confronted with a critical choice in his second term, and with two years left in that term, he opted to call an election and have the people decide which path to take. The people chose the path offered them by Edward Seaga, who, at the time, was accusing Manley of being a puppet of Fidel Castro and of the Soviet Union's and insisting that the PNP was indistinguishable from the Workers' Party of Jamaica, the pro-Soviet Communist party.[73]

It occurred to very few at that time that someone bent on tyranny was unlikely to submit himself and his party to the uncertainty of a democratic election.

It is not clear to me that Seaga appreciates fully, even today, the strength of Manley's fundamental commitment to the principles of liberal democracy. He focuses single-mindedly on a critique of Manley's socialism combined with praise for Manley's desire to end the unjust conditions under which the majority of Jamaicans had long laboured. Yet he mischaracterises the fact that Manley – having written a book entitled *A Voice at the Workplace* – had passed legislation granting workers in the private sector precisely that, even if not in the same way that they had a voice in the sugar workers' cooperatives that he decries. Seaga cannot, it appears, present Manley in any terms other than those of the dichotomous oppositions of the Cold War. This, I suspect, is due not so much to a fundamental misunderstanding of Manley, though that may be involved, as to a desire to ensure that the first draft of history is as favourable to Edward Seaga as possible.

In the end, however, Seaga strives within limits to be fair to Manley. He recognises that Manley, like himself, was animated by love of country and that his goal was the good of the people. It cannot be expected that he would see that good in the same way that Manley did. It would be asking a great deal from someone who had built a lifetime's career on their rivalry.

**Notes**

1. Edward Seaga, 'River Maid, River Maid,' *Jamaica Journal* 32, nos. 1–2 (2009) [1969]: 17.
2. The last was Sir Howard Cooke, who was Governor-General from 1991 to 2006. He was a member of the Parliament of the Federation of the West Indies from 1958 to 1962. He thus entered public life before Seaga and left it after him.
3. Edward Seaga, 'A Life on a Cultural Mission,' *Jamaica Journal* 32, nos. 1–2 (2009): 12–13.
4. Seaga, 'A Life on a Cultural Mission,' 13.
5. Edward Seaga, *My Life and Leadership, Volume I: Clash of Ideologies, 1930–1980*. (Oxford: Macmillan, 2009), 32–33.
6. Ibid., 34.
7. Ibid.
8. Ibid., 67.
9. Ibid.
10. Ibid., 68.
11. Ibid.

12. Edward Seaga, 'The Haves and the Have-Nots, So Little Has Changed': Farewell Address to the House of Representatives, 18 January 2005,' in Edward Seaga, *Revelations: Beyond Political Boundaries* (Kingston: The Edward Seaga Research Institute, 2009), 9.
13. Equivalent, at the time, to $US840. To provide a sense of what that money could buy, it is worth remembering that at the time the value of gold was fixed at $US35 per troy ounce. It has been pointed out to me, by Brian Meeks, that Lloyd Best had claimed authorship of the 'Haves and Have-Nots Speech'. If so, Best was showing a less able grasp of statistics than in his celebrated essay on the plantation model of development a few years later.
14. Ibid.
15. Ibid.
16. Seaga, 'The Haves and the Have-Nots, So Little Has Changed,' 11.
17. Ibid., 13.
18. Ibid., 14.
19. Ibid., 15.
20. Seaga, *Clash of Ideologies*, 210.
21. Ibid., 214–16.
22. Ibid., 216.
23. Ibid.
24. Ibid.
25. It is possible that Seaga had been exploring the possibility of staking out a position on the left during the period when he had 'withdrawn from active politics'. Manley's proclamation of democratic socialism as PNP policy foreclosed that option. More than one young radical of the period recall having been approached by Seaga during that period (personal communications).
26. Seaga, *Clash of Ideologies*, 219.
27. Ibid., 223.
28. Ibid.
29. Ibid.
30. F.S.J. Ledgister, *Michael Manley and Jamaican Democracy, 1972–1980: The Word is Love* (Lanham, MD, Lexington Books, 2014), 110.
31. Ibid.
32. Seaga, *Clash of Ideologies*, 225.
33. Ibid.
34. Ibid.
35. Ibid., 226.
36. Ibid.
37. Ibid., 227.
38. Ibid., 229.
39. Ibid., 230.
40. Ibid., 231.
41. Ibid.
42. Ibid., 231–32.
43. Ibid., 233.
44. Ibid., 234.
45. Ibid., 235.
46. Ibid., 235.

47. Ibid.
48. See, for example, Ibid., 303–304.
49. Ibid., 305.
50. Ibid., 321.
51. Edward Seaga, *Change in the Caribbean* (Kingston: Agency for Public Information, 1980), 13.
52. Seaga, *Clash of Ideologies*, 333.
53. Ibid., 7. Seaga says of himself 'My ancestry connects to Lebanon, Scotland, India, and Africa'. It is intriguing to see that the first page of his memoir includes a connection to an ancestor who arrived in the British Isles with William the Conqueror.
54. Seaga, *Clash of Ideologies*, 127–28.
55. Edward Seaga, 'Walter Rodney and the Course of Black Nationalism,' in *Revelations: Beyond Political Boundaries*, Edward Seaga, 115 (Kingston: The Edward Seaga Research Institute, 2009).
56. Ibid.
57. Seaga, 'Walter Rodney and the Course of Black Nationalism,' 117.
58. Ibid., 118.
59. Ibid., 119.
60. Ibid.
61. Ibid., 120.
62. Ibid., 120–21.
63. Ibid., 123.
64. Ibid., 125.
65. Ibid.
66. Ibid., 125–26.
67. Ibid., 126.
68. Ibid., 126-27.
69. Martin Luther King, *Letter from A Birmingham Jail*, http://www.africa.upenn.edu/Articles_Gen/Letter_Birmingham.html (Accessed July 17, 2012).
70. Seaga, 'Walter Rodney and the Course of Black Nationalism,' 127–28.
71. Ibid., 129.
72. Quoted in Patrick E. Bryan, *Edward Seaga and the Challenges of Modern Jamaica* (Mona, Jamaica: University of the West Indies Press, 2009), 302. A one-time advisor of Manley's noted that at Manley's funeral Seaga was seen to salute as the coffin was lowered into the ground. This gesture astonished observers close by (personal communication).
73. Waters, *Race, Class, and Political Symbols*, 211–12.

# 6 | *Characteristics of the Grenadian Revolution and the Caribbean Situation*

Maurice Bishop interviewed by Rupert Lewis

Following is the text of an interview with Maurice Bishop, Prime Minister of the People's Revolutionary Government of Grenada. The interview was conducted on May 11, 1982 by Rupert Lewis. It was first published as 'Grenada: History, Revolution, US Intervention'. Latin America: Studies by Soviet Scholars No. 4, *Social Sciences Today* USSR Academy of Science, Moscow, 1984, 108–24.

RL: Comrade Bishop, how do you characterise the Grenadian Revolution and what is the justification for this assessment?

MB: Fundamentally, as a national democratic, anti-imperialist revolution, involving the alliance of many classes, including sections of the small bourgeoisie but under the leadership and the dominant role being played by the working people and particularly the working class, through their vanguard party the New JEWEL Movement.

This alliance and the dominant role of the working people in it, can be seen, for example, in the composition of the People's Revolutionary Government (PRG) itself. That is to say, in the ruling council of the government, in which can be found small and middle businessmen, small farmers, middle strata professionals, but with the party dominant. This can be seen too, but to a lesser extent, in the Cabinet, where there is one middle-size business man.

Our national democratic path can also be seen from the existence of a mixed economy but with the state sector dominant. In fact, while domestic investment as a whole has doubled from some $34.5M to $78M between '79 and '81, state sector investment in this same period has nearly quintupled from some $15M to over $74M.

The other sectors in the economy are of course the private sector and the cooperative sector. Within the state sector there is now a National Commercial Bank (NCB) for the first time which was established to begin to assume gradual control of the financial institutions in the country.

We have also established a Marketing and National Importing Board (MNIB), which has the responsibility of importing a number of items – at this point essentially the most important items from the point of view of the consumer – sugar, rice, cement, such the like, and also has the responsibility for marketing the internal produce of the farmers in our country.

We have also established a state corporation called 'Grenada Resorts Corporation' (GRC) which now owns a number of hotels in the tourist sector and therefore the state, for the first time, is into that area of economic activity.

Many new state enterprises involved in production have also been established. In the area of agro-industries for the first time, in the area of fisheries for the first time and now too there is an expanded agricultural enterprise, which is attempting to bring idle lands into production and making this sector for the first time a productive and profitable undertaking.

The state has also moved to control the public utilities and to expand the infrastructure in the country. This can be seen in the present control by the state of the Telephone Company, of the Central Water Commission and or the Electricity Company. In the area of infrastructure the most dramatic evidence is the new International Airport project which is now well underway and is expected to be complete towards the end of next year.

We have also started on a major road reconstruction, maintenance and repair programme. This is both in the area of main roads and feeder roads so that farmers are now better able to get their produce out from the hillsides. In that area too, a lot of work has been done in the supply and distribution of water. At this point, after three years, we are now able to supply about two million more gallons of water every day and that has made a substantial impact on the life of the people.

We have also ordered some new electricity generators which would give us greatly increased electrical output in the country. Likewise, we have a contract now signed with the German Democratic Republic for a new telephone system, the installation of which should be completed over the next 18 months to two years.

All in all, this has represented a massive investment, and, in fact, last year, over 90 per cent of all new investment in the country was done by the state. In this way, we hope to continue the process of gradual disengagement from imperialism, we are also trying to develop new trading ties, particularly with the countries of the socialist world and we believe that this will help us to lay the basis for socialist construction.

In the area foreign policy, I think our national democratic path can also be seen. Firstly, in the firm principled foreign policy orientation that the government has pursued in our support for the world revolutionary process, the national liberation movements and the struggles of the working class internationally.

Internally we have begun to develop a people's revolutionary democracy, where the people are being put at the centre and focus of all events in the country, where the people are being involved in all aspects of national life and are being encouraged to participate in everything that is taking place in the country.

One way in which we are doing this is through our organs of popular democracy. Through these organs, the masses of people are being able on a regular basis to meet in their parish and zonal councils and there to receive reports on what is happening in the country, to receive reports from their mass organisation, to receive reports from the party, to receive reports about how programmes of the revolution whether milk distribution, or the housing repair programme, or the Center for Popular Education literacy programme, whatever the programme, to receive reports.

Likewise, to receive reports from top bureaucrats and managers in the bureaucracy and in the state sector so that on any given day the manager of the Central Water Commission or of the Telephone Company or of the Electricity Company, or a public health inspector, or a price control inspector might be called up to come before these parish councils and there to give an account of what is happening in his particular area of work.

These workers also hold their own monthly workers parish council (meetings), these being peculiar to the workers only and a similar kind of agenda is held for those occasions.

Likewise, the women and the youth hold their monthly general meetings and have similar discussions on matters that are important to them.

We have also as part of this phase – this national democratic stage – spent some time in trying to restore, and indeed, to expand the fundamental rights of the people. In the area of restoration, we have repealed the Essential Services Act of 1978 which was passed by the Gairy dictatorship. Under that Law, 11 of the most essential categories of workers, including the dockworkers, lost their right to strike.

The Public Order Act of 1974 was also repealed; under that Act the masses no longer had the right to use loudspeakers at public meetings. And this affected not just meetings during the year but meetings even during election campaigns.

The Newspaper Act, laid down that $20,000 had to be deposited before a newspaper could be published.

And finally, the Prohibited Literature Act, under which progressive, revolutionary, socialist and communist literature was banned from the country, was also repealed.

In the area of expansion, we have passed the Trade Union Recognition Act under which the workers of our country for the first time now have the right to form and to join Trade Unions of their choice. This has laid the basis for greatly expanded activity among workers in trade unionism.

We have also passed an Equal Pay Decree in the state sector so that the women of our country now receive equal pay for equal work. We have ended the policy of sexual discrimination, so again women are now able to go into areas where previously they were unable to find work. The Maternity Leave Law, likewise, has ensured that the women of our country, for up to three months during their pregnancy and just after their pregnancy are able to receive leave with pay.

Likewise, in the last three weeks in fact, we have passed two more pieces of legislation. One, the Workmen's Compensation Law, under which compensation for injuries, including permanent disablement and loss of life received in the course of work, have now been substantially increased.

A Rent Restriction Law has also been passed. Under that law, landlords will no longer have the right to arbitrarily evict tenants, furthermore over the next three months all landlords will have to go before a Rent Assessment Board. The Board itself is made up of ordinary laymen coming from the particular parish. There'll be such boards for the six parishes on the mainland of Grenada. And in this way, we hope that the abuse by many landlords in charging high rents and in arbitrary evictions would be ended.

In the area of the state apparatus, the old Gairy army was disbanded. The new army, which is based on the youth, has been reorganised, new training programmes have been established and apart from that a militia based on the people, in other words, a part-time arm, has also been created. We have also begun a policy of reorienting and reorganising the police force after having removed the criminal elements from that force.

In the area of bureaucracy a re-training programme is also going on, particularly through the In-service Training Unit (ITU) which, over a period of three years, is hoping to train or retrain most categories of civil servants in the bureaucracy. We have also begun a process of democratisation of the bureaucracy and we have made the bureaucrats, particularly top bureaucrats, responsible and accountable to the people, primarily through making them go before the zonal and parish councils and the worker parish councils to give an account of their stewardship and to explain the policies of their particular department or ministry directly to the masses.

We have also spent a lot of time over these past three years in trying to develop a new political culture, and to raise the cultural, scientific and material level of the people. This has been done in several ways.

In the area of education, we embarked in the first year on a literacy programme, which did have the effect of wiping out most of the illiteracy in our country. In its second phase, which begins in June, we are going to be concentrating on functional literacy and, in this stage of the programme, we hope to involve some nine thousand adults in adult education leading up to the primary school leaving examinations and 'O' levels.

We have also in this area developed worker education classes. These are based in the villages and at the work places – 23 villages and in about 59 workplaces. In the school system, curriculum reform is going on at this very moment and an intensive Teacher Training Programme is also underway. The Teacher Training Programme seeks to train all of the primary school teachers in the system at the same time. The old system was to bring together about 50 of them for two years. At the end of that training about half would have left the country. So really you were training about 25 people every two years. Under this new approach, we are trying to train all 500 or so of the untrained primary school teachers at the same time over the three years.

We have also democratised the mass media. We have given maximum assistance as Party and Government to the mass political organisations and to the trade union movement – all as part of this process of ensuring mass participation by the people of our country.

We have also spent a lot of time in the area of trying to develop new attitudes towards local production among the workers of our country. Here, we have been emphasising the fact that this is their revolution, this is their country, this is their government; that the benefits, which they have been receiving, are benefits which they have worked for, and benefits which would continue to come once the productive base of the economy can be expanded. Here too, we have spent much time in providing scientific training to different sections of the working class in our country. A Fisheries School has been opened, The Agricultural School has been reopened, the National In-service Teacher Education Programme has been established for the primary school teachers, the In-service Training Unit is meant to train the worker in the Public Sector and at the same time the whole process of national planning has been introduced for the first time in our country.

These new attitudes too, are being developed through the system of emulation which this year in particular we have begun to make a lot of strides in getting institutionalised. The principle of no commercial secrecy at the workplace has also helped in that process so that all of the books, all of the accounts, all of the figures, all of the returns, in all work places in the public sectors are now open to discussion by all of the workers on a monthly basis. The system of profit-making, too, has helped to make that process easier to implement.

And finally, through the production and productivity committees, the disciplinary and grievance committees and the emulation committees the workers are assured of a greater say at the workplace in helping to run the country.

RL: Can I ask about the role of the New JEWEL Movement as a vanguard party in guiding the Revolutionary process? What has been your experience in the situation in Grenada?

MB: In general terms, the first thing that I want to say is that the party tries to ensure that its presence is felt everywhere. We try, as a party, to take the initiative on all revolutionary, social, political, economic and defence processes. We try to be in constant, organised contact with the masses, getting their views and opinions, listening to and learning from them and involving them in the implementation of all major decisions.

The party has over the years been active in mobilising the masses and in helping them to become more organised through encouraging them to join the mass organisations. This is certainly so for the National Youth Organisation which is the major mass organisation of youth in our country, for the National Women's Organisation which is the major mass organisation of women in our country, for the pioneers, which is the major mass organisation for the young children between five and 13 in our country. This is also true of the militia where the people are involved in readying themselves to defend their country, and in the Community Work Brigades (CWB) which are voluntary organisations engaging in voluntary community work, particularly on the weekends.

In the area of trade unions, the atmosphere for greatly expanded trade unionism in the country was laid by the Trade Union Recognition Law (TURL), which I mentioned before, and is today being continued further through the production committees and the emulation committees which I had also mentioned before. But apart from this we have been encouraging, as party, the whole process of democratisation of the trade unions themselves through encouraging meetings of the unions, at the level of branches and what not. And we have also been encouraging the workers in the trade unions to themselves take a more active part in all decisions that were normally made in the past by the leaders alone. The forms of encouragement that we have been giving include providing transport to the workers to go to and from meetings and generally giving them all possible forms of moral and material support for whatever activities they engage in within the union.

The party has also been very active in the area of helping to raise the consciousness of the masses as a whole through our programmes of mass political education, some of which I've already mentioned, worker education classes at the villages and in the work places, parish and zonal councils and worker parish councils, and, in more recent times, this can perhaps best be seen through discussions which took place on the economy and more so around the question of the 1982 Budget and the first national plan of our country which was implemented this year. These discussions started in January, when over eleven hundred members of different mass organisations were brought together for one-day discussions and series of workshops on the economy, which was held in our National Conference Centre.

Coming out of those discussions, 25 zonal councils were held around the country. At these zonal councils, members of the bureaucracy, particularly top managers, went out and assisted our party comrades in presenting the facts about the economy to the masses, attempting in that way to demystify the whole budgetary process and indeed the economy, trying to get the masses more and more acquainted with the economic concepts that are used, trying to get them to understand that the economy is something that should be of deep concern to them, that it has daily relevance to their own lives, trying to get them to discuss the problems in the economy which they themselves can identify and indeed have identified over the years. And trying to get them to come up with ideas, recommendations for solutions and finally to help them create the necessary structures to ensure that they can have an ongoing part in implementing whatever ideas are agreed upon.

That whole process was extremely important and we think it has had a pretty fundamental impact on the level of economy consciousness of the masses in our country today.

The party has also played a very active role in the attitude we have taken to the democratisation of the media and the impact that it has had on the revolutionary media that is being created in the country. We have taken the decision that the masses must see themselves on television, the masses must hear themselves on the radio, the masses must read what they have written in their newspapers and see their own photographs in the newspapers. Their views, their ideas, their suggestions, their criticism, their comments are therefore dominant right now in the mass media. In this way, we have begun to develop a genuine free media and particularly a genuine free press, no longer a bourgeois controlled press. In fact, the party has crushed bourgeois rule and monopoly over the established press, over the former bourgeois press and has established working people control of the media today.

If you compare very quickly the situation before the revolution and that prevailing today, I think you can get some idea of what I am talking about at this point. Before the revolution, there were two newspapers in this country: the *Torchlight* and the *West Indian*. The *Torchlight* was a privately owned newspaper and, in fact, had to close down on more than one occasion because of different laws and different forms of harassment under Gairy.

The *West Indian* was the government newspaper that only reflected the government's point of view, and really was only a mouthpiece for the dictator [Eric] Gairy himself.

By contrast, today, there are over 15 newspapers that come out regularly in the country. Apart from the national newspaper now called the *Free West Indian*, there is also the party paper *The New Jewel*; there is an organ for the urban workers, the *Workers Voice*; there is an organ for the rural worker, *Cutlass*; an organ for the small and middle farmer, *The Fork*; an organ for the women and one for the youth. That one is called *Fight*; there is an organ for the Revolutionary Armed Forces, *Fedon*, named after one of our heroes; there is also an organ for the media workers themselves and several such other organisations, amounting in all, like I said, to 15 new organs that presently exist in the country.

We have also, as party, attempted to develop a patriotic, anti-imperialist consciousness in the Armed Forces. The party branch in the army, for example, is primarily responsible for morale of the troops, for discipline and for political and academic education for the soldiers. That question of academic education in fact is a key question, because you must remember that the army today is based on the youth, who were the unemployed youth under Gairy and many of them did not have the opportunity of receiving any formal academic education, or received very limited academic education, and therefore that's a critical aspect of the work of the party within the Armed Forces.

Through the party committees also, the party has begun to play a more and more prominent role in the area of monitoring and supervising the economy. These party committees have the responsibility of looking at different sectors and sections of the economy and of making regular reports to the party's economic bureau as to what is happening within the particular sector for which they have the responsibility of ensuring that as fast as problems come up and are identified, that solutions are found to those problems, and therefore bottlenecks do not arise, or when they arise they are solved quickly. The work of these party committees has been very important in this area.

We have also moved to appointing as chairpersons of the Board of Directors, leading party comrades. This, of course, is to ensure that they are able to lead, to guide, to direct the work of the particular state enterprise for which they are given responsibility. To ensure too, that they are to counter all vestiges of corruption and waste which was a traditional problem in the state sector. To ensure that they are able to combat any signs of economism among the workers and, of course, most critically of all, ensure that production and productivity are encouraged and pushed forward. They ensure that these state enterprises become profitable and productive. They have been chosen for this function because they are the best qualified leadership, they have the necessary scientific training, the necessary outlook to give the best possible leadership and to ensure that targets set are reached.

The party is deeply involved in helping to organise activities that large sections of the masses are most interested in. This relates particularly to the areas of sports and culture.

In the area of sports, the party has been involved in helping to build multi-purpose concrete courts around the country so that there would be more sporting facilities available to the youth and the people of our country. We have also been involved in identifying the major football fields, cricket pitches and what not that are in need of repairs, and then organise to have them repaired through voluntary work.

Likewise, in the area of culture, the party has been encouraging the formation of new culture groups and providing basic rudimentary materials such as box guitars. We have been helping to sponsor competitions, and through the work of the party and community many new community centres are being built. And these centres will, of course, help to provide the physical facilities for the further development of culture in our country.

Finally, the party most of all attempts to lead the process through example, through recruiting the best elements from among the workers, the small farmers, the youth, the women, the intellectuals in our country. We are particularly conscious of the fact that we are operating from the position of being a ruling party and therefore the danger of opportunists trying to seek membership is one that we are very conscious of; hence, we have increased the tightness of selection and recruitment of members into the party.

Party members, of course, are obliged to engage in ideological study, and practical, consistent concrete work on behalf of the party and the revolution on a daily and weekly basis and, indeed, are expected to lead those areas of practical and concrete work. They are expected to be in front, to lead, not because they are party members, but because of their work.

All party comrades must also abide with all the internal norms of the party such as in the areas of criticism and self-criticism and in the practice of democratic centralism.

I think it's important to conclude this by saying that all of this activity by the party is possible today because of its historical experience. Our party was built in underground conditions, in the days when repression was very common, when party members on a regular basis were being imprisoned, brutalised and tortured [and] were forced to develop underground techniques for producing our newspaper and thereafter selling our newspaper. Our party, therefore, has been steeled in battle and has produced over the years members of a certain quality and calibre, who have operated within the context of a strict, disciplined organisation. Within our ranks today, therefore, we have the finest fighters in the work places and villages, among the workers, among the youth and among the women.

Our party at this time, therefore, is a vanguard in deed and not just a vanguard in name as our party has had to lead and today still leads the struggles of the working class and the working people.

RL: What do you see as the main problems facing the Grenadian Revolution and how are these being tackled? Some of these have already been mentioned in terms of your answer to the character of the Grenada Revolution. Can you just identify what you see as the main ones now?

MB: The two main problems as far as we are concerned today, would be, firstly, the threat from imperialism and, secondly, building the economy in the context of the world capitalist crisis that we face today.

To take the first one first – the threat from imperialism – this has been for us a total and all-round threat. It has taken the form of propaganda destabilisation that has been quite massive over the years. It has also taken the form of an economic squeeze on all fronts, indeed of economic aggression against our country. It has taken the form of internal terrorist and counter-revolutionary activity, prompted, encouraged, supported and incited by imperialism in their attempts to stir up internal counter-revolutionary elements.

And today, increasingly, it has taken the form of a direct military threat, a military threat which could eventually take the form of direct marine invasion, or of mercenary invasion, against our country. At this point in time, that threat is by far the most serious threat we face – the threat of military intervention.

It's necessary to say that all of the other threats we have faced from imperialism, the propaganda threat, the diplomatic threat and the economic aggression have basically failed. And that is why today the threat of military intervention has been placed so highly on the agenda. Notwithstanding the attempts at economic squeeze against us, the fact is they have had very limited success. They have not been able to deter the traditional friends of Grenada from continuing to give assistance to the revolution. Nor have they been able to stop us in our attempts to diversify our relationships and to develop new relations with the countries of Eastern Europe, the countries of the Socialist World and, indeed, with the countries of Western Europe.

So today, in fact, we have very good relations with countries like Canada, Venezuela, the ten-member grouping of countries in the European Economic Community (EEC) and increasingly with different countries of the Socialist World. We have also seen the excellent relations with the Arab states that are members of OPEC – Libya, Algeria, Syria, and Iraq being the most prominent in terms of our relations of co-operation with these countries.

They have had real problems in getting the economic squeeze to have an effect on our economy, largely because we have never had strong trading commercial relations with the United States. Indeed, we have very little economic relations with the United States. They have been unable to bring that pressure directly to bear on us, and they have had to rely on trying to influence their friends and on trying to intimidate other countries from providing economic assistance and, in this, they have not been very successful.

Likewise, their propaganda attacks against the Grenada Revolution have not been as successful as they would have hoped. It has had only marginal impact on tourist activity in our country. It did have the effect, last year in particular, of somewhat reducing the number of tourists who came to our country. But as against that, many more non-traditional tourists and other people came to our country for the first time to see what was happening for themselves. People who are not in the least concerned about the propaganda being put out by the United States imperialism.

Likewise, once we moved to counter-attack with our own propaganda, once we moved to try more and more to get the truth of the Grenada Revolution out to the region and to the world, it did begin to have the effect of neutralising the propaganda attacks by imperialism.

Last November, for example, we had our first ever international Solidarity Conference with Grenada, right here in St George's and there were 112 delegates coming from 41 different countries and from all five continents of the world and this solidarity conference, in fact, was extremely important.

We have also been able to broaden and deepen our work with friends, supporters, democratic and progressive forces in different countries around the world. This can be best seen through the increase in the number of Friendship Associations with Grenada. In the United States alone today, there are now over 15 different chapters of United

States/Grenada Friendship Associations with Grenada. And all of this has had the effect of cutting back on the extent of the propaganda damage which would otherwise have been done.

The situation, therefore, that imperialism faces today is one of internal consolidation on the military and political fronts and reasonable progress on the economic front. That is why they are forced more and more to resort to the external threat, that is why they are forced more and more to resort to almost complete reliance on a military intervention in order to roll back the revolutionary process. We believe that is by far the biggest problem we face, the greatest danger.

The way in which we have responded to this aggression is through alerting our people to the danger, always informing them about the facts, getting them more and more involved in the Militia so that whenever such a threat materialises the people themselves will be in a position to defend the country and the revolution. And equally, by alerting world public opinion to the danger we are able to rely on the power and force of international solidarity and international public opinion on ensuring that the threat is neutralised or delayed for as long as possible.

The second main problem is the question of the economy and building the economy in the context of imperialist attempts to destabilise us, and also in the context of the world capitalist crisis which continues today. Our country traditionally has had a very dependent relationship with the capitalist world. We have had to depend on them both to sell our products and to buy the manufactured items which we need.

In that situation, of course, our terms of trade have continued to deteriorate and we have found ourselves, in common with other developing countries around the world, faced with tremendous economic difficulties internally, which have aggravated the cost of living and the job situation.

In responding to this situation, we have been attempting to develop greater self-reliance within the economy, by growing more of our food, producing more of the items that we use in the country and in that way hoping to cut back on our imports, to save very scarce foreign exchange and create new jobs.

We have also been attempting to develop and expand the productive base in the economy, particularly through diversifying our agricultural production and moving into the area of agro-industrialisation based on the crops that we produce and expanding the fisheries and Fishing sector in the country.

Additionally, we have been attempting to diversify our economic relations and links; particularly, we have been trying to develop trading and commercial ties with the socialist world and generally to find new trading partners.

Internally, we have been developing and encouraging new worker attitudes to production and productivity and we have been trying as best as we can to apply science and technology, creatively applied through skills training at all different levels to the productive process in the country.

RL: Finally comrade Bishop, what is your assessment of the present political situation in the Caribbean, in the light of [Ronald] Reagan's Caribbean Basin Initiative (CBI)?

MB: The CBI is, in our view, a response by imperialism to the revolutionary upsurge in the region. This upsurge has been on the rise since, certainly, 1979. This can be seen from the Grenada Revolution in March 1979, the Nicaragua Revolution in July and, in between these two, a popular upsurge overthrowing the right-wing government of Patrick John in Dominica and the electoral victory of progressive forces in St. Lucia. A few months later in Suriname, in February 1980, we also saw another victory of the progressive forces.

All of this had the effect of seriously shaking imperialism. Imperialism, therefore, had to organise a fight-back and this fight-back, it must be said, had the effect of returning right-wing governments to power in Dominica and St Lucia. However, the United States understands that the deep underlying objective and material basis for this upsurge is because astronomical unemployment, high living costs, internal repressive mechanisms of control and institutionalised poverty still exist.

Imperialism will also understand very well, as we do, that none of the right and centre-right governments in power in the region today are able to rule with any decisiveness. They are also in power, but they are not able to be as decisive as they would like. Indeed, even when the left forces are small, or weak, or divided, the independent upsurge and challenge of the masses nonetheless pose a threat to the ruling establishment.

In Barbados too, which has long been advertised as being a model of stability for the Eastern Caribbean, today there is tremendous industrial unrest and activity in that country.

In Jamaica likewise, a very powerful left still exists, and this no doubt has implications for how fast and with what degree of success the right wing can pursue their policies.

I want to repeat that right and centre-right forces are in power, but they are not able to rule decisively. The balance of forces at this point is not decisively in favour of the right or the left and, therefore, they are not able to have a decisive grip on state power.

We believe that this will continue and, indeed, heighten because the economic situation is deteriorating in the midst of these countries. In fact, more and more of them are now coming under the grip of the International Monetary Fund (IMF). There are IMF Programmes now for St Vincent, St Lucia, Dominica, Antigua, and discussions are now going on between the government of Barbados and the IMF, and an IMF programme could well come on stream for that country very shortly.

As we know, the IMF recipe is a recipe for disaster because the programme always seeks to get the right countries out of the particular economic crises at the expense of the workers. And, therefore, at a minimum, industrial unrest will increase. This we can already see happening in Jamaica, in Barbados and elsewhere in the region where there are tremendous signs of such heightened industrial activity.

Class contradictions can only heighten in this situation and because of the pro-imperialist outlook of the ruling circles, they will be unable themselves to develop programmes that will deal with the real problems that the masses face.

It must be said too that at this time the masses of the region are able to observe an alternative path to development. They are watching very carefully the experiments in Grenada and Nicaragua which are popular, democratic and revolutionary processes with deep growing participation by the people and in which independent economic paths are being stressed. Together with the example of Cuba, which has been around now for the past 23 years, all of this poses a very serious threat for imperialism. They understand very well that on the forefront of the consciousness of the masses and on their immediate agenda is an alternative to the dependent, capitalist, pro-imperialist Westminster hypocrisy of economic and political developments.

It is for these reasons that Reagan today speaks of Grenada, for example, exporting the virus of communism. It is for these reasons likewise, that Prime Minster Tom Adams of Barbados is able to allege that the main threat coming from Grenada is not a military threat, as suggested by Reagan, but what Adams describes as an ideological threat. The power of example of the Grenadas, the Nicaraguas and the Cubas is precisely what imperialism today is most afraid of.

This, of course, also explains the attempts to isolate us in the region, the attempts to develop a programme of military intervention in Nicaragua and their continuing ambition to overthrow the consolidated revolutionary process in Cuba.

The reality in the region today also includes armed uprisings in countries like El Salvador and Guatemala. Elsewhere this reality is being expressed in the form of mass demonstrations and protests and everywhere it is taking the form of, at a minimum, mass discontent. This is the region, therefore, that Reagan has to deal with at this point and I think the CBI has to be seen, in part, as Reagan's response to this new regional reality.

In exactly the same way as the Alliance for Progress which John F. Kennedy had put forward on March 11, 1961, was essentially a response to Cuba, so too, today we have to see the CBI as being a response to Nicaragua and Grenada, coming on top of Cuba. The CBI must therefore be firmly located in the context of the revolutionary upsurge in the region as a whole.

The main characteristics of the CBI itself: its divide-and-rule aspect, its patent attempt to try to re-colonise the region, its attempt to use geography in a political way in its exclusion policies for certain countries, its hope of creating an anti-Cuba, anti-Nicaragua, anti-Grenada axis, these characteristics will certainly help to ensure the failure of the CBI plan. In fact, almost all sectors of public opinion and strata have serious reservations, of one kind or another and to one degree or another, about the CBI. This is true of right-wing forces, of centre-right forces, of the established labour movement, and of the regional bourgeoisie in general. All are concerned, sometimes for different reasons, about aspects of the Plan. In some cases, there are complaints about the fact that the amount of money being provided is too small. Others are concerned about the effects that this could have on the regional integration movements which have been built up over dozens of years of struggle.

Still, others are concerned, including private sector interests, about the possible effects of transnational exploitation at the expense of the local private sector and many are concerned about the military component which the Plan includes, a military component which in fact represents the real reason for the US vision of the CBI. It is the mechanism which was devised by Ronald Reagan and his warlords to provide further military assistance to the junta in El Salvador, in particular.

The situation in the region, therefore, remains dynamic and explosive. The revolutionary ferment will definitely continue and will be given expression in different forms and ways. This is our judgement about the present situation in the Caribbean region.

# 7 | *Blowing the Abeng:*
*Rupert Lewis and the Rebuilding of Caribbean Socialism*

Paget Henry

The focus of this paper, rebuilding Caribbean socialism, is a part of my larger response to the dramatic rises in levels of social inequality that have marked the last three neoliberal decades, the financial collapse they produced in 2008, and the hardships of its aftermath. As Thomas Piketty's book, *Capital in the Twenty-First Century*, makes clear, these increasing levels of inequality are global phenomena. In the US, we now have hedge fund managers and corporate CEOs who make anywhere between $9million and $1billion in annual income, while there are over ten million households making less than $12,000 annually (Schweickart 2011, 90–95). In the Caribbean, we too have seen the simultaneous increases in the number of millionaires, the number and size of ghettos, and disturbing increases in crime rates. But a rebuilding of Caribbean socialism in response to global neoliberalism can only rest on a set of clear and detailed critiques of the mistakes, theoretical and practical, made in the past by the Caribbean Left. I cannot think of a better way of joining in this celebration of the thought of Professor Rupert Lewis than by enlisting his work in this critical prolegomena to the next attempts at socialist transformations of the political economy of the post-colonial Caribbean.

**Transformation and Its Dimensions**

To grasp the significance of the contributions of Professor Lewis to Caribbean intellectual and political life, we must focus our attention on the challenges of post-colonial transformation in the 1960s and '70s. These challenges arose from the push to end British colonial rule and the economic dominance of its local allies, the planter classes of the region. This long and protracted struggle gained new intensity and momentum in the 1930s as the contractions in external demand produced by the Great Depression began to work their way through Caribbean economies. Neither the colonial political elites nor planter/

merchant economic elites were able to make adequate constructive responses to this major crisis of Western capitalism.

The planters, who in the mercantile period had been a part of the leading faction of the British bourgeoisie, had, since the rise of competitive and industrial capitalism in the second half of the nineteenth century, been forced to join the marginal factions of this class. Not only were Caribbean planters losing ground to textile manufacturers, they were also unable to transform and industrialise their sugar industry and in the process integrate Caribbean economies and expand domestic markets. Only through such a major restructuring could they have restored earlier levels of capital accumulation and their importance to the British state. This combination of declining strategic importance and the resurgence of popular resistance to colonial rule was the context in which the territories of the English-speaking Caribbean secured their political independence from Britain.

This defeat of the planters brought to the fore the issue of the class that would replace them. As we now know, they were for the most part replaced by local political elites of petit bourgeois background. However, in cases like Antigua and Barbuda, the planters were replaced by leaders of working-class background. These local political elites have governed the territories of the regions with the assistance of local petit bourgeois economic elites and with even greater reliance on white foreign capitalists. This pattern of dependent governing partnerships followed from the underdeveloped state in which colonial exclusion from the major sectors of the economy had left Caribbean bourgeois and working-class groups. Particularly among Afro-Caribbeans, where this exclusion was most extreme, entrepreneurial traditions had been decimated and thus were even more unable to compete in the economic order of the post-colonial period.

Under these conditions, it very quickly became clear that the new governing elites, although doing better than the planters, would also not be able to integrate and industrialise the region's economies and insert them more competitively into the circuits of the international economy. The first major signs of this leadership crisis were the singular independence of Jamaica and Trinidad in 1962. By 1968, these new political leaders were encountering both productive difficulties in their economies and popular resistance in their polities. In 1970, there was a major uprising in Trinidad that almost toppled the regime of Eric

Williams. These movements of popular resistance were calling for changes in inherited race relations, for more socialist approaches to the difficulties of economic development and to regional integration. Thus, the challenge confronting these socialist alternatives was to succeed in these areas where the planters and the first generation of local political leaders had failed.

### Lewis and the Movements for Radical Transformation

One of the many reasons we are celebrating the work of Professor Rupert Lewis is the scholarly way in which he has helped us to understand the nature and meaning of these challenges to the first generation of Caribbean post-colonial leaders, and the kinds of difficulties that they would present for strategies of socialist transformation. However, Lewis did not just write about these movements, he was also an active participant. In a masterful and revealing essay, 'Learning to Blow the Abeng', Lewis not only describes some of these anti-establishment movements but also his own involvement. He tells us that in 1969 the Abeng group 'was a moment of coming together of a variety of trends – Rastafarians, Garveyites, businessmen,...lawyers, UWI academics and disillusioned grassroots PNP activists' (1997, 6), of which he too was a member. This larger movement, 'of which Abeng was a part, was a response to Manley's, Bustamante's and Shearer's maltreatment of the Rastafarian and Black Power movements' (1997, 7). Lewis was also a member of the Workers Party of Jamaica (WPJ). Formed in 1978, and headed by his university colleague, Dr Trevor Munroe, this party was 'modeled on the CPSU which we considered the party of Lenin' (1997, 13). Lewis also discusses the 1970 uprising in Trinidad, the 1979 revolution in Grenada and the impact of the latter's implosion on the WPJ.

As a result of these deep involvements with the above movements, Lewis's writings on this period of attempted socialist transformation are both theoretical and practical. His scholarly contributions have been particularly strong with regard to issues of racial and socialist resistance to the new local elites and also to the rebirth of Pan African impulses and ideals. In regard to the latter, we think immediately of his extensive work on Marcus Garvey. This work includes: *Marcus Garvey: Anticolonial Champion*, the volume, *Garvey: Africa, Europe, the Americas*, edited with Maureen Warner-Lewis, and *Garvey: His Work and Impact*, edited with Patrick Bryan. Further, we think of his work at Liberty Hall, Garvey's headquarters and the new journal *76 King Street*, the address in Kingston of those headquarters. With regard to the experiences of socialist resistance and attempts at transformation, we think immediately of his major work on Walter Rodney, *Walter Rodney's Intellectual and Political Thought*. It is now time for us to get deeper into these intellectual contributions made by Lewis, and what they tell us about his generation's attempts at Caribbean transformation.

## Lewis and the Intellectual Dimensions of Transformation

Among Lewis's earliest publications was the landmark reader in Caribbean politics that he co-edited with his colleague Dr Trevor Munroe. This 1971 reader, *Readings in the Politics and Government of the West Indies*, helped to establish the academic field of Caribbean politics, and also to solidify the department of political science at the University of the West Indies (UWI), Mona. What is really important about this volume for us is its multi-dimensional approach to Caribbean politics. It opens with an essay on the Caribbean family and its impact on the political values, attitudes and behaviour of citizens. This multi-dimensional approach to politics will become one of Lewis's primary trademarks along with the epistemic challenges of bringing these dimensions together, which others were often working hard to keep apart.

Lewis's work on Garvey was a major effort at rescuing his image from the distortions of his detractors and political rivals, while at the same time keeping the focus on his ideas about anti-black racism and Pan Africanism. His full-length study, *Marcus Garvey: Anticolonial Champion*, is a masterful portrait of Garvey, which is both carefully crafted and highly informative. Garvey was and still is a highly controversial figure about whom much has been written. Three features in particular have distinguished Lewis's account from earlier ones. First, is the balanced and judicious nature of his scholarship. Second, is the illuminating way in which the book links Garvey to a local tradition of protest with roots in the 1865 Morant Bay Rebellion, and which was continued through figures like Theophilus Scholes, Robert Love and Alexander Bedward. With the contributions made by Garvey, the foundations of the Rastafarian Movement were laid. Third, and finally, is the detailed account of Garvey's years in Jamaica (1929–34) after his politically motivated imprisonment and deportation from the US.

After describing in detail Garvey's activities in the years following his return to Jamaica, Lewis goes on to deal directly with Garvey's theoretical treatment of the class/race issue and the practical problems of the relationship between Garveyism and the international working class movement. His treatment of this issue is important for our theme of re-building Caribbean socialism. At the same time, it illustrates well the strong tendency in Lewis's thinking toward reconciling different or opposing analytic approaches to the politics of post-colonial transformation in the Caribbean. He was convinced at the time that this transformation required 'an alliance between the national liberation movement and the international working class movement' (1988, 126). In other words, it required a linking of the struggles against racism and class oppression, and thus between movements like Garveyism and socialism.

Given the above view, Lewis suggested in this book that Garvey's 'exclusive equation of "race" with "nation" was scientifically and historically unsound' (1988, 125). This exclusive equation made it too difficult to take adequate account of other social factors that were vital for liberation. Lewis is here attempting to correct an excessive epistemic claim on Garvey's part in order to make room for other relevant factors, particularly class. In short, at the same time that this work is a vital contribution to our understanding of Garvey, it also tackles very directly the difficulties of bringing together issues of class, race and culture in projects of post-colonial transformation.

Lewis's work on Walter Rodney builds on and advances the work done on Garvey. His book, *Walter Rodney's Intellectual and Political Thought* was the first and still is the only full-length study of this outstanding scholar and activist from Guyana. Just as he did not want us to forget Garvey, so also he did not want us to forget Rodney. In the introduction to this book, Lewis tells us: 'part of my concern in writing about Walter Rodney is to develop a political dialogue with my students in Caribbean Political Thought and my children who were born in the 1970s' (1998, xiii). Another portion of Lewis's concern in this work was to make more explicit and accessible the evolution of Rodney's political thought and its significance for the larger Caribbean intellectual tradition. In particular, Lewis feared that by the late 1980s, Rodney's 'pioneering work on African history and his Pan African activism in Tanzania' had become obscured (1998, xiii). Consequently, he saw the need to bring together Rodney's 'African and Caribbean intellectual and activist contributions for they constituted a whole' (1998, xiii).

In the course of realising this aim, Lewis introduces us to Rodney's Marxism, his Pan Africanism and how he attempted to link them both theoretically and practically. In dealing with Rodney's Marxism, Lewis uncovers its roots in the influences of Cheddi Jagan's People's Progressive Party (PPP); the influences of scholars like Eric Williams, Lloyd Best, and Norman Girvan during his undergraduate years at UWI (Mona) from 1960 to 1963; and finally the influence of C.L.R. James during his graduate years at the School of Oriental and African Studies (SOAS) in London. Rodney was a member of that now famous Marxist study group that James led. As such, he was a member of an up-and-coming third generation of Caribbean Marxists who were eager to try their hands at post-colonial transformation. The first generation, who were of Garvey's era, included Hubert Harrison, W.A. Domingo, Richard Moore and Cyril Briggs. The second included George Padmore, C.L.R. James and Claudia Jones. Each of these generations of Caribbean Marxists made distinct intellectual and practical responses as they were confronted with different political economies, racial situations and global conjunctures. Lewis's concern in this work is with the contributions of his and Rodney's generation of Caribbean Marxists.

In developing Rodney's Pan Africanism, Lewis uncovers its roots in Rodney's experiences of race in Guyana; discussion groups on the Mona Campus; his contacts with Rastafarians while an undergraduate; and finally Rodney's strong desire while in graduate school to know more about Africa and how it has influenced the Caribbean. The strength of this interest produced his dissertation at SOAS, 'A History of the Upper Guinea Coast, 1545–1800', which was later published as a book with the same title. Lewis provides us with a portrait of Rodney as a strong but not dogmatic Pan Africanist with deep Marxist roots. Thus, compared to Garvey, he was a very different kind of Pan Africanist, as he was also a very different kind of Marxist from Padmore or James.

In spite of the significant differences between Garvey and Rodney, these two men and their struggles with race and class domination, have been the primary lenses through which Lewis has viewed the problems of post-colonial transformation in the Caribbean. However, this use of them as lenses did not mean for Lewis that they got everything right. As we will see, Lewis often catches both men in moments of dogmatism that resulted in strategic or practical decisions of poor quality. At the same time, the fact that he never brought these two wings of our political tradition together as a black democratic socialist formation is indicative of the depths of these internal tensions. Let us now take a closer look at Lewis's examination of Rodney's Marxism.

**Lewis, Rodney and James**

Lewis often works out significant portions of his thinking through critical dialogues with the positions taken by figures such as Garvey, James, Franz Fanon, Rodney and the Rastafarians. Consequently, a good way in which to grasp his thoughts on the problem of socialist transformation is by situating him in the discursive space defined by the convergences, divergences and tensions between the Pan African/socialist positions of James and Rodney. Lewis has navigated this particular space with great skill, insight and care. He is indeed a distinguished Professor of this important domain of Caribbean thought. It is from this particular space that he has been blowing the Abeng in both socialist and Pan Africanist directions.

In order to grasp the significance of Lewis's critiques of Rodney and their importance for our project of re-building Caribbean socialism, we must be clear on a number of key concepts used by both James and Rodney, but were defined implicitly or rather loosely. The most important of these were the concepts of racial capitalism, socialism and how immediately it could be implemented, the petit bourgeoisie, and Caribbean post-colonial political economy. Both James and Rodney linked race and capitalism in their texts, but the nature of these linkages remained implicit and thus not systematically elaborated, as in the cases of Cedric Robinson and Sylvia Wynter. As a result, these implicit linkages were invoked on ad hoc bases by both thinkers in different ways, leading to different moments in which race would be eclipsed or under-represented. In such moments of divergence, Lewis often sides with James.

In spite of its importance, socialism remains one of the loosely defined concepts of the Caribbean Left. For both James and Rodney, there were important subjective and objective dimensions to the concept of socialism. In broad terms that encompass both of these dimensions, socialism was the activist/discursive response of workers to their exploitation and dehumanisation on the plantations and within the factories of capitalism. This often-insurrectionary response included projects for the full re-humanisation of workers and the ending of their poverty. As such, they had to address issues of political and economic self-determination for workers, the de-proletarianisation of their identities and the cultural autonomy to redefine and assert their humanity. However, the socialist formulations of specific demands emerging from these insurrectionary projects have been the work of petit bourgeois intellectuals like Karl Marx, Friedrick Engels, Vladimir Lenin, James, Rodney and Claudia Jones. In addition to the classic Marxist contributions to these theoretical formulations, James and Rodney included the de-negrification of Afro-Caribbean identities and the de-coolietising of Indo-Caribbean identities in their socialist projects. However, there were significant differences between the two in regard to how the various aspects of this socialist vision – economic self-determination, racial equality, or political self-determination – would be implemented and how immediately.

The petit bourgeoisie was a class stratum that was very important for James, Rodney and Lewis. In *Walter Rodney's Intellectual and Political Thought*, Lewis tells us that what emerges from Rodney's work is not just a critique of imperial capitalism but also 'a dissection of the domestic political elite that assumed political authority from the colonisers in Africa and the Caribbean as well as an analysis of the processes of recolonisation' (1998, xvii). Rodney was highly critical of these elites and saw their quick removal from power as an important step towards socialist transformation in our region. James's views of the Caribbean political elite and their local economic counterparts are well known. He emphasised their exclusion from the centres of power and production during the colonial period, their tendencies to identify with Western capital and hence their inability and unpreparedness for leading a worker-centred programme of change in the post-colonial period. However, given that workers were also excluded from the above centres of power and production, James was more cautious in his dismissal of the Caribbean petit bourgeoisie. In *Party Politics in the West Indies*, he emphasised the kind of popular democratic practices that workers needed to engage in if they were to overcome the legacy of their long exclusion from being full and equal participants. Particularly on this question of the petit bourgeoisie we can see Lewis leaning much closer to James's position.

On the nature of Caribbean political economy, there were significant divergences between James and Rodney. James saw Caribbean political economies within the framework of his broader theory of state capitalism (1968), while Rodney saw them within the framework of the theory of dependent or peripheral capitalism that had been developed by the New World Group and the Latin American and African schools of dependency theory. The influences of these schools on Rodney's thinking are very evident in his well-known text, *How Europe Underdeveloped Africa*. Lewis did not get into these particular sets of differences between James and Rodney on Caribbean political economies but selected a yardstick of his own. That yardstick was how effectively and efficiently post-colonial economies were run and how clear was the evidence that they were alleviating the poverty of workers. This is the yardstick by which Lewis will measure Rodney's economic claims.

With these conceptual clarifications in mind, let us return to Lewis's critical reading of Rodney and look at some of the more specific points that he makes.

### Lewis, Rodney and Socialist Transformation

Rodney's vision of socialist transformation and its prospects for realisation in the Caribbean and Africa are best seen in his responses and contributions to the building of Ujamaa socialism in Tanzania in the 1960s and '70s. Although very supportive of President Julius Nyerere, Rodney had a more expansive, immediate and anti-petit bourgeois vision of socialist transformation in Africa. Consequently, there were parts of Nyerere's socialist programme that Rodney supported quite strongly and also parts of which he was highly critical. He supported Nyerere's emphasis on self-reliance, and his nationalisation of major sectors of the Tanzanian economy. These moves were, for Rodney, the beginning of a socialist order in Tanzania. The success of this young socialist nation would depend on how effectively these initial moves were executed. Effective execution would include paying close attention to those technical and organisational details, which, if ignored, have the potential to generate short-term crises, such as shortages, which could delegitimise and destabilise the regime. Given the earlier experiences of the Soviet Union, Eastern Europe and China, it was obvious by the 1970s that socialist regimes had their own economic and political crisis tendencies, which in conditions of maturity could lead to the collapse of young socialist states. From Lewis's account, Rodney did not pay sufficient attention to these organisational and technical issues that were internal to socialist economies and polities. Indeed, he suggests Rodney assumed that these were routine problems that would be taken care of and resolved. Thus, Lewis notes: 'Rodney can be criticised for overestimating the extent to which the relevant social structures were being built' (1998, 141).

In contrast to this inadequate attention paid to these technical and organisational issues, Lewis points to the close watch that Rodney kept on ideological matters. He describes in detail the many ideologically oriented debates and papers that Rodney was engaged in or wrote while he was in Tanzania. From these works, it would appear that Rodney's primary emphasis was on the ideological vision guiding the process of socialist transformation. In this regard, the class position of the leaders and major thinkers became extremely important. In addition to being strongly pro-worker, the ideological vision that Rodney wanted to see in place had to be firmly anti-imperialist, anti-capitalist, anti-racist, committed to socialism and to African unity. These were the crucial yardsticks by which Rodney marked off political differences, and were thus the grounds for ideological critique or attack. These practices had the potential for factional fighting and in some cases pushed Rodney to attack without the strategic resources to deal with likely counter-attacks.

It is this spirit of ideological critique and measurement that emerges from Lewis's analyses of papers by Rodney such as 'Tanzanian Ujamaa and Scientific Socialism', or 'African Socialism'. Lewis suggests that, in the first of these essays, Rodney attempts two ideological tasks: first, to legitimise Nyerere's Ujamaa socialism by demonstrating its closeness to scientific socialism; and second to differentiate Ujamaa socialism from what had been called African socialism. Both of these were highly problematic undertakings as the notion of scientific socialism was a highly contested one, and also because Nyerere had linked his socialism so directly to African socialism (1968, 2–5).

Further, in this paper, Rodney associated African socialism with the negritude of Leopold Senghor and thus saw it as being without much socialist content. But this was a very narrow reading of African socialism as it was also embraced by a leader like Kwame Nkrumah, who linked it to Marxian socialism through his philosophy conscienceism. Further, one got the impression that Rodney was quite uncomfortable with Nyerere's theorising of African socialism as a societal projection of the solidarity, collective responsibility and mutual support of an extended family.

Lewis's critique of this paper by Rodney also pointed to the fact that it minimised the significance of the nascent stages in which both the working and bourgeois classes existed in Tanzania, and the difficulties they would create for any attempt to apply scientific or classical Marxian socialism to this young nation. Indeed, Lewis stated very paradoxically the major challenge arising from the nascent stages of class development in Tanzania: that is, the need to encourage the 'internal capitalist development' upon which the application of scientific socialism could rest (1998, 143). This may not be the best or the most tactful way to state the problem, but it makes the vital point regarding the appropriate levels of entrepreneurial, planning and managerial capabilities that are necessary for a modern socialist project to succeed.

Another important example of Rodney's practice of ideological critique and attack that Lewis discusses was his position on the urgency of continental African unity. This position was outlined in the paper that he sent to the Sixth Pan African Congress, 'Aspects of the International Class Struggle in Africa, the Caribbean and America'. Lewis tells us that this paper 'was a sharp critique of post-independence regimes in Africa and the Caribbean, and that he was especially critical of the exclusion of non-governmental radical parties by ruling parties' (1998, 170). At the heart of this critique was the petit bourgeois character of these regimes. For Rodney, they were reformers not revolutionaries. On this point, Lewis quotes Rodney as follows: 'In the very process of demanding constitutional independence, they reneged on a cardinal principal of Pan Africanism: namely the unity and indivisibility of the African continent' (1998, 174).

Making use of a letter that James wrote to Rodney in response to his paper, Lewis points out some of the significant differences between the two on some of these issues. In his letter, James makes it clear that in spite of differences on specific positions, he has no quarrel with

Rodney about political ideas. In other words, there is no need for a major ideological battle here over the petit bourgeois nature of African and Caribbean post-colonial governing elites. Rather, the real issue at stake, says James, is 'who, what, where, and when we can get some of these ideas across' (1998, 171). The elder Marxist was here raising the practical issue of how do we get these good political ideas into the hearts and minds and interpersonal relations of the people and even some of these petit bourgeois leaders. James was not convinced by Rodney's open attack on African political leaders. Indeed, he suggested that it was a blunder.

On the whole, Lewis tends to side with James in the course of this exchange with Rodney. In James, Lewis recognised a position that was more tactful and nuanced, while at the same time being fully aware of the petit bourgeois nature of post-colonial regimes. With an eye ever turned to praxis, Lewis raised two questions of his own. First, was it possible that 'Rodney underestimated the significance' of the actions of progressive post-colonial regimes? (1998, 179) And second, how does one build socialism in post-colonial societies without the skills and cooperation of the petit bourgeoisie?

In short, through this extended critique of Rodney's socialist practice, Lewis was not only completing his exposition of Rodney's intellectual and political thought, he was also making clear his own views on the theory and practice of socialist transformation in post-colonial societies. The critique of Rodney made clear many of the unresolved theoretical and practical issues. On the theoretical side, the remaining challenge was achieving more equitable theoretical spaces for race and class. On the practical side the challenge was that of building socialism with an underdeveloped working class and a reformist but necessary petit bourgeoisie.

## Lewis and the Problem of Socialist Transformation Today

We can update this view of the problem of socialist transformation by looking briefly at Lewis's 2001 paper, 'Reconsidering the Role of the Middle Class in Caribbean Politics'. In contrast to the more retrospective glance of his Abeng paper, this essay was written with a definite look ahead. It focused directly on the prospects for socialist transformation in the wake of the collapse of the revolution in Grenada, the democratic socialism of Michael Manley in Jamaica, and other socialist experiments that came out of the upheavals that challenged the first generation of post-colonial leaders. The collapse of these socialist experiments in the Caribbean was, in turn, followed by the dramatic fall of state socialism in the Soviet Union and Eastern Europe. Consequently, the paper is a frank look at the failures of various socialist experiments in the Caribbean region and what should come after. In many ways, its recommendations follow directly from the criticisms Lewis made of Rodney's socialist praxis and also that of the Workers Party of Jamaica (WPJ).

At the end of the Abeng paper, we got a more chastened commitment to socialism. That chastened commitment was expressed in language borrowed from Derek Walcott: 'some form of socialism, evolved from our own political history, is the only hope for the archipelago' (1997, 16). At the end of this paper, on reconsidering the role of the middle class, there remains a definite commitment to transformation, but there are no clear indicators of its socialist nature. For Lewis, just about all of the problems raised in his critique of Rodney's socialist praxis are still with us, with no real new or innovative solutions on the horizon. Consequently, this essay reflects a receding of the project of a socialist transformation.

There are, of course, several factors motivating this retreat, even though only some of them are developed in detail. The first is the meaning of socialism in the period after the collapse of our Caribbean experiments and the fall of state socialism in the Soviet Union and Eastern Europe, China, Vietnam and, most recently, Cuba. The need for theoretical and practical elucidation in the wake of these events is both necessary and urgent. What are we to make of the re-introduction of the market in all of these societies? Does it spell the end of central planning or a rescaling of it? What of the communal/cooperative roots of African and Afro-Caribbean socialism to which Walcott referred? Lewis's papers are calls for increased clarity on these issues.

Second, and very important for Lewis, is the politics of our socialist movements and the regimes they have produced. The politics of these movements and regimes have been infected with levels of dogmatism that were far too high. These excessive levels of dogmatism led to destructive factional fights, which, in turn, became the basis for autocratic styles of rule that contradicted the goals of popular proletarian democracy. Lewis is crystal clear on the need to address this problem in new and creative ways.

A third factor motivating Lewis's retreat from a socialist transformation was the weak economic foundations of our socialist movements and regimes. Lewis points out the many times that Rodney was wrong about the Tanzanian economy and the fact that it collapsed from problems of shortages, mismanagement, and poor planning. Lewis's works are alarm bells sounding the crisis of confidence that has engulfed socialist economics.

Fourth, for Lewis there remains the vexed question of the kind of engagement that Caribbean socialist movements and regimes should have with the petit bourgeoisie. We have seen the consistency with which he has asserted that past engagements have been rather impractical and unrealistic. Further, as we have noted, Lewis has stressed the fact that in post-colonial Caribbean societies the petit bourgeoisie displays wide variation along the ideological spectrum. In doing so, he is concerned that the Left has underestimated the potential of alliances with progressive elements of this governing class. Closely related to this concern is Lewis's even more pointed question: can Caribbean socialism be built without the skills and contributions of this class? In his paper on the role of the middle class, we get the strongest statement that there can be no transformation, socialist or otherwise, without the contributions of this class. Indeed, his position is that a strengthening of this class, particularly its entrepreneurial capabilities, is one of the conditions now required if transformation is to take place.

The fifth factor motivating Lewis's retreat from his earlier socialist position is his continuing fear that tendencies towards excessive dogmatism around the class issue will result in the eclipsing of the race issue. Closely related to the eclipsing of the race issue is that of the eclipsing of culture, and in particular, African culture. Lewis's continuing work on Garvey at Liberty Hall and the journal, *76 King Street*, are indicators of these concerns. In other words, the Caribbean socialism of the future must not only be less dogmatic but also much more dialectical.

Sixth and finally, there is what Lewis calls 'the raw wound of Grenada' (1997, 14). On this wound, Lewis is very clear:

the murders of Maurice Bishop and other party leaders were criminal acts that were justified on ideological grounds, on the characterisation of Bishop as a petit bourgeois and Coard and his allies as proletarians. It was classic Stalinism. The effects of those tragic days not only ended the Grenadian Revolution but it brought down the curtain on Anglophone-Caribbean radicalism for the rest of this century (1997, 14).

From these six crucial points, we can get a rather clear idea of the intellectual and practical work that the Left would have to do before it could put on the political agenda a credible alternative to the still crisis-ridden neoliberal order that has been imposed on the economies of the region by the policies of globalising financial and commodity markets, and by our debt-driven relations with the International Monetary Fund (IMF).

**Lewis's Concerns: Two Responses**

The first step in an appropriate response to Lewis's genuine concerns must be some very good reasons for rebuilding our Pan African/Marxist or black democratic socialist tradition after its defeats and collapses. The major reason for repairing it is that this tradition has been and still contains our most consistent activist and discursive responses to our encounter with Western racial capitalism. As Lewis's work so clearly demonstrates, this has, for the most part, been a black democratic socialist tradition with a mixed economic base that has strongly resisted the Stalinist model of state socialism and full centralised planning. Further, this mixed economy has always included the communal and solidarity orientations of Caribbean peasants and the lumpen-proletariat. From revolting slaves like Ottobah Cugoano and Toussaint Overture, to Garvey, James, Rodney, Lewis and Derek Walcott's call for some form of socialism, this has been the dominant record of our political voice. Over the past decade, I have certainly felt this black socialist response rising in me with greater strength. This paper is very much a product of that response. To abandon this historic political voice would mean silencing ourselves and having to speak through voices that are not our own. To avoid such silencing and self-alienation, we must rise to the challenge of repairing this tradition and restoring its vitality and vision.

The need to act now becomes clearer every day as we watch the intense pushback coming from the right wing of Western capitalism, the faction that has dominated Western political economy since the early 1980s. This pushback has been on both class and race fronts, giving this expanding global system new racial and class inscriptions. For example, since coming to power in the US, these conservative and pro-business elites have prematurely eliminated the federal affirmative action programmes of the 1960s, and are now very busy imposing post-reconstruction type restrictions on the voting rights of African Americans and other minorities. These voting restrictions are closely related to policies of mass incarceration. Today, it is estimated that 'hundreds of thousands' of African Americans are disenfranchised (Higginbotham 2013, 189–91). On the class front, the same set of elites have significantly disempowered American workers, white and black, by putting them in direct competition with cheaper Chinese labour and weakening their trade unions. These neoliberal policies were counter-responses to the growing power of American labour and to the demands for a New International Economic Order (NIEO), which emerged from movements in the third world like those described by Lewis. Through our importing of foreign capitalists, and Western control of organisations such as the IMF and the WTO, these neoliberal economic theories have entered Caribbean discursive and policy-forming spaces, displacing the economic theories produced by our black democratic socialist tradition.

These disturbing trends cannot be reversed without a vigorous reclaiming of our tradition. However, to work at rebuilding it, we must assume that the passions, visions, and ideas about freedom that have animated the major popular upsurges of this tradition are still alive in us and in the rising generations, and are still seeking realisation in the social world. Of course, we could be wrong in this assumption, as so much has changed since the 1970s. For example, it could be argued that higher levels of consumption, the distractions of the Internet and shifts in the demographic composition of Caribbean working classes have so sedated and divided these classes that they could never be the insurrectionary forces they were in the 1930s and 1960s. This is clearly an important issue, which can only be definitively resolved by evidence from future upsurges by the Caribbean masses. Only then will we be able to know for sure that the theories of our tradition are still in sync with the political subjectivity of the majority of the population.

Assuming the persistence of these longstanding black democratic socialist impulses and ideals, it becomes clear from Lewis's critique of both Garvey and Rodney regarding the kind of intellectual and organisational work that must be done if this tradition is to be renewed and re-enter the debates about the future of our region. Given the comprehensive and detailed nature of Lewis's critique, I cannot here respond to all of the concerns noted above, but will select two for extended commentary.

**Between Race and Class**

The first of Lewis's concern that I will address is the persisting competitive tension between class and race, as the two have remained in battles for both conceptual and political space. In my view, the roots of this persistent problem are to be found in a well-known area of philosophical dependence that we must now overcome. Whether it is Christianity, liberalism or Marxism, the manner in which we have appropriated these imposed or imported ideas did not give us access to their operating manuals. That is, access to the a priori or always already presupposed categoric foundations or conceptual schemes of these discourses. In other words, we appropriated and mastered the explicit concepts, arguments, empirical claims and projections of these discourses while leaving un-mastered their underlying a priori schemes. As a result, there were deeper transcendental dimensions to these discourses that we were reluctant or unable to unlock and explore, and thus remained dependent on Western Christians, Marxists or liberals to make significant changes at these foundational levels. This is the legacy of philosophical, or more specifically, transcendental dependence that must now be broken if we are to have better ways of linking class and race that reflect more faithfully our socio-historical experiences. We really should not have expected white Western Marxists to provide us with a mode of linking class and race that would reflect our realities and experiences.

Fortunately for us, Cedric Robinson and Sylvia Wynter have begun the kind of a priori or transcendental analysis of the foundational concepts of imposed and imported discourses like liberalism or Marxism, which we will have to master if we are to achieve more satisfactory linkages between class and race. In his classic work, *Black Marxism*, Robinson subjects the medieval categoric inheritances of Western Marxism to a breathtakingly detailed analysis. This brilliant transcendental analysis reveals very clearly the manner in which concepts such as whiteness, slavery, class and their opposites were linked to a priori formations that Marxism inherited from the European medieval period. Robinson then goes on to suggest that it was the whiteness of concepts, which were transcendentally embedded, that explain why blacks such as George Padmore, C.L.R. James, W.E.B. Du Bois, Richard Wright and Aimé Césaire experienced the difficulties they did inside Communist parties – difficulties that echoed those described by Lewis in Marxist parties of the Caribbean. This speaks of a deep categoric inheritance that has been working against our experience of race and needs to be removed. To do so, we can join Robinson in the transcendental practice that he calls 'an anthropology of Marxism' (2001).

Equally important in achieving transcendental independence is the epistemic historicism of Sylvia Wynter. Like Robinson's, Wynter's work is also at the level of a priori conceptual schemes that ground the discourses we routinely use. Both of these thinkers have been pioneers on our path to full philosophical responsibility for the a priori foundations of all the discourses that we use; and both have worked on the transcendental foundations of Marxism (Henry 2006, 374–80). With regard to the more effective linking of class and race, it is precisely to this deeper level of conceptual schemes that Wynter directs our focus. Particularly relevant here is her suggestion that by the time that James was writing *Beyond a Boundary*, he had broken quite clearly with all mono-conceptual frameworks, such as an exclusive labour or race-theoretic one. Wynter suggests that the transcendental foundations of James's thinking had by that time become 'pluri-conceptual' in nature. In other words, James had found his way to a new and more complex dialectic. Thus, at the a priori level of his thinking, James now had multiple conceptual schemes of race, class, culture, and level of education operating simultaneously, the permutations of which he could now dialectically engage or analytically manipulate.

Drawing on the example of James, Wynter goes on to suggest that the conceptual scheme that grounded Western political economy and made possible concepts like exchange value and market was not a mono-conceptual transcendental formation. Rather, it was a pluri-conceptual one that also gave birth to a reductionist, and hence subordinate, concept of a 'law of cultural value' and its related notions of cultural exchange and cultural accumulation. At the heart of this subordinate schema of cultural value was the figure of the pieza or the general category of human exchange. The pieza was the conceptual instrument through which equivalences were established between a wide variety of racialised and oppressed groups. Within the framework of this discourse of human exchange, each of these groups was assigned a colour inferior to white and negatively stereotyped. Africans ceased being Yoruba, Akan or Baluba and became 'negroes' or blacks; Native Caribbeans and Native Americans ceased being Taínos, Seminoles or Navahos and became 'Injuns' or 'the red man'. Thus, at the same time that the discourse of exchange value was being generated for the trading of different types of commodities, another was also being developed to conceptually facilitate the racial ranking and exchange of human beings of different races, genders and ages. Wynter thinks that it is the simultaneous operating of these two conceptual schemas in the European mind that holds the key to more systematic notions of racial capitalism. Further, her work and Robinson's point us in the direction of the transcendental anthropology that we must employ in revising our notions of black democratic socialism.

**Rethinking Socialist Economies**

The second of Lewis's concerns that I will address is that regarding the viability of socialist economies in general, and in particular, the ones that we have so far imagined and established. In my view, this issue of economic viability is the biggest challenge confronting the rebuilding of socialist traditions in our region and elsewhere. Lewis's critique of Rodney made it very clear that a strong anti-capitalist stance is not a substitute for sound socialist economic policies. The collapse of the state socialist economies that followed the demise of our socialist experiments, and the re-introduction of markets in cases where they were eliminated are the primary sources of this issue of the viability of socialist economies. Thus, even after the Great Recession of 2008, we can still hear the cry of TINA – there is no alternative to capitalism.

For our black democratic socialist tradition, the first issues that we need to acknowledge are the differences in economic outlook between the Pan Africanist and the socialist wings of our political tradition. Garvey's strong pro-capitalist sentiments would have clashed with Rodney's strong socialist impulses. But all is not lost in this opposition as there are important points of convergence. Both wings have a history of strong communal and solidarity economic practices, which derive from their roots in the peasant and lumpen sectors. If we are to produce a form of socialism from our own politico-economic history, then the ideals and economic strivings of these collective, labour-oriented visions must be an integral part of it. Thus, as in the case of the revolution in Grenada, we will have to get past that ideological conflict that Rodney had with African socialism. The bonds of collective solidarity that exist in these communities are structures we can build on.

From the perspective of the Marxist wing of our tradition, the big issues to be addressed are clearly the fundamentals of socialist economic theory and practice in the light of the re-introduction of the market that has taken place in just about all of the formerly state socialist societies. This re-introduction of the market has presented the biggest challenges for those societies that adopted the Stalinist model of centrally planned economies in which the market was suspended by law and replaced by a central plan. This plan determined levels of production and prices, allocated resources and coordinated input-output relations. Further, the authoritarian politics associated with this model was a major source of the resistance that brought down these Stalinist models. It was the possibility of this type of resistance that led James, in the 1930s, to predict state capitalist futures for these regimes.

This retreat from central planning is less of a problem for us, as we never completely suspended the market. Clive Thomas's *Dependence and Transformation* contains the most systematic model of a socialist economy that our tradition has produced. Not only is it a mixed model, it addressed issues of dependence that Western models did not have to. Judged in the light of the Grenadian and other Caribbean socialist experiments, I think that the levels of planning capability assumed by Thomas are too high. But these are the issues that must be decided in the light of local conditions. The following is one of the major lessons that we have learned about central planning from the state capitalist turns of the former state socialist economies: the project of an economy that is completely centrally planned is too big an undertaking for any state. There are just too many moving details to monitor and stay on top of for even the best state bureaucracy. That the tasks of economic production, management and investment must be shared with the private sector is an unmistakable lesson growing out of the fall of the state socialist economies. In these societies, the state took on much more than it could in fact launch and manage.

When we add to these cases the repeated turning to the state by liberal capitalist economies, particularly after times of crisis, two important consequences follow: first the usefulness of James's theory of state capitalism for understanding the present conjuncture; and second, we now have good empirical grounds for thinking of market and plan as partial principles of economic organisation that may in fact be complementary rather than diametrically opposed. As we rethink this issue, it is important to recall that markets are older than capitalism and that the distinctiveness of the latter has been its project to make markets a universal principle.

On this issue, there is Lewis's clearly stated concern that the Caribbean Left needs to reconsider the Fabian socialism of the Caribbean Nobel Laureate, Sir Arthur Lewis (1998, 143). The latter's ideas on mixed economies were major influences on the rural reforms of Deng Xiaoping, the leader of China who followed Mao Tse-tung (Chang 1993). Chinese economists often refer to this period between 1979 and 2010 as the Lewisian phase of the Chinese economy. Thus Yinxing Hong, economist and Provost of Nanjing University, did just that in a major address at Brown University in December of 2011. He outlined the current transition from this Lewisian phase that China was undertaking, and noted in passing that in some rural areas posters of Arthur Lewis replaced those of Mao.

In short, the above considerations make it clear that Professor Rupert Lewis's economic concerns can only be addressed by rebuilding our political tradition on the principles of a mixed economy, principles that are transcendentally rooted in pluri-conceptual schemas, and not the pure or mono-conceptual ones of either market or plan. At the a priori level of our thinking, economic visions and practices must be anchored in pluri-conceptual frameworks that will allow us to move more dialectically between cooperative, plan and market, and in ways that reflect our capabilities and aspirations. Within the context of these changes in our basic frameworks, we must then decide what sectors of our economies will be state controlled and why. The 'why' would then have to include reasons such as guarding against the limitations of the market, correcting for social inequities, protecting workers and accumulating and investing portions of the surplus on their behalf. In other words, the justifications for the state will be on the grounds that it is different from and can correct the market, and not because it is inherently better.

We would therefore be looking at some type of mixed economy with increasing possibilities for worker self-management, which we can call market socialist without being absolutely attached to it. The nature and viability of the firms in which workers participate in the management will have to be carefully theorised and practically tested. In this economic model, in spite of its participatory aspects, the position of the workers would still be a subordinate one. Leadership will still be in hands of the petit bourgeoisie. On this point, I am very much in agreement with Lewis. If their exclusion from the centres of power during the colonial period left the petit bourgeois classes unprepared for post-colonial leadership, this problem is only compounded in the case of workers who were even further removed from these centres.

On this point, V.C. Bird's 1940s black democratic socialist experiments in Antigua and Barbuda are particularly instructive. Bird and his trade union-based colleagues were overwhelmingly of working-class background. Further, as a result of leading the anti-colonial struggle they not only gained control of the state, but also succeeded in forcing the planters to leave and making the state the owner of their extensive land holdings. In other words, a group of working-class leaders were not only solidly in power, but also had control of the major sectors and resources of the economy. All of Antigua and Barbuda's prime ministers have been of working-class background except for Lester Bird, who was the son of V.C. Bird. A strong case could be made that Antigua and Barbuda is the most proletarian of Caribbean nations. Yet, in spite of this distinct political heritage, today the roles of both the petit bourgeoisie and foreign capitalists in its governing coalitions are just about the same as those territories in which the petit bourgeoisie replaced the planters (Henry 2009, 105–30).

But if we are not to repeat past patterns of economic failure, then every effort must be made to widen the outlook and improve the entrepreneurial and managerial capabilities of both the working and petit bourgeois classes. The model of mass education outlined in James's *Party Politics in the West Indies* is a good place to begin practices of participatory learning and exercises in self-management among workers.

## Conclusion

As I look beyond the current state capitalist conjuncture that has followed the collapse of state socialism and the Great Recession of neoliberal capitalism, I see, rising out of the recently repaired financial bubble, an informatic global economy in which productive routines have incorporated the revolutions in information and communications technology. The leadership of this new global economy is now up for grabs. In October of 2014, the GNP of China surpassed that of the US for the first time with GDP expected to follow in the next ten years. The social framework of this new informatic economy will be determined by the group of countries that will lead it. Whoever wins the leadership of this new economic order, the big question for us will be: has this new informatic order made easier or harder the tasks of integrating, industrialising and inserting our economies more competitively into its global markets? In other words, will it be easier or more difficult to complete the tasks left undone by the planters and the subsequent generations of post-colonial leaders who replaced them?

At the moment, it is difficult to say for sure, as I am unable to see clearly what exactly is around this particular historical bend. But what remains crystal clear is the region's need for a strategic response to this arriving order, which grows out of our political traditions and also reflects our political and economic capabilities. Re-systematising the best elements of our political heritage in the light of past failures and the demands of the arriving informatic era is the only credible proactive response that we can make. As we undertake this re-thinking of the troubled state of our black democratic socialist tradition, we must take careful note of Lewis's criticisms of contradictions in our thinking and errors in our practice. To ignore these pinpricks from his blowing of the Abeng would only compound these earlier problems and increase the probability of another round of socialist failures.

However, the consequences of not rebuilding our black democratic socialist tradition will be another round of dependent, externally-driven growth, and thus a rather passive response to the informatic phase of the global economy. If this external dynamic comes in the form of capitalists from the West, growth will most likely bring with it a reinforcing of existing patterns of entrepreneurial dependence, social inequality, urban ghetto formation, and rising crime rates. If it comes from China, it is still too early to say with comparable certainty what the results will be. In either case, if we are to shift into a higher gear, to stop spinning our wheels, the time has come for us to once again join with other progressive groups and countries to help in the shaping of this new order. We can only be a contributing part of such a group if we repair and revitalise our black democratic socialist tradition, which has gotten us through so much on our long journey to the future that now confronts us.

## References

Chang, Kyung-Sup. 1993. The Peasant Family in the Transition from Maoist to Lewisian Rural Industrialization *Journal of Development Studies* 29, no.2 (January): 220–44.

Higginbotham, Michael. 2013. *Ghosts of Jim Crow*. New York: New York University.

Henry, Paget. 2009. *Shouldering Antigua and Barbuda: The Life of V.C. Bird*. London: Hansib.

———. 2006. Wynter and the Transcendental Spaces of Caribbean Thought. In *After Man, Towards the Human*, ed. Anthony Bogues. Kingston: Ian Randle Publishers.

James, C.L.R. 1962. *Party Politics in the West Indies*. San Juan, Trinidad: Vedic Enterprises.

——— 1986. *State Capitalism and World Revolution*. Chicago: Charles Kerr.

———. 2013. *Beyond a Boundary*. Durham: Duke University Press.

Lewis, Rupert, and Trevor Munroe. 1971. *Readings in Government and Politics of the West Indies*. Kingston: Dept. of Government, University of the West Indies.

Lewis, Rupert. 1988. *Marcus Garvey: Anticolonial Champion*. Trenton: Africa World Press.

———. 1997. Learning to Blow the Abeng. *Small Axe*, no.1.

———. 1998. *Walter Rodney's Intellectual and Political Thought*. Kingston: The Press, University of the West Indies.

———. 2001. Reconsidering the Role of the Middle Class in Caribbean Politics. In *New Caribbean Thought: A Reader*, ed. Brian Meeks and Lindahl Folke. Kingston: University of the West Indies Press.

Lewis, Rupert, and Maureen Warner-Lewis. 1986. *Garvey: Africa, Europe, the Americas*. Kingston: ISER.

Lewis, Rupert, and Patrick Bryan. 1991. *Garvey: His Work and Impact*. Trenton: Africa World Press.

Nyerere, Julius. 1968. *Ujamaa: Essays on Socialism*. London: Oxford University Press.

Piketty, Thomas. 2014. *Capital in the Twenty-First Century*. Cambridge: Harvard University Press.
Robinson, Cedric. 2000. *Black Marxism*. Chapel Hill: University of North Carolina Press.
———. 2001. *An Anthropology of Marxism*. London: Ashgate Publishing.
Rodney, Walter. 1974. *How Europe Underdeveloped Africa*. Washington, DC: Howard University Press.
Schweickart, David. 2011. *After Capitalism*. New York: Rowan & Littlefield.
Thomas, Clive. 1974. *Dependence and Transformation*. New York: Monthly Review.
Wynter, Sylvia. 1992. Beyond the Categories of the Master Conception: The Counter-doctrine of the Jamesian Poiesis. In C.L.R. James, *Caribbean*, ed. Henry, P & P. Buhle. Durham: Duke University Press.

# 8 | *Echoes of the Bandung Movement in the Caribbean and China's Presence in the Region Today**

Rupert Lewis

Abstract

*The ideas of Bandung had echoes in the anti-colonial and decolonisation movement in the Anglophone Caribbean from the 1950s to the 1970s. These echoes were signals of international solidarity that emerged among the political leadership and radicalised publics in Asia, Africa, Latin America and the Caribbean. That sense of solidarity has been replaced by pragmatic business relations in the era of global neoliberalism and the growing role of China and other ex-colonies as economic powers. There is an urgent need for renewal of mutually beneficial political association among ex-colonial countries. The spectres of racism and racial stereotypes need to be confronted in the building of stronger economic relations. These racial stereotypes arise from the growth of anti-black racism over the past five hundred years. Similarly, racial stereotypes of Chinese and other peoples of Asia are rooted in colonial histories. New political relations cannot be based exclusively on trade and economic relations but on an explicit elaboration of ideas that can encourage discussion, debate and the development of institutions. These new political ideas can build on shared principles in an anti-racist direction which help to restore human dignity to international relations.*

The statement accompanying the programme poses very important questions about how we think about the present and notes that 'ex-socialist, ex-colonised and ex-third world countries seem to have emerged as the leading edge of global capitalism.' We therefore need to critically reflect 'on the histories, the trajectories and the conditions of the world being transformed'. The statement further poses the question: 'Are these rising economies with a revolutionary and anti-imperialist past, able to break the conquering and exploitative logics of capitalism, or simply to reproduce what they were fighting against?'

These questions are being posed in the context of the post-Cold War world, the fall of Eastern European communism and the global systemic reach of neoliberal ideas and structures. And this context means that there is no clear line between the Bandung conference of 1955 and the 60th anniversary in 2015. If we examine the goals of Bandung, the historical evidence suggests that the scale of the economic relations between China and Africa and China and Latin America provides policy options and opportunities that were unthinkable in the last half of the twentieth century. In thinking about past solidarities we have to be hard-headed about present-day possibilities and how new solidarities can be shaped.

The broad goals of Bandung of the 29 Asian and African countries that met in Indonesia in 1955 were:

> To promote goodwill and co-operation among the nations of Asia and Africa, to explore and advance their mutual as well as common interests and to establish further friendliness and neighbourly relations.
>
> To consider social, economic, and cultural problems and relations of the countries represented.
>
> To consider problems of special interest to Asia and Africa of racialism and colonialism.
>
> To view the position of Asia and Africa and their people in the world of today and the contribution they can make to the promotion of world peace and co-operation (Wright 1956, 13).

These are sufficiently broad perspectives that can still serve as valid guidelines to solidarity in the twenty-first century. However, one would have to add Latin America, Central America and the Caribbean, as well as other regions desirous of this global connection, to those identified above.

## Bandung movement in the English-speaking Caribbean

I will selectively identify some markers of the Bandung movement in the English-speaking Caribbean. Asia is a far cry from the Caribbean geographically. However, given the presence of Indians and Chinese in the region since the nineteenth century, the Asian presence is part of our cultural and economic landscape. The Caribbean is a cross roads of global cultures of Africa, Asia, Europe and the indigenous peoples of the Americas. The political echoes of Bandung in the Caribbean were heard in the mass mobilisation of Eric Williams, the Trinidadian intellectual and politician, in 1956, at the time when he organised the People's National Movement (PNM) and led Trinidad and Tobago to independence in 1962. He served as Prime Minister until his death in 1981. Bandung served as a banner of political solidarity against colonialism which was a system of white supremacy and economic domination against peoples of Asia, Africa, Latin America and the Caribbean. But for Williams, it was also a metaphor for the unity between the descendants of enslaved Africans and indentured Indian labourers and how they could live in one nation as nationals and not as colonial subjects (Ryan 2009, 109; St. Pierre 2015, 77).

There are few witnesses in the Caribbean to the events that took place in Indonesia 60 years ago. Although there were no independent states in the Anglophone Caribbean at that time, political demands were being made for independence by some political parties. Independence first came to Jamaica and Trinidad and Tobago in 1962. So the Bandung conference was a source of inspiration coming from the actions and aspirations of Asian and African countries. However, there are still some who can recall the echoes of Bandung in Caribbean politics in the 1970s and early 1980s. Echoes of Bandung were to be heard in the 1970s when radical currents and social movements developed out of Rastafari, Black Power, civil rights protests and the programmes of social democratic political parties. It was the decade when four Caribbean nations – Guyana, Trinidad and Tobago, Jamaica and Barbados – recognised and developed diplomatic relations with Cuba in opposition to the US. It was also the decade when Guyana and Jamaica established diplomatic relations with China in 1972 and other Caribbean territories followed suit later on. The thinking at the time was geared towards the development of a multi-polar world that would transcend the bi-polar universe that characterised the Cold War and where newly independent states were coerced into choosing between the US and the Soviet Union. Rejection of this bi-polar choice led many ex-colonial countries in the direction of the non-aligned movement and the right to choose one's friends (Singham 1986).

Echoes of Bandung were to be heard in the speeches of Michael Manley, Prime Minister of Jamaica in 1972–80 and 1989–92. These echoes were also heard in the broadcast journalism of Peter Abrahams, the South African born journalist and novelist, for much of the last half of the twentieth century. In Manley's speeches and in Peter Abrahams's broadcasts, the hope that the non-aligned movement would come into its own economically through self-reliance was frequently expressed.

The idea of non-alignment is now outdated because the communist bloc imploded and collapsed. Conceptions of self-reliance and, in some cases, autarky were abandoned by China as an economic route and replaced instead by pragmatic economic policies. This integration into global trade and markets contributed to millions being lifted out of poverty and resulted in the emergence of Chinese entrepreneurs as well as the largest expansion of the middle classes. The lessons of the past 35 years of economic development are profound, given the conceptions of socialism that prevailed in 1955, and which would have informed the thinking of the political leaders who gathered in Indonesia. These are matters for urgent discussion as there is no straight line between Bandung 1955 and our present conjuncture. What lies in between Bandung and now has not been adequately examined from the standpoint of those countries which were signatories to the Bandung declaration.

We are also witnesses to a new international economic order in the making evidenced by the emergence of China, India, Brazil, South Africa, Turkey and other states whose economic growth rates have been impressive. The economic growth of China has led to the global spread of its investments and influence and the emergence of an infrastructural bank.

The echoes of Bandung in the Caribbean are faint today but can be revived in the coming years. However, that depends on political leadership that can interpret the new global realities which, in my view, are now more propitious to the ideas of Bandung which called for economic development for ex-colonial countries, respect for political sovereignty and a say in international relations on key issues of peace, social development, human rights and the reduction in environmental degradation. Political leadership in the Caribbean requires an orientation that strengthens regionalism among the Caribbean's small states and the discouragement of tendencies towards parochialism and short-term frames of reference. This is necessary to combat the region's political fragmentation with its micro-nationalisms predominating over the efforts to develop a relevant twenty-first century regional voice. The English-speaking Caribbean states are a micro-region in the wider Americas which have a population of 800 million people of Spanish and Portuguese speakers. This English-speaking region has a combined population of just over six million people with the smallest territory, St Kitts and Nevis, having 50,000 and the largest, Jamaica, 2.7 million, according to 2010 figures.

The preoccupation of the people of this region is with two issues. First, there are economic issues and second, there is the challenge of high homicide rates. The negative impact of the economic crisis on economies that rely on tourism and remittances from their nationals in North America and Britain is still being felt, especially by the mass of the population. Caribbean countries are recovering slowly from the consequences of the world financial crisis of 2008. Jamaica has been in the harness of fiscal discipline of the International Monetary Fund (IMF) because of its indebtedness that was in the region of 140 per cent of the Gross Domestic Product (GDP) in 2012 and which is being reduced. However, major infrastructural loans have been supplied by China and this is resulting in the completion of a major highway from the South to the North of the island. The agricultural sector is underdeveloped and much hope is based on the Business Processing Outsourcing (BPO) sector and the development of infrastructure that policymakers hope will be similar to transhipment ports in the Panama Canal or Singapore.

The second principal challenge after the economy is that Jamaica, Belize and St Kitts and Nevis are in the top ten countries with high homicide rates. High homicidal rates are connected to transnational narcotics and gun trade in the region and linked to the demand for drugs in the US. Given these challenges, it is not surprising that there is much interest in the region in developing economic relations with China by governments and business people.

## Caribbean–China Relations

Indicative of this interest in China was the publication in 2014 entitled, *The Dragon in the Caribbean: China's Global Re-Dimensioning Challenges and Opportunities for the Caribbean*, by economist Richard Bernal. This text encourages Caribbean governments and businesses to take advantage of the investment opportunities being opened for trade with China. Opportunities arising from Chinese investments are uppermost in the thinking of Caribbean states with some aligning themselves with Taiwan for reasons of money and others with China. Jamaica and Guyana have had diplomatic relations with China since 1972 and the People's National Party (PNP) in Jamaica has good party-to-party relations with the Communist Party of China. In Guyana, party-to-party relations were initiated by Forbes Burnham when he was Prime Minister. Trinidad and Tobago has had relations with China since June 1974. Other countries that have recognised China are Barbados (1977), Antigua and Barbuda (1983), the Bahamas (1997), and Dominica which has had relations with China since 2004. Belize had relations with China in 1987–89 and shifted to Taiwan since 1989; Grenada has moved between China and Taiwan; in 1985–89, it recognised China and in 1989–2005 it shifted to recognise Taiwan. Since 2005, Grenada has re-established relations with China. St Lucia had diplomatic relations with Taiwan from 1984–97, China from 1997–2007 and is now back with Taiwan.

St Vincent and the Grenadines has had diplomatic relations with Taiwan since 1981. So there is competition between these two Asian states for diplomatic relations with the micro-states of the Caribbean. And, in some cases, decisions on these matters are made on the basis of money and not on any political principle. So the Anglophone Caribbean micro-states have no common policy position with regard to relations with China.

## The Existential Situation of African People and Chinese in Jamaica

Allow me to comment briefly on the existential situation of Chinese in Jamaica. Historically, Chinese migration followed the routes of the British Empire from South China where Hakka-speaking Han Chinese migrated from the middle of the nineteenth century to find work in agriculture and infrastructural projects such as the Panama Canal. These Chinese migrants opened shops and over time became an economic force in the retail trade. In the economic and political crisis of the 1970s in Jamaica, many of them migrated and prospered in Canada, with two Jamaican Chinese becoming billionaires in Canada. Those Chinese who remained, made investments to enhance their retail operations with modern supermarkets.

The creolised Chinese have been joined by a new generation of Chinese migrants who have gone into retail business in working-class areas in several towns.

Mainland Chinese politics has always impacted the Chinese community. I grew up hearing of battles between the Kuomintang and the Communists in Chinatown in Kingston. After 1989, when there were student demonstrations in China, I attended a meeting of the Chinese community in Kingston which was open to the public, and the audience was divided between those who supported the Chinese state and those who were on the side of the students. Today, there is an active discussion about Chinese investments in the region by all sectors of society. However, no one frames this discussion historically with respect to the Bandung tradition. It is, therefore, timely to have the Bandung framework resurrected by intellectuals and political leaders.

**China in Rising Africa**

Pan African-minded Jamaicans watch with interest the growth of influence of China in Africa. Many were pleased with the new African Union building in Addis Ababa constructed by the Chinese government. However, as a reader of Howard French's journalistic book *China's Second Continent: How a Million Immigrants are Building a New Empire in Africa* (2014), while I note Howard French's American bias, I was dismayed by the racial stereotypes that Chinese investors and business people brought to bear on Africa. Are Chinese investors, who express racial stereotypes of African people, breathing new life into old forms of oppression?

Professor Said Adejumobi, an African scholar, noted in an assessment of China's relationship with the African continent:

> In sum, China is now Africa's biggest trading partner, with a trade volume of over $200 billion annually, leaving the United States and Europe in a distant second and third respectively. The massive trading relationship between China and Africa is not a coincidence – it is something actively promoted by African governments and also encouraged by China's new market orientation policy. However, the relationship does not stop at economics and trade; there is also a growing social dynamic. Hitherto uncommon, inter-marriages or conjugation are occurring with a new breed of African-Chinese or Chinese-Africans being born, creating unprecedented identities and social spaces (Adejumobi 2015, 11).

The latter social dynamic and sexual relations have been part of Caribbean nation formation since the nineteenth century. Chinese people are less than one per cent of the Jamaican population which is over 90 per cent of people with an African heritage, but there is a much larger percentage of the population which claim both African and Chinese heritage. There is therefore a racial dimension to Sino-Jamaican relations.

Jamaican Chinese are well integrated into Jamaican society but are regarded as a relatively privileged sector although there are poor Chinese to be seen but not in large numbers. Chinese musicians and producers have been central to the development of Jamaican popular music. And Trinidadian Chinese are heavily involved in the famous carnival and cultural life of that country. And the same can be said for Suriname and other territories in the region with a Chinese presence. Chinese have also been active in political life in the region.

**Twenty-first Century Solidarity**

At the Bandung conference, the focus was on building Asian–African solidarity, asserting political sovereignty and non-interference from the big powers, overturning colonial rule and preventing neocolonialism in the early years of the Cold War. The African American writer, Richard Wright, who was excited by the prospects of this conference representing the majority of the world's people, wrote a book entitled *The Color Curtain: A Report on the Bandung Conference.*

The 'color curtain' referred to global racial discrimination. The emergence into the international arena of the brown and black peoples of Asia and Africa was heralded by Richard Wright and many others as an opportunity to undermine racism through the achievement of sovereignty from Europe. Few would argue with the fact that the iron curtain is coming down with the latest rapprochement between Cuba and the US. After more than 50 years, this rapprochement signals engagement between these two neighbours with a view to resuming bi-lateral relations.

Removing the colour curtain remains a persistent and difficult challenge which needs to be addressed. The fact that the UN has declared that the next decade 2015–2024 is to be marked as the International Decade for people of African descent is significant. The declaration notes that 'people of African descent represent a distinct group whose human rights must be promoted and respected. Around 200 million people identifying themselves as being of African descent live in the Americas' (UN 2015). Millions more live in other parts of the world, outside of the African continent, in Europe, the Indian Ocean, the Middle East and Asia.

Any discussion of the legacy of Bandung must deal with the persistence of racism on a global level particularly against dark-skinned people.

In conclusion, I hope we can frame a project that may be consistent with the Bandung ideals. Among these are basic aspirations: respect for each other, an end to racial discrimination, a better life with freedom from hunger, unemployment, war and violence. There needs to be a radical shift from the old power balances of the last half a millennium. This shift should be reflected in the balance of power within all international institutions. The development of new institutions such as the emergence of the Asian Infrastructural Bank (AIB) is an indication of this thrust.

While co-operation at the level of the state and political parties is important, civil society interactions and intellectual exchanges that impact on knowledge development and exchange need to be encouraged.

**Acknowledgement**

This paper was delivered at the Bandung – Third World 60 Years forum held in Hangzhou, China, April 17–19, 2015 and published in *Inter-Asia Cultural Studies* 17, no. 1 (2016):52–57.

**References**

Adejumobi, Said. 2015. Beyond the Money and the Infrastructure. In *New African* (March): 10–12.
Bernal, Richard. 2014. *Dragon in the Caribbean: China's Global Re-Dimensioning Challenges and Opportunities for the Caribbean*. Kingston: Ian Randle Publishers.
Ryan, Selwyn. 2009. *Eric Williams: The Myth and the Man*. Kingston: University of the West Indies Press.
Singham, A.W., and Shirley Hune. 1986. *Non Alignments in an Age of Alignments*. New York: Lawrence Hill and Co.
St. Pierre, Maurice. 2015. *Eric Williams and the Anticolonial Tradition: The Making of a Diasporan Intellectual*. Charlottesville and London: University of Virginia.
United Nations. 2015. *2015–2024 International Decade for People of African Descent*. http://www.un.org/en/events/africandescentdecade/. Accessed November 29, 2015.

Wright, Richard. 1956. *The Colour Curtain: A Report on the Bandung* Conference. New York: World Publishing Co.

# 9 | *Quobna Ottobah Cugoano: Black Radical Heretic or Black Radical Liberal?*

Charles W. Mills

'Black radicalism' has, in recent years, become the preferred umbrella term for designating the political philosophies of blacks in Africa and the African Diaspora seeking to end racial subordination through radical social transformation. Credit for its coinage is standardly attributed to Cedric Robinson's now-classic *Black Marxism: The Making of the Black Radical Tradition*, originally published more than three decades ago.[1] The great virtue of the term is its potential breadth of reference. While excluding – obviously – accommodationist politics, it can encompass a wide variety of political outlooks, not just varieties of black nationalism, black communitarianism, and black Marxism, but (I would claim) at least some varieties of black liberalism, not to mention syntheses and hybrids of these positions. But clearly, location under such a capacious umbrella is only the first step in characterising a putatively emancipatory ideology. One then wants to know in what ways it needs to be differentiated from other candidates, and how it stands up in competition with them. A black radicalism, yes; but of what kind?

In this chapter, I look specifically at the eighteenth century 'black radical' African anti-slavery theorist Quobna Ottobah Cugoano,[2] and the way he is characterised by Anthony Bogues in his important text, *Black Heretics, Black Prophets: Radical Political Intellectuals*.[3] I will argue that Cugoano is far less 'heretical' than he is represented by Bogues – or, perhaps better, that Bogues mis-identifies the nature of his 'heresy'. In my opinion, Cugoano can best be seen as an eighteenth-century black ex-slave Christian liberal who, writing a hundred years after the seventeenth-century white slave-owning Christian liberal John Locke, is developing ideas quite congruent for the most part with a Lockean worldview, once extended to the human population as a whole. Thus, Cugoano can be viewed as engaging in an anti-racist retrieval of a liberalism whose dominant varieties would become increasingly racialised with the growth of the European empires.[4] But this anti-racist black radical liberalism is, I would claim, still a *liberalism*.

**Heretics and Prophets**

Let me begin by saying something about Bogues's book, and its significance. *Black Heretics, Black Prophets* is an invaluable contribution to the contemporary project of Africana theorists excavating, reclaiming, rethinking, and reconstructing a distinct Africana political tradition. After the Second World War, the Holocaust, the (partial) discrediting of racism by Nazism, and global decolonisation, modern Western political philosophy retroactively sanitised its racial past, presenting itself as universalist and all-inclusive rather than generally complicit (as it was) with international Euro-domination. Bogues's book is an important mapping of a global black tradition of political resistance to this unacknowledged international white polity, from Quobna Cugoano in the 'black Atlantic' through Ida Wells-Barnett and W.E.B. Du Bois in the US and Julius Nyerere in Tanzania to Walter Rodney, Bob Marley, and the Rastafari in the Caribbean, not to mention C.L.R. James everywhere. Bogues distinguishes what he sees as two 'significant stream[s] of black intellectual production', that of 'heresy' and that of 'redemptive prophesy'.[5] The heretics include Cugoano, Wells-Barnett, James, Du Bois, Nyerere, and Rodney; the prophets include Bob Marley and the Rastafari.

Since we are taking Cugoano as our key figure, we will limit ourselves to the first stream – the heretic. For Bogues, the transition to 'heresy' begins with Du Bois' 'double consciousness', the internal psychological 'strife' that arises from being socialised into Western categories that 'negate one's self', leading to a radical 'second sight':

> Coping with modernity that negated one's humanity created not only counter narratives of modernity's history, practices, and meanings but also a dilemma for the Africana intellectual in the West—to *be in* and *of* the West, and yet to create inside the West an identity, a personhood which required that the West, in the words of Fanon, be left behind...To remain consistently radical, to rupture the boundaries that confine, the Africana radical thinker transforms "double consciousness" into heresy.[6]

Heresy involves the challenging of orthodoxy:

> [B]lack radical intellectual production engages in a double operation – an engagement with Western radical theory and then a critique of this theory...breaking the epistemic limits established by the Western intellectual tradition...For the black radical intellectual, "heresy" means becoming human, not white nor imitative of the colonial, but overturning white/European normativity - in the words of Robert Marley, refusing "what you wanted us to be"....[H]eresy is a constructive project, sometimes developing a different set of political and social categories.[7]

Now, I am in broad agreement with much of what Bogues says here – certainly on the existence of an alienated black radical consciousness, the need for counter-narratives of modernity, the insistence on one's personhood in the face of discourses that overtly or subtly seek to undermine it, and the project of constructing categories in some sense different. Where I diverge is on the question of what exactly this 'heresy' involves and how 'different' these categories actually are.

In focusing on this issue, I am continuing a friendly debate Bogues and I have been having for more than a decade now on the extent to which a mainstream white apparatus of concepts, values, and theoretical frameworks can be drawn upon by Africana thinkers seeking black, and more generally anti-racist, emancipation. Bogues was one of the very first commentators on my 1997 book, *The Racial Contract*, and reviewed the book in print not once but twice.[8] I, in turn, answered some of his criticisms in a *Small Axe* symposium, and in an essay on the possibility, contra Audre Lorde, of using the master's tools (here liberalism and contract theory) to dismantle the master's house.[9] My argument is basically that many bodies of Western theory have a radical potential that is under-appreciated – indeed not even recognised as such – because of their racialisation, so that by de-racialising them we can, to a significant extent, 'retrieve' them for the black radical project. This is uncontroversially the case for Marxism, as attested to by the very title of Cedric Robinson's book, and by the fact that three of Bogues's 'heretics' (James, Du Bois, and Walter Rodney) were themselves Marxists, or at least strongly influenced by Marxism. But it is far less conceded for liberalism. So the obvious question is posed: is Marxism any less a product of Western theory than liberalism? And, if at least significant elements of the former can be retrieved, then why not the latter also?

## Retrievalism vs Anti-Retrievalism

To provide some historical perspective on the matter, let us put the debate into a broader trans-racial context. For the problem is not at all confined to race, since there are longstanding (intra-white) feminist and Marxist variants on the same theme. Indeed, my term is a tribute to C.B. Macpherson's famous attempt decades ago to 'retrieve' liberal-democratic theory for the left.[10]

A body of oppositional theory is seeking to challenge the existing oppressive order, whether conceptualised primarily as class society, patriarchy, or white supremacy, and the natural question raised is: what is the relation between the values of this theory and the norms of mainstream liberal theory, such as freedom, equality, autonomy, self-realisation, individual rights, and so forth? Are there, in fact, any distinctively socialist values, for example, a utopian (as against backward-looking) communitarianism transcending the liberal norms, the rights and freedoms, of mutually antagonistic selves in bourgeois class society? Or is the socialist project normatively parasitic on mainstream liberal-democratic values informed *by* the realities of bourgeois class society, so that real freedom, equality, and self-realisation for the majority require the communist transformation of the relations of production that currently make these ideals unachievable for all but a few? Similarly, should feminists be feminist liberals, seeking the extension of liberal rights and freedoms across gender barriers, and rethinking the private/public divide accordingly?[11] Or should they reject all 'male'/'androcentric' theory in the name of distinctively sororal values, however conceived of? So, though race is distinctive in that the white working class and white women are still part of the white family in a way that blacks were not, the terms of contestation and the opposing positions should themselves be quite familiar.

I suggest that there are at least four ways in which a value, or a system of values, can be problematic in its formulation or instantiation. First, it might simply have been restricted in scope to some subset of humans, rather than being extended to humans in general. Property rights for men only, freedom and equality just for white people, and so forth. Second, it might have been deployed in such a way as to be axiologically insensitive to factors that hinder its realisation, but which are not recognised in its particular formulation. For example, a liberty that is restricted to 'negative' freedoms from interference, and does not reflect how liberty may also be constrained by systemic socio-economic disadvantage. (The traditional left critique of 'freedom' as a value when deployed one-sidedly by the right to defend laissez-faire.) Or, relatedly, a schedule of rights that only recognises negative Lockean rights of non-interference and not positive welfare rights, despite the fact that the ability to lead a meaningful life will arguably require the latter also. (The traditional left case for expanding recognised basic 'rights'.) Third, the value itself may be so causally related to privilege that it is intrinsically suspect, and should not be salvaged in any form. For example, the 'possessive individualism' that C.B. Macpherson diagnosed as characteristic of some varieties of liberalism,[12] or straightforwardly sexist and racist values – 'natural' male superiority and machismo, racial 'purity', and so forth. Finally, the system of values may be deficient, lacking crucial goods by whose absence it is overall impoverished in comparison to alternative possibilities. In this case, completely new values not derivative of the already existing ones, however extended or expanded, may be required.

So when we say that the values of a particular body of theory are problematic, obviously it needs to be clarified in which sense we mean, since, depending on the nature of the problem, there are fundamental differences in the diagnoses and corresponding recommendations we would make to fix it. Is it just that the value was restricted in its population scope? Or that it needs to be tweaked in a different direction, or filled out with a complementary content? Or that its intrinsic and ineluctable relation to the maintenance of illicit group privilege requires that it be jettisoned altogether? Or that the axiological set has a gap in kind and not merely in scope or content? Different answers will be appropriate according to the category into which it falls. And relatedly, the claim that 'new' values are required will need to be scrutinised and justified in the light of this taxonomy.

Retrievalists will be insistent that while a minority of liberal values fall into category (3), most actually fall into categories (1) and (2), and that, before proclaiming the need for values in category (4), we need to check and see whether extending and expanding values in categories (1) and (2) cannot do the job – indeed, whether what are being represented as putatively new category (4) values are not in fact familiar categories (1) and (2) values less recognisable as such precisely *because* of this broadening of scope. From the fact that these values have usually been employed in exclusionary ways, it does not follow, retrievalists claim (whether of class, gender, or race), that many of them cannot still be appropriated if suitably modified. Anti-retrievalists, on the other hand, will be insistent that attempts to demarcate (1), (2), and (3) are doomed to failure, since (1) and (2) collapse *into* (3), thereby necessitating brand new values in category (4).

Now I locate myself in the retrievalist camp insofar as the point of my work has been to explore how liberalism, Enlightenment principles, and social contract theory can be harnessed to an emancipatory anti-racist agenda. I locate Bogues in the anti-retrievalist camp because, as I read him, he sees such an attempted operation as ultimately conforming to rather than 'deviating from orthodoxy' and thereby failing to '[break] the epistemic limits established by the Western intellectual tradition' as 'heretical' black intellectuals should. Thus, in the 'Opening Chant' of *Black Heretics, Black Prophets*, he describes 'theories and frameworks which currently reject the privileged position of the Western episteme' but which nonetheless 'are themselves rooted in the conceptual protocols of this tradition'.[13] And it is clear from his earlier critical reviews of *The Racial Contract* that he puts me in this category. As he writes in the *Small Axe* symposium on the book:

> [C]onstructions of freedom were built within [social contract] frameworks that could accommodate slavery and servitude...Mills's critique of contract theory is an external one. His is not an interior criticism that explodes the contract theory at its deepest levels... There is a basic tension in *The Racial Contract* between the historical construction of race in a set of exploitative power relations and a programme that is limited by the acceptance of the interior norms developed within social contract theory – namely, that of liberalism.[14]

So liberalism and the Enlightenment should be rejected:

> If the *practices* of liberalism reveal an inadequate emancipatory logic, then can it give social equality and therefore freedom to racially oppressed groups and others who are dominated? If not, then do we require another theory of emancipation?...[T]he Enlightenment is problematic for any project of human emancipation that has to break the confines of the Western intellectual tradition. The quest I would suggest for radical black intellectuals is one that Fanon proclaimed years ago: leave Europe behind and create a new humanism.[15]

And in his later *Constellations* review, he cites Cugoano as one possible source for this new black vision:

> [Black] struggles for political equality and the rights of citizenry challenged the foundational structure of the society and gave new forms to old questions. This means that political values like the meanings of equality and freedom are themselves transformed... It is the fact of these different questions, other than those raised by the contract theory, which makes the theory of the racial contract such an inadequate tool for grappling with the inner logic of racial domination...[F]ormer slaves [like Quobna Cugoano] began a distinct tradition in counterpoint to western modernity, liberalism, and western political thought. Their writings critiqued the eighteenth-century notions of the contract, particularly its English version, and exposed its exclusion of Africans.[16]

So in general, Bogues contends, the black radical tradition requires the rejection of liberalism, even when deracialised. Instead we need to follow the example of 'heretical' theorists like Cugoano, who, at least according to Bogues, 'began a distinct tradition', one involving the 'transformation' of political values, thereby giving rise to 'another theory of emancipation', that breaks with the Enlightenment in the name of 'a new humanism'.

**Quobna Cugoano and John Locke**

I now want to argue against Bogues's anti-retrievalism. My strategy will be very simple. I will use the theorist, Quobna Cugoano, whom he takes as an exemplar of the 'heretical' black radical tradition in chapter 1 of his book, and make the case that Cugoano's values are virtually all readily derivable from deracialised liberalism. So Bogues's own poster boy for anti-retrievalism is, I claim – contra Bogues – actually himself a retrievalist, thereby dramatically undermining Bogues's overall thesis. My reference point will be right-wing Lockean liberalism, not because I endorse such a position myself, but because this is the variety of liberalism that would have been dominant in the period, and which Cugoano would have known.

Kidnapped at 13 in 1770 from his Fante village and sold into slavery, Quobna Ottobah Cugoano would be transported first to Grenada and then to England, where he would eventually achieve his freedom, and become an 'emancipationist' activist.[17] Vincent Carretta, the editor of the Penguin edition of his book, points out that this position – the demand 'to outlaw slavery and free all slaves immediately' – was an unusual one at the time, demarcated from 'abolitionists' who were only targeting the slave trade:

> In his *Thoughts and Sentiments [on the Evil of Slavery]* (1787), Cugoano raised the most overt and extended challenge to slavery ever made by a person of African descent. He was also the first English-speaking African historian of slavery and the slave trade and the first to criticise European imperialism in the Americas...[The book was by] far the most radical assault on slavery as well as the slave trade by a writer of African descent, at a time when attacks on slavery as an institution were very rare.[18]

Clearly, then, Cugoano is eminently deserving of the 'black radical' honorific, and Bogues's decision to open his book with the emancipated African emancipationist is completely justified. But does this emancipationism make Cugoano a black heretic by Bogues's standards? Let us compare him with the seemingly quite incommensurable figure of John Locke, whose *Two Treatises of Government* was published almost exactly a century earlier, in 1689.[19] Here, we have a white political theorist who was not merely *not* an ex-slave, but someone who had earlier himself had investments, through the Royal Africa Company, in Atlantic slavery, and who had a crucial role in writing the Carolina constitution, which gave masters absolute power over their African slaves. Yet, unlikely as it may seem, the similarities are numerous.

To begin with, both men were, by the standards of their time, 'radical' theorists. This might be difficult to accept for Locke, considering his establishment stature as one of the founders of liberalism. But it needs to be appreciated that liberalism was, in its time, a radical doctrine – a challenge to absolutist monarchy, unconstrained government, and assumptions of the natural inequality of (white) 'men'. Indeed, so radical was the *Two Treatises* that the prudent Locke left it unsigned in his lifetime, only acknowledging his authorship in a codicil to his will added shortly before his death.[20] For many years it was thought of as an ex-post facto justification of the 1688 'Glorious Revolution', and only with Peter Laslett's scholarship has it been recognised to be a call *for* revolution, written before it. The *Second Treatise* would go on to become one of the most influential political works in modern history, drawn upon not just by the American and French Revolutions, but also the later nineteenth-century Latin American revolutions against Spanish rule.

Secondly, both books are unequivocally Christian texts. Emphasis on this point is particularly appropriate considering Bogues's 'heretic' category, which of course, he meant metaphorically, in a secular sense, but which is classically associated, from modernity onwards, with religious dissent. Locke's *First Treatise* is a tediously detailed scouring of the Old Testament to disprove the claim of the absolutist Sir Robert Filmer that 'men' are naturally unequal because of their lines of descent from Adam's different children, so that present-day Christian kings rule by virtue of their superior blood. The *Second Treatise*, starting off from this refutation of the patriarchal position, then sets out to show what the real foundation of government should be, relying throughout on the Christian natural law tradition. Likewise, *Thoughts and Sentiments* is a religious tract from beginning to end, with numerous references to biblical authority and Christian natural law. However, 'heretical' Cugoano may have been in other respects, it certainly did not extend to his adopted religion! Indeed, like another famous work in the black diasporic political tradition – Frederick Douglass's 1852 'What to the Slave is the Fourth of July?' speech – its argumentative strategy is basically to appeal to the author's co-religionists, his fellow-Christians, *in the name of their religion*, to condemn slavery.

Finally, and most importantly, both the *Second Treatise* and *Thoughts and Sentiments* are ringing affirmations of the foundational norm of natural human equality and equal natural rights, and the revolutionary implications of that norm for the governments and institutions of their day. In the case of Locke, of course, we know that this proclaimed equality did not seem to extend to African slaves (or even white women, feminists would charge). A large secondary literature has centred on resolving this seeming contradiction, with a range of explanations being put forth: Locke as a hypocrite who did recognise black equality, but was seduced by pecuniary considerations; Locke as genuinely believing the enslaved Africans had been captured in a just war, thereby forfeiting their natural rights; and, most straightforwardly, and my own preferred candidate, Locke as a racist who was not even thinking of Africans when he enunciated those inspiring sentiments about human equality. So, in keeping with the framework sketched at the start, Locke would then be the exponent of a 'racial liberalism', in which key terms and assumptions in the apparatus are so racialised that they are restricted in their scope to whites. Locke and Cugoano would be in agreement that 'men' had equal natural rights, and that respect for these rights mandated the overturning of institutions built on their denial, but in disagreement on the population covered by the 'men'.

Is this a minor disagreement? Of course not – it is huge, and hugely consequential in its implications. But my point, contra Bogues, is that Cugoano's 'heresy', insofar as it exists, consists primarily in demanding the extension of these rights to blacks, with all the corresponding revolutionary ramifications throughout the normative and sociopolitical system that such an extension would require. It is in this extension that his radicalism inheres, not, as Bogues is claiming, in a rejection of liberalism as such. Rather, the whole text is thoroughly imbued with a liberal spirit throughout.

Let me now try to make my case for this claim by beginning with Bogues's ten-point summary of Cugoano's position:

The major political ideas of Cugoano can be distilled into the following themes and propositions:

1. Opposition to African slavery.
2. A theory of history that conflates Enlightenment concerns surrounding geography and climate empiricism with a Christian notion of monogenesis.
3. An overarching framework of natural liberty that is located in the emergence of civil society and not in a state of nature.
4. That natural liberty is enriched rather than diminished by the growth of civil society.
5. That natural liberty and monogenesis mean that all 'men' (heathens, pagans, Christians) have property, civil, and political rights.
6. That racial slavery is evil and contrary to divine law, natural human law, and 'common humanity'.
7. That a consequence of racial slavery is restitutions to Africans who had suffered because of the trade.
8. That colonialism and colonial conquest are contrary to civilization (civil society), natural law, and divine law.
9. That society should be constructed as a common harmonious community which looks after its poor.

10. A definition of natural liberty as self-ownership, and a critical attitude to the British crown and its involvement in the slave trade.[21]

Now look at this list, bearing in mind that Cugoano is, for Bogues, one of the paradigm representatives of a black radical tradition whose axiology supposedly makes a clean break with European liberalism, even when deracialised. I suggest that the immediate thing that will strike the reader familiar with liberal principles is how utterly *non*-incompatible, *non*-discontinuous, *non*-incommensurable it is with the liberal tradition, once liberalism has, as prescribed, been purged of its racism. Indeed, with one or two exceptions, all of his principles seem to me to be compatible, as emphasised, not merely with liberalism in general but with deracialised right-wing Lockean liberalism in particular, and where they are not so compatible it is not necessarily an improvement upon Locke.

Let us begin with the points that refer to slavery (#1, 6, 7, 10), and compare them with the *Second Treatise*. Assume that the Locke-as-racist interpretation is the correct explanation for his seeming flagrant inconsistencies. Deracialising Racist Locke, then, we need only ask what this reconstructed figure – call him (unimaginatively) Anti-Racist Locke – would have thought of Cugoano's proposals.

Locke's starting-point is freedom, and in a deracialised Lockeanism (as against actual Lockeanism) all men, regardless of race, are in 'a *State of perfect Freedom*' and a '*State* also *of Equality*' (§4). So 'The *Natural Liberty* of Man is to be free from any Superior Power on Earth... The *Liberty of Man, in Society*, is to be under no other Legislative Power, but that established by consent' (§22). Clearly, this rules out racial slavery (#6), since racial slavery presumes that some 'men' are natural slaves by race, and this could be no more true than Filmer's claim (refuted by Locke in the *First Treatise*) that some men were naturally superior to others by birth. Locke does permit slavery in certain circumstances, when people have been guilty of a serious transgression of natural law. So, for example, if the prosecutors of an unjust war, a war of aggression, are defeated, they may legitimately be executed or enslaved by the victors (chapter xvi). But this is a justification on the grounds of wrongdoing, not race or nationality. Moreover, Locke explicitly rules out the enslavement of their wives and children, or the taking of any of their property other than that necessary to pay restitution. So this principle could hardly be used to justify African slavery (#1), which – even if Locke had convinced himself was limited to prosecutors of an unjust war – was hereditary. He would likewise support the second part of #10, that the British crown should be condemned for its involvement in the Atlantic slave trade, which is in violation of natural law and natural liberty. Locke explicitly stipulates that the victim of transgressions of natural law has 'a particular Right to seek *Reparation* from him that has done it' (§10), so deracialised Lockeanism would strongly endorse #7, the call for restitutions by Anti-Racist Locke, including demands from Racist Locke himself, as a former investor in the trade.[22]

What about liberty (#3, 4, 5, 10) and possible variations in human entitlements to it because of racial ancestry (#2)? Locke, like David Hume, was one of the key empiricists of early modern philosophy, but unlike Hume, whose polygenetic racism was notoriously displayed in his essay 'Of National Characters',[23] Locke was a monogenist. Monogenism does not, of course, rule out racism, but here we are dealing with Anti-Racist Locke, who would endorse environmentalist Enlightenment accounts of natural human variation that did not imply racial inequality (#2). Locke is famous for linking liberty to self-ownership, telling us that 'every Man has a *Property* in his own *Person*' (§27). So even if Racist Locke did not think of people of colour as fully or at all self-owning, this would not be the case for Anti-Racist Locke (#10), who would fully agree that all men have 'property, civil, and political rights' (#5).

The relation in #3 and #4 between natural liberty and civil society requires a more complicated story. Bogues says that Cugoano 'seems to operate with no such historical fiction' as a state of nature, and that he 'collapses all forms of liberty into "natural and common liberty." There is no separation in Cugoano's thought between different forms of liberty.'[24] If this gloss is correct, then it seems to me a deficiency of Cugoano's thought rather than a virtue, in that crucial distinctions are being obliterated. Even if you don't believe in a literal state of nature, the language of 'natural liberty' captures the normative principle that we *should* be free, independent of what particular governments have prescribed. That's the whole point in the natural rights tradition of distinguishing natural and civil rights – that one can then criticize the actual civil rights one has in a particular society in the name of the natural rights one has, and therefore the civil rights one *should* have. As Locke writes in the *Second Treatise*: 'The Obligations of the Law of Nature, cease not in Society...Thus the Law of Nature stands as an Eternal Rule to all Men, *Legislators* as well as others' (§135). If Cugoano really collapsed all forms of liberty together, as Bogues says, then I don't see this as an improvement upon Locke, but a regression, since in an oppressive society, one's severely constrained liberties will then be taken to limit the liberties one *should* have.

Consider now #4. In the Lockean state of nature we have the right ('power' for Locke) to preserve ourselves within the limits of natural law and the right to enforce natural law against transgressors (§4, 6–9, 11–13, 128). With our entry into civil society, we have to allow the first to be regulated by civil law while we have to give up the second entirely (§129–30). But this is not a loss overall, since while the Lockean state of nature is not as lethal as the Hobbesian one, it is still a 'Condition, which however free, is full of fears and continual dangers' because of the absence of codified legislation, impartial judges, and official enforcers of executive power (§123–26). So we come out ahead, and this would seem to be obviously compatible with Cugoano's position (even if he did not believe in a literal state of nature) that natural liberty is thereby enriched.

Finally, we have #8 and #9. Given Locke's principled opposition to wars of aggression, and conquests resulting from wars of aggression (chapter xvi) – which in his incarnation as Anti-Racist Locke would be racially inclusive – colonial conquest is clearly ruled out, so there is agreement on #8 also. As for #9: Locke's political community is to be bound by natural law, whose aim is *'the preservation of Mankind'* (§135), and he did think we had some charitable obligations to the poor. But they are pretty weak, so here, perhaps, one would admittedly have to turn to left-wing liberalism for an endorsement of Cugoano's position (though one wonders how strong *he* envisaged such statist welfare commitments as being). However, such demands are a longstanding part of the left-liberal tradition (contested, of course, from the right), whether couched in terms of utilitarian social welfare or positive welfare rights, so these ideas are certainly not alien to liberalism in the broader sense.

Where then are the radically new values, the startlingly different conceptions of liberty, that we were promised? With the exception of

#9 (that can be accommodated by left-liberalism) and #3 (which just seems wrong to me), all of Cugoano's 'major political ideas' can be readily translated into the language of deracialised right-wing Lockean liberalism. This does not at all mean (I will elaborate on this at the end) that he does not deserve credit for them, but that his contribution does not consist, as Bogues is claiming, in 'transforming' values and coming up with a new axiology of the kind I demarcated above as (4), but rather of carrying out an extensional and expansionist exercise to redress problems of types (1) and (2).

Moreover, my dubiousness that Cugoano's thought really represents the kind of radical break that Bogues imputes to it is reinforced by his own further characterisation of Cugoano after his initial ten-point summary cited above. Consider the following passages from Bogues:

> Cugoano's foundational assumption was that there existed a state of natural freedom which each person had. Slavery therefore was not just about brutality or inhumane conditions, but at root was the taking away of the freedom made possible by natural liberty. That robbery of natural liberty was therefore slavery's worst element. This was a view of natural liberty very different from that promulgated by the mainstream natural rights thinkers of the period.[25]

But compare Locke's own view on natural rights and freedoms:

> [W]e must consider what State all Men are naturally in, and that is, a *State of perfect Freedom* to order their Actions.... [H]e who attempts to get another Man into his Absolute Power, does thereby *put himself into a State of War* with him; It being to be understood as a Declaration of a Design upon his life... for no body can desire to *have me in his Absolute Power*, unless it be to compel me by force to that, which is against the Right of my Freedom, *i.e.* make me a Slave.... This *Freedom* from Absolute, Arbitrary Power, is so necessary to, and closely joyned with a Man's Preservation, that he cannot part with it, but by what Forfeits his Preservation and Life together. (§4, 17, 23)

So how is Cugoano's position radically different from Locke's? Is it in the values themselves? Surely not; it is in the racial scope of the values.

Similarly, Bogues claims that:

> Cugoano argues that slavery is evil because it is contradictory to three elements: justice, humanity in a collective sense, and reason - that most celebrated dimension of the European Enlightenment. This is

different from the descriptions of slavery as evil by both the radical natural right thinkers of the period and the white abolitionists.... Other writers, such as Paine, Diderot, and Montesquieu, would suggest that slavery was against natural liberty, but *reason* - none would venture there.[26]

Again, I see this as just false. Locke again:

> The *State of Nature* has a Law of Nature to govern it, which obliges every one: And Reason, which is that Law, teaches all Mankind, who will but consult it, that being all equal and independent, no one ought to harm another in his Life, Health, Liberty, or Possessions... In transgressing the Law of Nature, the Offender [for example, the would-be enslaver] declares himself to live by another Rule, than that of *reason* and common Equity (§6, 8).

Bogues on the putatively 'heretical' character of Cugoano's views of natural rights:

> For Cugoano, the fundamental natural right was the right of the individual to be free and equal, not in relationship to government but in relationship to other human beings. This, I want to suggest was not only a radicalised version of natural rights but also, at the time, a heretic one.[27]

And I in turn want to suggest that it was not; for as Locke said:

> [W]e must consider what State all Men are naturally in, and that is, a *State of perfect Freedom* to order their Actions...A *State* also *of Equality*, wherein all the Power and Jurisdiction is reciprocal, no one having more than another: there being nothing more evident, than that Creatures of the same species and rank...should also be equal one amongst another without Subordination or Subjection (§4).

Bogues on another aspect of Cugoano's supposed originality:

> Cugoano, unlike other radical natural rights thinkers of the period, claims that the laws of civilization are derived from divine laws, and therefore they enhance rather than diminish man's natural rights.[28]

Nothing original about this; Locke again:

> The *State of Nature* has a Law of Nature to govern it, which obliges every one...The Obligations of the Law of Nature cease not in Society...Thus the Law of Nature stands as an Eternal Rule to all Men, *Legislators* as well as others. The *Rules* that they make for other

Mens Actions, must...be conformable to the Law of Nature, i.e., to the Will of God, of which that is a Declaration (§6, 135).

In sum, I do not see that Bogues has made the case 'that there existed in Cugoano's slave narrative a political counter narrative that moved in a different direction than the political horizons of the Enlightenment'.[29] What we have in Cugoano is an eighteenth-century black Enlightenment liberal demanding the extension of white liberal values to a population racially excluded from their scope. As Bogues himself characterises Cugoano's achievement:

> Cugoano sees natural rights as "common rights," and applies these rights to African slaves. *In doing this he universalises natural rights in ways others did not* [my emphasis]. ...Cugoano's dethronement of blackness as curse and badge of inferiority was astonishing for its time, given the normative weight of hegemonic whiteness naturalised as the universal self.[30]

In other words – and exactly as I said at the start – Cugoano sought to develop a black natural rights liberalism that was simultaneously a radicalism in its extension to blacks of values previously limited to whites. But, contra Bogues, the radicalism inheres not in the axiological newness of the values (unless their extension to blacks is, definitionally, taken to make them new, which trivialises the claim) but the 'astonishing' insistence, with all its world-overturning implications, that norms applicable to whites should indeed be applicable to blacks also.[31] In my book, that makes him a retrievalist.

## Conclusion

Finally, let me pre-emptively address some possible misunderstandings of my claim, and its associated assumptions.

I am *not* saying that Locke, for example (or fill in your alternative white Enlightenment candidate), was 'really' a closet anti-racist, or that his 'essential' position was somehow an anti-racist one. The point is that even if he was a racist, it is a non sequitur to argue from the importance of this kind of *exposé* to the conclusion that reconstructed and sanitised versions of the theory are therefore impossible or worthless. If Locke did not think of blacks as fully, or at all, self-owning, it does not follow that a theory based on natural rights, including self-ownership, cannot be valuable when extended to blacks. Racial retrievalism argues that reconstructed (expanded, deracialised, rethought) versions of liberal values can be used to advance an anti-racist agenda; racial anti-retrievalism argues that they cannot. This is the substantive issue, which we must not lose sight of.

Nor should it be thought that a pro-Enlightenment position, as I have characterised it above, leaves one in thrall to 'European' ideas. That would be to suppose that only Europeans have had the concepts of (to cite one familiar gloss) rationalism, objectivism, universalism, and egalitarianism. But, in fact, these ideas have appeared in all the world's cultures, though not necessarily developed to the same extent. In his *Reclaiming the Enlightenment*, Stephen Bronner suggests: 'The belief that enlightenment values are somehow intrinsically "western" is surely parochial and most likely racist.... [L]iberal and cosmopolitan values usually identified with western thinking in general and the Enlightenment in particular were expressed in any number of nonwestern societies – including the three great civilizations of India, China, and Islam.'[32]

To characterise Cugoano as a black Enlightenment theorist, then, is not at all to diminish his achievement. I am in complete agreement with Bogues on the significance of the conceptual breakthrough represented by Cugoano's rejection, against the wisdom of the age, of the axiom of black inferiority, and the courage it must have taken to challenge white scholarly authority. Who cannot admire the boldness of his blow against the racial orthodoxy of the time? Who cannot applaud his vision? Where we differ is in how this 'heretical' intellectual feat should be characterised. For Bogues it is an anti-Enlightenment act carried out in the name of trans-Enlightenment values; for me, it is an anti-racialised-Enlightenment act carried out in the name of the deracialised Enlightenment, thus turning Enlightenment principles upon themselves. I think this characterisation is the more accurate one and that Bogues's own words inadvertently give us proof of its correctness.

In sum, Bogues's black heretic is, I would claim, simultaneously a black canonist.

# Notes

1. Cedric J. Robinson, *Black Marxism: The Making of the Black Radical Tradition* ([1983] 2000: Chapel Hill, NC: University of North Carolina Press, 2000).
2. Quobna Ottobah Cugoano, *Thoughts and Sentiments on the Evil of Slavery, and Other Writings*, ed. Vincent Carretta (New York: Penguin, 1999).
3. Anthony Bogues, *Black Heretics, Black Prophets: Radical Political Intellectuals* (New York: Routledge, 2003).
4. See Uday Singh Mehta, *Liberalism and Empire: A Study in Nineteenth-Century British Liberal Thought* (Chicago, IL: University of Chicago Press, 1999) and Jennifer Pitts, *A Turn to Empire: The Rise of Imperial Liberalism in Britain and France* (Princeton, NJ: Princeton University Press, 2004).
5. Bogues, *Black Heretics*, 12–16, 16–20.
6. Bogues, *Black Heretics*, 14.
7. Ibid., 13.
8. Anthony Bogues, 'Race and Revising Liberalism,' *Small Axe: A Journal of Criticism*, no. 4 (1998): 175–82; Anthony Bogues, 'Review of *The Racial Contract*, by Charles W. Mills,' *Constellations* 8, no. 2 (2001): 267–72.
9. Charles W. Mills, 'Reply to Critics,' *Small Axe: A Journal of Criticism*, no. 4 (1998): 191–201; Charles W. Mills, 'Rousseau, the Master's Tools, and Anti-Contractarian Contractarianism,' *CLR James Journal: A Review of Caribbean Ideas*, Special Issue: Creolising Rousseau, ed. Jane Anna Gordon and Neil Roberts 15, no. 1 (2009): 92–112.
10. C.B. Macpherson, *Democratic Theory: Essays in Retrieval* (New York: Oxford University Press, 1973).
11. Ruth Abbey, *The Return of Feminist Liberalism* (Durham: Acumen, 2011).
12. C.B. Macpherson, *The Political Theory of Possessive Individualism: Hobbes to Locke* ([1962] New York: Oxford University Press, 2011).
13. Bogues, *Black Heretics*, 3.
14. Bogues, 'Race and Revising Liberalism,' 177–78.
15. Ibid., 179, 181.
16. Bogues, 'Review,' 270.
17. Carretta, introduction to Carretta, ed., *Thoughts and Sentiments*.
18. Carretta, introduction, xvii, xx–xxi.
19. John Locke, *Two Treatises of Government*, ed. Peter Laslett (New York: Cambridge University Press, 1988 [1960]). I will follow the convention of citing in the text the paragraph numbers of the *Second Treatise*.
20. Peter Laslett, introduction to the *Two Treatises*, 4.
21. Bogues, *Black Heretics*, 35.
22. See Bernard Boxill, 'A Lockean Argument for Black Reparations,' *The Journal of Ethics* 7, no. 1 (2003): 63–91.
23. David Hume, 'Of National Characters' (1753–54 version), excerpted in Emmanuel Eze, ed., *Race and the Enlightenment: A Reader* (Cambridge, MA: Blackwell, 1997).
24. Bogues, *Black Heretics*, 44, 43.
25. Ibid., 36.
26. Ibid., 36, 38.
27. Ibid., 45.

28. Ibid., 41.
29. Ibid., 45.
30. Ibid., 36, 45.
31. These sentences come from the conclusion of my brief discussion of Bogues in Carole Pateman and Charles W. Mills, *Contract and Domination* (Malden, MA: Polity, 2007), 247–48.
32. Stephen Eric Bronner, *Reclaiming the Enlightenment: Toward a Politics of Radical Engagement* (New York: Columbia University Press, 2004), 31.

## 10 | *Jean-Jacques Dessalines and the Haitian Revolution:*
Global Agency of Universal Modernity

Clinton A. Hutton

'[V]ow before me to live free and independent, and to prefer death to anything that will try to place you back in chains' – Jean-Jacques Dessalines, January 1, 1804, Declaration of Haiti's Independence.

Jean-Jacques Dessalines became the leader of the anti-slavery revolution in Saint Domingue at the juncture of its transformation into the anti-slavery national liberation revolution of Haiti which led to the declaration of independence on January 1, 1804. Dessalines thus became the founder of the Haitian nation state on January 1, 1804. This fact alone made/should make Dessalines a global historic figure of immense ontological importance.

This was not to be the case, however. In the pantheon of global leaders engaging in the identity construction of modernity, Dessalines could not find a place. Yet he belonged there. He was, objectively, a central defining figure of modernity, despite the rituals of obscurity and marginality to which he was, and continues to be subjected, in the narratives of certitude spun in the epistemic and intellectual culture of occidental empireism, the assumed, unimpeachable source of thinking, knowing and constructing meaning and certifying the nature of things.

The Haitian nation state and the revolution which gave birth to it, constitute perhaps, the single most important source of the ontological defining material of modernist universal humanism to have hitherto emerged in history. Put another way, the Haitian nation state and the revolution which gave birth to it, constitute the most important epistemological and ontological/cultural sources for framing, defining and articulating a modernist universal humanist ethos beyond the realm of the racial contractarian model.

The narratives of the Haitian Revolution, even when authored by supportive progressives, have been, to a great extent, constructed within an occidental epistemic culture which denied the existence of an indigenous/autonomous cognitive and intellectual agency in blackness and its pioneering role in raising a category of humanist values in modernity that would mark the genesis of the epistemology and culture of equality, justice and freedom as universal categories. Before Haiti and its revolution, modernity rested primarily on the agency of a new model of empire driven mainly by the emergence and development of a number of sovereign European and diasporic European super nation states such as Britain, France, Spain, Germany and the US.

These European super nation states were united by a racial contract denoting the superiority of whiteness in the global ordering of humanity while competitively engaging each other, or forming alliances with each other, to appropriate or to otherwise subject non-European spaces and peoples (deemed as non-sovereign humans) in a global division of the world among these European states.

The epistemological and ontological values of modernity that the Haitian Revolution has given to the world were long recognised by Haitian revolutionaries and other black abolitionists in the Americas as flowing from the cognitive, epistemological and intellectual culture and agency of enslaved Africans in Saint Domingue. While progressive twentieth-century scholars such as Eugene Genovese, C.L.R. James, Robin Blackburn, Susan Buck-Morss and David Geggus have mostly and variously argued that the Haitian Revolution was, indeed could have been, nothing more than the realisation or extension of the principles and values of the French Revolution/ Enlightenment/Western civilisation, African abolitionist thinkers of the nineteenth century such as Pompée Valentin Vastey (Baron de Vastey), Frederick Douglass, William Wells Brown and James Theodore Holly have, from the outset, asserted that the values and principles of the Haitian Revolution were historically original, epochal, and embraced a kind of modernity that had a universalist vision of equality, justice and freedom.

The conceptual/philosophical approaches in the narratives of the Haitian Revolution are thus the tales of the articulation of two distinct kinds of epistemologies, two distinct ways of thinking, knowing and constructing meaning; two distinct ways of explaining and articulating the logic and significance of the Haitian Revolution. The pervading view was/is that Africans lacked cognitive agency and, hence, the capacity to conceptualise freedom, justice and the principles and values requisite for the modernist development of civilisation and the making of history. This tale is more or less associated with James,

Blackburn, Geggus, Genovese, Buck-Morss and others, although there are important differences and emphases among these thinkers.

So normative has this view become, that the assertion that the philosophical and intellectual basis of the Haitian Revolution emanated from the French Enlightenment/European epistemic culture is taken to be a truism and constitutes the epistemological basis and compass of the majority of the progressive scholars of the Haitian Revolution.[1] A crucial logic of this episteme in Haitian Revolution studies is raised by Geggus and Genovese. They have argued that black anti-slavery insurrections prior to the upsurge of bourgeois revolutions and white abolitionism were aimed at restoring the African primitive state of nature. These black anti-slavery insurrections and their leadership were thus deemed inconsequential to the march of civilised humanity and modernity, or more affirmatively, fettered such a march. These insurrections were, hence, not progressive. They were restorationist, that is, they were aimed at restoring Africans to what they were before slavery.

Only with the advent and spread of bourgeois enlightenment ideas and culture among a core of *'creole slaves'* were black anti-slavery efforts deemed to have any historical value. In this regard, Eugene Genovese notes that 'The brilliance with which Toussaint L'Ouverture claimed for his enslaved brothers and sisters the rights of liberty and equality – of universal dignity – that the French were claiming for themselves constituted a turning point in the history of slave revolts and, indeed, of the human spirit' (Genovese 1979, xix). The implications here are not in doubt. The 'rights of liberty and equality – of universal dignity – that the French were claiming for themselves constituted a turning point in the history of slave revolts and, indeed, of the human spirit', values apparently absent in black anti-slavery character, thought and agency prior to what Genovese had concluded to be the occidental epistemological and ontological transformation of the character of Africans, which made it possible to also transform their thoughts and actions into civilising outcomes.

It is within this epistemic context evident in Genovese's Haitian Revolution/ 'slave revolts' narrative, that issues of the nature/character and scope of leadership and the motives and principles of 'slave revolts' are viewed and articulated. In this context, pre-1791 'slave revolts' were deemed to be devoid of the claims of 'the rights of liberty and equality – of universal dignity' because, in Genovese's logic, up to that time in history, black anti-slavery leaders never possessed the values, principles and the words/ rhetoric to articulate 'the rights of liberty and equality – of universal dignity'. Hence, prior to the Haitian Revolution with its acquired signatures of 'the rights of liberty, equality [and] universal dignity', black anti-slavery actors in David Geggus's estimation, 'rarely demanded freedom as a right' (Geggus 2002, 37).

And they could not in Geggus's logic, because they were so mired in their primitivist epistemologies and ontologies that their triumph over these constituted the basis upon which they would be able to become agency of the rights of liberty, equality and universal dignity. Put another way, only when Africans, especially their leaders, were free, not from slavery, but from themselves, from their own primitivist epistemologies and ontologies, would they become the agency of the rights of liberty, equality and universal dignity.

The most profound impediment that Africans must overcome to achieve freedom from slavery, in Geggus's and indeed, Genovese's logic, was not their enslavement by Europeans, but freedom from themselves, from the 'zoological garden' of the geography of their birth and of their inferiority.

When Africans were not free from themselves, as evident in the restorationist epoch of their resistance to slavery, according to Geggus, enslaved Africans 'rarely demanded freedom as a *right.*' This view found common ground with Genovese, whom Geggus cited: It was only after 'the revolution in France, [that] American slaves turned from 'restorationist' rebellion to 'bourgeois-democratic' revolution and sought for the first time to eradicate slavery as a system and to come to terms with the modern state and world economy' (Geggus 2002, 37).

For Geggus, Genovese et al., the genesis of black anti-slavery as a kind of rationalist expression of the Enlightenment and bourgeois freedom only became possible with the emergence of a class of 'creole slaves' and 'freed men' in whom primitivism/Africanism had been defeated and enlightenment/Europeanism triumphed. In this logic, the epistemology and culture of happiness, dignity, freedom and rationality, the essential humanity of Africans emerged only with their emancipation, not from slavery, but from themselves, the consequence of the exposure of 'creole slaves' and 'freed men' to occidental socialisation.

In the logic of Geggus, Genovese et al., the process of emancipating blacks from their Africanist state of knowing and being was simultaneously transforming them into the agency of modernist anti-slavery, such as the Haitian Revolution. In this mode of conceptualising, analysing and articulating the Haitian Revolution, the extent of the occidental epistemological and ontological presence in the revolutionary process would determine the nature of the assessment of the value and relevance of the revolution to the development of modern civilisation.

The evidence of this can be found everywhere in the progressive narratives of the Haitian Revolution. Susan Buck-Morss (2000) argues, for example, that:

> For almost a decade, before the violent elimination of Whites signalled their deliberate retreat from universalist principles, the Black Jacobins of Saint-Domingue surpassed the metropole in actively realizing the Enlightenment goal of human liberty, seeming to give proof that the French Revolution was not simply a European phenomenon but world-historical in its implications (835–36).

Here, Buck-Morss is passing judgement on two leaders and leadership styles evident in the Haitian Revolution, one whose agency allowed the revolution to surpass France 'in actively realising the Enlightenment goal of human liberty' and the other, whose agency signalled a 'deliberate retreat' of the revolution from the 'universalist principles' of this goal. The first of the two was Toussaint L'Ouverture, who led the revolution for almost ten years. During that time, the Haitian Revolution, in Buck-Morss's assessment, upheld 'universal principles' of liberty, indeed, it *'surpassed'* France in this regard. The second leader implicated was Jean-Jacques Dessalines, who became leader of the Haitian Revolution when Toussaint L'Ouverture was seized by the French and taken to France in 1802. Dessalines then presided over what Buck-Morss calls 'the violent elimination of Whites' which signalled that the revolution had deliberately retreated from 'universalist principles'.

Under Dessalines' leadership, the Haitian Revolution had thus become a revolt against civilisation, a revolt against the principles and values of 'the Enlightenment goal of human liberty'. It had reverted to the status of pre-1791 'slave revolts' with their restorationist ontologies, the agency of blackness devoid of Enlightenment. The constraining power of the Enlightenment, of rationality, justice, liberty, love and dignity, had so declined with Toussaint L'Ouverture's departure, that it led to the triumph of anti-occidental forces under the leadership of Dessalines. Such is the intended or un-intended logic of Buck-Morss.

In this context, it was not the French Revolution or the European nations which supported slavery as an integral part of the global order they were making, that Buck-Morss fingered for deliberately retreating from universalist principles when the French launched a bloody campaign to abolish the Haitian Revolution and re-impose slavery, it was the victims of this campaign who were to be blamed.

It was not the violent elimination of blacks by whites which signalled a retreat from 'universalist principles', it was apparently the opposite, the violent elimination of whites by blacks. After all, if black people killed white people to prevent their extermination or re-enslavement, they would be in breach of a more serious crime, a crime against civilisation: the attack on the moral, rational, cognitive, intellectual, aesthetic, spiritual, inventive, entrepreneurial and certificatory agency of modernity.

Moreover, it would appear in Buck-Morss's logic that the centuries of European enslavement of Africans never prevented Europeans from articulating 'universalist principles' and from being deemed the cognitive agency and nativity of these principles. These 'universalist principles', however, were not inconsistent with slave-making and its maintenance, in the same way that the European revolutions which amplified these principles were not inconsistent with the making and maintaining of slavery. These revolutions were global status quo phenomena consolidating a world order in which slave-making was a defining ontological principle. Indeed, they were not inconsistent with Haitian revolutionary Pompée Valentin Vastey's articulation of the dystopian landscape in which French enslavement placed Africans in Saint Domingue:

> Haven't they committed unheard-of cruelties until then unknown to humankind? Haven't they burnt, roasted, grilled and impaled alive the unfortunate slaves? Haven't they sawn off the limbs, torn out the tongues and teeth, torn off the ears, and cut off the lips of their Blacks? Haven't they hung men upside down, drowned them in sacks, crucified them on planks, buried them alive, crushed them in mortars? Haven't they forced them to eat human shit? And, after

having flayed them with the whip, haven't they thrown them to the ground to be devoured by worms, or onto anthills, or lashed them to stakes in the swamp to be eaten alive by mosquitoes? Haven't they put men and women into barrels spiked with nail[s], closed at both ends, and rolled them from the top of mountains, hurling the unfortunate victims inside into the abyss below? Haven't they had these miserable blacks savaged by trained dogs, until these mastiffs, full of human flesh, refuse any longer to act as instruments of the torturers who then finish off the half-eaten victims with the thrust of a knife or bayonet? (Arthur and Dash 1999, 29)

In Buck-Morss's logic, blackness devoid of the guiding principles and culture of occidental ontologies and epistemologies will necessarily lead blackness back into the state of nature (a condition worse than European enslavement), back into what Georg Hegel calls a 'zoological garden,' or a 'primitive state of nature,' or 'a state of animality' (Eze 1997, 128) where 'the arbitrary rule of the senses, the energy of the sensuous will' (137) characterised their nature of existence. This was the fate/object of 'slave revolts' before the Haitian Revolution, before the occidentalisation of blackness in Genovese's and Geggus's thoughts and what the Haitian Revolution reverted to when the Whites were violently eliminated in Buck-Morss's estimation.

In this logic, blackness in Saint Domingue-Haiti did not possess the will and cultural and intellectual ability to come out of the primitive state of nature by itself, or indeed, to remain in the state of man on its own accord. In this logic, blackness required the agency of whiteness to keep it on a rationalist/humanistic path of existence. Apparently, this is a debt that blackness eternally owed to whiteness. Eric Williams's (1964) observation and assessment of the epistemology of British historians may well be applied here: 'The British historians wrote almost as if Britain had introduced Negro slavery solely for the satisfaction of abolishing it' (182).

In the logic of Buck-Morss, the Haitian Revolution retreated from 'universalist principles' because its acquired European qualities, its acquired occidental values, its creole enlightenment ethos deteriorated – nay, collapsed under Dessalines's leadership, under his resurgent or unrestrained Africanism, under the agency of *neg ginin*, of African men and women, the majority of whom were born Kongolese, who could scarcely speak a word of French. Here the victory of restorationism over the revolution's acquired 'universalist principles' was directly related to the deterioration in the state of Europeanism in the leadership of the Haitian Revolution, which made that revolution incompatible with the state of man. To put it bluntly, in Geggus's et al., formulation, 'the elites among the enslaved/black population of Saint Domingue derived their "sombodiness", their nature of being, from their creole birth and socialisation into a European way of knowing, feeling and doing' (Hutton 2005, 81).

In the epistemology of Buck-Morss and Geggus et al., the Haitian Revolution is assessed and articulated not on the basis of its deeds and rhetoric compared to the English, American and French revolutions, but primarily on the basis of the extent of the presence of Occidentalism in the epistemic and ontological culture, especially of the leadership of the revolution.[2] In this respect, under Toussaint L'Ouverture's leadership, the Haitian Revolution was rated highly for embracing the principles and values of the Enlightenment/Western civilisation and was deemed, to some extent, to be even bolder in articulating and implementing these principles and values, compared to the French Revolution, a reflection of the high presence or prevalence of Occidentalism in the Haitian Revolution, while the French Revolution was meandering from moderation to leftwing extremist terror, to proclaiming abolition, to rightwing coup d'état and purges, to renouncing emancipation and the launching of a military expedition to restore slavery in Saint Domingue-Haiti.

It is within this epistemological context that Genovese's statement, which is cited above, makes sense. Here it is again:

> The brilliance with which Toussaint L'Ouverture claimed for his enslaved brothers and sisters the rights of liberty and equality – of universal human dignity – that the French were claiming for themselves constituted a turning point in the history of slave revolts and, indeed, of the human spirit (Genovese 1979, xix).

Buck-Morss's high commendation of the Haitian Revolution for upholding 'universal principles' on the one hand, and her denunciation of it for deliberately retreating from these principles on the other hand, reflected in the logic of her position a recognition of the ontological presence and application of Western principles and values in that revolution for almost ten years under Toussaint L'Ouverture and the catastrophic disuse and absence of these, under Dessalines, after L'Ouverture's departure.

In the following statement, Robin Blackburn is in clear disagreement with Susan Buck-Morss about the presence, followed by the virtual death, of the Enlightenment in the Haitian Revolution. It never died for Blackburn. On the contrary, it was precisely because of its presence why Haitian revolutionaries were able to defend their revolution against Napoleon Bonaparte's determination to abolish it and re-impose slavery.

> One of Napoleon's grave miscalculations, when he set out to reconquer St. Domingue and re-enslave the blacks, was to underestimate the extent to which liberty and equality had become the religion of the former enslaved....Part of the grandeur of the great Revolution in St. Domingue-Haiti is that it successfully defended the gains of the French Revolution against France itself (Blackburn 1988, 259).

For Blackburn then, the culture of the Enlightenment which Africans in Saint Domingue-Haiti acquired, was central to the defence of the Haitian Revolution against Napoleon Bonaparte's counter-revolution, while for Buck-Morss, there was precious little left in the Caribbean Revolution to defend, as the oxygen of Enlightenment, the Haitian Revolution's ontological ethos, was sucked out of it by a resurgent Africanism. Either way, the Haitian Revolution possessed something that was not of its own making, its cognitive agency, its identity/ontological corpus, the very reason for its existence.

This author's analysis of James's construction of Toussaint L'Ouverture's agency in the Haitian Revolution is mindful of this epistemological problematic:

> C.L.R. James' ontological construction of Toussaint L'Ouverture as 'a typical representative of the French Revolution' was simultaneously a construction of the Haitian Revolution under his leadership as such. 'That was why in the hour of danger,' James notes, 'Toussaint, uninstructed as he was, could find the language and accent of Diderot, Rousseau, and Raynal, of Mirabeau, Robespierre, and Danton.' Moreover, James asserts that Toussaint L'Ouverture 'in one respect excelled them all,' these intellectual agencies of the French Revolution. 'For,' James notes, 'even these masters of the spoken and written word, owing to the class complications of their society, too often had to pause, to hesitate, to qualify' and thus could not defend the freedom of blacks without reservation, as Toussaint could (Hutton 2011, 534).

For James, it was Toussaint L'Ouverture, 'a typical representative of the French Revolution', who was the unswerving defender of the French Revolution, its principles, values and goals, not the French authors of the revolution themselves, and all because of Toussaint's genius in internalising the Enlightenment principles, values and goals and consistently defending them more than their authors and even from their authors, who could not defend freedom for Africans without reservation, as Toussaint could.

In the narratives of progressive scholars such as James and Geggus, Toussaint L'Ouverture's facility for grasping occidental cultural values, principles and goals and weaving them into the epistemological and ontological corpus of the Haitian Revolution, into its moral compass, enlightened vision, rationalist ethos and universal pathway, was the marker of his creole enlightenment identity and agency. After all, he could read and write. He exuded 'sophistication' and possessed a secularism which triumphed over magico-religion, *Vodou*. Moreover, he was a Christian. The compassion with which he was treated in enslavement and his experience as a freedman, as well as his general association with whiteness, were deemed to be clues to his enlightened demeanour and the nature of his leadership style.[3]

Toussaint L'Ouverture's visa to the world of the Enlightenment was all of these combined, but especially his literacy. It was because of his command of literacy that Toussaint L'Ouverture was able to access and grasp the ideology of the French Revolution/white abolitionist thought and to apply it as a guide for action and for defining the Haitian Revolution. Herein lie Toussaint L'Ouverture's defining strength and the rationale for C.L.R. James to deem him 'a typical representative of the French Revolution' (James 1938, 256).

Toussaint L'Ouverture's ontological and agential transformation to Enlightenment fellow occurred with his reading of Raynal. Toussaint L'Ouverture's 'road to Damascus' moment came, in James's estimation, when he discovered Raynal's book, *Philosophical and Political History of the Establishments and Commerce of the Europeans in the Two Indies*. This book, 'famous in its time, came into the hands of the slave most fitted to make use of it, Toussaint L'Ouverture' (James 1989, 24–25), according to James.[4] Indeed, because of circumstances of history, including what James posits to be some of the inadequacies of other leaders of the Haitian Revolution: 'Toussaint alone read his Raynal' (82).

It was Raynal's book that James posits to be the harbinger of the epistemological and intellectual basis of the Haitian Revolution and only so, because of Toussaint L'Ouverture's access to it and his grasp and use of it to give the revolution reason, a consequence of his facility for literacy and other traits which made him 'a typical representative of the French Revolution.' Overall, '[n]one of the other leaders of the Revolution was able to match Toussaint's quality, according to James, because they were fettered with disabilities of the slave system which Toussaint was protected against. While Toussaint had probably never been whipped since his childhood,' Jean-Jacques Dessalines grew up on savage beatings and abuses and, even though he was the most famous of Toussaint's generals and some thought he excelled Toussaint 'in military genius,' James asserts that 'it was late in life before he learned to sign his name' (Hutton 2005, 29–30). Furthermore, argues James, Henri Christophe, who 'listened to the talk [about the French Revolution] in the hotel where he worked [as a waiter] but had no constructive ideas, could neither read nor write [although] he learned to speak French with remarkable fluency [unlike Toussaint, and] astonished the French by his knowledge of the world' (30).

While Toussaint L'Ouverture fitted the ontological profile of enlightened agency of the Haitian Revolution and 'a typical representative of the French Revolution', on account of his literacy and other acquisitions of Occidentalism, Dessalines was being categorised as the other. He was best at the borderline of enlightenment and restorationism. He possessed less of the ontological traits that would signal his emancipation from Africanist ontologies and epistemologies, the antithesis of L'Ouverture's acquired Enlightenment status.

While Toussaint L'Ouverture was constructed as a man of literacy, sophistication and Christianity, who was measured/reasonable, rational and capable of expressing love, empathy, forgiveness and justice in the Judeo-Christian sense, Jean-Jacques Dessalines was constructed as a brute. He was deemed to be illiterate, unforgiving, un-empathetic, unreasonable and pathologically murderous, characteristics which led to 'the violent elimination of Whites' under his leadership of the Haitian Revolution and its 'deliberate retreat from universalist principles'.

Even though it is not true that Dessalines was illiterate,[5] we see the development of a logic in Haitian Revolution scholarship where the correlation between the extent of literacy and illiteracy determined the levels of brutality, reason, Africanism and Europeanism in the assessment of the revolution and its leadership at any given time. This defies the reality of slavery and colonialism which the Haitian Revolution eviscerated in Saint Domingue-Haiti. Was Donatien Rochambeau, the French General who took over from General Victor-Emmanuel Leclerc, Napoleon Bonaparte's project for restoring slavery to Haiti, illiterate? It was he who presided over 'the appalling murder of Jacques Maurepas, one of the first black generals to join the French. In front of his wife and daughter, he was dragged on board the French admiral's ship in the bay and bound to the main mast. Then, his epaulettes hammered into his shoulders with long nails, a cocked hat was nailed on his head, and he was savagely whipped. He died without a word, tears flowing down his face' (Dayan 1988, 186).

In this theatre of horror directed by Rochambeau, Jacques Maurepas, his wife and children and some 400 men under his command, were ritually desecrated and killed in a spectacular dramatisation. Dessalines responded to this performance with a swift resolve to overwhelm and paralyse the French with awe and fear. He gathered an equal number of French soldiers he took as prisoners and executed them in full sight of Rochambeau (Beard 2002, 122).

This resolve was articulated in the declaration of independence speech which Dessalines made January 1, 1804:

> And you precious men, intrepid generals, who, without concern for your own pain, have revised liberty by shedding all your blood, know that you have done nothing if you do not give the nations a terrible, but just example of the vengeance that must be wrought by a people proud to have recovered its liberty and jealous to maintain it, let us frighten all those who would dare try to take it from us again; let us begin with the French. Let them tremble when they approach our coast, if not from the memory of those cruelties they perpetrated here, then from the terrible resolution that we will have made to put to death anyone born French whose profane foot soils the land of liberty.[6]

There is a tendency among some scholars to write about Dessalines's violent political acts as if they happened without context, without reason, as if they were all expressions of the state of his inferiority, of his untamed state, of his nature, a man unfettered by the virtual absence of enlightenment from his ontological corpus; the bringer of death embracing the primitivist state of nature.

The French enslavement of Africans with its dystopian rituals of desecration, blood and pain to command labour in perpetuity, without pay and dignity; the French pretence at fraternity which lured Toussaint L'Ouverture into imprisonment and death, and Maurepas and his family and soldiers to a carnival of death; the French restoration of slavery in Guadeloupe and its determination to do likewise in Saint Domingue-Haiti and the French policy of kidnapping and enslaving Haitians along the Santo Domingo-Haitian border, which lead to the Haitian invasion of Santo Domingo in 1805 (Bellegarde-Smith 2004, 75), are contextual issues often ignored by some Haitian Revolution scholars in their assessment of Dessalines. Jean-Jacques Dessalines became the third national leader of the Haitian Revolution after Boukman 'Zamba' Dutty and Toussaint L'Ouverture. He was perhaps the revolution's best military tactician and strategist and the figure that most engendered fear and doubt in the British, French and Spanish troops about their ability to destroy the will, fortitude and psychological corpus of Haitian revolutionaries and their revolution.

'The Haitian Revolution was a profoundly global historical phenomenon. It ushered into human consciousness a way of thinking, knowing and doing that was out of step with, and antithetical to, the global order of slave-making, colonial subjection and the racist ordering of humanity' (Hutton 2007, 16). The truth is, the English, Americans and French who made revolutions, did not do so because they wanted to change the racialised slave-making colonial order that Europeans were responsible for creating, neither were the European states which did not produce revolutionary outcomes. Trouillot (1995) notes that, 'the very deeds of the revolution were incompatible with major tenets of dominant western ideologies' (95).

The end of slavery, the *raison d'être* of the Haitian Revolution, placed Haiti in a unique modernist historical position. It was the first nation state authority in a global historical context to assert that a person's right to his or her own body was sovereign and inviolable. Moreover, the Haitian revolutionary authority declared to the world, the collective right of a people to self-determination/national sovereignty, the defence of which Dessalines articulated in blunt, uncompromising language: 'In the end we must live independent *or die.*'[7] The principle of 'racial equality was the Revolution's philosophy of respect and of justice and social relationship' (Hutton 2007, 22).

The truth is, whatever scholars thought of him, Jean-Jacques Dessalines was a central agential figure in the epistemological and ontological construction of the Haitian Revolution and its defence, and the core modernist values it gave to the world: the unimpeachable right of a person to his/her body; the right of a people to self-determination and racial equality as the basis of human intercourse, above all, empathy and fairness.

Jean-Jacques Dessalines was thus one of the most important historical figures of the modern age, indeed, of any age. He was the leading historical agency and the ontological embodiment and personification of the Haitian Revolution as the anti-slavery/anti-colonial, anti-hegemonic alternative and antithesis to the global European order which collapsed with the global tide of national liberation after the second twentieth century war of the European empires came to an end in 1945. Today, Dessalines is a *lwa* in the *Vodou* pantheon, the only leader of the Haitian Revolution to be deified.

**Notes**

1. There is another category of progressive Haitian Revolution scholars which is not as categorical in its assertion of the singularity of Western epistemology and ontology as the basis of what ought to be considered the modern humanistic values of the Haitian Revolution or the measurement of what is deemed to be good about the Haitian Revolution and its place in the global order.

    This epistemological and ontological category began with Haitian revolutionaries such as Pompée Valentin Vastey, as well as black abolitionists in the Americas such as Frederick Douglass, who were still struggling to end slavery. Vastey (1969) notes that:

    > *Hayti has no general history written by a native of the country. The few detached fragments which we possess are chiefly from the pens of European writers, who have principally confined themselves to those parts more immediately connected with themselves, and who, when led by the subject to speak of the native inhabitants, have done so with that spirit of prejudice and partiality which never fails to appear whenever there arises a question involving the competition of Blacks and Whites' (15). So from the beginning, there was concern among Blacks about the use of a White epistemology rooted in the 'spirit of prejudice and partiality' to construct the existence of Blackness as inferior and subordinate and Whiteness as superior and sovereign.*

    Vastey rejects this characterization, so too Frederick Douglass, the prominent Black anti-slavery campaigner in the United States of

America. To him, the Haitians Revolution was a singular historical phenomenon with pioneering modernist universal principles rooted in the agency of enslaved Africans:

> *I regard her as the original pioneer emancipator of the nineteenth century. It was her one brave example that first of all startled the Christian world into a sense of the Negro's manhood.... Until Haiti struck for freedom, the conscience of the Christian world slept profoundly over slavery. It was scarcely troubled even by a dream of this crime against justice and liberty. The Negro was, in its estimation, a sheep-like creature, having no rights which White men were bound to respect, a docile animal, a kind of ass, capable of bearing burdens, and receiving stripes from a white master without resentment, and without resistance. The mission of Haiti is to dispel this degradation and dangerous delusion, and to give to the world a new and true revelation of the Black man's character* (Foner 485).

These epistemological and ontological issues, as well as others, including views about the nativity, history and global impact of African cognitive and intellectual agency from early antiquity, were part of the geography of contemporary African diasporic defence of the Haitian Revolution. It should be noted that a cohort of progressive twentieth century and twenty-first century scholars has been relying less on the normative Western epistemological mode of formulating and articulating the Haitian Revolution story. They are at various stages of embracing an African diasporic derived/inspired epistemology or one combining European and African diasporic. They range from Price-Mars (1983), to Trouillot (1995), to Dayan (1998), to Fischer (2004), to Hutton (2005), to Nesbitt (2008).

2. A fundamental problem with this episteme is that it obscures the search and visioning of the Haitian Revolution through an African/African diasporic epistemological, cosmological and cultural complex. Hence, this author's endeavour to address this issue in Hutton (2005, 2007 and 2011).
3. See Hutton (2005, 78–81) for a discussion of Geggus's discourse on Toussaint L'Ouverture and the Haitian Revolution which he led as expressions of creole enlightenment epistemology, ontology and political praxis.
4. For an extended discussion on this issue, read Clinton Hutton *The Logic and Historical Significance of the Haitian Revolution and the Cosmological Roots of Haitian Freedom* (Kingston: Arawak Publications, 2005), 28–31. Also, read Nick Nesbitt, *Universal Emancipation: The Haitian Revolution and the Radical Enlightenment* (Charlottesville and London: University of Virginia Press, 2008), 48–65, for more on Toussaint L'Ouverture's literacy and the articulation of Enlightenment cognitive and intellectual agency in the Haitian Revolution.
5. See Deborah Janson, 'Hegel and Dessalines: Philosophy and the African Diaspora,' *New West Indian Guide* 84, no. 3–4 (2010): 271–72.
6. See the Haitian Declaration of Independence, 1804 today.duke.edu/showcase/haitideclaration/declarationstext.html. Accessed August 17, 2012.
7. Ibid.

**References**

Arthur, Charles, and Michael Dash, eds. 1999. *A Haiti Anthology: Liberté*. London, Princeton and Kingston: Markus Wiener Publishers, Latin Bureau and Ian Randle Publishers.

Bellegarde-Smith, Patrick. [1990] 2004. *Haiti: The Breached Citadel*. Toronto: Canadian Scholars' Press Inc.

Beard, John R. 2002. *The Life of Toussaint L'Ouverture: The Negro Patriot of Hayti: A Drama of the Black Napoleon, 1853*. This edition edited by Michael W. Perry. Seattle: Inkling Books.

Blackburn, Robin. 1988. *The Overthrow of Colonial Slavery 1776–1848*. London and New York: Verso.

Buck-Morss, Susan. 2000. Hegel and Haiti. In *Critical Inquiry* 26, no.4 (Summer): 821–65.

Dayan, Joan. 1998. *Haiti, History, and the Gods*: 1995. Berkley, Los Angeles, London: University of California Press.

Eze, Emmanuel Chukwudi, ed. 1997. *Race and the Enlightenment: A Reader*. Cambridge, USA, Oxford, UK: Blackwell Publishers Ltd.

Fischer, Sibylle. 2004. *Modernity Disavowed: Haiti and the Cultures of Slavery in the Age of Revolution*. Jamaica, Barbados, Trinidad and Tobago: University of the West Indies Press.

Foner, Philip S. 1955. *The Life and Writings of Frederick Douglass: Reconstruction and After*. Vol. IV. New York: International Publishers.

Geggus, David Patrick. 2002. *Haitian Revolution Studies*. Bloomington and Indianapolis: Indiana University Press.

Genovese, Eugene. 1979. *From Rebellion to Revolution: Afro-American Slave Revolts in the Making of the Modern World*. Baton Rouge and London: Louisiana State University Press.

*The Haitian Declaration of Independence, 1804*. https://today.duke.edu/showcase/haitideclaration/declarationstext.html. Accessed August 17, 2012.

Hutton, Clinton. 2005. *The Logic and Historical Significance of the Haitian Revolution and the Cosmological Roots of Haitian Freedom*. Kingston: Arawak Publications.

———. 2007. The Historic Values of the Haitian Revolution and the Making of the Modern World. *The Jamaican Historical Review*. XXIII: 36–61 and 69–81.

———. 2011. The Haitian Revolution and the Articulation of a Modernist Epistemology. *Critical Arts: South-North Cultural and Media Studies* 25, no. 4 (December): 529–54.

James, C.L.R. 1938. 1989. *The Black Jacobins: Toussaint L'Ouverture and the San Domingo Revolution*. 2ed. New York and Toronto: Vintage Book.

Jenson, Deborah. 2010. Hegel and Dessalines: Philosophy and the African Diaspora. *New West Indian Guide* 84, no. 3–4:269–75.

Nesbitt, Nick. 2008. *Universal Emancipation: The Haitian Revolution and the Radical Enlightenment*. Charlottesville and London: University of Virginia Press.

Trouillot, Michel-Rolth. 1995. *Silencing the Past: Power and the Production of History*. Boston: Beacon Press.

Vastey, Baron de. 1969. *An Essay on the Causes of the Revolution and Civil Wars of Hayti*... 1823. Tr. from French by W.H. M.B. New York: Negro Universities Press.

Williams, Eric. 1964, reissued 1994. *British Historians and the West Indies*. New York: A&B Books Publishers.

# 11 | *The Sett Girls and the Pedagogy of the Streets:*
*An Aural Black Counterpublic**

Linda Sturtz

Christmas was coming to pre-emancipation Jamaica.[1] New merchandise, perhaps only slightly sea-weary, appeared on quaysides again now that ships could reach the island after the end of the long hurricane season; fowls were being fattened and cloth was measured out for the annual allocation of work clothing to the enslaved people. Enslaved people marshalled their savings, often accumulated from a year's sales of foodstuffs in the Sunday Markets, to purchase luxury goods.[2] Amidst these preparations for merriment, planters and local officials worried about unruly crowds of enslaved and free revellers while local militias prepared armed men to police Kingston and towns in 'country'. To prepare for potential unrest and intimidate possible rebels, white men were called up for patrol duty during the holiday period, allowing the white population to believe that armed forces could protect them from the power of freedom-seeking revellers. Militia service for white men, like special foods and the distribution of 'gifts', characterised the island's festivities and were so taken for granted by residents that militia service featured in the published fiction of the period.[3]

Amidst the festive disarray the world was not so much 'turned upside down' (at least from enslaved peoples' perspective) but flipped right-side up. But the planters, who constituted the minority of the population, feared disorder. The threats were palpable but de-centred. During the holidays, enslaved people and free blacks would move into the streets and public places in organised groups. Queens and their bands of Sett Girls – groups of women and girls who paraded at Christmas – would commandeer the thoroughfares and with the better-known John Canoe bands, they ruled the soundscapes of the island. In this, they occupied a counterpublic that displayed a de facto Caribbean Pan Africanism that established the background against which formal intellectual and political movements, like those of Marcus Garvey, emerged in subsequent generations.[4]

How do we interpret these events? Were festivities merely examples of the total dominance of the enslavers that extended even to the recreational activities of the enslaved? Were they simply safety valves for the enslaved people's outrage that, if not channelled, would erupt into more overt rebellion? Or, alternatively, could the festivities be understood as 'strategies' by which oppressed people responded to the 'tactics' of the enslavers to dominate the lives of the enslaved? Scholars studying systems of domination more generally and power dynamics in early modern slavery have provided ways of thinking about the competing efforts to control the slaves' autonomy and self-expression.

Scholars, including Michel de Certeau, James C. Scott, and Jean Baudrillard, working outside the Caribbean have outlined approaches to analysing covert struggles that are central to understanding how people crafted meaningful lives in the midst of oppression. Michel de Certeau outlines how to understand the 'tactics' by which oppressed people resisted the 'strategies' of the oppressors by creating spaces of autonomy and by re-fashioning the goods and ideas of the oppressors to serve their own needs and convey their own messages. In this framework, the Sett Girls' appropriation of public streets and private spaces ordinarily in the control of the planters and their representatives demonstrates the performers' tactics in the face of whites' efforts to use their own strategies to control the island.[5] Along the same lines, James C. Scott stresses how, within systems of domination, the oppressed seek social 'weapons' or 'hidden transcripts' that allow them to resist those systems.

> Every subordinate group creates, out of its ordeal, a 'hidden transcript' that represents a critique of power spoken behind the back of the dominant. The powerful, for their part, also develop a hidden transcript representing the practices and claims of their rule that cannot be openly avowed. A comparison of the hidden transcript of the weak with that of the powerful and of both hidden transcripts to the public transcript of power relations offers a substantially new way of understanding resistance to domination.[6]

Scott points out that hidden transcripts are, in fact, typically expressed openly, though in disguised forms, and that the 'rumors, gossip, folktales, songs, gestures, jokes and theater of the powerless' are vehicles for 'insinuate[ing] a critique of power while hiding behind anonymity or behind innocuous understandings of their conduct.' These forms of insubordination are what Scott refers to as the 'infrapolitics of the powerless.' The Sett Girls' holiday processions provide an example of such a covert critique of the power of the planters. In a similar vein, another scholar, Jean Baudrillard stresses the ways that covert and seemingly mundane, everyday acts like cooking constitute practicing the 'revolutionary micrology of the quotidian.' These become a means of resisting established authority 'just as a single ironic smile effaced a whole discourse, just as a single flash of denial in a slave effaced all the power and pleasure of the master. The more hegemonic the system, the more the imagination is struck by the smallest of its reversals.'[7] The Sett-Girls' ironic smiles flashed throughout their festive processions and resounded in sonic equivalents.

Scholars have delved into more nuanced studies of the particular ways that power relations and reconfiguration of them operated in plantation societies in the Americas.[8] More recently, historians have delved into the ways the repertoire of resistance to slavery included not only violence but also assertions of self and community in holiday celebrations and artistic creativity. Stephanie Camp has outlined the ways that enslaved women in the antebellum US used control of space, time, and objects to experience their bodies as 'an important site not only of suffering but also (and therefore) of resistance, enjoyment, and potentially, transcendence.' Illicit dances held well beyond the space of the holidays sponsored by the enslavers provided a space for this enjoyment.[9] Saidiya V. Hartman offers a contrasting view, which stresses the power of the enslavers in the US over the expressive cultures and recreations of the enslaved.[10]

Scholars of the Caribbean, including Clinton Hutton and Carolyn Cooper, have focused on the ways that expressive cultures foster public agency in Jamaica.[11] In this manner, the Sett Girls used the tactics of their performance to contest the Jamaican elites' negative depiction of themselves as women. According to a 1796 account, the Christmas season in Jamaica was ushered in by processions of Sett Girls who 'greet us with their mating song, as a preparative to days of delight and dissipation' and prepared the island's residents for a time when 'a kind of Roman *equality* [prevailed] between the slave and the master that must not be invaded. The Sett Girls processed through the city in a quasi-military manner, with ranks of jewellry, of silks, of fine linen, parading our streets.' The Setts entered city homes with 'licentious liberty', accompanied by 'violins, thrum-thrums, tamborines [sic] &c. &c.'[12] Although the boundary between master and slave may have been broken down, hierarchies within the processions were observed strictly. Performers could use their songs and dances as ways to convey subversive messages through the superficially harmless songs they chanted in the street. As such, the performances conveyed 'hidden transcripts' about their understandings of their own roles in society and their thoughts about enslavers.[13]

In urban areas, women could process with the accompaniment of several fiddles, a tabor, and pipe while other troupes retained more traditional instruments such as the horse's teeth, goombays, and other types of drums. In Kingston, a fashionably dressed Sett with their band of European instrumental musicians, 'familiarly' entered the homes of their audiences, danced for a half an hour, and were treated to cake and wine. One anonymous author was astonished at the cost of the 'cloathes and ornaments' worn by the Setts. This 1797 observer believed the competition over who was the finest dressed among Kingston's Sett Girls led to dangerous 'excess', with the 'slaves of one party assaulting and ill-treating those of the others'.[14] Bands of women and girls who paraded at Christmas prepared outfits that matched those of other members of their groups. For the most prosperous and organised Sett Girls groups, this could include new dresses made of freshly imported fabrics sewn in a common style, as is apparent in Belisario's print of the 'Red Set Girls'. For rural and more frugal groups, the bands might limit their decorations to a ribbon of the same colour. In either setting, members of the Setts created alliances among band members while simultaneously demonstrating to audiences of outsiders that the group shared a common bond. Within hierarchical organisations of their own making Sett Girls groups hired musicians, composed songs, and devised costumes.[15] The complexity of the groups varied across time and by circumstances, but what they shared was the creation of collaborative and often ranked organisational structures under the direction of the women and girls themselves.

The two best-known sources documenting the Sett Girls in the period in which they flourished are those by Matthew 'Monk' Lewis and Isaac Mendes Belisario, and both of these present images of the Sett Girls that supported the status quo power that existed in Jamaica when they were produced. In the first, Monk Lewis recorded his introduction to the Christmas bands in *Journal of a West Indian Proprietor* and in the second, artist Isaac Mendes Belisario depicted Setts in his images of island life that later circulated as water-coloured engravings. These two texts have become the canonical portrayals of the Sett girls in the pre-emancipation and early apprenticeship periods.[16] Both emphasise the ways that the performers enjoyed the costumes, dances, and public performances that occurred during the festive season between Christmas and New Year's Day. For Lewis, at least, the message was that the form of bondage prevalent in the British West Indies was benevolent, and he concluded that William Wilberforce would have needed to revise his views on abolition if he had seen the joyous Sett Girls and their male counterparts, the John Canoes, performing in Jamaica. Reprints of the Sett Girls images from Belisario's portfolio still frequently adorn the walls of respectable public places in Jamaica, indicating their on-going appeal. At a musical comedy staged for a 'family' audience at the University of the West Indies – Mona in January 2014, the young characters in the play, set in the present, planned a masquerade on the John Canoe model in which the women proclaimed they wanted to be Sett Girls in their drama. These pretty-pretty, sanitised Sett Girls appear wholesomely attractive and posed no more threat to viewers in 2014 than they did to Monk Lewis.[17]

Elsewhere, I have traced the foundations of the Sett Girls groups in the Pan Africanist festivities of the island-born generations in the late eighteenth century, whose young people began moving from the ethnically specific celebrations of their parents and grandparents' generations and also contrasted their performances with the dances and music of newly enslaved Africans who continued to arrive on the island.[18] Here, I want to focus on how the Sett Girls' bands functioned as an aural black counterpublic. In effect, the Sett Girls and their contemporaries among the island-born, second and third generation of African Jamaicans, created a trickle-up, de facto Pan Africanism.

The importance of the 'public sphere' for understanding the political developments of the late eighteenth century has been debated among scholars who draw on the work of Jürgen Habermas. In these discussions, the significance of the public sphere and especially the growing print culture features prominently. Increasingly, however, scholars have pointed out the importance of 'counterpublics' as spaces where disfranchised persons establish their own identities in the midst of silencing and oppression. These scholars of counterpublics criticise the narrower view of the 'public sphere as a "parade of legitimations" that "affirm the illusory" identification of middle-class economic interests with the general social interests.' Instead, counterpublics allow disfranchised persons to 'reclaim a measure of subjectivity despite being positioned as the instruments, objects, or properties of the middle class.' As such, the counterpublic allows a 'social and discursive challenge to the power of the White male property owners who make up civil society'.[19]

The significance of music in transmitting information was abundantly evident in 1791. In the midst of white fear in Jamaica that unrest in St Domingue would lead to local insurrection, one observer noted that enslaved people in Jamaica had been 'very inquisitive' to find out about any news from the nearby island and that in order to pass along that information to wider audiences of equally eager auditors, 'they have composed songs of the Negroes having made a rebellion at Hispaniola, with their usual chorus to it.'[20] By setting lyrics to music, singers could repeat information in an easy-to-remember format for oral broadcast of news from estate to estate. In this case, the 'counterpublic' provided the means of conveying information without resorting to print, or even written information. In this manner, lyrics like the Sett Girls songs, composed each year by the participants, provided a means to offer a commentary on recent events and spread that information to members of the community and to audiences beyond the local groups. The soundscapes of the streets of Jamaica became a means of circulating information and teaching audiences about the values of the performers, values that contrasted with those imposed by the planter elite.

The Sett Girls provide insights into what some scholars have referred to as a 'Black counterpublic' at work on the island – not the sole black counterpublic, but certainly a significant public self-expression. Several projects have sought to recover the 'texts and testimonies' of the enslaved and free black populations of the West Indies while acknowledging the phenomenal difficulties of finding voices in traditional print sources. Simultaneously, efforts to discover a black counterpublic, most notably in the early National Period in the US, have focused on the print culture created by African American organisations such as Prince Hall Freemasonry in northern cities in the

US shortly after the Revolutionary War. While the words of free and enslaved people of colour rarely make it into print, never mind public discourse, in the West Indies during slavery, apprenticeship, and early full-free periods, the Sett Girls in particular and the power of music in general, do provide an opportunity to consider how women chose to represent themselves.[21]

In Jamaica, non-print 'publications,' including the Sett Girls' parades, allowed for the formation of black counterpublics during the late eighteenth century and early nineteenth centuries. In their processions and preparatory rehearsals, black and coloured women created a ritual for public self-presentation that portrayed themselves as actors in command of public spaces and in charge of the soundscapes of the island. White audiences were mesmerised by the festivities, simultaneously attracted to and terrified by the processions.

In the late eighteenth and early nineteenth-century contexts, authorities attempted to contain the temporary occupation of the streets even as they conceded control of spaces and soundscapes during the holiday period. In an 1823 account of the procession of a set, ongoing noise overwhelmed the house:

> Of course, it was impossible to attempt either conversation or sleep, whilst this racket continued, and we had to sit in dull melancholy contemplation of this saturnalian festival, which had neither moderate cheerfulness or innocent frolic to render it interesting, where all was beastly drunkenness and brutal noise.

The sound itself served as a type of aggression in spaces usually under the dominion of the planters. Through noise, according to one account, the revellers controlled households even as they refused to perform their usual tasks. One guest reported that:

> The lady of the house apologised for being compelled to give us a cold dinner, and to make us wait upon ourselves. As she said it was impossible to interrupt the enjoyment of the negroes, by exacting any attendance from them at such a season.[22]

The full significance of how the Sett Girls' parades allowed the participants to assert their own temporary autonomy and aesthetics along with their choices of how to structure their celebrations became apparent during the Apprenticeship period (1834–38) and afterward. No longer willing to serve simply as hands to work in fields, rural sugar workers cemented their solidarity with each other and with townspeople while demonstrating their independent wills when they struck work to go to town to enjoy the Sett Girls' processions. The collective strength of the Sett Girls' bands appealed to audiences of African Jamaicans, men as well as women, who could revel in the message of autonomous control of the streets the Sett symbolised.

In his letter to Lord Seaford in 1839 on the conditions of Seaford's Jamaica estates and the potential for profits there, Thomas M'Neel, who managed those plantations, reported on his negotiations with the workers over their schedules and pay. M'Neel seethed that they had already decided they preferred to devote Fridays and Saturdays to cultivating their own provision grounds rather than earning extra income by working longer hours on the estates. In addition, they demanded to be paid by the day, not by the task. Then on December 19, they decided to quit work entirely. M'Neel fumed 'I do not know what came over the whole of the people on the Montpelier's, they 'struck work' and refused to proceed again on any terms until after the holidays.' M'Neel hired additional hands but finding a workforce at this critical period in the crop cycle proved daunting because most people preferred to celebrate the holidays instead, 'the greater part feasting, and going about from place to place'. M'Neel heard rumours that many had travelled to Montego Bay to 'see some great turn-out of the reds and blues' – the two local Setts.[23] The Montego Bay Sett Girls were famous enough to lure rural estate workers who travelled to Montego Bay to see the 'great turn-out' of the city's competing Setts of Reds and Blues. They were so renowned that even Mr M'Neel understood their magnetic appeal. With workers' decisions about how to allocate their time and labour in new ways, formerly lush cane fields had become fallow grass lands while cane and coffee crops were left unharvested by 1839. Obviously, the Sett Girls – even the spectacularly attractive Montego Bay bands – and their audiences were not solely responsible for this turn of events, but their processions represented the desire of African Jamaicans to establish their own hierarchies of time management and self-representation.

Sometimes the groups composed tunes and lyrics for their bands and although M'Neel left no record of the lyrics to the Montego Bay Sett Girls' songs, other writers did. More than 35 years earlier, Maria Nugent reported on the sets she heard during her tour of the northern part of the island. After watching a review of the local militia with her husband, Jamaica's Royal Governor at the time, Mrs Nugent reported 'Immediately, sets of singing women sent me word of their approach. They danced, and sung several songs; some made in honour of General N. and some of me, till we were heartily tired of them.'[24] Composing occasional pieces, either to honour an individual or an event, and repeating tunes and lyrics that jarred audiences initially charmed by the songs\ were characteristics commonly reported by white audiences. In celebrating the Governor and his wife in their songs, these 'sets of singing women' honoured the Nugents, claiming an affectionate link and elevated public status through their expressed loyalty but also establishing an aesthetic of their own that framed the Nugents' status in the eyes of the performers within the musical tastes of the performers, an aesthetic at odds with that of their Anglo-Jamaican audience's own customs. The Nugents could reject the songs and dances prepared in their honour or adapt to the tastes of the performers and thereby accept the tribute paid to them. That musical tribute, however, would be paid in the performers' own terms.[25]

Later Governors found themselves overtly mocked and mimicked in parades by the Setts. During the Earl of Mulgrave's administration (1832–33), Isaac M. Belisario recounted descriptions of the processions in Falmouth that mocked the controversial governor and 'several other distinguished characters' who were impersonated 'by negroes in full costume, as closely imitating their models in this respect as possible'. Belisario and his Falmouth informer claimed the depiction of the officials failed because the performers 'had lost sight of one grand requisite to comple[te] the resemblance, viz. – ease of manner, and consequently, their deportment being strangely at variance with that of their originals, rendered such mimic actions truly amusing.' Another way of interpreting the portrayals, however, would be to see the performers transforming the mannerisms of the officials deliberately, as part of an intentional effort to create a caricature of those in authority. Mulgrave served as governor during a tense period in which he found himself at odds with the island assembly who resisted metropolitan efforts to craft a plan for emancipation of the enslaved.[26] An observer on St Kitts and Nevis, in the eastern Caribbean, understood the significance of ridiculing the manner of the whites in the holiday celebrations on that island: 'their little funds are spent in harmless amusements – in adorning their persons, and giving Christmas and other holiday entertainments, in which it is their delight to mimic the manners of the Whites.' Although this correspondent believed the mockery was 'harmless', he clearly did understand that the performers intentionally ridiculed the habits of those who enslaved them and that perfect imitation would have undermined that function.[27] In this way, the humour of carnivalesque moments, when normally subordinate persons became empowered to mock their oppressors, inverted the hierarchy of non-carnival 'ordinary time' when enslavers persistently and publicly ridiculed the customs, manners, and appearance of the enslaved.[28]

The words to the songs were only rarely transcribed by reporters, but a few authors who had observed Sett Girls performances wrote about the lyrics the Setts composed, allowing us to hear how the performers' songs provided them with a means of singing thinly-veiled subversive public comments about a world that usually demanded deference or silence from them. In a lightly fictionalised account published in an 1823 newspaper, the reporter described the first Christmas back in Jamaica experienced by a creole girl after her return from her education in England. During the 'Saturnalia', as he called the event, the women sang lyrics that reflected African Caribbean women's admiration for the fashion of that year, in that instance the 'dandy' figure who was incorporated into the praise song. The song was lined out initially by 'The ma'am, as she is called, or head lady of the party', who 'sung the burden of the song, consisting of one couplet or stanza, and then all joined in the hideous chorus, interspersed with shouts and screams, capering and jumping. The song of the year, always of their composition, is framed on the last fashionable idea or word they pick up, which, on this occasion, happened to be *Dandy*.' The lyrics for that year's song were as follows:

> Happy year to Massa, Misses,
> Happy year to sweet young Misses;
>     Walk in go shew the Dandy.
> Happy year to Massa stranger;[29]
> Happy year to al the family;
>     Walk in go shew the Dandy.
>
>     CHORUS
> Walk in go shew the Dandy,
> Walk in go shew the Dandy;

Happy year to all good negers,
Walk in go shew the Dandy.'

Although these lyrics appear deferential on the surface, other elements of the performance indicate the subtexts the singers wished to communicate, and the gestures that accompanied the lyrics and confrontational acts that made up the performance reveal a more complex context for this seemingly obsequious song. The white author dismissed the skill of the dancers suggesting they failed to live up to the aesthetics of European-Jamaican dance.

> The chorus and dance were accompanied by so many frightful grimaces and ridiculous antics, that I could not help thinking the creatures before me, bore a stronger resemblance to apes and ouran-outangs, than to rational beings...They went on with this overpowering riot for about half an hour incessantly, when they paused...and seeing two decanters of Madeira from the sideboard, emptied them to the health of their massa and misses; they then brought in a bottle of new rum, strongly impregnated with aniseed, their favourite liquor, and nearly stifled the young mistress, forcing her to swallow some in pledging their health and happiness.

The context for the song consisted of 'an overpowering riot' that included aggressive movements, seizing elegant decanters of wine and spirits usually off limits to the slaves, and consuming the forbidden beverages in full view of their master and mistress. Their final gesture, veiled as tribute, occurred when they forced the terrified creole daughter of the family to swallow the harsh aniseed-flavoured liquor they favoured but repelled a proper lady accustomed to sipping more refined beverages. By reading against the grain of the author's mocking commentary that insults the performers, we can hear and see the singers' own hidden message embedded in their song and dance and we can see that the performance, seen in totality, established that the words the party sang mocked the family and the belligerent tone was apparent in the movements. Even the writer admitted that the 'toasts' to the daughter were a 'caricature', with wishes that 'she might live hundreds of years, have a rich fine gentleman for a husband and plenty of negers, fine dresses, and other fine things' concluding with a final toast in which the female leader 'uttered a rhapsody of prophane nonsense and cant, quite shocking to Christian ears.'

In this not-so-hidden transcript, the enslaved seized temporary authority from the masters and through their collective revelry they celebrated the aesthetics of people whose rhapsody appeared nonsense to outsiders. Buried in the subtext of this author's account the 'dandy' celebrated an alternative splendour to that of the white audience and advanced an artistic agency of the community's own making. The women of the Sett and their followers indeed, 'walked in', uninvited, to spaces normally off limits to them and engaged in behaviour that displayed their own taste, their own representation of a powerfully subversive fashionability represented in the figure of 'the dandy'. The Setts' parade of style went beyond mere ephemeral forms of beauty suggested in European-defined 'fashion' and claimed an aesthetics of their own making that assaulted the eyes of the whites. The performers only agreed to leave after receiving a Christmas gift from each targeted member of the audience. As this incident indicates, the songs the enslaved composed could celebrate the joys of stylish life as well as the more profound interests of political life – like revolution in St Domingue. Even public celebration of the seemingly trivial aspects of community joy – like merriment focused on the dandy – confirmed the celebrants' own style, norms, and fashions.[30] Women whose appearances were mocked as resembling 'ourang-outangs' (an image also invoked in Edward Long's 1772 *History of Jamaica*) were wondrously altered when they became Sett Girls in their holiday finery. The 'ma'ams' of the Sets became the Fairy Godmothers who transformed members of their bands into Cinderellas for the holidays. There would be no rescue for the dancers once the midnight hour chimed, though, and they were expected to return to work for another year.

The extent to which the Sets controlled public spaces is also apparent in the story of the Dandy song. The effect of this song's performance was to terrify the audience, especially the young creole woman who had recently returned from England. The anonymous author of the newspaper article lightly mocked the creole miss in the audience who fled to her room and bolted the door to escape the dancers, refusing to emerge until her father demanded that she come out to give the dancers their Christmas 'gift'. Intimidating the audience seemingly constituted part of this group's agenda, and the white patriarch demanded a suitable performance of noblesse oblige from his daughter who had forgotten the script for interaction between enslaved and enslaver during her time abroad.[31]

Under the guise of festive joy, noisy aggression reminded the enslavers of the delicate balance of power among the residents of the estates. In this instance, the appeal of the au courant 'dandy', advancing his virtues in an aggressive context of the holiday season and demanding 'gifts' before leaving the audience in peace, established an alternate aesthetic hierarchy to the one that predominated on days when the exuberantly clad Sett Girls returned to their serviceable workday oznabrug outfits. The 'little revolutions' of the holidays, performed on verandahs of great houses and based on aesthetics determined by the performers themselves, offered normally disempowered persons a sense of pride in their own creativity and provided them with the stages and soundscapes in which to communicate that sense of self.[32] The raucously public display of collective self-confidence and the concerted assertion of a distinctive aesthetic sensibility by the population normally disdained by whites as demonstrating a gaudy, unrefined, and inferior taste nevertheless appealed both to enslavers and to a labour force released from the quotidian 'downpression' that characterised the other 51 weeks of the year.[33] Were these celebrations a form of resistance, a means for enslaved and newly emancipated people to assert their own selfhood and to claim public spaces as their own? Or do they make sense only as the product of the elite establishment who sometimes provided willing or unwilling support for the events? How do we make sense of a practice embedded in the structures of power that held the performers in submission?[34]

Music allows us to move beyond those silences and grasp the values of peoples whose words are otherwise lost to printed archives.[35] Reports on the Sett Girls' activities, even when written by a hostile or dismissive narrator, provide a means for careful readers to tease out the meanings embedded in the songs and the solidarity produced by community-building groups who organised the holiday processions. Following Maureen Warner-Lewis's example, this essay explores some of the ways that we can understand the tactics of the Sett Girls, especially the ways they used sound to wrest temporary control of landscapes and to convey to their audiences their own beliefs within the strategies of oppression imposed by the planters. The essay also discusses one set of reported lyrics that appeared in an account of a holiday celebration. Through their processions, the Sett Girls conveyed the power of their unified groups and the organisational integrity of their bands, communicated their respect for the wisdom and power of older women in their midst, and flaunted their own aesthetic sensibilities. Thus, they offered a 'pedagogy of the streets,' reaching not only the white audiences whose written reports foregrounded their own presence in the events, but also the black spectators who embraced the Sett Girls' positive images of black and brown womanhood.

Furthermore, planters believed that labourers would work harder during the rest of the year if they were permitted some recreation. Individual planters wanted to control the musical landscapes of their estates, often claiming an interest in the workers' health and availability for the next day's labour, but conversely, they wanted to permit some music to sustain the spirits of the slaves and to improve atmosphere on the estates. While overseers in the ameliorationist period could be expected to address this issue, plantation manuals from earlier decades had also pointed out the significance of music to the successful operation of an estate. Plantation management manuals provided directions to overseers about how to organise holidays on the estates to achieve higher levels of productivity and to prevent the outbreak of rebellion.

In one of the most bizarre instruction books for new planters, James Grainger, in *The Sugar-Cane*, presented his lessons to newcomers in verse. He advised masters to encourage cultivators to permit singing and dancing on the slaves' holidays and in the evenings.

> On festal days; or when their work is done;
> Permit thy slaves to lead the choral dance,
> to the wild banshaw's melancholy sound.[36]

Grainger, like Sir Hans Sloane before him, recognised the distinctive nature of slaves' own celebrations, confirming they would organise their dances to the sound of the 'wild banshaw', comfortingly familiar to the slaves but 'melancholy' to the European's ear.[37] The actual dance the enslaved people enjoy comes across as a reverie but is interrupted by the fearful voice of the enslaver who cautions that limits must be imposed on the celebrations – notably that drumming and alcoholic beverages be prohibited – because of the danger that might develop from the inclusion of these.

But let not thou the drum their mirth inspire;
Nor vinous spirits: else, to madness fir'd,
(What will not bacchanalian frenzy dare?)
Fell acts of blood, and vengeance they pursue.

Drumming, along with drinking alcohol, might inspire them to 'vengeance' presumably against the masters.[38] John Dovaston, who also wrote an instruction manual for new planters with an eye toward publication, insisted that in the long run, granting holidays would make slaves better workers so effective planters should 'provide a Violin or Banshaw for one of your most skilfull Slaves to lead them to the Dance'. Doing so would make the slaves more docile labourers, Dovaston claimed. 'These small concessions would provide cheer to the workers' and 'give their Labour and Slavery a greater appearance of Freedom, and make their burden seem lighter, and they will with ease and Willingness go out to their labour, and pursue the same without the Means of the Whip.' But planters should also limit their workforce's holiday 'mirth' and restrain them from over-indulging in 'Wanton Gamboles' because violence that threatened the larger public peace could erupt during these celebrations. He was especially worried about people who left the estates for the towns to dance in John Canoe processions:

> in Towns they [Negroes]sho:d be restrained drumming and dancing of the Johnny Cooney, and no Liquors or Moneys to purchase it be given them by the Inhabitants which wo:d prevent their Intoxication & danger of riots.[39]

Into the 1820s, whites believed that Christmas revelry was both dangerous to public order and, conversely, necessary for urban masters who wished to sustain the productivity of their workers by placating individuals in the workforce. As a result, these urban masters were resigned to giving the performers even longer periods of holiday. Observing Sett Girls' processions in 1829, missionary Waddell Hope, who was no friend of slavery, described how:

> In the towns, two parties or 'Sets' of girls, called from their dresses 'reds and blues,' paraded the streets in rivalry, followed by crowds of both sexes and all ages. The young women who led, gaily dressed, sang sweet airs to improvised words; their followers swelling the chorus...The three days became a week among the town slaves, who

made a Saturnalia of a Christian festival, spending the time in the grossest rioting. The result of so much license or licentiousness, it was hoped, would be great good humour, to prepare the slaves for another year of ill-requited toil.[40]

Managing enslaved peoples' collective recreation was a delicate balancing act for a planter who wanted to operate a profitable estate or an urban master who wanted to maintain control of his workforce. Subverted desires would foster malaise while frenzied celebrations, especially those fuelled by drumming and alcohol consumption, stirred up concerted rebellion.

Newly arrived planters read instruction manuals alerting them to the problematic nature of raucous celebrations organised by enslaved people and learned that their traditional festivities must be both permitted and controlled if estate owners wanted their properties to become prosperous sugar producers. White fears of black control of landscapes and soundscapes were apparent in their calling out the militia for guard duty in the period between Christmas and New Year's Day. An 1831 report described the custom of militia control of the holidays:

> As there is so much indulgence granted to the Negro population at Christmas, in holidays, allowances of provision, liquor, &c. it is natural to suppose, various excesses will be committed; and it has, therefore, been the invariable custom for the militia regiments to assemble a few days previous thereto, when the commanding officer fixes the point, of renedezvous expected to be found, in case of need; and on some occasion, it has been the practice to appoint a regular guard for duty, during the continuance of this always somewhat lawless season.[41]

Thus, white officials acknowledged the radical potential embedded in this temporary appropriation of geographic and sonic spaces. No matter how hard the pro-slavery interests attempted to co-opt the celebrations to represent their own status or to invoke holiday celebrations as evidence of contentment, planter fear of the underlying danger implicit in music and public performance surfaced at moments of crisis.[42]

In the 1820s, a white newcomer reported on his startling introduction to island life at Christmas, when he realised with dismay that once martial law was declared he would be expected to parade along with the island residents even though he thought 'all of them [the enslaved people] I have as yet seen, seem harmless creatures.'[43] William Beckford, an estate owner who defended planter society, lamented the decline of Christmas celebrations in England and was even more appalled at the situation in Jamaica where 'this festival is hardly kept'; nevertheless he believed that planters by necessity moderated their own merriment in order to police the activities of slaves during the holiday season.

> You observe, indeed, the White people riding from one plantation to another, and returning perhaps overcharged with liquor at night, when it is doubly incumbent upon them, at such a season of riot and inebriety [Christmas], to keep themselves sober, and to preserve a proper authority upon the plantation.[44]

Beckford took for granted that with the workers' own celebrations likely to explode into disorder or riot, the white population would need to avoid overindulgence themselves.

By the 1830s, the threats posed by the holidays had become more palpable, and one officer of a royal naval ship that had been called in to police the island both noted the charm and levity of urban Jamaica at the holidays and the danger that lay just beneath the surface. He marvelled at the Kingston market, loaded with 'fruits of the most exquisite taste' and noted with delight the arrival of the 'gentle fair within several miles of the vicinity, [who] added to the elegance of the market by their presence, and courtesy to the black peasantry.' In the midst of the festive marketplace 'sets of dancing girls possessed the streets, in the enjoyment of that degree of hilarity almost peculiar to the blacks, in whatever part of the globe they may be existing.' Even in the midst of this glee, he expressed anxiety: 'Notwithstanding these demonstrations of apparent quietude and satisfaction on the part of the slaves, the experienced colonist could observe some circumstances which excited suspicion as to the reality of that contentment, of which their sportive amusements above-mentioned are indicative.'[45] When rumors circulated that a rebellion might occur and that the docks at Portland were 'menaced' by local 'negroes,' his vessel was ordered to Port Antonio on Christmas morning. Upon arriving there, the sailors discovered that the edgy white residents of Portland had already placed the local militia under arms in anticipation of a New Year's Day insurrection. The reason why the unnamed Navy vessel was available on the island at such short notice was that:

By a standing order of the Colonial Government, and as a measure of precaution, a man-of-war is despatched a few weeks prior to Christmas, to the different ports of the island, for the purpose of depositing at the several military posts and forts a supply of ball and pistol cartridges; and during the holidays, a company of the militia is called out for the preservation of order, and to overawe the numerous and unbridled assemblage of the blacks. The – [unnamed ship]had fortunately been employed on the service during the latter part of the month of November, and the early part of December, and it was on her return from the execution of this service that she was lying in Port Royal harbour, and so suddenly ordered to Port Antonio on Christmas morning.

To ensure that any potential rebels in Portland fully recognised the presence of the armed forces, the ship's commander exercised the entire company twice a week and a smaller division every day in view of the townspeople. He reinforced his message about the military presence to Portland residents who lived well outside of town by ordering his crew to shoot off blank cartridges every afternoon and arranging for every gun on his ship to fire three rounds a day so that 'their reverberation amongst the hills and mountains caused the report of our artillery to be heard at the distant estates, a circumstance' he claimed 'which very materially contributed to the suppression of the rebellion.' Faced with this overwhelming firepower, the potential rebels held off their uprising, waiting for the ship's departure to improve their chances of success. Instead, the militia took advantage of the delay to apprehend those they believed to be the leaders on the rebellious estates. Elsewhere on the island, treaty-bound Maroons allied with the British forces secured the rebels who had hidden in canefields and turned them over to the white authorities while regular troops and militia forces pacified 'turbulent districts' on New Year's Day of 1832.[46] Although the power of the Christmas celebrations remained hidden prior to emancipation, the full radical potential became apparent in the 1840s.[47] Attempts by officials to shut down the John Canoe processions in 1840/1841 resulted in violent riots.[48] Beneath the surface of the celebrations that had amused planter, merchant, and labourer alike was a threat embodied in a public presentation of traditions. Furthermore, many of the Anglo-Jamaican audience members for the pre-emancipation events may have had little awareness of the multiple messages conveyed in them. In his brilliant analysis of the religious dimension of John Canoe Celebrations, Kenneth Bilby points out that performers 'in the "public" world, including the spaces most clearly dominated by Europeans' could 'embody the spirits at the same time that they concealed them from unknowledgeable onlookers; the two kinds of "masking" could conceivably occur simultaneously.'[49] As Mary Turner pointed out, African Jamaicans visited graves of their deceased friends and relatives at Christmas following on the feasts held at the funeral and on the ninth and fortieth days after burial. Christmas could have different meanings for each group of celebrants.[50] Like the 'hidden transcripts' James C. Scott described, the Jamaican Christmas celebrations could convey multiple messages to various audiences, deliberately concealing some of their most confrontational elements until a moment like the 1840 riots, when power structures were being reconfigured in the aftermath of emancipation.[51]

The counterpublic in modern Jamaica still includes non-print sources, as Rivke Jaffe's insightful work on graffiti in early twenty-first century Jamaica demonstrates. According to Jaffe, graffiti allows painters 'to voice their opinions in the broadest way possible and re-write the city in doing so.' Jaffe cites Henri Lefebvre, who discusses the 'struggles over cultural meaning and the social production of space' distinguishing between official space as designated by state planners and maps and 'a more informal perceived space – the everyday spatial practices of popular life – and the lived space of artistic and imaginary representations, the location of more transformational or subversive practices.'[52] Jaffe points out how 'states implement spatial schemes to rule over their subjects', but equally how citizens resist those 'strategies' through spatial 'tactics' in their everyday uses of spaces. By these means, 'citizens can reinforce, contest, or subvert the dominant power structure.'[53]

Through their processions, the Sett Girls asserted their claims within 'the safety of collectivity' to control public spaces and to define themselves, as women, in the very public spaces where they often faced attempts by white women and men to demean them, to define them in more limiting and limited ways.[54] In the aftermath of emancipation, the full importance of the processions became apparent when Kingston Mayor Hector Mitchel attempted to ban the parades in 1840.[55] Celebrants refused to acquiesce to this authority and riots broke out. For a variety of reasons, the Sett Girls declined as a public phenomenon.⁵⁶ Further research is required to discover what the remnants of the groups remained and how their traditions persisted. Olive Lewin's study on early Brukins, the celebrations that commemorated Emancipation, suggests that similar colour-coded groups of female dancers prevailed in that form.⁵⁷ More recently, scholars have suggested that Dance Hall queens functioned as successors. What is evident, however, is that the sonic landscape created a black counterpublic well before emancipation.

Sett Girls' performances demonstrated the continuing balancing act African Jamaican women performed in criticising, resisting, negotiating, and modifying the hierarchies they inhabited while also shaping their worlds.⁵⁸ In conclusion, while the words of free and enslaved people of colour rarely make it into print, never mind elite public discourse, in the West Indies during slavery, apprenticeship and early full-free periods, the Sett Girls provide an opportunity to consider how women chose to represent themselves and perform their collective identities. We need to listen carefully.

*Funding for the research and writing of this paper was provided by a National Endowment for the Humanities Grant at the John Carter Brown Library in 2012–13 and a Sanger Summer Fellows grant from Beloit College in 2014. I am grateful for the suggestions of Dereck Burdett, Amy Bushnell, Jack Greene, Ana Honatilla, Beatrice McKenzie, Debra Majeed, James Robertson, Frances L. Ramos, April Shelford, Holly Snyder, Lisa Voigt, Nicole Weber, Sandra Young and the staff at the John Carter Brown Library.*

## Notes

1. The process of emancipation in Jamaica, initiated by an 1833 act of the British Parliament, began in 1834 with a period of continued bound labor euphemistically called 'Apprenticeship'. 'Full Free' only came about on August 1, 1838 after Apprenticeship was deemed unsustainable.
2. Sir William Young, *The West-India Common-place Book: Compiled from Parliamentary and Official Documents; Shewing the Interest of Great Britain in its Sugar Colonies, &c* (London: Printed For Richard Phillips, 1807), 201.
3. Anonymous, *The Peregrinations of Jeremiah Grant, Esq; the West-Indian* (London: G. Burnet, 1763). Concern about unrest during Christmas waxed and waned in the 50 years prior to emancipation. Mary Turner points out that by 1823 the militia was no longer called up at Christmas. Tensions re-emerged, however, as English missionaries began arriving. Trigger-happy militia men in St Ann's Bay under the instigation of Rev. George Wilson Bridges precipitated violence at Christmas in 1826. Mary Turner, *Slaves and Missionaries* (Kingston:

University of the West Indies Press, 2000), 107, 119–120. In practice, planned war as well as spontaneous disorder occurred at holidays, when the authorities and their troops were preoccupied or inebriated. See Court in Antigua, St. Patrick's Day revolt in Montserrat and, more recently, Fidel Castro's guerrilla attack on the Moncada Barracks in Santiago on *Carnaval Santiaguero* on July 26, 1953, the Saint's Day Carnival for that location. David Barry Gaspar, *Bondmen and Rebels: A Study of Master-Slave Relations in Antigua* (Durham: Duke University Press, 1993), 248–51; Michael Craton, *Testing the Chains: Resistance to Slavery in the British West Indies* (Ithaca: Cornell University Press, 1982), 132; Michael Craton, 'Decoding Pitchy Patchy,' *Slavery and Abolition* 16 (1995): 14–44; Yvonne Daniel with Catherine Evleshin, *Caribbean and Atlantic Diaspora Dance: Igniting Citizenship* (Urbana: University of Illinois Press, 2011), 116.

4. Nicosia Shakes effectively outlines the links between art and mental emancipation in Garvey's thought and art in 'playmaking', and in performative arts in which 'speech, dress and bodily movements combine'. Shakes argues that '[i]n the Garvey Movement and in Garvey's thought artistry furthered the second emancipation: Firstly, it was pedagogical. That is, it was an educational, edifying tool aimed at creating a space for dialogue and expression about the form of this emancipation and the way it would be achieved. Secondly, it was propagandistic in its confrontation and subversion of the White supremacist thinking. Thirdly, it was contemplative and imaginative; it channeled the wishes and hopes of a future redemption of Africa and people of African descent.' Although the Sett Girls operated in far more localised settings, one can find all three elements Shakes finds in Garveyite arts in the eighteenth- and nineteenth-century women's performances. Nicosia Shakes, 'Composing the Second Emancipation: Black Radical Intelligence in Marcus Garvey's Philosophy,' Rupert Lewis Conference, October 11, 2013. I am grateful to Ms Shakes for sharing her work-in-progress.

Other kinds of holiday processions occurred elsewhere in the Caribbean and Latin America, and became far more elaborate in the Catholic settlements where confraternities organised these events. Occasionally Africans in the Americas were required to process in these religious festivals, though the Christmas season processions often occurred on the Day of the Three Kings (January 6). See, for example, Rachel Sarah O'Toole, *Bound Lives: Africans, Indians, and the Making of Race in Colonial Peru* (Pittsburg: University of Pittsburg Press, 2012), 117; Elizabeth W. Kiddy, *Blacks of the Rosary: Memory and History in Minas Gerais, Brazil* (University Park: Pennsylvania State University Press, 2007), 88. For Puerto Rico, see Edward Bliss Emerson, *The Caribbean Journal and Letters, 1831–1834*, ed. by José G. Rigau-Pérez (San Juan, Puerto Rico: Published online by the author, 2013), 173. http://edicionesdigitales.info/biblioteca/Emerson. pdf.

5. Michel de Certeau, *The Practice of Everyday Life* (Berkeley, CA: University of California Press, 1984). For the Sett Girls, for example, commerce and consumer culture provided the tools for creating costumes, music, and a total carnivalesque practice that allowed them to resist the planters' strategy of labelling African Jamaican women as mere laboring drudges.

6. As James C. Scott asks, 'How do we study power relations when the powerless are often obliged to adopt a strategic pose in the presence of the powerful and

when the powerful may have an interest in overdramatising their reputation and mastery?' If we take all of this at face value we risk mistaking what may be a tactic for the whole story. Instead, I try to make out a case for a different study of power that uncovers contradictions, tensions, and immanent possibilities.' James C. Scott, *Domination and the Arts of Resistance: Hidden Transcripts* (New Haven: Yale University Press, 1993), xii–xiii.
7. Jean Baudrillard –'Simulacra and Simulations - XVIII. On Nihilism,' Translated by Sheila Faria Glaser. http://www. egs. edu/faculty/jean-baudrillard/articles/simulacra-and-simulations-xviii-on-nihilism/; Jean Baudrillard. 'On Nihilism,' in *On the Beach*, transl. Sheila Faria Glaser, vol. 6, Spring 1984, 38–39.
8. The nature of the cultures of Africans in the Americas and the attendant implications for power dynamics and, indeed, public policy, has been at the foundation of the twentieth-century historiography of slavery in the US. A full analysis of this historiography is impossible here, but for a remarkably concise overview of the classic literature, see Drew Gilpin Faust, 'Slavery in the American Experience,' in *Before Freedom Came: African-American Life in the Antebellum South*ed, ed. Edward Campbell, Kym Rice, and Drew Gilpin Faust (Richmond: Museum of the Confederacy and University of Virginia Press, 1991), 6–7.
9. Stephanie M.H. Camp, 'The Pleasures of Resistance: Enslaved Women and Body Politics in the Plantation South, 1830–1861,' *The Journal of Southern History* 68 (2002): 540.
10. Saidiya V. Hartman, *Scenes of Subjection: Terror, Slavery, and Self-Making in Nineteenth-Century America* (New York: Oxford University Press, 1997).
11. The connections between artistic creation, community cohesion, and spiritual agency, especially in masquerades and mourning practices is outlined in Clinton Hutton 'The Creative Ethos of the African Diaspora: Performance Aesthetics and the Fight for Freedom and Identity,' *Caribbean Quarterly* 53, no. 1/2 (2007): 144; Carolyn Cooper, *Noises in the Blood: Orality, Gender, and the 'Vulgar' Body of Jamaican Popular Culture* (Durham: Duke University Press, 1995), xii.
12. 'Tipsey' of Bumper Hall, 'The Ritual of Christmas,' *Columbian Magazine* 1 (December 1796): 445–56.
13. Scott, *Domination and the Arts of Resistance*, xii–xiii.
14. 'Parties,' *Columbian Magazine* [Kingston] 2 (1797): 6–7.
15. Drawing on archaeological excavations in Virginia, Jillian Galle concludes that 'enslaved women and men used several different consumption strategies to solidify social and economic relationships within precarious and rapidly changing environments. Signalling theory, derived from evolutionary theory, illuminates the contextual factors that structured slaves' consumer choices and provides a model for understanding their choices as the result of dynamic and mutually beneficial behaviors.' In this context, we can see Sett Girls' consumption going beyond the obvious expressions of identity and actually establishing cooperative bonds among the women and girls who participated. For the significance of 'signaling behavior' in displaying consumer goods, see Jillian Galle, 'Costly Signaling and Gendered Social Strategies among

Slaves in the Eighteenth-Century Chesapeake: An Archaeological Perspective,' *American Antiquity* 75(2010): 19–43.

16. The Belisario prints received sustained attention in two volumes commemorating the artist, his life, and the context of his trans-Atlantic Jewish ties. Both volumes include gorgeous facsimile reproductions of his work, including the Sett Girls prints. Jackie Ranston's impressive research has uncovered new information about the artist, Jackie Ranston, *Belisario: Sketches of Character, a Historical Biography of a Jamaican Artist* (Kingston, Jamaica: Mill Press, 2008). The essays in the Yale volume highlight the ways that West African traditions were translated into the Sett Girls and John Canoe celebrations performed in Jamaica in Belisario's day. See especially, Robert Farris Thompson, 'Charters for the Spirit: Afro-Jamaican Music and Art,' 89–101; Gillian Forrester, 'Sketches of Character,'. 424–35; and Barbaro Martinez-Ruiz, 'Jonkonnu/John Canoe,'. 463–71, all in *Art and Emancipation in Jamaica: Isaac Mendes Belisario and His Worlds*, ed. By Tim Barringer, Gillian Forrester, and Barbaro Martinez-Ruiz, (New Haven: Yale Center for British Art, 2007). For a fascinating study that considers the multiple layers of tradition that shaped the Sett Girls, see Sara E. Johnson, *The Fear of French Negroes: Transcolonial Collaboration in the Revolutionary Americas* (Berkeley, CA: University of California Press, 2012), 122–56.

17. For a scholarly view that highlights the power of the enslavers in expressive culture, see the work of Yvonne Daniel. She argues the holiday processions displayed the performers' skills, but even more, asserted the prestige of the enslavers. Daniel, *Caribbean and Atlantic Diaspora Dance: Igniting Citizenship*, 118.

18. Although Hilary Beckles focuses on Barbados, his delineation of musical developments in the late eighteenth century, bringing together African and creole practices, are worth noting here. Hilary Beckles, '"War Dances": Slave Leisure and Anti-Slavery in the British-colonised Caribbean' in *Working Slavery, Pricing Freedom: Perspectives from the Caribbean, Africa and the African Diaspora*, ed. Verene Shepherd (Kingston, Jamaica: Ian Randle Publishers, 2002), 223–46.

19. Joanna Brooks, citing the work of Oskar Negt and Alexander Kruge in Joanna Brooks, 'The Early American Public Sphere and the Emergence of a Black Print Counterpublic.' *William and Mary Quarterly* 62 3rd ser. (2005): 70. For the role of music and the soundscape in forming the Black Counterpublic in the age of Marcus Garvey, see Clare Corbould, 'Streets, Sounds and Identity in Interwar Harlem,' *Journal of Social History*, 40 (2007): 859–94. For a more confrontational counterpublic, voiced by the rebels at Stono, in South Carolina, see Jack Shuler, *Calling Out Liberty:The Stono Slave Rebellion and the Universal Struggle for Human Rights* (Jackson: University Press of Mississippi, 2011), 99.

20. TNA CO 137/87:164.

21. Brooks, 'The Early American Public Sphere and the Emergence of a Black Print Counterpublic,' 73.

22. *Jamaica Journal*, May 10, 1823.

23. This name appears variously as M'Neel and M. Neel in the documents but I have standardised it to M'Neel. Extract From Letter of Thomas M. Neel to

the Right Hon. Lord Seaford, dated January 8, 1839, *Return to an Address of the Honourable The House of Commons dated 19 March 1839*, 49–50.
24. Entry for March 27, 1802, Maria Nugent, *Lady Nugent's Journal of Her Residence in Jamaica from 1801 to 1805*, ed. by Philip Wright and Verene Shepherd (Kingston, Jamaica: University of the West Indies Press, 2002), 80.
25. For an account of the various elements that enter into the 'presentation of self in everyday life,' and, I would add, in the non-everyday life of holidays, along with the interactive construction of the site of performance, see Erving Goffman, *The Presentation of Self in Everyday Life* (Garden City, NY: Doubleday, 1959).
26. I.M. Belisario, *Sketches of Character: In Illustration of the Habits, Occupation, and Costume of the Negro Population, in the Island of Jamaica, Drawn after Nature, and in Lithography* (Kingston, Jamaica: privately published by the artist, 1837): no page number, but on the text page for 'Queen or Ma'am of the Set Girls.' Wilbur Devereux Jones, 'Lord Mulgrave's Administration in Jamaica, 1832–1833,' *The Journal of Negro History* 48, no. 1 (1963): 44–56.

When Lord Sligo arrived in Jamaica as successor to Mulgrave as Governor in 1834, he was welcomed by a variety of entertainments by townspeople in Kingston and Spanish Town, among them women who could very well have been members of the Setts. Writing from King's House in Spanish Town, he praised the dancing women in the welcoming party: 'From their novelty, the Antics of the Females dancing and waving boughs in both their hands amused me very much.' Other bands of Sett Girls waved branches as part of their processions, and this appears to be similar to those processions; nevertheless, since this display would have occurred during his first days on the island, he would not necessarily have been aware that the dancing women were part of a larger festival complex. Lord Sligo to Rt Hon. E.G. Stanley, Secretary of State for the Colonies, April 15, 1834, Lord Sligo Private Letter Book 1834, 2, National Library of Jamaica.

27. *The St. Christopher Advertiser*, July 24, 1827; See also, 'How Christmas Was Spent One Hundred Years Ago, *Gleaner*, Dec. 22, 1900, 11: 'Their songs were for the most part in burlesque of some custom or person and afforded no end of amusements.'
28. The classic treatment of the power of humor and inversion of orders is M.M. Bakhtin, *Rabelais and His World* (Bloomington: Indiana University Press, 1984), see especially 5, 11, 13.
29. 'Massa Stranger' refers to the writer who observed the festivities.
30. 'Philanthropy,' 'To the Editors of the Jamaica Journal,' *Jamaica Journal*. May 10, 1823. '*Philanthropy*' makes further contributions to the *Jamaica Journal* in later issues.
31. The story concluding with the usual trope presented by white pro-slavery observers who invoked the Christmas performances as evidence of performers' contentment under slavery when the author invoked the famous abolitionist: 'Oh! That Mr. Wilberforce could witness this scene.'
32. Erving Goffman, *The Presentation of Self in Everyday Life* (Garden City, NY: Doubleday, 1959).
33. Shane White and Graham White. '"Us Likes a Mixtery": Listening to African-American Slave Music.' *Slavery & Abolition* 20 (1999): 22–48.

34. 'Downpression' is voiced in the Rasta lexicon of creative word play. Scott, *Domination and the Arts of Resistance*, 19.
35. Scholars have been encouraged by Professor Warner-Lewis to explore songs as a form of 'residual text' of a period engulfed in silences. Maureen Warner-Lewis, 'The Thoughts and Moods of Slave Songs of the Caribbean,' The George Carlington Simmons Annual Lecture, Frank Collymore Hall, Bridgetown, Barbados and Union College, Maracas, Trinidad, 14 and 15 November 2006, 4. I am grateful to Professor Warner-Lewis for providing me with a copy of this paper.
36. James Grainger, *The Sugar-cane: A Poem, In Four Books*, book iv (London, 1764), 1, 582–85.
37. Grainger defines the 'banshaw' as 'a sort of rude guitar, invented by the Negroes. It produces a wild pleasing melancholy sound.' n. to p. 157. On Sloane's study of Jamaican music, see Richard Cullen Rath, 'African Music in Seventeenth-Century Jamaica: Cultural Transit and Transition,' *The William and Mary Quarterly* 50 (1993): 700–26.
38. Ironically, observers expressed surprise at the infrequency of inebriation among the labour force. Richard Rath has pointed out that Anglo-Jamaicans enacted laws against musical gatherings and drumming among the African-Jamaican population by 1688 and codified the legislation in 1717. In the interval, Barbados and St Kitts had also regulated drumming and horn blowing, both associated with African martial music. Richard Cullen Rath, *How Early America Sounded* (Ithaca, NY: Cornell University Press, 2003), 79.
39. Codex Eng 60, John Dovaston, 'Agricultura America, or improvements in West-Indian husbandry considered, wherein the present system of husbandry used in England is applied to the cultivation or growing of Sugar canes to advantage...by John Dovaston, of the Nursery, Twyford, wrote in the year 1774'...2 vols. (Twyford, Berks, 1774– May 16, 1790), 159, ms at the John Carter Brown Library, R.I. Dovaston planned unsuccessfully to publish his work.
40. Hope Masterton Waddell, *Twenty-Nine Years in The West Indies and Central Africa: A Review of Missionary Work and Adventure: 1829-1858* (London: T. Nelson and Sons, 1863), 17.
41. Bernard Martin Senior, *Jamaica, As It Was, As It Is, and As It May Be: Comprising Interesting Topics for Absent Proprietors, Merchants &c. and Valuable Hints to Persons Intending to Emigrate to the Island: Also an Authentic Narrative of the Negro Insurrection in 1831; With A Faithful Detail Of The Manners, Customs and Habits of the Colonists, and a Description of the Country, Climate, Productions, &c., Including an Abridgment of the Slave Law* (London: T. Hurst, 1835), 175–76.
42. For a view that stresses the control of the enslavers in the celebrations of the enslaved, see Saidiya Hartman, *Scenes of Subjection: Terror, Slavery, and Self-making in Nineteenth-century America* (New York: Oxford University Press, 1997). Elsewhere, Hartman poses questions about how to understand culture and resistance: 'How do objects of property advance political claims and make their gestures legible? What forms do slave politics assume: appeals and freedom suits, arson, poisoning, plotting, fleeing, infanticide, collective action, praying, suicide, loving, child-rearing, and imagining a future other than that of captivity? Should not a comparative project be able to think across

a wide spectrum of actors, practices, and beliefs? Is the enslaved a political actor like others; and, if not or if so, what role, if any, did the millions of enslaved Africans play in the abolition of slavery and the end of slavery in the Americas?' Saidiya Hartman, 'Review of Abolition of *Slavery and Antislavery*,' by Seymour Drescher, *The American Historical Review* 115 (Oct. 2010): 1,105.

43. 'Journal of ------- --------- of Loanhead near Rathven, Banffshire,' National Library of Scotland – MS 17956, edited by Patricia Jackson: Jamaican Family Search online. University College London, 1823–1824. http://www.jamaicafamilysearch.com/members/JournalAlexanderInnes.htm. The editor notes 'The name of the author is not on the manuscript. However, references in the text lead to other evidence indicating that the author is Alexander Innes (1792–1875), an officer in the British army.

44. William Beckford, *A Descriptive account of the Island of Jamaica, with Remarks upon the Cultivation of the Sugar-Cane, throughout the different Seasons of the Year, and chiefly considered in a Picturesque [!] Point of View; Also, Observations and Reflections upon what would probably be the Consequences of an Abolition of the Salve-Trade, and the Emancipation of the Slaves*, 2 vols. (London: T. and J. Egerton, 1790), vol. 1, 387.

45. 'The Christmas holidays appointed by the Colonial Legislature of Jamaica were ushered in by the observance of the usual festivities amongst the black population: — the negroes from the several parishes and from the mountains carrying the produce of their own grounds to the nearest market, to exchange them for the more grateful aliments of beef, pork, &c, or for the purchase of the more elegant possessions of civilised life.': 26. 'An Eye-Witness Sketch of the Late Insurrection in Jamaica: An Extract from the Private Journal of an Officer of H.M.S. _____. [left blank in the published version]' *The United Service Journal and Naval and Military Magazine*. 1833. Part III, (London 1833): 26–29.

46. *United Services Journal*, (London 1833): 30. At emancipation, sonic intimidation from warships was turned on the planters when Governor Sligo used these same tactics to stare down white Jamaicans who threatened violence against their freed labor force. He sent a new-fangled steam ship to intimidate the planters of St Ann's parish and ordered the ship's guns fired 'as supposed for a Pilot, but really [the percussion] conveyed to all the district where the disturbance existed the information that a man or war & troops had arrived.' Lord Sligo Private Letter Book 1834, National Library of Jamaica, MS 281, 136. For the variety of ways African-Jamaicans participated in the events of 1831–32, demonstrating the 'deeply disturbing lack of Black solidarity in these wars,' see Verene Shepherd, *I Want to Disturb My Neighbour*, 122–36. Shepherd reminds us that 'we cannot treat the Black population of the Caribbean as an undifferentiated mass.'

47. Barbara Bush discusses Cubah, elected the 'Queen of Kingston', dismissed in Edward Long's *History* as 'a mere carnival character,' but sentenced to transportation after the 1760 uprising. Her ultimate execution suggests her powers were respected not only by the Coramantins of Kingston who had enthroned and crowned her prior to the rebellion, but also by white enforcers of the law. Barbara Bush, *Slave women in Caribbean Society, 1650–1838* (Kingston, Jamaica: Heinemann Caribbean, 1990), 72.

48. Swithin Wilmot, 'The Politics of Protest in Free Jamaica – the Kingston John Canoe Christmas Riots, 1840 and 1841,' *Caribbean Quarterly* 36, no. 3/4 (1990): 65–75.
49. Kenneth Bilby, 'Surviving Secularization: Masking the Spirit in the Jankunu (John Canoe) Festivals of the Caribbean,' *NWIG: New West Indian Guide/Nieuwe West-Indische Gids* 84 (2010): 210.
50. Mary Turner, *Slaves and Missionaries*, 55.
51. Scott, *Domination and the Arts of Resistance*.
52. Jaffe points out that the graffiti may contain a conservative dimension, and messages in 'these social texts' also contributed to 'the maintenance of the city's class, political and sexual orders.' Rivke Jaffe, Kevon Rhiney, and Cavell Francis, '"Throw Word": Graffiti, Space and Power in Kingston, Jamaica,' Caribbean Quarterly 58 (2012): 3.
53. Certeau, *The Practice of Everyday Life*.
54. In her inimitable style, Judith Butler establishes the power of performance in the creation of identities. If 'the various ways in which a body shows or produces its cultural signification, are performative, then there is no preexisting identity by which an act or attribute might be measured.' Instead, 'reality created through sustained social performances means that the very notions of an essential sex and a true or abiding masculinity or femininity are also constituted as part of the strategy that conceals gender's performative character.' In the second edition of her classic *Gender Trouble*, Butler delves into the ways that race factors into the performances of gender, 'thus opening the performative possibilities for proliferating gender configurations outside the restricting frames of masculinist domination....' Butler's approach to performance suggests ways that the Sett Girls critically shaped alternative ways of being women (collectively) in Jamaica, a significance that highlights the power of their acts to do more than merely reflect gender(s) – as established by various sectors of Jamaican society. Judith Butler, *Gender Trouble: Tenth Anniversary Edition* (London: Routledge, 1999), 215; Brooks, 'Counterpublic,' 77.
55. Wilmot, 'The Politics of Protest'.
56. Linda Sturtz, 'The "Sett Girls" Have Torn up their Dresses: Change and Continuity in an African-Jamaican Celebration for a session on "A Religious "Triangle Trade": Black Women and Missionary Agendas in Anglo-American Atlantic Empires,' Berkshire Conference of Women Historians, Toronto, May 2014.
57. Olive Lewin, *Rock It Come Over: The Folk Music of Jamaica* (Kingston, Jamaica: University of the West Indies Press, 2000), 114–17.
58. For a discussion of this balancing act between resistance and accommodation see Steve Buckridge, *The Language of Dress: Resistance and Accommodation in Jamaica, 1760–1890* (Kingston, Jamaica: University of the West Indies Press, 2004), 106. For a discussion of the role of dress in establishing honour of enslaved and emancipated peoples elsewhere in the Americas along with the 'pageant of dress in public', see Tamara J. Walker, "He Outfitted His Family in Notable Decency": Slavery, Honour and Dress in Eighteenth-Century Lima, Peru,' *Slavery & Abolition* 30 (2009): 383–402.

# Bibliography

Anonymous. *St. Christopher Advertiser*, July 24, 1827, 1.
Anonymous. *The Peregrinations of Jeremiah Grant, Esq.* London: G. Burnet, 1763.
Bakhtin, M.M. *Rabelais and His World*. Bloomington: Indiana University Press, 1984.
Baptist, Edward E., and Stephanie M.H. Camp. *New Studies in the History of American Slavery*. Athens: University of Georgia Press, 2006.
Baudrillard, Jean. 'Simulacra and Simulations – xviii. On Nihilism.' The European Graduate School, n.d., website.
Beckford, William. *A Descriptive Account of the Island of Jamaica: With Remarks Upon the Cultivation of the Sugar-Cane, Throughout the Different Seasons of the Year, and Chiefly Considered in a Picturesque Point of View; Also Observations and Reflections Upon What Would Probably Be the Consequences of an Abolition of the Slave-Trade, and of the Emancipation of the Slaves*. 2 vols. London: Printed for T. and J. Egerton, 1790.
Beckles, Hilary. 'War Dances': Slave Leisure and Anti-Slavery in the British-Colonised Caribbean.' In *Working Slavery, Pricing Freedom: Perspectives from the Caribbean, Africa, and the African Diaspora*, edited by Verene Shepherd, 223–46. Kingston, Jamaica: Ian Randle Publishers, 2002.
Belesario, Isaac Mendes. *Sketches of Character: In Illustration of the Habits, Occupation, and Costume of the Negro Population of Jamaica, Drawn after Nature, and in Lithography*. Kingston, Jamaica: Privately published by the Artist, 1837.
Besson, Jean, and Barry Chevannes. 'The Continuity-Creativity Debate: The Case of Revival.' *New West Indian Guide/Nieuwe West-Indische Gids* 70, no. 3/4 (1996): 209–28.
Bettelheim, Judith. *Cuban Festivals: An Illustrated Anthology*. New York: Garland Publishing, 1993.
Bettelheim, Judith, and Fernando Ortiz. *Cuban Festivals: A Century of Afro-Cuban Culture*. Kingston, Jamaica: Ian Randle Publishers, 2001.
Bilby, Kenneth. 'Surviving Secularization: Masking the Spirit in the Jankunu (John Canoe) Festivals of the Caribbean.' *NWIG: New West Indian Guide/Nieuwe West-Indische Gids* 84, no. 3/4 (2010): 179–223.
Bilby, Kenneth M. *Drums of Defiance: Maroon Music from the Earliest Free Black Communities of Jamaica*. Sound recording. Washington, DC and Cambridge, MA.: Smithsonian/Folkways, Distributed by Rounder, 1992.
Brooks, Joanna. 'The Early American Public Sphere and the Emergence of a Black Print Counterpublic.' *The William and Mary Quarterly* 62, no. 1 (2005): 67–92.
Browne, Howe Peter, Lord Sligo, to Rt. Hon. E[dward] G[eorge] [Smith-] Stanley. Private Letter Book, 1834, MS 281, National Library of Jamaica, Kingston.
Buckridge, Steeve O. *The Language of Dress Resistance and Accommodation in Jamaica, 1760–1890*. Kingston, Jamaica: University of the West Indies Press, 2004.
Burton, Richard D. E. *Afro-Creole: Power, Opposition, and Play in the Caribbean*. Ithaca, NY: Cornell University Press, 1997.
Bush, Barbara. *Slave Women in Caribbean Society, 1650–1838*. Kingston, Jamaica: Heinemann Publishers (Caribbean), 1990.
Butler, Judith. *Gender Trouble*. London: Routledge, 1999.
Camp, Stephanie M. H. 'The Pleasures of Resistance: Enslaved Women and Body Politics in the Plantation South, 1830-1861.' *The Journal of Southern History* 68, no. 3 (2002): 533–72.

Camp, Stephanie M. H. *Closer to Freedom: Enslaved Women and Everyday Resistance in the Plantation South Gender and American Culture*. Chapel Hill, NC: University of North Carolina Press, 2004.

Certeau, Michel de, Luce Giard, and Pierre Mayol. *The Practice of Everyday Life*, Volume 2, Living and Cooking. Minneapolis: University of Minnesota Press, 1998.

Cooper, Carolyn. *Noises in the Blood: Orality, Gender, and the 'Vulgar' Body of Jamaican Popular Culture*. Durham, NC: Duke University Press, 1995.

Corbould, Clare. *Becoming African Americans: Black Public Life in Harlem, 1919–1939*. Cambridge, MA.: Harvard University Press, 2009.

Craton, Michael. *Testing the Chains: Resistance to Slavery in the British West Indies*. Ithaca, NY: Cornell University Press, 1982.

———. 'Decoding the Pitchy-Patchy: The Roots, Branches and Essence of Junkanoo.' *Slavery & Abolition* 16, no. 1 (1995): 14–44.

Daniel, Yvonne. *Caribbean and Atlantic Diaspora Dance: Igniting Citizenship*. Urbana, IL: University of Illinois Press, 2011.

Dirks, Robert. *The Black Saturnalia: Conflict and Its Ritual Expression on British West Indian Slave Plantations*. Gainesville: University Press of Florida, 1987.

Dovaston, John. Agricultura America, or Improvements in West-Indian Husbandry Considered, Wherein the Present System of Husbandry Used in England Is Applyed to the Cultivation or Growing of Sugar Canes to Advantage...By John Dovaston of the Nursery, Tryford, Wrote in the Year 1774...Codex Eng 60, John Carter Brown Library, Providence, RI.

Emerson, Edward Bliss, and José G. Rigau-Pérez. *The Caribbean Journal and Letters, 1831–1834*, edited by Jose G. Rigau-Perez. San Juan, Puerto Rico: Universidad de Puerto Rico Biblioteca Digital Puertorriqueña, 2013. http://bibliotecadigital.uprrp.edu/cdm/ref/collection/librosraros/id/1701 (accessed June 18, 2014).

Faust, Drew Gilpin. 'Slavery in the African American Experience.' In *Before Freedom Came*, edited by Edward D.C. Campbell, Kym S. Rice and Drew Gilpin Faust, 1–19. Richmond, VA: The Museum of the Confederacy, 1991.

Forrester, Gillian. 'Sketches of Character.' In *Art and Emancipation in Jamaica: Isaac Mendes Belisario and His Worlds*, edited by T.J. Barringer, Gillian Forrester and Barbaro Martinez-Ruiz, 424–35. New Haven, CT.; London: Yale Center for British Art in association with Yale University Press, 2007.

Galle, Jillian E. 'Costly Signaling and Gendered Social Strategies among Slaves in the Eighteenth-Century Chesapeake: An Archaeological Perspective.' *American Antiquity* 75, no. 1 (2010): 19–43.

Gaspar, David Barry. *Bondmen and Rebels: A Study of Master-Slave Relations in Antigua*. Durham, NC: Duke University Press, 1993.

Gerstin, Julian. 'Tangled Roots: Kalenda and Other Neo-African Dances in the Circum-Caribbean.' *New West Indian Guide/Nieuwe West-Indische Gids* 78, no. 1 & 2 (2004): 5–41.

Gilmore, John, and James Grainger. *The Poetics of Empire: A Study of James Grainger's the Sugar Cane*. New Brunswick, NJ: Athlone Press, 2000.

Goffman, Erving. *The Presentation of Self in Everyday Life*. Garden City, NY: Doubleday, 1959.

Grainger, James. *The Sugar-Cane: A Poem in Four Books, with Notes*. Dublin: William Sleater, 1766.

Great Britain. *Return to an Address of the Honourable the House of Commons Dated 19 March 1839, 1839*.

Hartman, Saidiya. 'Abolition: A History of Slavery and Antislavery.' *American Historical Review* 115, no. 4 (2010): 1,103–106.

Hartman, Saidiya V. *Scenes of Subjection: Terror, Slavery, and Self-Making in Nineteenth-Century America*. New York: Oxford University Press, 1997.

'How Christmas Was Spent One Hundred Years Ago.' *Jamaica Gleaner*, December 22, 100, 11.

Hutton, Clinton. 'The Creative Ethos of the African Diaspora: Performance Aesthetics and the Fight for Freedom and Identity.' *Caribbean Quarterly* 53, no. 1/2 (2007): 127–49.

[Innes, Alexander?]. 'Transcript of "Journal of ------- --------- of Loanhead near Rathven, Banffshire," Ms. from National Library of Scotland – Ms 17956.' edited by Patricia Jackson: Jamaica Family Search Online, University College London, 1823–1824. http://www.jamaicanfamilysearch.com/Members/JournalAlexanderInnes.htm

Jaffe, Rivke, Kevon Rhiney, and Cavell Francis. '"Throw Word": Grafitti, Space and Power in Kingston, Jamaica.' *Caribbean Quarterly* 58 (2012): 1–20.

Johnson, Sara E. *The Fear of French Negroes: Transcolonial Collaboration in the Revolutionary Americas*. Berkeley, CA: University of California Press, 2012.

Jones, Wilbur Devereux. 'Lord Mulgrave's Administration in Jamaica, 1832–1833.' *The Journal of Negro History* 48, no. 1 (1963): 44–56.

Kiddy, Elizabeth W. *Blacks of the Rosary: Memory and History in Minas Gerais, Brazil*. University Park, PA.: Pennsylvania State University Press, 2005.

Kubik, Gerhard. 'Analogies and Differences in African-American Musical Cultures across the Hemisphere: Interpretive Models and Research Strategies.' *Black Music Research Journal* 18, no. 1/2 (1998): 203–27.

Lewin, Olive. *Rock It Come Over: The Folk Music of Jamaica*. Kingston, Jamaica: University of the West Indies Press, 2000.

Mair, Lucille Mathurin, Hilary Beckles and Verene Shepherd. *A Historical Study of Women in Jamaica: 1655–1844*. Kingston, Jamaica: University of the West Indies Press: Centre for Gender and Development Studies, 2006.

Martinez-Ruiz, Barbaro. 'Jonkonnu/John Canoe.' In *Art and Emancipation in Jamaica: Isaac Mendes Belisario and His Worlds*, edited by T.J. Barringer, Gillian Forrester and Barbaro Martinez-Ruiz, 463–71. New Haven, CT; Yale Center for British Art in association with Yale University Press, 2007.

McDaniel, Lorna. *The Big Drum Ritual of Carriacou: Praisesongs in Rememory of Flight*. Gainesville: University Press of Florida, 1998.

Miller, Joseph C. 'Retention, Re-Invention, and Remembering: Restoring Identities through Enslavement in Africa and under Slavery in Brazil.' In *Enslaving Connections: Changing Cultures of Africa and Brazil during the Era of Slavery*, edited by José C. Curto and Paul E. Lovejoy, 81–121. Amherst, NY: Humanity Books, 2004.

Morgan, Jennifer L. *Laboring Women: Reproduction and Gender in New World Slavery Early American Studies*. Philadelphia: University of Pennsylvania Press, 2004.

Nugent, Maria, Philip Wright and Verene Shepherd. 'Lady Nugent's Journal of Her Residence in Jamaica from 1801 to 1805', University of the West Indies http://site.ebrary.com/id/10342240.

Nunley, John W., Judith Bettelheim, Barbara A. Bridges, and St. Louis Art Museum. *Caribbean Festival Arts: Each and Every Bit of Difference*. Saint Louis, MO: Saint Louis Art Museum, 1988.

Philanthropy, (pseudonym). 'Letter to the Editor.' *Jamaica Journal* (1823).

Ranston, Jackie. *Belisario: Sketches of Character: A Historical Biography of a Jamaican Artist*. Kingston, Jamaica: Mill Press, 2008.

Rath, Richard Cullen. 'African Music in Seventeenth-Century Jamaica: Cultural Transit and Transition.' *The William and Mary Quarterly* 50, no. 4 (1993): 700–26.

———. *How Early America Sounded*. Ithaca, NY: Cornell University Press, 2003.

Roberts, Helen H. 'A Study of Folk Song Variants Based on Field Work in Jamaica.' *The Journal of American Folklore* 38, no. 148 (1925): 149–216.

Scott, Julius. '"Negroes in Foreign Bottoms": Sailors, Slaves and Communication.' In *Origins of the Black Atlantic*, edited by Laurent Dubois Scott and Julius Sherrard, 69–94. New York: Routledge, 2010.

Senior, Bernard Martin. *Jamaica, as It Was, as It Is, and as It May Be: Comprising Interesting Topics for Absent Proprietors, Merchants, & C., and Valuable Hints to Persons Intending to Emigrate to the Island*. London: T. Hurst; etc., 1835.

Shakes, Nicosia. 'Composing the Second Emancipation: Black Radical Intelligence in Marcus Garvey's Philosophy.' Black Radical Thought, Pedagogy and Praxis: A Conference in Honour of Professor Rupert Lewis, University of the West Indies, Mona, 2014.

Shepherd, Verene. *I Want to Disturb My Neighbour: Lectures on Slavery, Emancipation, and Postcolonial Jamaica*. Kingston, Jamaica: Ian Randle Publishers, 2007.

———. *Working Slavery, Pricing Freedom: Perspectives from the Caribbean, Africa and the African Diaspora*. New York: Palgrave, 2002.

Shuler, Jack. *Calling out Liberty: The Stono Slave Rebellion and the Universal Struggle for Human Rights*. Jackson: University Press of Mississippi, 2009.

Stallybrass, Peter, and Allon White. *The Politics and Poetics of Transgression*. Ithaca, NY: Cornell University Press, 1986.

Sturtz, Linda. '"The Sett Girls Have Torn up Their Dresses": Change and Continuity in a Jamaican Celebration.' Paper presented to The Berkshire Conference of Women Historians. Toronto, May 2014.

Thompson, Robert Farris. 'Charters for the Spirit: Afro-Jamaican Music and Art.' In *Art and Emancipation in Jamaica: Isaac Mendes Belisario and His Worlds*, edited by T.J. Barringer, Gillian Forrester and Barbaro Martinez-Ruiz, 89–101. New Haven, CT: Yale Center for British Art in association with Yale University Press, 2007.

'Tipsey' of Bumper Hall (psuedonym). 'The Ritual of Christmas.' *Columbian Magazine* 1 (1796): 445-6.

Turner, Victor W. *The Anthropology of Performance*. New York: PAJ Publications, 1986.

Waddell, Hope Masterton. *Twenty-Nine Years in the West Indies and Central Africa: A Review of Missionary Work and Adventure: 1829–1858*. London and New York: T. Nelson and Sons, 1863.

Walker, Tamara J. '"He Outfitted His Family in Notable Decency": Slavery, Honour and Dress in Eighteenth-Century Lima, Peru.' *Slavery & Abolition* 30, no. 3 (2009): 383–402.

Warner-Lewis, Maureen. 'The Thoughts and Moods of Slave Songs of the Caribbean.' The George Carlington Simmons Annual Lecture. Bridgetown, Barbados and Maracas, Trinidad, 2006.

White, Shane, and Graham White. '"Us Likes a Mixtery": Listening to African-American Slave Music.' *Slavery & Abolition* 20, No. 3 (1999): 22–48.

White, Shane, and Graham J. White. *The Sounds of Slavery: Discovering African American History through Songs, Sermons, and Speech*. Boston: Beacon Press, 2005.

———. *Stylin': African American Expressive Culture from Its Beginnings to the Zoot Suit*. Ithaca, NY: Cornell University Press, 1998.

Wilmot, Swithin. 'The Politics of Protest in Free Jamaica – the Kingston John Canoe Christmas Riots, 1840 and 1841.' *Caribbean Quarterly* 36, no. 3/4 (1990): 65–75.

Young, William. *The West-India Common-Place Book Compiled from Parliamentary and Official Documents; Shewing the Interest of Great Britain in Its Sugar Colonies*. London: Printed for R. Phillips, 1807.

# 12 | 'Sankofa':
Garvey's Pan Africanism, Negritude, and Decolonising Narratives

Mawuena Logan

> In no way should I dedicate myself to the revival of an unjustly unrecognized Negro civilization. I'll not make myself the man of any past. I do not want to exalt the past at the expense of my present and of my future...I am not a prisoner of history. I should not seek there for the meaning of my destiny...I am not the slave of the Slavery that dehumanized my ancestors.
> – Frantz Fanon *(Black Skin, White Masks)*

In the 1920s when Marcus Garvey spoke of 'back-to-Africa,'[1] his detractors, mainly in the African Diaspora, ridiculed him and took his words literally to mean: 'pack your bags and move to Africa.' It is, however, arguable that what the Harlem Renaissance and later Negritude poets achieved in verse, Garvey accomplished with a catch phrase that has come to define, unfortunately and narrowly, his movement and work. This 'back-to-Africa' ideology was not confined to a physical return to Africa, and could be likened to the concept that the Sankofa bird in Akan art and cosmology embodies regarding the centrality of the past to the present – the past as a prerequisite for understanding the present in order to envision the future. 'Sankofa' literally means, 'go back and fetch it'; the 'it' refers to the 'usable past'. It is this idea that is artistically captured in the Sankofa bird whose head is facing the opposite direction of its forward-moving body. This essay establishes how Pan Africanism, Negritude, and Garvey's metaphorical 'return to Africa' (symbolised by the Sankofa bird) intersect and interrelate, and argues that these movements and ideologies, no matter how antiquated, remain key ingredients in the struggle toward decolonisation in the Black Atlantic world. These components retain their relevance in spite of the claim that the narrative of decolonisation has been eclipsed by globalisation.[2] Aimé Césaire's historical play, *A Season in the Congo* (1966), will be shown here to exemplify this premise.

The epigraph above speaks to a perennial question writers of African descent have been pondering since Olaudah Equiano's *The Interesting Narrative of the Life of Olaudah Equiano*, or *Gustavus Vassa, the African, Written by Himself* (1789): What of Africa? Slavery? The Past? Franz Fanon's rejection of history and the past should be understood in post-modernist terms, but it is one thing to be enslaved by history, and another to be informed by that history. Proclaiming the end of history, as we know it, for its fictionality, post-modernists privileged memory for its dialectic character. Pierre Nora, in his article, 'Between Memory and History: Les Lieux de Mémoire,' distinguishes memory from history:

> Memory is life, borne by living societies founded in its name. It remains in permanent evolution, open to the dialectic of remembering and forgetting...susceptible to being long dormant and periodically revived. History, on the other hand, is the reconstruction, always problematic and incomplete, of what is no longer; history is a representation of the past (3).

'History' and 'memory' are terms that are deployed in discussions about how the past is remembered or represented. Both terms have a history that dates as far back as the pre-modern age when history served to preserve the memory of authority figures and heroes; therefore history could not possibly claim neutrality or objectivity because it was meant to serve the interests of the ruling class, legitimising their rule, and hence, unreliable. Memory which can also be faulty and selective, allows, however, for a re-evaluation of what history may have obscured or glossed over in its attempts to be in line with 'specific functions of the state'. Memory studies, according to Aleida Assmann, 'reflect a desire to claim the past as an important part of the present...to reassess it as part of individual autobiographies and the way individuals position themselves in a wider historical perspective' (6). Claiming the past and positioning the self in a wider historical context is what the Sankofa bird symbolises as used here: it reclaims the past in the present for future generations. This past is not an ideal but a 'usable past'. Yet, it is not usable if it is unchallenged, nor is it usable when it becomes a nostalgic recollection of past achievements. How usable, then, is a past that is inglorious, filled with centuries of systemic humiliation and dehumanisation?

When the Sankofa bird takes a glance at the past it sees, among other things, slavery and colonisation. While these tragic events in and of themselves have no redeeming qualities vis-à-vis the victims and perpetrators, they nevertheless speak to the spirit of survival, courage, resilience, and bravery on the part of the victims. We miss/undermine all that when we reject that (usable) past. Renowned abolitionist Lloyd William Garrison, in his Preface to Frederick Douglass's *Narrative of the Life of Frederick Douglass, an American Slave* (1845), wrote:

> It may, perhaps, be fairly questioned, whether any other portion of the population of the earth could have endured the privations, sufferings and horrors of slavery, without having become more degraded in the scale of humanity than the slaves of African descent. Nothing has been left undone to cripple their intellects, darken their minds, debase their moral nature, obliterate all traces of their relationship to mankind; and yet how wonderfully they have sustained the mighty load of a most frightful bondage, under which they have been groaning for centuries! (37).

Like the Sankofa bird, we can glimpse that past as we race towards the future of globalisation, because the present is a present within the past: that is, there is no present (or future) without a past. Literary movements such as the Harlem Renaissance and Negritude have attempted to challenge the 'single story', the Eurocentric perspective, to reclaim this usable past. Garvey's call for a return to Africa, far from being confined to a physical return, is a return to this past.

While there have been antecedents to Garvey's Pan Africanism, the latter's influence on African nations cannot be overstated.[3] Garvey's success, impact, and political ideas, should not be measured in terms of their immediate success, or by the 'historian's success story' (Clarke 1974, 413), as contemporary scholarship has a propensity to diminish or discredit his impact and success.[4] In the main, African intellectuals were conversant with and endorsed Garvey's Pan African objectives and economic goals, but remained sceptical about Diasporic leadership in general and Garvey's 'colonisation' schemes in particular. Referring to the Ghanaian lawyer, philosopher, and nationalist, Kobina Sekyi, a Garvey supporter who contributed poems to Garvey's newspaper, the *Negro World*, historian John Henrik Clarke argues that the African Diaspora, 'in spite of its race consciousness and pan-Melanism, had inherited Anglo-Saxon prejudices against the African and [was] ipso facto disqualified from assuming any political leadership in the African continent' (Clarke 1974, 410).[5] A propos, we may recall the Liberian precedent where native Liberians were compelled to be 'apprentices' in American Liberian homes in order to become 'legal' citizens of their own country. Barry Chevannes's words echo the thoughts of Kobina Sekyi: 'the truth is that Africa has been and remains a problem for us descendants of the enslaved Africans, personal and social...a matter of psychology and politics...but also of identity, a source of much angst and disquiet....To be correct, it is not Africa so much as Europe that is the problem—the rupture, the commodification, the contempt and humiliation, the lies, the love-hate, the patronage, the racism, the colorism, and now the denial' (5).

To wit, the physical black empire that Garvey's Pan Africanism entailed could not have been possible for the simple fact that the whole continent, with the exception of Ethiopia and Egypt, was at that time, under colonial rule, a reality that made it difficult for Garvey's organisation to take root and for its sympathisers to be open and candid about their affiliation with the Universal Negro Improvement Association (UNIA). The *New Negro* was even banned in many African countries and in the Caribbean by the colonial metropole. It is no coincidence that Garvey was imprisoned on bogus mail fraud charges and deported after serving two years in jail, and that his dream of establishing a settlement in Liberia for the black Diaspora never materialised.[6] Garvey's 'back-to-Africa' is a philosophy, a brand of Pan Africanism that 'worries' (to use Charles Johnson's term), or challenges accepted and formal 'historical' interpretations of the Black Atlantic World, the same way the Sankofa bird entreats us to take stock and control of our own story/past. Hence, when the *Negro World* refused to take skin lightening and hair straightening ads (which would have brought financial benefits to the struggling newspaper), it was to force us to ponder and revisit what the colonial and single story has done to our sense of self and thereby to self-evaluation.

Aimé Césaire's play, *A Season in the Congo*, documents the thwarting of a Pan African agenda and the dream foreseen for the Congo by Patrice Lumumba, a man whose Pan Africanism, not unlike Garvey's metaphorical back-to-Africa, invites us to re-evaluate the past. Like Garvey in the 1920s, Lumumba in the 1960s became a target and a victim of colonial regimes and their cold war politics.

## A Season in the Congo

Published in 1966, A *Season in the Congo* is a historical play that chronicles the decolonisation of the Congo in the 1960s, and the West's (namely British, American, and Belgian) involvement in the assassination, a year later, of the country's first democratically elected Prime Minster, Patrice Lumumba. Primarily a literary movement, Negritude, however, embodies a political agenda and an ideology that are clearly Pan African. Césaire, a founding father of the Negritude movement in the 1930s, was a Pan Africanist; in other words, Pan Africanism represents an ideology, or a sentiment that can be traced back to the forced removal of Africans from their homeland. It has been manifested in different ways, from Kunta Kinte's refusal to adopt his slave name, Toby, in *Roots*, to Negritude poetry, Garvey's movement, and Pan African Conferences and Congresses. As Colin Legum opines, 'Pan-African is not, and never has been, a unified or structured political movement. It is a movement of ideas and emotions: its recent political history has been a search for a viable political organisation' (quoted in Le Baron 1). As a literary movement and phenomenon, Negritude could be said to have a built-in Pan Africanism that is intellectual and political. *A Season in the Congo* speaks to decolonisation, Pan African Unity, and the ways in which the past could be put to use.

In an interview with Nicole Zand, Césaire describes the play thus: *A Season in the Congo* 'is a slice of life in the history of a people. So Lumumba is not Patrice Lumumba; he is, before everything else, a symbol of a man, a man that identifies with the Congolese reality and with the Africa of decolonisation, an individual that represents a collectivity' (quoted in Ojo-Ade 2010, 159). This process of decolonisation is made manifest in the protagonist's (Lumumba's) speech during Congo's independence celebration ceremony in 1960 at which the Belgium King (in the character of Basilo) is present. The latter pays tribute to his predecessors, 'first to Léopold, the founder, who has come here not for taking or dominating, but to give and civilize' (Act I, Scene 6). Lumumba then takes the floor and charts a path that would lead to the decolonisation of the Congo after years of Belgian rule. He speaks of taking up all the laws and revising them and taking 'all the parts of the old building from top to bottom for the Congo. All that is bent will be straightened....' He demands 'the union of all' (Act I, Scene 6). Lumumba's rejoinder obviously tells a different story that is all too often forgotten or taken for granted by the colonialists: 'We are those who were dispossessed, struck, mutilated... spat upon. Cookboys, chamberboys, laundryboys, we were a people of boys...' (Act I, Scene 6). The atrocities committed against the people of the Congo – in the name of a 'civilizing mission' in general, and King Léopold in particular – have been well documented. According to Adam Hochschild, '...the major legacy Europe left to Africa was not democracy as it is practised today in countries like England, France, and Belgium; it was authoritarian rule and plunder. On the whole continent, no nation has had a harder time than the Congo in emerging from the shadow of its [colonial] past' (301). In 1883, a year before the infamous Berlin Conference that occasioned the partition of the African continent, King Léopold counselled his Africa-bound missionaries in these words:

> Pastors, you are certainly going to evangelise, but that evangelisation is inspired by our great principle...the interest of the Metropolis. The essential goal of your mission is not to teach the Negroes to know God...Your essential role is to facilitate the administrators' and industrialists' task. Your knowledge of the gospel will allow you to find texts recommending and urging them to love poverty...Avoid developing the spirit of criticism in your schools. Teach the pupils to believe, not to reason...' (quoted in *L'Afrique répond à Sarkozy*, 25–26).

It was this legacy of manipulation, duplicity, and indoctrination that the Congo and all colonised people had to confront. The task of decolonisation, then, involves a critical evaluation of the past to explain the present-day post-colonial (neocolonial) Congo.

Lumumba's Pan Africanism links the struggle of the Congo to that of the rest of the continent and beyond on several occasions. He appeals to members of his Senate: '...Africans, my brothers, Mali, Guinea, Ghana, to you beyond the borders of the Congo, we cry. Africa, I am screaming to you...Or do they believe the hand of Africa is too short to deliver us? I know well that colonialism is powerful. But I swear by Africa: all united, all together, we will pierce the monster by the nostrils' (Act I, Scene 11). He refers to Northern Rhodesia (Zambia, today) and Southern Rhodesia (present-day Zimbabwe), Angola, and South Africa where millions are 'dispossessed, parked in townships' (Act II, Scene 11). So, what does independence mean for the Congo and by extension for the continent? The playwright suggests, using the character of the sanza player: 'No more ethnic fights. Don't let colonialism divide and rule! Let us rise above these tribal quarrels! Let there no longer be Bengalas, Bakongos, Batetelas among us, but only Congolese!' (Act I, Scene 5). While this internal unity seems to be a prerequisite for a Pan Africanism that would foster a diasporic alliance, these internal divisions persisted and were exacerbated by neocolonial rule after formal independence.

As suggested earlier, external forces were at work to thwart the future of the new Nation State. Lumumba's demise has a historical precedent in the person of Marcus Garvey who became a target of American secret agencies, namely the FBI, for being a 'communist Negro agitator.' In the Congo, it is as though history is being repeated. Larry Devlin, Central Intelligence Agency (CIA) Station Chief in the Congo (2007), discloses US complicity in Lumumba's demise:

> For those who think we should not have attempted to remove Lumumba from power, I can only say that I believed that his lack of understanding of world politics and his dalliance with the Soviet Union made him a serious danger to the United States. We were after all, involved in a major war, albeit a cold one (131).

Without a doubt, Belgium, the former coloniser, was equally involved in the death of Lumumba.[7] Critic Femi Ojo-Ade summarises the consequences and collateral damage of the Cold War in the Congo: 'It should also be recalled that the West led by the United States, was clearly against Lumumba and in support of Katanga whose mineral wealth they were targeting. Labeling Lumumba a communist was tantamount to sending him to his grave' (175).[8] Césaire, once again attuned to the history of colonialism and of the Cold War that is fought between superpowers on African soil, reminds us of the precarious state of affairs in the Congo, not only due to internal divisions (some of which could be attributed to the colonial policy of 'divide-and-rule'), but also motivated by the so-called white man's burden and a perceived fear of communism. Great Western Ambassador, a character in the play, soliloquises: '…Ah well, people should know that we are not just policemen, we are also firemen of the world! Firemen designated to circumscribe the fire lit everywhere by Communist pyromania! I say 'everywhere!' in the Congo, as elsewhere! Greetings to the good listener!' (Act I, Scene 13). One should hasten to add that, if anything, most African countries upon independence were either 'non-aligned' or socialist leaning, not communistic.

Césaire's choice of literary medium or genre is worthy of note: that he chooses to represent the decolonisation of the Congo in a dramatic form speaks to his awareness of the tragic and delicate nature of the process of decolonisation and self-rule, especially when the colonial master is bent on destroying and crippling the new Nation State at birth. Césaire deploys literary devices such as metaphors and symbols that speak to his subject matter. Throughout the play the sanza player becomes the voice of the masses, the people's conscience, a griot of sorts, a historian that is not acknowledged in history books; his incorporation in the play suggests the many ways in which the past is remembered, forgotten and misrepresented. His voice, while not official, tells the story of the Congo from a Congolese perspective. It is a voice that is critical of the colonial modus operandi, and the internal divisions and neocolonial forces soon to render independence nominal in the Congo. Césaire uses birds in the play to symbolise the aspirations, pride, and freedom that underlie the vision of Lumumba who identifies, for instance, with the toucan: 'I want to be a toucan, the beautiful bird, to be all over the sky, to announce to races and languages that Kongo is born to us, our king! Kongo, may he live!' (Act I, Scene 6). The character of the madman in the play could be read as a metaphor for the psychological damage done to the colonised; he intones: 'I went down the river to find the White men who left my village, and I did not find them at all; the whites have left the village and the Black men are bad! Black men are cursed by God...'– an indication of the 'evil we must still conquer' as Lumumba argues (Act II, Scene 1).

Negritude, despite the undue negative attention it had attracted, is still arguably a valuable tool for thinking through many cultural, political, and social issues. The colonial legacy that has confronted the continent remains with the Diaspora today. Whether we are deploying and discussing Pan Africanism, Negritude and Harlem Renaissance writing, or Afro-centricity and post-colonial theory, we are perusing theories that are all steeped in the idea of reclaiming the past and positioning ourselves in a wider historical context. Negritude writing, like the symbolic Sankofa, has to look back and selectively preserve memories that are worth preserving, while incorporating new ideas wherever they come from, because no culture is an island.

Collective memory haunts us still, as when Femi Ojo-Ade queries:

> Why Africa [or Pan Africanism] when Africans themselves seem to have accepted their fate as the wretched of the earth that must flee their homes for havens in places that may, indeed, be a euphemism for hell? Why Africa when Africans in the Diaspora refuse and reject any notion of solidarity with the ancestral land of shame... even as their mainstream masters...subtly remind them, constantly, of their affiliation to Africa? (2).

Sekyi, Chevannes, and Ojo-Ade highlight the internal divisions, individual and collective, that were engendered by the colonial encounter and that must be trounced for a true and organic Pan Africanism to be born and nurtured. Pan Africanism in its multiple manifestations is still relevant today because some of the forces that occasioned its birth have not abated but rather metamorphosed: the humiliation, racism, colourism, denial, contempt, and lies that Chevannes outlined are the real elephant in the room, so to speak. Césaire's play, like the Sankofa bird, takes us back to revisit that inglorious past of chattel slavery and colonial rule in order to lay the colonial ghost to rest. Sadly, the Congo is not unique: many African and post-colonial societies across the globe have achieved only flag independence; the real liberation, which is becoming more of a dream in the age of globalisation, still awaits, inasmuch as colonialism itself represents an 'epochal era in Africa'[9] and by extension in the global South.

## Notes

1. According to historian John Henrik Clarke, the 'back-to-Africa' concept was introduced into the social thought of Jamaica by J. Albert Thorne [born in Barbados] while Marcus Garvey was growing to manhood' (1974, 27).
2. Simon Gikandi, in *Globalization and the Claims of Postcoloniality* argues that pioneering post-colonial theorists have become cultural (post-colonial) theorists of globalisation, implying that globalisation has usurped or claimed post-colonial criticism.
3. Personalities and Heads of State, such as Kwame Nkrumah (first President of independent Ghana in 1957); Leopold Sedar Senghor (first President of independent Senegal in 1960 and father of Negritude); Patrice Lumumba (the first Prime Minister of independent Congo in 1960); Julius Nyerere (the first President of independent Tanzania in 1962); Jomo Kenyatta (first President of independent Kenya in 1964); Sekou Toure; Steve Biko; and recently Nelson

Mandela, to name just a few, were students of Garvey's political philosophy and had embraced his Pan Africanism and nationalism.

4. See James Weldon Johnson's *Black Manhattan* (1930); David Cronon's *Black Moses: The Story of Marcus Garvey and the Universal Negro Improvement Association* (1955); John Hope Franklin's *From Slavery to Freedom: A History of Negro Americans* (1967); Theodore Draper's *The Rediscovery of Black Nationalism* (1970); Clarence Walker's *Deromanticizing Black History* (1991).

5. Sekyi has argued that what Garvey and other African American Pan Africanists need to realise is that, 'republican ideals in the crude form in which they are maintained, in theory, at least in America go directly against the spirit of Africa, which is the only continent in the whole world peopled by human beings who have in their souls the secret of constitutional monarchy....' (quoted in Clarke 1974, 411).

6. As Manning Marable and others contend, British and American governments (the FBI under the directorship of John Edgar Hoover) were instrumental in destroying and discrediting Garvey and his movement. According to Theodore Kornweibel, the FBI recruited black agents who infiltrated Garvey's movement and spied on its leader. The same tactics were used to track and eliminate other black leaders, such as Rev. Martin Luther King Jr., Malcolm X, and the Black Panther Party. (Refer to Kornweibel's *'Seeing Red': Federal Campaigns Against Black Militancy, 1919–1925* (1999). As we shall see, the CIA, among other government secret services, had a hand in Lumumba's demise.

7. In 2002, after parliamentary inquiry, the Belgian government assumed partial responsibility for Lumumba's murder but the US has not done so to date, even though according to Stephen Weissman, former Staff Director of the US House of Representatives' Subcommittee on Africa, there is ample evidence that the US had a hand in Lumumba's demise. See allAfrica.com (August 1, 2010).

8. The question of the mineral-rich province of Katanga was at the heart of the scramble in the Congo. Just a few days after independence, the Belgium Army provoked a mutiny in the Congolese military that started the secession of the Katanga, headed by Moïse Tshombe, and backed by Belgium troops sent by the government and 'multinational monopolies such as Union Minière controlled by the French, Belgian, British, and US capital.' Lumumba appealed to the UN to no avail, and consequently sought support from some African countries as well as the Soviet Union. As Hakim Adi and Marika Sherwood write, 'foreign monopolies completely dominated Congo's economy and felt that their profits were now being threatened by Lumumba and his government. At this time Congo produced over half of Africa's tin and silver, over 85 per cent of its diamonds and was an important producer of uranium' (115).

9. In 'Colonialism and Social Structure,' Iheanyi J. Samuel-Mbaekwe argues that for a more comprehensive critique and understanding of colonialism, we need to consider it as constituting an 'epochal era in Africa' because it shares the same attributes of epochs, and therefore comparable to the Industrial Revolution and the French Revolution. According to Samuel-Mbaekwe, colonialism 'embraces social formations whose dimensions even the most imaginative actors in the colonial situation could not predict' (36). See *The Colonial Epoch in Africa*, Vol. 2 (1993), edited with Introduction by Gregory Maddox.

# References

Adi, Hakim and Marika Sherwood. 2003. *Pan-African History: Political Figures from African and the Diaspora since 1787.* New York and London: Routledge.
Assmann, Aleida. 'Transformations between History and Memory.' *Social Research* 75:1 (2008): 49–72.
Cesaire, Aime. *A Season in the Congo.* 2010. London, New York, and Calcutta: Seagull Books.
Chevannes, Barry. 2006. *Betwixt and Between; Explorations in an African-Caribbean Mindscape.* Kingston: Ian Randle Publishers.
Clarke, John Henrik, ed. 1974. *Marcus Garvey and the Vision of Africa.* New York: Vintage Books.
Cronon, David. 1960. *Black Moses: The Story of Marcus Garvey and the Universal Negro Improvement Association.* Madison: University of Wisconsin Press.
Devlin, Larry. 2007. *Chief of Station, Congo: Fighting the Cold War in a Hot Zone.* New York: Public Affairs.
Douglass, Frederick. 1845. Reissued 1986. *Narrative of the Life of Frederick Douglass, an American Slave.* New York: Penguin Books.
Draper, Theodore. 1970. *The Rediscovery of Black Nationalism.* New York: Penguin Books.
Equiano, Olaudah. 1789. Reissued 2007. *The Interesting Narrative of the Life of Olaudah Equiano, or Gustavus Vassa, the African, Written by Himself.* Boston and New York: Bedford/St. Martin's.
Franklin, John Hope. 1971. *From Slavery to Freedom: A History of Negro Americans*, 3rd Edition. New York: Alfred Knopf.
Gikandi, Simon. "Globalization and the Claims of Postcoloniality." *South Atlantic Quarterly* 100: 3 (2001): 627–58.
Hochschild, Adam. 1999. *King Leopold's Ghost.* Boston and New York: Mariner Books.
Maddox, Gregory and Timothy K. Welliver. 1993. *Colonialism in Africa*, Vol. 2. *(The Colonial Epoch in Africa)*. New York: Garland Publishing, Inc.
Marable, Manning. 1998. *Black Leadership.* New York: Columbia University Press.
Nora, Pierre. "Between Memory and History: Les Lieux de Mémoire." *Representations* 26 (Spring 1989): 7–24.
Ojo-Ade, Femi. 2010. *Aimé Césaire's African Theater.* Trenton, NJ: Africa World Press.
Gassama, Makhily, ed. 2008. *L'Afrique Répond À Sarkozy: Contre Le Discours de Dakar.* Paris: Editions Philippe Rey.
Walker, Clarence E. 1991. *Deromanticizing Black History: Critical Essays and Reappraisals.* Knoxville, TN: The University of Tennessee Press.

# 13 | *Arthur Lewis: Mild Afro-Saxon or Militant Anti-Racist?*
*Lessons from His Struggles and His Disparagement by Other Black Power Advocates*[1]

Mark Figueroa

**Introduction**

Arthur Lewis's self-conscious efforts and achievement in the struggle against racism are not widely recognised. Previous studies provide relevant material (Tignor 2005; Mine 2006; Matera 2008; Chartier 2012; Whittall 2012; Ingham and Mosley 2013) but I am not aware of any comprehensive discussion of Lewis as an anti-racist.[2] I therefore documented, in some detail, his role as someone who fought against racism in his own way. In doing so, I set this against the way in which he was characterised by some critics who ostensibly shared a common opposition to racism. Given his significance and the extent to which he has been mischaracterised and misinterpreted, the examination of his praxis in this field is itself interesting. Yet, the contrast which I highlight between his contribution and its reception may be of greater import for future efforts against racism and other forms of discrimination.

Lewis's case poses the question as to whether it may be possible to achieve greater social change where coalitions are built which focus on shared perspectives, an approach that contrasts with the divisive politics manifested in many Caribbean societies, and more generally within the contemporary world. My motivation is based on the many years which I spent as an activist and a desire to use lessons from history to share some of what I think I have learnt from the struggles of the fraction of my generation which sought to change the world. My concern is to emphasise the value of dialogue as I believe that our societies need to be less tribal and more cohesive and our discourses less polemical and more convergent. This is what much of my work on Arthur Lewis is about. Although he is interesting in himself, he is rarely the main issue; he is a hook.

In what follows, I show how Lewis was portrayed as a stooge by some of his successors, who did not take the time to know him or dialogue with him, although their lives overlapped with his for many years. I then speak to Arthur Lewis's background and the racist challenges he faced; look at his anti-racist activism, his role as a path-breaker and his writings on Africa, race and ethnicity. It is primarily in the latter section that I touch on his relevant academic works. I then consider his limitations with respect to issues of culture, and comment on the choices that he made within the struggle against racism, following which I conclude.

**Lewis's Anti-racism and the Black Studies Controversy**

In his first published monograph, Lewis suggests that 'everyone is conscious of the efforts of white people to maintain their supremacy and their privileges. These things reveal themselves...in social clubs, in official functions, in church...but the form which is most resented is the reservation of certain appointments...for white men' (1939, 13). In his submission to the Moyne Commission, the same point is included but with a sharper statement that 'the coloured population is perfectly conscious of the efforts of the white minority to "keep the nigger in his place"' (1938, 8). Here, Lewis's register contrasts with his better known profile as a development economist, who in his later years was often seen in a conservative light. Despite this, his anti-racist passion was well understood by those close to him.

> Perhaps...there are two Arthur Lewis's (sic). One the brilliant economist...whose easy phrase masks great originality and depth of thought...who is softly spoken, good natured...with a sharp tongue, it is true, but its edge is blunted by keen wit. The other feels passionately on problems of colour...Arthur Lewis cares about many things...he is a lover of music, literature and art...But what moves him as nothing else is the problem of colour. People who have met this side of him sometimes even assert that he is obsessed by racial problems, though, in fact, they could...be astonished by his objectivity.

> Sometimes with friends whom he trusts he will recount incidents when he...experienced...discrimination...he will talk jocularly... prepared to admit that white men...are the same as black men in the mass but undertones are there. Every...incident, a sensitive listener will feel, has wounded him, even if he can be so understanding about colour prejudice (*West Africa* October 12, 1957, 965).

Lewis's passion arose in part from his general belief in 'equal opportunities for equal talents' (1955a, 171) but more so, it was personal. 'I wanted to be an engineer, but neither the colonial government nor the sugar plantations would hire a black engineer' (1986, CP, Vol. 1, xxxiv).[3] Lewis (1939, 11–14) presents the racial situation in the various West Indian colonies. He notes a range of social and political problems arising from the British application of the colour bar and related policies of social exclusion. He stresses that the French adopted a different policy, and intimates that one result is that 'those educationally most fitted to lead the West Indies' were generally excluded from playing this role. When Lewis set off, as an Island scholar, to read for a degree at the London School of Economics (LSE), he was therefore generally aware of the discrimination he might face. By the time he came to make his submission to the Moyne Commission, he had already experienced such discrimination which I discuss below.

Lewis's interest in race persisted throughout his life. Indeed, it was in his 55th year that he wrote an article which caused considerable controversy (1969). At that time, pressure was building on prestigious US universities to develop Africana programmes. Simultaneously, some black power advocates, who were critical of integrationist tendencies, called for the building of economic power, based on the communities where persons of African heritage lived. While being generally supportive of Africana programmes and the keeping of community enterprises in the hands of its members, Lewis was critical of separatist tendencies. At the base of this was Lewis's belief in the universality of humanity as well as his vision of a race-less society (1971, CP, 2,339). In addition, he saw the USA as being very different from the Caribbean and Africa. He contrasted the latter two, where he had witnessed political movements seeking state power on behalf of the majority, with the US, where 'blacks are only 11 per cent of the population, and have neither claim nor prospect of capturing the Congress, the executive… or the Supreme Court for themselves alone' (1969, CP, 1,518).

Lewis was more inclined to recommend Africana studies for persons who knew nothing of the Africana experience 'to whom this will come as an eye opener' (1969, CP, 1,528). He felt that US students of African heritage would do better to take only a few Africana courses as they needed to study engineering, medicine, chemistry, economics, law, agriculture or other such fields to ensure that they won a fair share of top jobs in major US corporations. His estimate was that they were

11% of the US population but had two per cent of the top, four per cent of the middle and 16 per cent of the jobs at the bottom, with as much as 40 per cent of some at the very bottom. With the high failure rate of business start-ups and the limited employment potential of community economies, he focused on the corporate sector where the majority would be employed.[4] He also noted that:

> Neither is black America going to be saved by a Marxist revolution. Revolution takes power from one set of persons and gives it to another...it does not change the hierarchical structure of the economy. Any kind of America that you can visualise...capitalist, communist, fascist...is going to consist of large institutions...It will have people at the top...in the middle, and...at the bottom. Its leading engineers, doctors, scientists, and administrators—leaving out a few top...politicians—are going to be recruited from a small number of highly select colleges. The problem of the black will essentially be the same (1969, CP, 1,531).

**Polemics versus Dialogue**

Lewis's remarks were not well taken by black power advocates in the Caribbean. For nine months during 1969, the *Abeng* newspaper was an important outlet for black power advocacy in Jamaica following Walter Rodney's exclusion in 1968. The Editorial Committee included George Beckford, Robert Hill, Rupert Lewis, and Horace Levy, who was later replaced by Trevor Munroe. *Abeng* was enthusiastically welcomed by the left wing of my generation. In an article 'Arthur Lewis & Black Power' (August 16, 1969, 4), Lewis is portrayed as a stooge for his economic and political ideas. He is criticised for limiting his view of black power to the capture of 'the central legislature and executive and judicial powers'[5] as opposed to 'control of our economic resources' which by implication were 'better left in the hands of the imperialist.'

He is identified as an agent of his employers (the *New York Times*, Princeton University and the *Gleaner*, all of which published his views) who would not have a job, 'If black power meant conscious blackman – with the help of all colour and class—taking control ... of economy and society, and turning it to the service of himself and mankind.' *Abeng* suggests that for the blackman, the enemy was the same in both the US and Jamaica and that he should take on his historical role to 'lead the attack of the American working class to make human a system which has grown powerful by dehumanising rich and poor alike'. Lewis is decried for proposing education in 'white culture to get eleven per cent of all the Mammon Babylon has to offer' and he is described as a 'black knight of the Empire' who 'has had a long history of planning brown management of white power – (inside and outside of the universities).' *Abeng* concludes that, 'the understanding of white-hearted blackmen like Lewis...will remain dim so long as they remain apart from the black masses on the move' and that 'they will be used by white power in its attempts to foul up the movement.'

Lewis was also styled an Afro-Saxon by some of his critics, notably Lloyd Best, who probably coined the term as he often created such catchphrases. Best also suggested that Lewis was 'not a West Indian Economist' (2004, 87) and that 'He was epistemologically an Englishman' (2003, 426).[6] The replacement of Anglo with Afro suggests a lack of consciousness where persons of African heritage take on Englishness, alienating themselves from their roots. As such, Lewis was attacked for his political, economic and cultural orientation by fellow anti-racists, despite the fact that many of those who were closest to him saw race as the issue about which he was most passionate.

### Lewis's Family Background and Racial Self-Confidence

In his autobiographical sketches, Lewis recounts few incidents from childhood, but he does include one in affirming his anti-imperialism. He recalls that his father, who he indicates died when he was seven, took him 'to a meeting of the local Marcus Garvey association' (1986, CP, Vol. 1, xliv).[7] As such, his father appears to have inculcated in him an awareness of race along with the self-confidence he needed to succeed, qualities which Lewis suggests were later re-enforced. 'My mother had brought me up to believe that anything that they can do we can do' (1985, CP, 2,077–78). This anecdote is significant as it illustrates how central race was to Lewis's consciousness. He often pointed to racial aspects of an issue, when other economists would not have considered them. In such cases, he gained nothing personally from bringing race to the attention of his audience, many members of which would have preferred if race were left unmentioned. Lewis's family was of mixed racial heritage and Lewis's mother was relatively light-skinned. Lewis's siblings varied in complexion; he was darker than his mother and his brother Allen who became a well-known jurist and later Governor and

Governor General of St Lucia, as well as Chancellor of the University of the West Indies (UWI). In the Caribbean, such families sometimes produce children with identity issues. Alternatively, they can produce children who are accepting of the kinds of racial difference which their families embody. Lewis appears to fall into the latter group. In his published work, he does not dwell on childhood incidents which caused him to confront problems associated with racial prejudice but he speaks to his racial experiences as a young adult in Europe (1936a). In later life, he underplays the considerable discrimination which he faced. 'I have been subject to all the usual disabilities – refusal of accommodations, denial of jobs...generalised discourtesy, and the rest of it' (1986, CP, Vol. 1, l). This was typical of Lewis's dominantly pragmatic attitude in such matters and was in keeping with another maxim taught to him by his mother. 'My mother taught us to make the best of what we have and that is what I have tried to do' (1986, CP, Vol. 1, l).

**Lewis's Activism as a Student and Young Academic**

At 18 years of age, Lewis arrived at the LSE to pursue a four-year B.Com Degree programme which commenced in October 1933. He soon became involved with organisations engaged in social action. Among these, his connection with various Fabian groups and associated tendencies within the British Labour Party are perhaps best known.[8] He was also quickly in touch with leading Pan Africanists in Britain. In a conversation which I had with him in 1989, he described George Padmore and C.L.R. James as his 'learning tree'. In early 1935, he was part of a group, including Amy Ashwood Garvey, Jomo Kenyatta, and Ras Makonnen (né George Thomas Nathaniel Griffith), which James brought together to form the International African Friends of Ethiopia (IAFE). By 1937, Padmore had linked with the IAFE to form the International African Service Bureau (IASB) for which Lewis prepared the pamphlet *The West Indies Today* (IASB 1938). Lewis was also involved in student activism, from at least 1934, when he represented the Student Christian Movement (SCM) and chaired the Council for Peace and Civil Liberties. This was an LSE student, anti-fascist coalition with representatives of political parties from the Marxist to the Conservatives, and other groups including the Jewish Union Society (JUS).[9] Meanwhile, Lewis was pursuing a successful academic career. He won the Roseberry and Leverhulme scholarships on completing his intermediate examinations and on graduation respectively. In 1934–35, he had won the Director's Essay Prize, and the following academic year received an honourable mention for his essay on *The Evolution of the Peasantry in the British West Indies* (1936) (*LSE Director's Reports* various years). The first of these essays has not come to light, but the latter demonstrates that his race concerns were featuring in his academic work. In Britain, there were many publications which accommodated anti-racist positions, a full catalogue of which is not available. It is therefore likely that he wrote other articles on race-related issues which have not come to light, but it is clear that he was seeking to have his views heard. For example, he wrote letters to the editor of the *New Statesman* in the 1930s (LP 51/6) and for less well-known journals, but space does not allow for a listing of these here.

The British organisation which best represented his anti-racist perspective was Harold Moody's League of Coloured Peoples (LCP). He is listed as joining the LCP in 1934, but he had already acted in an LCP play staged in November 1933 (The *Keys* 1934, 1, no.4: 87; 1934, 1, no. 3: 50). This suggests that he had not been in England for many weeks before he became involved with the LCP. By 1935 he was on the executive and in 1936, he served first as editor of the LCP's journal, The *Keys*, and then also as the Publicity Secretary. In 1937 he was back on the executive as an ordinary member and stayed for a number of years thereafter and between 1935 and 1938 he contributed four articles and a short story to the journal (The *Keys* various issues). The LCP campaigned for an end to the colour bar, which as I have noted was an issue that was embedded within the core of Lewis's psyche. Whittall reports that 'Members of the LCP took part in a bewildering array of public events during the 1930s and 1940s. Leading figures...Harold Moody, Una Marson...Arthur Lewis...addressed gatherings held by a range of groups around London and beyond' (2012, 201). The political orientation of the LCP can be gleaned from the inspiration behind the naming of The *Keys*. This was based on the piano metaphor associated with the Ghanaian, James Emmanuel Kwegyir Aggrey (1875–1927). Whittall also reported that as editor, Lewis like Marson, shifted the line of The *Keys* and presented racism not as arising from ignorance as Moody did, but from a systematic policy based on the economic foundations of empire (2012, 265). Lewis participated in

LCP delegations to the Colonial Office. This included a December 1939 meeting with the Secretary of State for the Colonies, where the issue of the colour bar was raised (UKNA CO 323/1692/4). He was also a lead spokesperson in August 1940, when the LCP presented its Memorandum on the Recommendations of the West India Royal Commission (UKNA CO 318/445/47), which he had helped to draft and which included a section on 'Racial Equality' (LCP 1940, 10). The LCP had its success, notably in challenging discriminatory employment practices at the port of Cardiff, a campaign which involved Lewis (The *Keys* 1935, 3, no. 2 and subsequent issues) and in removing discrimination in the granting of military commissions during the War (Tignor 2005, 47–52).

## Lewis's Experience of Discrimination

Lewis's experiences of discrimination must be set against the quality of his achievements including: first class honours, first in his class and a first in seven of his eight papers as reported in The *Keys* (1937, 5, no. 1: 6) along with the quote below, from one of his professors.

> My dear Lewis, I have been stupidly tied up here lecturing to a Summer School...so that I have not had a chance to say how magnificent I feel your B.Com. results to be and how fortunate I count myself in being able to claim you as "one of my students." The relief I get from the knowledge that a man may still do so brilliantly in spite of three years of me in quite indescribable.

With this background, Lewis was still unable to get a job as a clerk with the Port of Spain City Council, and his application to The *Economist* was rejected on the grounds that persons may be unwilling to give him interviews (Tignor 2005, 19). His application for a chair at the University of Liverpool was also rejected in 1947, despite the unanimous support of the selection board and the interventions of the Director of the LSE, himself a Liverpudlian. The Vice Chancellor suggested that the students might not be comfortable having him as a teacher.

Ironically, discrimination probably worked in Lewis's favour. Had engineering been open to him, he probably would have lived a much narrower life, so too, if he had been employed by the Port of Spain

City Council or at The *Economist* and not pursued graduate studies or an academic career. In addition, his inability to get a job may have made the leaders of the LSE more inclined to offer him a job. This they did with the blessing of the Board of Governors on a temporary 'experimental' basis (quoted in Tignor 2005, 21), and having proved his worth, he was promoted rapidly. His failure to gain a chair at Liverpool meant that he soon obtained one at the less parochial Manchester, which gave him a greater opportunity to shine.

Lewis's two sides are reflected in his reactions to the Liverpool experience. The Vice Chancellor's last suggestion was that Lewis 'visit Liverpool several times...so that the faculty, students, and community could get to know him'. Tignor reports that 'Lewis recoiled from the proposal that he visit "so that the public may be able to look at me and decide whether they can stand my appearance"'.[10] This acerbic quote from a letter dated July 4, 1947, sent by Lewis to his director Carr-Saunders contrasts with a more cheerful letter, dated July 15, 1947, which Lewis wrote from Jamaica to his Head of Department, Lionel Robbins. In this letter, Lewis opens with a report on the exciting time he is enjoying, travelling about, partying and socialising, having just got married. Then, in his penultimate paragraph, he suggested that by denying him a job based on colour, Liverpool had not lived up to what he had expected of an English university in 1947. He states that given LSE's superior academic environment, he is not really bothered as he would lose much going to Liverpool with the single gain of a higher salary (LSEA Robbins/4/1/3).

The latter response can be seen as more representative of what was perhaps Lewis's dominant side when he came face to face with racism. This may have been due in part to the fact that despite what he describes euphemistically as 'generalised discourtesy' he also had more positive experiences: 'some doors that were supposed to be closed opened as I approached them' (1986, CP, Vol. 1, l). He never accepted victimhood. His daughter Elizabeth told me (personal communication January 25, 2007) that he always said that when you face racism you must understand that the defect is not in you; the defect is in the racist person. Persons who knew Lewis closely, such as Robert Tignor, have confirmed the extent to which racism rankled him (personal communication May 7, 2014), but it did not demoralise him.

## Lewis's Struggles at the Colonial Office

Like many of his colleagues, Lewis worked for the British government as part of the war effort. Having previously been a consultant to Lord Hailey's Committee on Post-war Reconstruction in the Colonies, he moved full time to the Colonial Office in 1943, to be Secretary to the Colonial Economic Advisory Committee (CEAC). He resigned this post in November 1943, but continued to work on projects until 1946 with Frederick Meyer, his research assistant from 1942 (Meyer file, LSEA).[11] The CEAC was wound up later in 1946, and after a delay, Lewis was appointed to the CEAC's successor, Colonial Economic and Development Council (CEDC) in 1947. In 1951, he was also appointed to the Board of the Colonial Development Corporation (CDC).

The termination of Lewis's relationship with the latter two bodies was linked to issues of race. Ingham and Mosley note that 'in…1950… the Attlee government, decided to exclude Seretse Khama… future president of Botswana, from the Bamangwato territory of Bechuanaland [later Botswana]…to please the South African…regime' (2013, 98). In response, Lewis took a public stand.

> I consider the "Socialist" Government's action to be…cowardly…and insulting to the 400,000,000 coloured citizens of the Empire. As one of these, and to mark my disgust, I have…resigned my appointment to the Colonial Economic and Development Council (The *Manchester Guardian* March 11, 1950, 6).

Lewis was not reappointed when his first term as a CDC board member came to an end in 1953. Barbara Ingham and Paul Mosley explain, 'He had accused the Colonial Office of conniving at racial discrimination by giving preference to high-cost European labour over low-cost indigenous labour – in encouraging Central African Federation' and 'in Malaya…he was regarded as conspiring with another non-European to be disloyal' (2013, 84). The latter point related to his sympathy for a critical position towards the CDC. In the case of the Central African Federation (CAF), Lewis was also critical of the weak position adopted by those closest to him in the Labour party, including the Fabian Colonial Bureau. His main concern was that a federation of Nyasaland (Malawi), Northern Rhodesia (Zambia) and Southern Rhodesia (Rhodesia/Zimbabwe) was being constituted in a manner to allow for the extension of the power of the minority, which had already entrenched its South African type discrimination in Southern Rhodesia (Lewis to Nicholson March 5, 1953, FCBP 8/2). One of Lewis's talks, criticising the federation was broadcast in July 1952, and Lewis indicated in an interview that he was convinced that this contributed to his not being reappointed (The *Manchester Guardian*, May 18, 1953, quoted in Ingham and Mosley 2013, 82).

Lewis's service with the various Colonial Office bodies coincided with his membership in other bodies. He was a member of the Fabian Colonial Bureau Advisory Committee (FCBAC) from 1941 to the mid-1950s (FCBP hand lists 6–9) and on the Fabian Society Executive for a short period in the late 1940s (Fabian Society 1947, 2; 1948, 2). The December 17, 1941 Labour Party Advisory Committee (LPAC) on Imperial Questions agreed to recommend that Lewis be appointed as a member, and he probably remained a member until the Imperial name went out of style at the turn of the decade (see relevant committee minutes in LPA). Lewis prepared various memorandums for these bodies. He also made conference presentations, some of which were published, and especially later in the decade, was more involved in the mainstream media, writing commentaries for the press and making broadcasts for the British Broadcasting Corporation (BBC). Despite the economic flavour of the titles of his documents, they were not exclusively techno-economic. At minimum, Lewis set the position of the native peoples against that of the European settlers, officials or investors whereby the racial distinction was made clear. At times, he spoke directly to racially charged issues, for example when the Labour Party equivocated on the continued exclusion of Kenyans from some of the best lands in their country (1946). Elsewhere, his statements were more subtle but still pointed in a context where the intellectual and moral superiority of Europeans was often taken for granted. 'The natives of the colonies are inherently as intelligent as anybody else, given proper training and experience there is no reason why they should not manufacture as cheaply as anybody else' (1944, 4). He took on issues of race and ethnicity where others did not see them. In (1942), he notes the situation of Greek, German and British settlers in different parts of Africa as against Chinese settlers in Malaya, and elsewhere (1943) compares the role of Indians in East Africa with Syrians in West Africa. He notes that 'Indians and Chinese are regarded with no less hostility than Europeans in many territories because of the extent to which they export their profits' (1942, 14), all this while discussing what many economists would have taken as purely technical matters of capital flows to the colonies and the development of secondary industries. In fact, his comments in the latter memorandum were so pointed that they elicited a classic minute from a British Civil Servant. 'I think that perhaps Mr Lewis's account of the racial aspects of the licensing problem goes too far in the direction of frankness' (Sidney Caine, December 24, 1943 UKNA CO 852/482/2).

Lewis's concern regarding race never wavered throughout this period. This can be seen in positions taken at opposite ends of the period. The first was in 'The West Indian Outlook on International Affairs' presented at Chatam House. 'There is little doubt that if the West Indies...became...part of the USA there would be certain immediate economic advantages, but...the reason for the... opposition...to...absorption...is American racial policy' (1941, 5). Here Lewis's concern was that there was a 'rigid finality, that sense of imminent hostility' which was present, especially in the southern US and which stood in contrast to the more 'flexible' racial situation under British rule (1941, 4). The second was contained in a letter drafted in January 1947 on behalf of the FCB to the Colonial Office, on mining policy, in which Lewis alludes to the colour bar as well as associated elements of structural racism.

> We attach particular importance to the recommendations on recruitment of local personnel, and regret that they are not given greater precision in the memorandum...what steps are...being taken to eliminate the colour bar in mining in Northern Rhodesia [Zambia]...In...nearly all colonial territories Natives are excluded from managerial and technical posts...by custom...and...through the absence of...training; not only university training, but...opportunities of practical experience. We should like to know what...plans there are for selecting suitable persons to receive such training opportunities (1947, 2).

## Lewis in Manchester: Local and Global Activism

In his first years in Manchester, Lewis was still engaged with bodies associated with the Colonial Office. As time went by, he was involved in additional activities, which pulled him in different directions. He continued to provide memoranda and articles for Labour Party bodies, including for the journal *Socialist Commentary*, serving as an Editorial Board member from 1947. He was increasingly drawn into the economic issues facing Britain, and was closely associated with a number of Labour Party notables, including the Leader, Hugh Gaitskell (1956–63). His international work also expanded and he was on the United Nations (UN) panel of development experts (1951). He advised the Gold Coast/Ghanaian and Nigerian governments, and visited places like Burma (now Myanmar), Egypt, India, Malaya (now Malaysia), Sri Lanka and Thailand. Yet even as his activities were becoming more global, he intensified his activism at the local level. As might be expected, he opened his home to the West Indian students in Manchester (personal communication Ivo Desouza 1989) but more significantly, he became involved in community organisation in the districts where African and Caribbean residents of Manchester were most concentrated. In the midst of this, he was building a young family, as an engaged parent, and producing his most significant academic works (1954, 1955).

Lewis became active in the two adjoining inner city communities, Hulme and Moss Side, both an easy walk from his office at the University of Manchester. Ingham and Mosley (2013, chapter 5) provide a description of Lewis's efforts at community development and where not otherwise documented, this section draws on their work. Lewis sought to establish institutions which could assist disadvantaged persons, especially those of African heritage, to improve their technical competence and build their social networks and personal skills so as to improve their chances of employment and career advancement. To this end, he used his own contacts within the academy, local government, political and ecclesiastical institutions, and the business community to support the efforts of the residents of these communities. He became, in 1953, the Founder of the Hulme Evening Centre and the Founding Vice President of the Moss Side Community House Social Centre. His activism involved, not just garnering external support and chairing committee meetings, it also involved street-to-street mobilisation within the community and attendance at social functions where residents recall the Lewises as regulars on the dance floor (Interview, Victor Lawrence October 10, 2012, quoted in Ingham and Mosley 2013, 133).

In Manchester, Lewis's activism appears to have been more focused on discrimination among the working class. For example, he requested that the Fabian Colonial Bureau take up the case of the colour bar in the coal mines, and pledged financial support for any legal cases. Lewis was also engaged beyond the two communities mentioned. For example, he was on the invitation for a meeting involving the Manchester and Salford Council of Social Services and other civic groups on April 27, 1955, and he chaired the Manchester Council for African Affairs Race Relations Sub-Committee (LP 29/4). For the latter, he prepared a memorandum, a quote from which indicates how he differed from persons who wished to confront racism more directly.

> I think mass propaganda about colour prejudice does as much harm as good. It persuades hardly anybody who is already hostile, and sows seeds of prejudice in the minds of some people who would not otherwise have given any thought to the subject. The happiest community is that where race relations are not mentioned in the newspapers.... Others may disagree, I am sure, that the newspapers and religious and political and other organisations would be glad to cooperate if we wished to launch a campaign against colour prejudice, but I would prefer to stick for the present to the practical take outlined above (1953, 3).

## Lewis in Ghana, the Caribbean and the US

Lewis's move to Ghana and his earlier service to Ghana and Nigeria were motivated in part by issues of race. In 1955, two years before going to Ghana, at short notice (Tignor 2005, 146–48), he declined a request to serve as an economic advisor to the recently elected Labour Front government in Singapore despite the pleas of the secretary of the Fabian Colonial Bureau (Correspondence Selwyn-Clarke/ Lewis FCBP 10/2). Even when convinced that Nkrumah was totally off track, he was careful to avoid an acrimonious break as he did not wish the enemies of Africa to make capital of this (letter from Lewis dated December 11, 1958, quoted in Tignor 2005, 171). Indeed, he expresses his reluctance in critiquing the state of West African politics. Referring to the 'Pan African leaders' he states, 'I also share their goal of a free Africa, and it is only the defection of some from this goal that has wrung this pamphlet from me' (1965, 11).

Lewis expressed confidence that the leaders of the Anglophone Caribbean supported his ideas regarding race, perhaps best encapsulated in the Jamaican motto 'Out of many one people'. 'I believe in the open, egalitarian, raceless society which we do not have now, but to which most of our leaders are now committed' (1971, CP, 2,339). My assessment is that it was the formation of the Federation of which he was a supporter since his early teens (McCleery 1980, CP, 2,355-56) that spurred him to return to the region. He saw it as a decisive step towards his long held vision that, 'Out of a mosaic of complexions a new nation is beginning to arise which is neither European nor African nor Indian; it is the West Indian nation of the future' (1935, 4). Later, he returned once more as founding president of the Caribbean Development Bank (CDB) in 1970 once regional agreements were in place to move towards a Caribbean Common Market, starting with the formation of the Caribbean Free Trade Association (CARIFTA) in 1968.

Lewis's personal papers reveal that after he moved to Princeton in 1962, he maintained his interest in the struggle for racial equality. He worked with organisations such as the National Association for the Advancement of Colored People (NAACP) and was appointed to its Economic Policy Advisory Council. He cooperated with the Joint Center for Political and Economic Studies; a think tank for elected officials from US minority communities. In particular, he participated in the formulation of *A Policy Framework for Social Justice* (Kenneth Clark and John Hope Franklin 1983). He played a key role in the *Black Enterprise* Board of Economists, which projected the economic outlook for the magazine's target audience. He was a board member of the International Foundation for Education and Self-Help which seeks to use the skills of US persons of African heritage to support community based programmes in Africa. He also produced his more extensive publications on the race issues while in the US, including a number which related to the racial situation there.

**Lewis as Pioneer and Role Model**

If Lewis had done nothing more than pursue his career, he would have made a major contribution to the struggle for racial equality. Like other brilliant individuals of African heritage, he was an indictment against racist ideas and cleared the way for those who came after him to be treated more fairly even as he inspired them to seek higher goals and showed them that it was possible to overcome the challenges of racism. For many of his academic, state and other appointments and honours, he was the first for a person of African heritage but it is often difficult to unequivocally document this, and I do not attempt to make anything like a complete list of significant items. Lewis was conscious of his pioneering role. 'I...got used to being the first black to do this or that... to be a role model is a bit of a strain, but I try to remember that others are coming after me, and that whether the door will be shut in their faces...will depend... on how I conduct myself' (1986, CP, Vol. 1, 1 ). He is recognised as the first person of African heritage to hold an academic post at LSE and probably at a UK university – 1940, (at age 33) a full professorship in a British University – 1947, and at Princeton – 1962; and to be Principal of the University College of the West Indies (UCWI) – 1959 and Vice Chancellor of UWI – 1962, president of the American Economic Association (AEA) – 1983 and a Nobel Laureate in a scientific discipline – 1979.

In addition to many other academic and professional honours in the form of memberships and fellowships, he was awarded approximately 30 Honorary Degrees – 1954 to 1983, including those from some of the world's most prestigious universities such as Columbia, Harvard, London, Northwestern, Princeton and Toronto, located in eight nations in addition to the West Indies and in eight states of the USA; he was Deputy Managing Director of the UN Special Fund (forerunner to the UN Development Programme, UNDP), and chairman of the World Bank Research Advisory Panel (WBRAP). This list neither captures the full range of his service nor does it capture the impact that his successes had on persons of African heritage and others who faced discrimination. The latter can be seen in the invitations which he received from institutions in Asia, Africa and Latin America, including those to serve governments in the pre-independence period, when such positions were generally occupied by Europeans or North Americans. The nature of his impact is encapsulated in a tribute from Norman Girvan (1989, 19).

> In... preparing to write the entrance examination to the University College of the West Indies...I read that...Arthur Lewis was to become the...first West Indian Principal. Underneath the...headline was the picture of a man...balding, bespectacled, and unmistakably black. To my generation, the symbolism...was another shattering blow to the pervasive and debilitating images of colonial culture from which

we were...still striving to emerge....Lewis was at once a role model... and a repository of the aspirations of the young West Indian nation.

### Lewis's Writings on Africa, Ethnicity and Race

Space does not allow me to list Lewis's academic and professional publications specifically on Africa, ethnicity and/or race. These included two single authored books; one jointly authored book; and more than 15 other works, including short monographs, journal articles; and book chapters (Wilkinson 1999), not counting shorter items appearing mainly in more popular publications. Perhaps he could have qualified for a chair in Africana studies on these alone, and in the late 1970s he was in fact appointed as a Distinguished Visiting Professor in Social Sciences and Afro American Studies at Yale. Reviewing all his relevant works, including the more general ones, it is possible to trace how his focus shifted over the 50 years in which he wrote on race-related issues. His early works (1935–39) were characterised by his contestation of the prevailing ideas of Eurocentric white supremacy. These contestations continued into the next period but were more evident in his popular and unpublished writings. His more academic work in the 1940s and 1950s, along with those unpublished from his time with the Colonial Office, presented alternatives to colonial policy which, if implemented, would have had a significant impact on the position of persons of African heritage. This thrust persisted throughout his career, but in the 1960s, he was involved in the analysis of the economics and politics of post-colonial West Africa, and more broadly, from 1969, in the analysis of the political economy of race, primarily as it manifested itself in the USA.

### Lewis's Perspective on Race

Summarising Lewis's perspective poses many challenges. These relate to the extent of his work, the variety of topics dealt with, and the different audiences to which they were addressed. Lewis had a tendency to adjust his message depending on his audience, which requires that care be exercised in distinguishing what may be a shift in perspective from the tailoring of his position for rhetorical purposes. Bearing the above in mind, Lewis's position on issues of race remained quite consistent throughout his life, the exception being that he became more aware of more of the complexities involved and was probably somewhat less optimistic with respect to race relations as the years went by.

Lewis always took it for granted that there was no area of human endeavour in which persons of African heritage could not excel. For him, there were no fundamental differences in the capabilities of the world's peoples; it was the particularities of their histories which had caused their circumstances to differ so widely in the twentieth century. His ultimate vision for the countries with which he was most closely related was of a raceless society that would be typified by Haile Selassie's aphorism, presented in his speech to the UN General Assembly in 1963 and later rendered by Bob Marley as 'the colour of a man's skin is of no more significance than the colour of his eyes' (1976). He saw two other possibilities: racially/ ethnically homogeneous societies, including those created by partition, and plural societies. He did not spend much time on homogeneous societies but pointed to economic forces working against them as well as situations where they might be maintained. In his work on West Africa (1965), he discusses how the economics and politics of such plural societies might be managed. Here, he was looking at pluralism in the context of ethnicities, but his analysis could be extended to pluralism based on racialised differences. He paid particular attention to situations of uneven economic development and other disparities which existed between groups that had been brought together under various constitutional arrangements. He sought not to underestimate the challenges involved, but his stated preference was for situations where plural solutions would not have to be permanent. He saw how economic forces worked both in favour of and against racial equality and concluded that where it was achieved, sustained growth would have a positive effect although it would not be enough.

> People of different races, religions, and cultures have to learn to live peacefully…, and to develop pluralistic and federal institutions where this is the only way. Economic progress will help decisively, but racism has its own deep psychological springs that must be drained directly. To learn to live peacefully with each other is going to take a long time (1985a, 121).

Lewis was keenly aware of racism in both its structural and ideological forms, and hence its social significance and its role as a motivational factor. From his earliest works he used race as a central analytic category and he was personally invested in the struggle against racism. He had little tolerance for the perspective that persons of different races were different in moral character. Where he considered it warranted, he was just as critical of persons of African heritage as he was of the Europeans and their historical conduct towards Africa and its peoples. He had high standards and applied these without partisanship to persons of African Heritage. As a result, much of his writing can be seen as self-critical from a racial point of view. In particular, he was very critical of the post-independence leadership, especially in West Africa at a time when commentators were making excuses based on notions of the peculiarities of the African context.

Lewis saw the need for direct action to combat racism. In the US, he supported affirmative action, and more generally, he had a long record of anti-racist engagement. Despite this, he saw the long-term resolution of the problems of racism as taking place within the context of development. He neither saw the ultimate value of, nor possibility for, Black Power if it were not rooted in a process of socio-economic development, which built a solid economic foundation, banished poverty, replaced 'ignorance' with a 'scientific' perspective of the world, and brought to marginalised peoples the benefits of what he saw as the universalist achievements of humanity. Once this core idea is grasped, it then becomes clear that Lewis's entire life's work as a development economist embodied a desire to end racism and all other social ills like unemployment, which troubled him deeply. The transformation of tropical economies, societies and polities was, for him, part of an anti-racist praxis. This, in part, is the sense in which Lewis self-identifies as having 'spent all my adult life in black power movements' (1969, 1518).

Lewis's perspective on the differences between the political situation in the US and that of the Caribbean and Africa has been noted, but in each of these cases he had a common concern for economics and the need for different groups to get their fair share if they were to live together peacefully. This can be seen in early writings where he posited the need for land reform in the Caribbean, a position which he restates later in his career.

> What is now most urgently needed...is that the abolition of slavery should be taken a step further by destroying the economic foundations of slavery, and redistributing the land more equitably (IASB 1938, 25).

> The present distribution of land is the...legacy of...slavery...The consequences...are far-reaching...planters...bound together by... racial ties...combine to fix wages...the poverty of the masses contrasts shapely with the luxury of the landed aristocracy...the shadow of the plantation carries with it the touch of serfdom,...debasing mentally and spiritually the...labourer...such a concentration of property gives to the planters...political...power...always used to advance their... interests (1939, 48-9).
>
> The plantations are not all owned by whites, but the overlap is sufficiently great to be embarrassing...ownership of land carries with it income, social prestige and political power...concentration of these in the hands of a small minority has, throughout...history, proved to be a...cause of social upheaval....
>
> A community which is mixed racially needs, even more than other communities, to create for itself social and economic institutions which are broadly accepted. Now forms must be created which take the West Indian sugar industry "out of politics...or the West Indian Community will sooner or later...tear itself to pieces, and destroy the sugar industry in the process (1951, 1,226, 1,234–35).

Lewis was aware of political elements and identified the ways in which power was and could be used socially and economically. He was critical of the colonial constitutions and the extent to which the colonial officials integrated with the aristocracy rather than seeking to use their power to transform relations between the races. Despite this, he saw the need for a fundamental shift in the economic relationships. This explains, in part, his early interest in the Caribbean peasantry. Prior to the revolts of the 1930s, which opened the way to a political power, the peasantry provided a direct challenge by building an independent socio-economic basis for shifting power relations between the races, and he saw their presence as contributing to improved race relations.

> The plantation system intensifies class antagonisms by identifying them with racial divisions. Peasant agriculture has...the advantage that it softens...class...but also racial divisions...clear to any who compares...relations between black and white in peasant Jamaica and plantation Barbados (1936, 37–38).

As a democratic socialist/social democrat – a self-identification which he maintained to the end – (McCleery 1980, CP, 2,357) it was his hope that the leadership which emerged from the labour revolts of the 1930s would be able to take power and undertake policies which would break the hold which the minority had on economic, social and political power. Although considered by some in the Caribbean to be moving in the opposite direction, his widely misinterpreted policies of the 1950s were also aimed at ultimately placing greater economic power in the hands of local classes on a deracialised basis. 'That is why foreign businessmen should not be allowed into the country unless they play their part in training local people to do their job' (1953a, 26). 'This is why...countries...pass legislation...to compel foreign firms to open up managerial positions to local people' (1953a, 21–22) which he later identified as 'the most important control' to be placed on foreign investors (1984, 129).

When he turned to write about the US, he again focused on the economic. He spoke to the impact that the presence of economically powerful persons had on members of their race.

> A deficiency in entrepreneurship is bad for the image of a subordinate group. Entrepreneurs are one of the power units in the establishment, along with bishops, generals, landowners and secretaries of state. A group without its share in each of these lacks prestige. Its image is deficient, and image matters since there is much more image than substance in racial behaviour. Image apart, the group is also low in power, because entrepreneurs wield substantial power, not only over those they employ but in society at large (Lewis 1985a, 75–76).

In the short run, he did not foresee the possibility of achieving equality of wealth quickly (1985a, 2), but he saw no reason why persons of African heritage could not move within the foreseeable future towards getting a fair distribution of labour income. This required a shift of their position in the job hierarchy outlined above. Along with his rejection of revolution as a solution quoted above, came his rejection of Richard Nixon's notion of 'Black Capitalism' as well as separationist strategies within the Black Power movement.

> The world of the big corporations is an integrated world. There will be black grocery shops in black neighbourhoods, but in your lifetime... there isn't going to be a black General Motors...a few Negroes...will succeed in establishing sizeable...concerns. But the great majority, who start on this road, whether white or black, go bankrupt...To tell... blacks that this is the direction in which they must move is almost a form of cruelty (1969, CP, 1,522, 1,531).

Since the top jobs in the US mainly go to the graduates of a relatively small number of universities, Lewis argued for a strategy based on getting more young people into these institutions, but he did not see this as the main strategy. 'Probably the greatest contribution to black advancement would be to break the trade union barriers which keep our people out of apprenticeships in the building and printing trades, and prevent our upgrading or promotion in other industries' (1969, 1,524).

Given his relatively optimistic perspective with respect to the spread of development and the impact which the economy would ultimately have on racism, he tended towards the less confrontational approaches in the sphere of direct action. This was in keeping with his demeanour as well as his rationalist and modernist outlook. He gravitated towards organisations which appealed to the good sense of the authorities and which followed legal channels. He was also interested in those that opened opportunities for persons to participate in the economy and prepared them to take advantage of the openings which became available. Despite this, the weight he gave to the possibilities for reason, his pragmatism and his non-confrontational approach should not be confused with an attenuated aversion to racism. He generally sought to use more diplomatic language, but he could be quite combative in his writings as well as his personal interchanges. Indeed, when provoked, Lewis could be very sharp. An example of this was his review of *Africans and British Rule* by Margery Perham who was a leading academic Africanist and a supporter of the LCP. Lewis let none of this get in his way.

> To Miss Perham it is from his own savagery that the African needs protection; white exploitation is...merely...the inevitable if unfortunate accompaniment of the effort to civilise him...From the prosperous seclusion of Oxford it is easy to ride the high horse of cultural superiority, to belittle the wrongs of a people and magnify their faults. The book will go down well in the Colonial Office; it will please the settlers and doubtless be subsidised by...colonial governments. Africans fortunately are accustomed to being insulted. They will merely hope that Miss Perham will have learned a little manners before she settles down to write her next apology for imperialism (LCP Newsletter, September 1941, 128–29 quoted in Tignor 2005, 36).

Similarly, in an undated paper on 'Nationalism and Colonialism' which was written in the early 1950s, Lewis was quite caustic. Perhaps incensed by the proposals for the Central African Federation and thinking back to the recent War and its aftermath, he notes that it was not clear that the 'Europeans were any more fit to govern themselves' (c.1953, 6).

## Lewis's Over-estimation of the Universality of Cultural Values

Lewis's blind spot was on the question of culture. His acceptance of a rational modernisation metanarrative was rooted in what is generally referred to as the European Enlightenment, which left him with a level of Eurocentrism of which he was unconscious. In his early report on West Indian social conditions, he greatly overstates, with apparent pride, a process of acculturation.

> East Indians...are...recent comers...They...largely retain their languages, customs and religions. But they are fast becoming westernised...and their children, receiving a western education, are growing up with a European outlook.

> The bulk of the population...of African descent...have lost most of their African heritage, assimilating...ideas of their white rulers, and adapting...to European institutions. English is spoken universally (though there are remnants of a French patois) and Christianity has replaced the African religions (1939, 12).

Lewis tended to take his Eurocentrism as part of an enlightened universalism which embraced the best of world culture and rejected the pettiness of narrow nationalism as well as what he saw as the stultifying paternalism of those who would deny rapid development to the people of Africa. He notes that few persons who idealise 'small tribal societies on the verge of subsistence...show any desire to...settle... in such societies and to cut themselves off from modern hospitals, universities, concert halls, and the other luxuries which modern economic development can alone support' (1944, 2). His choice of examples was not accidental; he was trained in the European classical musical tradition and despite wider exposure, he regularly lapsed into accepting it as the norm. Ingham and Mosley discuss his tastes as an amateur musician who had strong views in this area; in particular, they record the occasion when he complains that 'one of his biggest grouses against the BBC is that it broadcasts so little classical organ music' (letter from Lewis November 21, 1952 LP 12/4, quoted in 2013, 293).

His commitments in this field no doubt allowed him to make various contributions; for example, while he lived in Jamaica he chaired the incipient board of the Jamaica School of Music, which sometimes met at his home (LP 32/7). He made a personal donation of £100 (over £2,050 today) to start a music fund to purchase instruments and records at UCWI (UCWI Council February 1960 min. 26). In contrast, he produced some very off-key public statements. While being positive on Caribbean achievements in the visual arts (his wife Gladys sculpted) he suggests that, 'In music we are...far behind...despite our... contributions to popular music, we have a dearth of...well trained musicians...especially...string players needed to maintain a symphony orchestra'(1971, 2,341). Paradoxically, this came after his statement in the same speech that 'human heritage includes...Hindu music... Ashanti music...the diatonic structure of jazz and the European classics' (1971, 2,340). Particularly in this area, he wore Eurocentric blinkers and became notorious for declaring during one of his first addresses to UCWI students that 'a false sense of nationalism has persuaded us that the steel band is a significant contribution to the world's heritage of music' (1960, 2,291).

Lewis was styled an Afro-Saxon by some who saw this as a severe indictment. He appears to have taken it as a compliment, defining himself in these terms as, 'a black man who can hold his own in competition with white people on their own ground' (1971, 2,332). He seemed bemused by persons who were:

> het up about... clothes we wear, or... hair styles, which seem to...be trivial and ever-changing phenomena...hardly worthy of the glance of the philosopher or statesman...though I recognise that...men have fought bitterly...about...wearing...a turban (1971, 2,333).

Prior to writing him off completely, the culturally aware reader may note that in the cited address at UCWI, he singled out a dictionary of Jamaican Dialect as one of the College's research achievements. His self-identity was as British West Indian who was coloured/black of African heritage, and we need to understand that each element had its particular significance.

## Undermining Racism in Many Ways

In considering Lewis's role in undermining racism, I make an allegoric reference to the Olympic Games, the history of which has witnessed two particularly poignant moments in the struggle against racism. In Berlin (1938), Jesse Owens's four gold medals challenged the racist propaganda of Adolf Hitler and the Nazis. In Mexico (1968), the demonstration by Tommie Smith and John Carlos was particularly dramatic, but fewer people know of the more understated stand taken by the Australian, Peter Norman who split the US duo to gain a silver medal in the 200m. On the podium, he joined the others in wearing an Olympic Project for Human Rights badge and like them, was never again chosen to compete in the Olympics. Memorable as this moment was, it is important to take note of the role which outstanding athletes like Arthur Wint, Leslie Laing, Herb McKenley, George Rhoden (Helsinki Olympics 1952); and Shelly Ann Fraser-Pryce, Sherone Simpson, Kerron Stewart, and Usain Bolt (Beijing Olympics 2008) among others have played in undermining racism. Lewis's approach was generally not that of Smith and Carlos. It is conjecture as to whether he would have done what Norman did. He may not have had the impact of the likes of Owens or Bolt, but with them all, he trod one of the many paths that have helped to undermine racism, and for this he should be recognised.

## Conclusion

Based on his social principles, socio-economic and political analyses, as well as his personal and professional experiences, Lewis was invested in issues relating to race and the struggle against racism. Within this field, he was persistent in his activism, academic and professional analyses, as well as his media and more popular interventions over five decades. During this time, the range of his involvements took a multiplicity of formats. As a person of African heritage he was a trailblazer who stood as an inspiration to many. He struggled self-consciously and undertook direct actions against racism. He also provided practical and intellectual leadership to institutions and organisations: as a teacher/ supervisor/ mentor and through his writings. He generated policy ideas which showed oppressed races how they might advance, and he could have contributed to an improvement in the welfare of millions of persons of African heritage. Unfortunately, those whom he advised directly generally failed to take advantage of his wisdom. It is primarily persons of Asian heritage who have benefited where states have followed economic paths similar to those he suggested, although the extent of his influence is yet to be extensively researched. He had a rough-and-ready pragmatism, and his ideas often proved more practical than many of his more revolutionist brethren with whom he made common cause. He was frank, and racially self-critical, neither being an apologist nor too partisan to point out weaknesses which required attention. He upheld universalist human values and was willing to serve all races and nations. He saw no value in being an oppositionist, especially during the early days of the independence movements, when it was important to prepare for the responsibilities of self-government. His perspective was not without its faults but he was often insightful. Despite his record, he has not always been remembered as an anti-racist fighter. In fact, until recently, he has suffered from erasure, for example, in terms of his role in the International African Friends of Ethiopia (IAFE) and the International African Service Bureau (IASB).

It is true that his written work was uneven and sometimes overemphasises features which could have been presented in a more nuanced form, but this was often influenced by the special message which he was seeking to address to his particular audience. Perhaps he was too optimistic. His posture within the cultural sphere was undoubtedly notorious in many respects, although he was not without redeeming features. He was not unique in exhibiting elements of Eurocentrism, a quality for which some other anti-racists of his era have been less chastised. These weaknesses set him on a different path from those of a more nationalist or cultural nationalist orientation. His non-confrontationalist style also set him apart from those who wished to challenge racism more directly and his focus on the economic foundations made him different from those who were more likely to emphasise the political. His desire to be realistic meant that sometimes he was more right and at other times those who had a more revolutionist orientation were better able to grasp what needed to be done. Yet, none of this suggests that the anti-racist movement benefited from the manner in which he was portrayed by many of his Caribbean critics. The focus on differences, the polemics and the ad hominem attacks tended to reduce the strength of the movement and to limit the extent to which all sections had access to its different histories, varied experiences and, indeed, its collective wisdom. The easy dismissal of Lewis was unfortunate. Indeed, it is ironic that it was when the Swedish sovereign handed him a prize that many of those who saw themselves as less Eurocentric began to re-appraise his worth. Looking back, it is of interest that at different times Harold Moody's LCP counted in and around his executive persons with as varied political positions as C.L.R. James, Peter Blackman, Una Marson, Arthur Lewis and Hugh Springer. In the 1930s, the LCP led by an anti-communist liberal Christian humanist, IASB led by an anti-Comintern Pan Africanist and the pro-Comintern communist led NWA (Negro Welfare Association) could find common cause against racism and were able to cooperate in presenting the Moyne Commission with a joint memorandum (UKNA 950/30). Without seeking to romanticise the past, the lesson of the Lewis case is that there is much to be said for broad cooperation within the struggle against racism and other social ills.

## Notes

1. This is a revised version of 'W Arthur Lewis and the Struggle for Racial Equality' presented to *Black Radical Thought, Pedagogy and Praxis: A Conference in Honour of Professor Rupert Lewi*s, UWI, Mona, October 10–12, 2013. It has been prepared with the research and editorial assistance of Rachel Folkes.
2. Lewis's activism as a student (including with the Student Christian Movement); an Anti-Colonialist, Anti-Imperialist, Anti-Fascist, Pan-Africanist, Peace Activist; a Fabian Socialist (and in the British Labour Party); an advocate for Caribbean Regionalism and other causes as well as his personal assistance to individuals of African heritage is yet to be adequately researched.
3. Pagination for Lewis's works included in his collected papers (CP) (1994) is for that edition.
4. Lewis expresses these views and quotes these figures in (1969, CP, 1522, 1527 and 1530–31).
5. This is a verbatim quote from (Lewis 1969, CP, 1518) although *Abeng* does not make this clear. Lewis identifies the objective quoted as: that of 'political movements' in countries with which he was familiar, where 'blacks are the great majority of the people' such as Jamaica and Nigeria.
6. This is not the place to contest Best's view, but it is clear that Lewis's most significant work (1954) and many others were rooted in his Caribbeanness (see Figueroa 2004).
7. A chapter of the Universal Negro Improvement Association (UNIA) started in St Lucia in November 1920 but it did not last. It was reconstituted in 1921 (Garvey 2011, cclv–cclviii).
8. By early 1935 Lewis offered to do a pamphlet for the New Fabian Research Bureau (1935). Extensively revised, it was published by the Fabian Society

(1939). He prepared items on race, colonialism and development for Labour Party related groups including the Advisory Committee on Imperial Questions and the Commonwealth Sub-Committee of the National Executive Committee. More is said on his Labour Party connections below.
9. Information on Lewis's involvement in the IAFE and its connection to the IASB are from (Matera 2008, 113–14). Reports relating to Lewis and the SCM are in the *Clare Market Review* (1934, 15, no. 1: 57; 1935, 15, no. 2: 43–44) and SCM minutes' books (LSEA LSE/UNREGISTERED/24/9-10). Lewis is also mentioned in the SCM files: A162, C73, J2, J10 and M81 in the University of Birmingham Archives (UBA). Archival references include an abbreviated archive name, collection and or box and or file number and sometimes item number as per the various cataloguing systems. The abbreviated and full names of the archives are listed in the references.
10. The account of Lewis's Liverpool experience is based on Tignor 2005, 38; he quotes letters, on Lewis's LSE file, between Vice Chancellor, Mountford, and LSE director, Carr-Saunders, and between the latter and Lewis (dated May 19, 1947 to July 14, 1947). I could not view these, as Lewis's LSE file was missing when I wished to view it in 2014 and 2015, and the relevant Liverpool Archive file was closed. Lewis's Manchester file was also missing.
11. Meyer was an Austrian émigré. He was one of the few persons who wrote with Lewis (Lewis and Meyer 1946, 1949) perhaps not by accident. 'All his life, Lewis would find himself better able to get on with exiles, like himself, than with WASPs' (Ingham and Mosley 2013, 98).

## References

*Abeng*. Kingston: Abeng Publishing Group.
Best, Lloyd. 2003. Reflections on the Reflections. In *Independent Thought and Caribbean Freedom: Essays in Honour of Lloyd Best*, ed. Selwyn Ryan, 423–41. St Augustine: SALISES, UWI.
———. 2004. The Lewis Tradition: Town and Gown. *The Integrationist* 2, no. 1: 78–92.
Chartier, Brittony. 2012. Reversing the Gaze: Wasu, The Keys and the Black Man on Europe and Western Civilization in the Interwar Years, 1933–1937. MA Thesis, Carlton University.
Clark, Kenneth, and John Hope Franklin. 1983. *A Policy Framework for Racial Justice*. Washington, DC: Joint Center for Political Studies.
Fabian Society. Various years. *Annual Report*. London: Fabian Society.
FCBP, Fabian Colonial Bureau Papers, Rhodes House Library, Oxford.
Figueroa, Mark. 2004. W. Arthur Lewis versus the Lewis Model: Agricultural or Industrial Development? *The Manchester School of Social and Economic Studies* 72, no. 6: 734–48.
Garvey, Marcus. 2011. *The Marcus Garvey and Universal Negro Improvement Association Papers, Volume XI: The Caribbean Diaspora, 1910–1920*, ed. Robert A. Hill. Durham: Duke University Press.
Girvan, Norman. 1989. Sir Arthur Lewis: A Personal Appreciation. In *Sir Arthur Lewis: The Simplicity of Genius*, 19–26. Cave Hill: ISER, UWI.
IASB, International African Service Bureau. 1938. *The West Indies Today*. London: IASB.

Ingham, Barbara, and Paul Mosley. 2013. *Sir Arthur Lewis: A Biography*. Basingstoke: Palgrave Macmillan.

*The Keys*. London: League of Coloured Peoples. New York: Kraus-Thomson Organization, 1976.

LCP, League of Coloured Peoples. 1940. *Memorandum on the Recommendations of the West India Royal Commission (Cmd. 6174) Prepared for H.M. Secretary of State for the Colonies*. London: League of Coloured Peoples.

Lewis, W. Arthur. 1935. *The British West Indies*. Typescript. Draft of a Pamphlet Prepared for the New Fabian Research Bureau. In Creech Jones Papers, Rhodes House Library, Oxford, 25/1a item 2.

———. 1936. *The Evolution of the Peasantry in the British West Indies*. Typescript of an Undergraduate Essay. Honourable Mention, Hugh Lewis Prize, LSE.

———. 1936a. A Peek at Denmark. *The Keys*. 4, no. 2: 21.

———. 1938. *Memorandum of Evidence to the West India Royal Commission*. In UKNA CO950/5c.

———. 1939. *Labour in the West Indies: The Birth of a Workers' Movement*. London: Fabian Society. London: New Beacon Books, 1977.

———. 1941. *The West Indian Outlook on the International Situation*. Presented to The Royal Institute of International Affairs, London, February 27.

———. 1942. *Some Aspects of the Flow of Capital into the British Colonies*. Memorandum to the Committee on Post War Reconstruction. Included as Appendix IV to (1943).

———. 1943. *The Development of Secondary Industries in the Colonial Empire*. Memorandum by the Secretary to the CEAC. In CO852/482/2 UKNA.

———. 1944. *Colonial Economic Development*. Draft Report to the CEAC Agenda Subcommittee. In UKNA CO990/7.

———. 1946. *Land Utilization and Settlement in Kenya*. Confidential Memorandum to the Labour Party Advisory Committee on Imperial Questions. In FCBP 46/2.

———. 1947. *Draft Letter to Colonial Office on Memorandum on Colonial Mining Policy*. Labour Party Advisory Committee on Imperial Questions, Paper no. 306. In LPA LP/ID.

———. 1951. Issues in Land Settlement Policy. *Caribbean Economic Review* 3, nos. 1 & 2: 58–92.

———. 1953. *Memorandum to Manchester Council for African Affairs Race Relations Sub-Committee*. In LP 29.

———. 1953a. *Aspects of Industrialization*. Cairo: National Bank of Egypt.

———. c. 1953. *Nationalism and Colonialism*. Typescripts. In LP 47/3

———. 1954. Economic Development with Unlimited Supplies of Labour. *The Manchester School of Social and Economic Studies* 22, no. 2 (May): 139–91.

———. 1955. *Theory of Economic Growth*. London: Allen and Unwin.

———. 1955a. A Socialist Economic Policy. *Socialist Commentary* 19 (June): 171–74.

———. 1960. *Address on the Occasion of the Matriculation of New Students at the University College of the West Indies, Mona, October 7, 1960*. Kingston: UCWI.

———. 1965. *Politics in West Africa*. London: Allen & Unwin.

———. 1969. Black Power and the American University. *University: A Princeton Quarterly* 40: 8–12.

———. 1971. On Being Different. *Bim* 14, no. 3: 3-9.

———. 1984. Development Economics in the 1950s. In *Pioneers in Development*, eds. Gerard Meier and Dudley Seers, 121-37. London: Oxford University Press.

———. 1985. *What Have We Learnt from Development*. Wildey, Barbados: CDB.

———. 1985a. *Racial Conflict and Economic Development*. Cambridge: Harvard University Press.
———. 1986. W. Arthur Lewis. In *Lives of the Laureates: Seven Nobel Economists*, eds. William Breit and Roger Spencer, 1-19. Cambridge: MIT UP.
———. 1994. *Sir William Arthur Lewis Collected Papers 1941–1988*, ed. Patrick Emmanuel. Barbados: ISER (Eastern Caribbean), UWI, 3 volumes.
Lewis, W. Arthur, and Frederick Meyer. 1946. *The Analysis of Secondary Industries*. Memorandum to the CEAC Industrial Sub-committee. In UKNA CO990/17.
———. 1949. The Effects of an Overseas Slump on the British Economy. *The Manchester School of Social and Economic Studies* 17, no. 3: 233–65.
LP, Lewis Papers, Seeley G. Mudd Manuscript Library, Princeton University.
LPA, Labour Party Archives, The People's History Museum, Manchester.
LSE, London School of Economics. Various years. *Directors Report*. London: LSE.
LSEA, London School of Economics Archives, London.
The *Manchester Guardian*. ProQuest Historical Newspapers. Accessed 29 May 2014.
Marley, Bob and the Wailers. 1976. *Rastaman Vibration*. Island Records IPS9383, LP, Album.
Matera, Marc. 2008. Black Internationalism and African and Caribbean Intellectuals in London, 1919–1950. PhD Dissertation, Graduate School-New Brunswick, Rutgers State University of New Jersey.
McCleery, William. 1980. Arthur Lewis on 'The Major Problem of Our Time'. *Princeton Alumni Weekly* 80, no. 19: 14–19.
Mine, Yoichi. 2006. The Political Element in the Works of W. Arthur Lewis: The 1954 Lewis Model and African Development. *The Developing Economies* 44, no. 3 (September): 329–55.
Tignor, Robert. 2005. *W. Arthur Lewis and the Birth of Development Economics*. Princeton: Princeton University Press.
UBA, University of Birmingham Archives, Birmingham.
UKNA, United Kingdom National Archives, Kew, London.
United Nations. 1951. *Measures for the Economic Development of Under-Developed Countries: Report by a Group of Experts Appointed by the Secretary-General of the United Nations*. New York: United Nations.
University College of the West Indies. 1960. *Council Minutes*. UWI Archives. UC-BV-2.
*West Africa*. Realistic Radial. October 12, 1957.
Wilkinson, Audine. 1999. *Sir William Arthur Lewis: A Bibliographic Portrait*. Cave Hill: ISER, UWI and http://www.uwi.edu/salises/arthur-lewis-page.php.
Whittall, Daniel James. 2012. Creolising London: Black West Indian Activism, and the Politics of Race and Empire, 1931–1948. PhD Dissertation, University of London.

# 14 | *Memory Gems of Revolution:*
*The Lived Experiences of Elean Rosalyn Thomas*

Linnette Vassell[1]

I reflect on the life and meaning of Elean Thomas as part of an effort to centre love in the practice of revolution, in the efforts to change Jamaica, that Rupert Lewis, myself, Elean Thomas and others such as (Elaine) Molly Wallace, Sharon Kelly and Clinton Hutton were a part of. Elean wrote a letter to me on September 20, 2002, in which she stated, 'No matter what, we have to take time to say, "I love you", to people, to trees, to flowers, to animals, to sky, to earth – ultimately to God (by whatever name called).' She was then living in Moore Town and I had written to tell her of the death of my mother in July of that year. It was the finality of death that had taught her two lessons, one of which was that need to share and to express love in the midst of all of life and for respect of all of life.

As *sistrens* and *breddrens* trying to build a nation through struggle, we experienced Elean as a rooted Jamaican woman, fierce in her love for justice, for liberation for all peoples oppressed, for the Jamaican people, black people, and passionate about the ordinary woman standing in the struggle of life. In all of this, love, manifested in action, was that struggle by women for wholeness, for family and community, 'because as long, as women take less, so long will women...children, men...ALL get less.'[2] Thomas was sure that love was not about the dolly baby type of woman, falling and losing the self in another. For when she explored this romantic side of *'A word more us-ed/ Yet more misunderstood/ More mystified, than, love'*, the meaning of the one strand she pulled and offered tentatively, was: *'in acceptance or rejection...in objective or subjective conditions/ You stand by me/ I stand by you.../Could this be Love?'*[3] This meaning of love, expressed as loyalty and solidarity...*In good times, or in bad/ In ups, or downs, or level/ In joy, or sadness/ In nearness, or in distance/ In acceptance or rejection,* came to define Elean Thomas (ET) and the things we had to learn as women and men in struggle.

Thomas has much to say to us, she has messages for children and for men and for women and for everybody. *Memory Gems* is the title of

Elean Thomas's unpublished collection of 'signposts along the road of living' which drew on her experiences, were reflected in her works, were exhortations...especially to women that, *'Until women learn, to make it/ With each other/We will never be able/To make it/ With men'*[4] and was knowledge taken from wall plaques in the homes of working people, reflecting the signs that guided their paths.

The location of Thomas's gravesite has been lost to us for now. On a search for the site at Church Pen cemetery on May 23, 2015, I shared the funeral programme with the cemetery manager. He said 'an important person like this should not be lost.' Many of the heroes of our struggles as Jamaican and Caribbean people are unknown women. Historical records favour men and often ignore the fact that many of men's achievements are made on the backs of women. This paper locates Elean Thomas as making a vast contribution, as a black woman who 'stan up' for progress at a very pivotal point in Jamaica's history, from the 1960s into the 1970s and to her death in 2004. It is part of creating a memory gem, as it were, a record that helps us locate our past, our present and paths for the future.

## Life and Death

After her funeral service in 2004, I wrote:

> We buried the body of my friend Elean Thomas-Gifford, ET, last week Saturday, June 5. She is back in her parish, interred at the Church Pen cemetery, near Old Harbour, where the bodies of her father Bishop David Thomas, founder of the Refuge Temple Pentecostal Church on Maxfield Avenue and of her beloved Uncle Natty also lay.[5]

As we watched the workmen shovel and lay the mortar to seal her grave, I bridged for a moment the pain of her passing within the hope captured in the graveside choruses led by Elder Currie and the band of choir members from Refuge Temple:

> *'meet me by the river someday...meet me by the river not far away...O when my Lord shall call me home...happy, happy home beyond the skies...meet me by the river someday'.*

Within the pause into the next chorus, the small band of five Rastafari Sistren who had been standing closely around, below the foot of the grave, raised a chant, and then others, bringing the African-Jamaican rhythm of the drum into the burial ceremony. They had come over to the funeral from Portland, where an all-night wake had been held at ET's home in Moore Town. (They were bound to be very tired, I thought.) One voice, raised above the rest, was blended by those of the other Sisters as they memorialised Sister Elean, Nana, Auntie. They spoke directly to her, not of her...how she had inspired them, had shared with them a Faith and a Livity. They said they could not even relate to many of the things they had heard about her at the church service. They knew her, the Sister said, as a woman who did not count high society, one who was struggling like them, with life.[6]

Thomas was born September 18, 1947, in Bellas Gate, St Catherine. In her autobiographical first novel, *The Last Room*, she paints a picture of the innards of rural Jamaica, of relationships, of people bound by family and land and people having conflicts over land but also bonding around important things of just being relatives. Thomas talks of her birth in the context of her mother's experience of getting pregnant as a single woman, surrounded by a multi-generational family at different economic levels, concerned with respectability. When Louise Duffus became pregnant at 19, she was sent away from the district to live with a relative in a remote place and to have her baby. She had started a sewing course that many young girls like herself were sent to do as preparation to make a living for themselves. Duffus sustained her family through employment as a weaver at the Ariguanabo Mills at Crescent in Spanish Town, a huge three-shift factory that milled cotton into fabric and was a lifeline for employment, especially for women. Elean lived with her mother 'in the humble circumstances of a tenement yard', recalled a schoolmate and friend from first to sixth form. She attended Miss Hall's Basic School in Old Harbour, Mrs Daniel's in Spanish Town, Crescent Primary and in 1959, went on scholarship to St Jago High School.

Elean would often pick up her friend Dorothy, whom she called DBurns, and give her a ride on her bicycle to school. They formed a small clique of four girls, including a Chinese girl whose parents owned a shop near to the school, and were very close. Sometimes at lunchtime they would go to the shop of her Chinese friend to cook and eat lunch before returning to school. DBurns recalls that from those early days in first form when they first met, to sixth form where she did English Literature, History and Religious Education at Advanced Levels (A

Levels), Elean was bright and full of confidence as a young woman. One of the strongest members of the school's debating society, she always questioned things, was very analytical, especially in discussing history and, if she did not agree with the teacher, she would say so and had the arguments to 'back up' her position. Her sense of social justice was nurtured in high school so that later, when she identified herself as communist, this did not come as a surprise. 'You see the people who work in the canteen? She and dem a fren...she would vex if anyone take step with Miss Ivy and would let you have it if anyone tried to disrespect her'.[7]

It was in her high school years that Elean's mother migrated to England and boarded her daughter with Sister Grant, described by another school friend, Carol, as a stalwart of the All Saints Pentecostal Church in Spanish Town.[8] The departure saddened Elean, and was a part of the pain that she spoke of as a foundational experience of her life. That period saw her also moving to live in Kingston and experiencing a certain rootlessness, living in different places, having lost her mother, as it were. She left high school, to teach in Kingston, at Strathford High School and St George's College, and worked in a bank in Cross Roads before going to the University of the West Indies to read political science and history. Thomas graduated in 1974 and thereafter worked as a journalist at the *Gleaner*. She later explained how the profession can lend itself to substance abuse – moving one from social drinking into habitual, and progressively to, addiction. Compounding the situation was always the pain of separation from her mother. She wrote in 1994: 'Nothing can be solved until, my relationship with my mother is solved. If only because she, birthed me, There is a part of me, Only she knows of, I cannot therefore be, whole, Until we are one again, As in the Womb'.[9]

Although they came together again later when ET went to 'rescue' her mother from the aloneness of the last room at a rented flat in London and took her back to Jamaica, mentally ill, the pain never went away. Part of that journey is told in her 1991 novel, *The Last Room*, which she dedicated in part to her mother. In this work, she spoke of the promise and pain of migration, the loss of family (the common and persisting experience of Jamaicans of the late twentieth and early twenty-first century) and of the rescue mission of a child, a daughter to a mother, herself also alienated in many ways.

Pain was not only of a personal nature in Thomas's life but impacted her politics. At the service of thanksgiving for her life, Apostle J.I. Clark Jr. had described ET as a 'Pentecostal Kid'. He said that the pain of people's lives which her father Bishop Thomas addressed in his ministry, had stayed with ET...and was expressed in her life, public activism and struggle for justice.

**Politics on the Left – The Political is the Personal**

Thomas was within the centre of the intense political battle of the Cold War politics which fought for the soul of Jamaica in the 1970s to the 1980s. Many of those of us on the Left felt that the traditional parties, the Jamaica Labour Party (JLP) and the People's National Party (PNP) had divided the people into two different tribes as it were, and because high prices and hardships did not impact the people on either side differently, our mission was to bring both tribes together to see their interest as one. ET had an explicit bias to the working class and the working people; she chose to stand with the people. She saw the Workers Party of Jamaica (WPJ) as an attempt to pull people across the divide and to talk about a new kind of Jamaica where the working people and those who stood with them would be a part of a movement to put our stamp on the country in a way that had not happened in history before. What distinguished this historical moment given previous efforts of those at the bottom to make a change was the prospect that, based on the political and social alignments in the country, the struggle for change could actually secure a strong enough foothold to move the people's agenda forward.

Elean was part of the ferment of the late 1960s on the campus at Mona which found its expression in this new left movement. She would have seen herself as a woman having a place and as having influence within it. She was among the leaders in the formation of the Workers' Liberation League (WLL) in 1974, which declared 'critical support' for the People's National Party and transformed into the Workers Party of Jamaica (WPJ) in 1978. She was the first and, for many years, the only female member of the Central Committee in the intensely male-dominated formation that was the party. ET also had a history of linkage with the trade union movement, grounding and organising with the Independent Trade Union Action Committee (ITUAC) at Wildman Street in downtown Kingston. Before my own entry into activist politics in 1975/76, I attended a few of their lectures and discussions about workers' rights.

Thomas's work as a journalist became a critical aspect of her activism. It had deepened her understanding of Jamaica's class contradictions which she could put to service as an executive member of the Press Association of Jamaica (PAJ) and at the Agency for Public Information (API) (now the Jamaica Information Service [JIS]) which she headed after the victory of the PNP under Michael Manley in 1972. Manley's time in office became a period of intense class clash in the country. It was an important area of collaboration between the PNP Left, styled as democratic socialist, and the communist WPJ. The WPJ's work in that area gave the PNP access to a cadre of trustworthy professionals it could rely on to defend the Left and who later became targeted when the JLP came to power in 1980. Thomas had also put her journalistic work into editing the *Struggle* newspaper which was the propaganda arm of the WPJ.

I saw Elean Thomas as someone that the 'ordinary members' of the party could relate to. She was serious, no nonsense-looking much of the time, but really a very warm person, very sisterly. People would have called her Sister Elean or ET in a genuine and sincere way because she was a Sister, real and grounded. She and Rupert Lewis brought a certain authenticity to how the party would have been viewed by others of us as members and maybe the wider public. She was fearless, a hard worker, strategic thinker and defender of the party.

From 1981 to 1984, Thomas was Chairperson of the International Commission of the WPJ with special responsibility for the Caribbean. Her role was to represent the party and serve as a bridge between the party and other fraternal bodies. That position brought her in close contact with the implosion of the Grenada revolution in 1983. She arrived in Grenada five days after the October 19 violence that saw the death of Maurice Bishop and other leaders and citizens of revolutionary Grenada, and remained there for two weeks. The Coards (who were at the centre of the internal conflict within the ruling New Jewel Movement, NJM) charged her with taking their children out of Grenada. She took that responsibility seriously and became a sort of guardian for them, settling them and helping to create a safe space for them in Jamaica. In the aftermath of the events, she would have been involved in internal party discussions on the Grenada situation, but more than everything, she herself did some hard thinking, for the whole situation affected her deeply. Recalling this some 20 years after, in an interview on IRIE FM radio in 2003, she explained why the 'terrible holocaust of Grenada' had affected her so deeply:

> Well, for a start, these were people I knew, and still know – those who are alive – very well. I was very close to Maurice Bishop, I am close to Phyllis Coard...you know Jacqueline Creft who died at Fort Frederick too was a very close and warm friend of mine. Then, I was the International Secretary of the Workers Party of Jamaica and as such was responsible for Caribbean relations and in the party, you have to go with the party line and I suffered for a number of years with a guilt that I did not agree with the line then, but I did not speak out so that politically, socially and personally those comrades were very close to me.[10]

Despite the pain, she dutifully took up between 1984 and 1987, service as the WPJ's representative to the Editorial Council of the World Marxist Review (WMR) based in Prague, Czechoslovakia where she overlapped with Rupert Lewis for a period. The WMR was the gathering of the intellectual force of the global communist movement where there were active discussions about issues in the international communist movement. There she established broad connections within the international socialist and communist movement. She remained in Prague beyond her desired stay and it became a very challenging period. She described it as such:

> It's for me a particularly challenging period – challenging for me to avoid vexation, depression and subjectivism. There are quite a few problems, personal/political (they can never be strictly separated – that's *not* dialectics) but the main one is that up to now the chances are one in a million that I'll be able to get home (i.e., Jamaica) when planned.[11]

She was not sure of the underlying reasons, but a letter that should have come from the WPJ to the WMR regarding her departure had not arrived as scheduled. Although she felt like 'tearing up and cussing', she drew, she said, on her training and experience to deal with the situation and shared a lesson in the process: 'Girl, any road that looks easy – shun it! There is something wrong with it! That is one thing I've definitely learnt.'[12] She was in a constant struggle to make ends meet, to deal with her responsibilities there and in caring for her mother in Jamaica for whom she had rented a house in Edgewater from a colleague and friend. By 1987, though still wearied, she had begun to work through a plan. She wrote:

> Since the letter, I sent to you from England and by the time I had gotten your letter, I think I have made some progress in sorting out in a more objective way my thoughts on the present and immediate future. In this respect, I think our thinking – yours and mine, coincide on all the fundamental questions, except that maybe I have developed a broader and more 'material' (as against sentimental) approach to the question of the interconnection between my own interest on the one hand and commitment/demands of other sources, including family.
>
> For example, I fully agree with you that my own ability to contribute significantly to strengthening 'that warm current', will be directly connected to my ability to preserve my mind and body, to survive, to live and not just on the margins of poverty and hustling. It was Marx who first said man has to eat before he can do politics and our own recent changes are trying to practically recognise this universal truth.
>
> But further, my ability to continue to care for and help Mama in any way much less to stabilise and strengthen that scene, more so depends on my strengthening in an all-round way my own material foundations.
>
> And on this, there are several elements to be considered (a) my own mental and physical situation – this cannot be taken lightly. If I am not careful – we could both end up with mental problems – then who would help who? I say this right out Lintin because sometimes even those close to one take for granted how delicate is the mechanism of the mind, how easily it can snap, even in supposedly strong people. And especially in situations where one has hosts of friends, comrades, supporters, admirers, etc., but where that loving support which can only come from blood – mother, father, sister, brother, auntie, uncle, child, life-partner – is not there. I don't say these things to frighten you or for pity (you know that) but rather to make the point that my decisions have to be first and foremost based on realism. [13]

So although, to a large extent, party practice presented as if there were no real choices for the good comrade between keeping up the pace of a rigorous party life and attending to personal and family interests, a most ardent leader had begun to question this.

## Shifting Politics – Centering Self in the Political

After the defeat of the Grenada Revolution, ET had begun to struggle intensely against the Marxist-Leninist orthodoxy of the WPJ. She tried more and more to centre herself within the cultural moorings of the Jamaican people and our African Caribbean history and heritage. She struggled to bring the personal, inter-personal and political together, striving for the realistic balance about which she spoke. Rupert Lewis, perhaps, best exemplifies the success of re-orienting oneself into the Jamaican historical and cultural context. His intellectual work, which centred on Garvey and Garveyism, was the major source that anchored him in the post-WPJ context as well as having the benefit of a stable family and home base.

But even in such circumstances, family and home had come under tremendous strain from party life with its demand for long and rigorous work and meeting schedules, commitment of finances (dues) and property to party work – the latter could be abused without explanation or apology – and the burden of care in the domestic sphere that would fall mainly on the women and, in exceptional cases, on a few supporting men. Where partners were both equally in the struggle, children could feel the pressure with unknown effects. The problems of single mothers would be even more challenging unless one had a superb support system. But, so caught up were we in the struggle, that many women like ET either did not have the time and space to think long-term to garner resources to acquire a home, or turned their minds from such pursuits from fear of being branded 'capitalist' by comrades in the party.

Many comrades, ET among them, believed that the cause to transform Jamaica for the benefit of the majority was laudable and just and therefore saw their personal sacrifices as necessary and worthy. Despite the contradictions and the mistakes in the process, many of us were proud that we had chosen to ally through the WPJ with a cause which placed in the forefront the interest of the majority, of so-called ordinary women and men, with their children. For the first time in modern Jamaican history, the hope was that, through securing changes in social and cultural life, in economic conditions and in the politics, the majority of our people would come to feel that they had a stake in the country. There was optimism for a new Jamaica, for the working people saw their sons and daughters whom they had sacrificed to educate, affirm commitment to giving back to community and building the kind of Jamaica that respected and built on their sacrifice.

The movement for change led by the PNP faced formidable challenges in the context of the politics of the Cold War, and manifested also in intense partisan political rivalry and economic sabotage mounted by opposing forces; it was an intense competition between what were defined as the forces of progress, on the one hand, and the forces of reaction, on the other. The WPJ was clearly allied to the forces of progress and had struggled to secure and to safeguard benefits on behalf of the working people; had raised consciousness and organisation among Jamaicans. However, it was itself not strong and rooted enough in the decision-making process and among the people to avoid the decisive political defeat of the progressive movement in 1980.

Elean applied herself to reflecting on these many aspects of the internal party life, including the gaps that needed to be filled in the work among women. This led her to explore as a major theme, women's role in life and politics – personal, interpersonal and organisational. In this aspect, her womanist standpoint comes to the fore as an understanding of the link between personal and community survival and liberation. She explains that she writes about women to women because on our backs are the burdens of many generations and that 'we who have dry peas have to seek fire.' In other words, women's challenges require specific types of autonomous mobilisation. So she challenged us as women to support each other, to speak to our pain and hopes, to struggle for ourselves and for the whole community, including children and men. In, 'You Ask Me Why',[14] she writes:

> You ask me why, I write about, women, to women.
> You say to me, women, are not the only, down-pressed, discriminated, down-trodden, deprived.
> So why, write about, women, to women.
>
> I write about my sisters, to my sisters.
> Because on our backs, was put the most heavy
> past-present-future, burdens.
> I write about my sisters, to my sisters
> Because, woman is the stone, that the builder refuse, but who is head
> of the corner, the unrealized foundation-stone.

> I write about my sisters, to my sisters,
> Because our ancestors say,
> it is those who have dried peas, that must seek a fire, hot enough to cook, those peas
> or she who feels it, knows it, and wants most, to change it.
>
> I write about my sisters, to my sisters, because as long as women, take less
> So long will women, children, men
> ALL
> Get less.
> You ask me why? That's why.

She therefore saw women's liberation as the route to the liberation of the whole people. She identified herself within the broad scope of the struggle of the people but also, specifically of the 'common woman'. In 'Lives of the Common Woman', she tells us:

> i am no muse, no scholar, no wise one, no poet
> i cannot, turn a rhyme, a metre, a phrase
> i am but one, of tens of millions of ordinary and common persons
> THE COMMON WOMAN, YET NOT COMMON TO ALL
> Who see and feel and live, THE WORLD, through the bare opaque window
> and in the midst of, The beating hot SUN, The drowning RAIN, The blasting Winds
> The unexpected joys, of Sunshine
> or tender MOON, Cooling Breezes, of the Space inhabited, by ordinary Common Persons...
> and in particular, The COMMON WOMAN
> And from what I see, and feel and live, Together with others, I try to make
> Word Photographs, Word Drawings, WORD PAINTINGS, WORD BEATS
> WORD Rhythms, from the lives, of the COMMON WOMAN.[15]

Thomas was also aware of the contradictions facing women within the WPJ and she was quite impatient with what she saw as petty, manipulative behaviour. She would have supported the development of guidelines for man/woman relationships in the Party. Democratic centralism basically demanded that everyone march in line, and this may have prevented her from taking a public stance on those issues, but this did not prevent her pointing out challenges and the need to address them. Commenting on the practice of special sessions of 'criticism and self-criticism' in the Women's Committee (WC) of the party, which could be quite bruising because, it was seen as being used to cut down one another as women, she questioned:

> How do we find the time and space to spend so much time in the WC talking about this individual's weakness and that one's idealism and the other one's promotion [?] *When do we discuss* the conditions of the domestic servant woman, the factory working woman, the rural field worker woman? The woman in Haiti, in Salvador, Nicaragua? When and where do we clarify our knowledge, and understanding of a *scientific view of the woman question?*
>
> Where and when do we discuss how to deepen the understanding of the Party on the particularities of our country on this question? When and where do we discuss how to link OWP[16] with broader international forces? When and where do we discuss the problems of women who don't work in the WC? When and where do we conduct leadership training so that *all* members of the WC can play their full part and responsibilities? When and where do we discuss our programme of action for uniting all the progressive trends in the entire women's movement?
>
> Now, get me clear, *nothing that I say must belittle the tremendous work, contribution and achievements of our comrade sisters in building the bedrock of the anti-imperialist women's movement in our country.* Many shortcomings are objectively rooted but we must also be clear that whenever we are spending more time and/or space discussing or being preoccupied with *inward* things instead of *outward* things – then something is wrong.[17]

As an inspiration for and a founding member of the Committee of Women for Progress (CWP) in October 1976, which was an 'arm' of the WPJ, her vision was that, among other things, the organisation should seek to unite women across the divisions of class position and political party division to address the interests of women. This mandate had been fulfilled with the CWP forming, with the PNP Women's Movement, a progressive alliance among women which resulted in the passage of the Maternity Leave Law for Women in 1979.

ET returned to this theme of the party and the organisations in which it had influence, placing priority on linking broadly with groups and organisations, in order to strengthen the struggle and to help the progressive movement to survive. In a long letter to the party leadership and membership in 1987 sent from the WMR, she stressed among many themes, the need for changes in the approach to leadership to one 'which allows comrades and non-Party people to develop and contribute independently, to think for themselves, to use their own experience and judgement' and to connect broadly among the people.[18]

## On Love and Being a Revolutionary

Elean Thomas believed in love. She understood what it meant. As a woman, as a human being, she always searched for companionship, for that oneness, for that empathy, for that ability to be able to be comfortable and to have a fabulous dance and intimacy that one hopes for in a truly reciprocal love relationship. When she decided to marry Lord Anthony Gifford (Tony), it was at one level a very conflictive situation – a black, communist, radical woman, marrying a white man from the heart of the colonial empire. Her long-time schoolmate DBurns tackled her about it....'You ET a marry a white man?' She said that ET said that the man was a 'conscious brother' and she liked his philosophy of life. Thomas and Gifford took that leap to marriage in September 1988 because she had found in him somebody who gave her comfort, emotional comfort and, I think, also material support. He was also someone with whom she could spar intellectually and he was a defender of the people's struggle, a human rights activist. She described Tony as a revolutionary person, a fine human being and a lovely man.[19] I would figure that she also meant a loving man, because he seemed that as well.

Thomas's marriage in 1988 coincided with the rethinking that had been underway for some time within the party which, in addition to issues of organisation and leadership, turned also on matters of personal desire and the work of revolution. Where party work had previously been expected to take precedence over personal desires, at that point in the life of both the party and ET, this ordering was being viewed differently. Returning to London, she pursued a graduate diploma in communications with the University of London, Goldsmith College. She continued her writing, publishing her second book of poetry in 1988 and her first novel in 1991. She resigned from the WPJ in 1989.

Thomas recognised, like many others, that the politics by itself is really nothing and the politics must be about people and their relationships in the different and diverse ways that we live our lives in the family, relationships between men and women, as within organisations and society. In other words, politics is about making people better and living better lives, and ET had reached a stage where she felt she could be in the struggle as well as try to build a relationship where she would have some intimacy as a woman. Elean and Tony returned to Jamaica in 1991, adopted a child legally, and many others informally. They tried to make a home and build that sense of having that close personal family amidst all of the contradictions of their lives.

**A Search for Meaning**

Although ET's politics shifted, it did not find a resting place. She tried to make meaning in the kind of 'livity' that she embraced, searching for ways to contribute to social action with meaning for people's liberation. As part of her search for new forms of politics, balance and struggle for service to community, ET, in 1991, developed Oil Nut, a self-help company dealing with education, communications and culture. The company pursued alternative education based on teaching children and young people Jamaican history. The Nanny Children's Workshop, which she also founded, focused on children. She extended links she had developed with Ghana, and in 1992, with Tony and others, organised the first Panafest Pilgrimage to Ghana under the Oil Nut banner. Coming out of this initial contact, the establishment of cultural links and collaboration between jamaica and Ghana became part of the mandate that she began to envision.

Through efforts to consolidate a new mission of enterprise, she started a small fish vending business, buying fish in Old Harbour Bay, for example, and seeking customers in and around the corporate area. Her friend DBurns was one of her customers. DBurns said she confronted Elean more than once on the question of what was happening in her life, because she saw that wandering spirit in her and feared that she was in trouble with substance abuse. She was right and ET was open in speaking to this in the 2003 interview on 'Running African', a feature focused on African connections that she had helped to establish at IRIE FM.

In the interview, she traced what she saw as the stages of alcohol addiction and linked it with the illness from sadness. She had developed that understanding from Arlene Mantle, a singer and lesbian, whom she had met in Moscow in 1987, who spoke of her own experience of abuse by her former husband and how this had brought the sickness of sadness in her life. She continued:

> It's the first time I'd heard that term, of sadness being an illness and as the alcoholism proceeded and I began to explore why I felt better drinking than not drinking (because that is the key that one needs to realise in addiction if we are to treat it properly...addicts do feel better using the substance than not you see) and then there are the many changes in my life.[20]

Grenada was one source of sadness. The other worse period was after the divorce in '98:

> because although Tony and I fully agreed that it was best for this to be, only married people who then become divorced understand what a traumatic thing this can be, because you are trying to rebuild your life at the same time I had left the Workers Party in 1989 and all that had happened to the communist movement and the left movement was also a source of sadness.[21]

She admitted that the alcohol abuse wasn't completely an aside in the break of the marriage, but analysed that:

> on my part I realised that a marriage between a black person and a white person, no matter the individual characteristics of the persons, have a very hard time working, especially when it is someone like me and someone like Tony Gifford, because as you know Tony is progressive. I am a Revolutionary, is, always will be.[22]

Thomas's embrace of Rastafari had become a central part of her life she said, and had played a big part of beating the habit in 2002. Moore Town she also saw as 'the place of her death and resurrection.' The Moore Town women who chanted at her burial met Elean at a stage of a journeying, a wandering that she had engaged in from previous years. This movement was both geographic and emotional, a seeking to find some balance in her life, to find peace and love and establish roots. She had moved about in St Andrew and Clarendon and finally in Moore Town, had received Maroon Community land and built a house, with support from her former husband. Here, it was said, she continued to struggle to set things right; for example, if she knew there was abuse she would chant out about it. She was therefore not sufficiently sensitive to the context in which she operated and felt justified that she had the liberty to just say what she wanted because an injustice had occurred. But this would evoke discomfort, if not resentment, among some folks. So she kept wandering.

**Lessons of a Woman in Struggle**

The life and experience of Elean Thomas reveals aspects of the especially tortuous journey of women in the struggle of life and living and the effects of the additional and multiple levels of responsibilities women carry in and for families. ET, like many women, searched, but did not achieve the balance that she wanted in her life, especially with her daughter and her mother. Manifestations of mental ill health, which she feared, came in the 1990s when the pressures of survival, the contradictions in her political context and the unravelling of her marriage came together to feed alcohol abuse. She died of brain cancer in 2004.

Thomas was an intense person. If you had a relationship with her, it was an intense, demanding one. The fact that her life was unstable economically, politically and emotionally, alerts us to pay special attention to who we are as human beings, as women, and as men in the process of engagement in the struggle for change and transformation in community. At the same time, her intense commitment and relentless work for the liberation of working people, black people, women, oppressed peoples everywhere, was the essence of who she was – an unrelenting fighter for revolutionary change on the battlefield of struggle.

**Notes**

1. With much thanks, respect and love to Maziki Thame who extended tremendous and unbelievable support to enable me to produce this paper.
2. Elean Thomas, *Before they Can Speak of Flowers: Word Rhythms* (London: Karia Press, 1988), 22–23.
3. Elean Thomas, *Word Rhythms From The Life of a Woman* (London: Karia Press, 1986), 54–55.
4. Ibid., 84.
5. Her Uncle Natty…'first taught me to be proud of my class, colour and sex… and who bequeaths me a heritage of struggle.' See Dedication in *Word Rhythms from the Life of a Woman*.

6. This was first written in June 2004, but it was not shared publicly.
7. Interview with Dorothy Noel, Friday May 6, 2016.
8. Conversation with Carol Charlton, Tuesday May 10, 2016.
9. Elean Thomas. Memory Gems (unpublished) Mama Louise, 1994.
10. Elean Thomas. Interview with Andrea Williams on 'Running African,' July 2003. Aired on IRIE FM Radio, Sunday May 30, 2004.
11. Elean Thomas to Linnette Vassell, June 19, 1986. Vassell Archives.
12. Ibid.
13. Elean Thomas to Linnette Vassell, March 11, 1987. Vassell Archives.
14. Thomas, *Word Rhythms*, 24–25
15. Elean Thomas. *Before They Can Speak of Flowers*, 22–23
16. The Organisation of Women for Progress (OWP) was the new name given to the Committee of Women for Progress (CWP) which had been formed in October 1986 under the influence of Elean Thomas and other activists and progressive women inside and outside of the WPJ. The name was changed from 'Committee' to 'Organisation' in the early 1980s and the OWP formed the Women's Resource and Outreach Centre in 1983 which became defunct by the mid-1980s.
17. Letter, June 19, 1986.
18. Elean Thomas. This is a letter to my Comrades of the WPJ, to the Leadership and To the Membership. Transcribed from tape received week of September 13–19, 1987. September 26, 1987. Vassell Archives.
19. Elean Thomas to Linnette Vassell, September 4, 1987 Vassell Archives.
20. Running African Interview.
21. Ibid.
22. Ibid.

# 15 | *Pedagogy and Leroy Clarke's Philosophy of Being, Freedom and Sovereignty*

Clinton A. Hutton

The power of philosophy
Floats through my head
Light like a feather
Heavy like lead.
– Bob Marley

Man of right is God in flesh –
Stop seeking God and be God.
– Priest Duggie (citing a Bobo Shanti Rastafari ontological concept).

Liberate the minds of men
And ultimately you will liberate the bodies
of men.
– Marcus Garvey

Welcome,
Welcome, O fine guests who congeal beyond
Endurances to link the pinnacles of Thought
In an addiction splendidly arisen above
Great spaces of palpitating climates.
See, the blessed heights of 'Art and Reason!'
– LeRoy Clarke

In a speech made by Marcus Garvey to an audience in Windsor, Ontario, Canada in 1937, the internationally renowned Pan Africanist leader and founder of the Universal Negro Improvement Association (UNIA), notes that it will require philosophy to save the African race from the consequences of slavery and colonialism. According to Garvey, 'It is an African Philosophy not platonic philosophy. It is going to be philosophy that will save this perishing race of ours' (Jacques Garvey and Essein-Udom 1987, 113).

Marcus Garvey's statement is, to a great extent, exemplified by LeRoy Clarke and his journey to the apotheosis of self, to El Tucuche. LeRoy Clarke (The Elder, Chief Ifá Ojé Won Yomi Abiodu) is a Master Artist of Trinidad and Tobago, poet, author and philosopher. For the last 45 years of Trinidad and Tobago's 51 years of independence, he has been weaving/beating/fashioning/'arting' into being a mode of existence depicting an image, an attitude and a language of sovereignty and freedom antithetical to the epistemology, ontology and cultural ethos of colonialism and neocolonialism.

Clarke's body of work comprising paintings and drawings, poetry/proses and essays constitutes a form of anti-colonialism and a re-creation of an Africa that was despised, disrespected, denigrated, feared, ridiculed, shattered and scattered into obscurity. This form of anti-colonialism and re-creation of sovereignty combines the political, but especially the cosmological/spiritual, epistemological, ontological and psychological into a way of life, which, to a large extent, denotes Clarke's evolving mode of existence. LeRoy Clarke lives philosophically and triumphantly over the philosophy and praxis of erasure and obscurity.

In the epistemological, ontological and psychological terrain in which Clarke thinks, creates, feels, acts and lives, development, freedom, sovereignty and identity continue to be tenuous for people of African descent so long as their sense of self remains problematic. Therefore, in Clarke's philosophical state of existence, the confused sense of self, or worse, pathological sense of self identified in the Europeanised ontological culture of Africa and the African Diaspora must be defeated. He thus put squarely on the development agenda of post-colonial society the principal elements of the philosophy of being: Who am I? Know thy self. To thyself be true.

The Occidental dystopian assault on the existential viability of First Nation peoples in the Americas and Africans who were enslaved and colonised by Europeans, has had an epochal agential impact on the psychological, epistemological and ontological culture of these peoples and their descendants as well as on the motive forces and beneficiaries of this Columbian project: Europeans and their descendants. It is this invention: a system of the fettering, debilitating myths of white supremacy and black inferiority, born of an evolving superstructure/neo-superstructure, shaping the meaning and ontology of power, authority and the narrative of existence, which LeRoy Clarke has spent the last 45 years of his life deconstructing and recreating an existence antithetical to the Columbian globalisation project and its neo-globalised manifestations.

LeRoy Clarke, who first exhibited works of his art in the national Independence Exhibition of Trinidad and Tobago in 1962 to mark that country's independence from Britain, would hold his first one-man show *Labour of Love* in 1966. A few years later, he would embark on a declarative journey of self-discovery imagining, imaging, deconstructing, recreating and articulating an identity devoid of the tenuous metaphysicality of colonialism, what Clarke (1981) calls 'Crumpled rainbow':

> Crumpled rainbow
> From Haiti to Trinidad and Tobago...
> To my task of broken mirrors,
> My archipelago! (6).

Colonialism has left 'a constellation of wombs waiting to be filled' (Clarke 1981:30) with the gestative materials of the recreation of self in what Clarke calls 'my archipelago.' In this archipelago called the Caribbean, Clarke notes:

> My bones are picked dry of scent
> they are marrowless staves
> that corrupt the road to stars....(71).

The journey to the stars, to the highest manifestation of self, has to be a creative process, requiring an agency of creativity. 'Who will rechart the ruins...?/Who will piece it together in its beginning...?/Who will utter the cipher...?' Clarke asks. His answer? 'A new poet':

> Who has collected words like nails
> stripped from his own fingers,
> each a testimony of burning lava... (72).

Clarke was confronted with the fact that the decolonisation of the political colonial state never meant the decolonisation of the state of the colonised mind, its mode of thinking, knowing, constructing meaning and existing. Hence, his conviction that a philosophy rooted in the 'blessed heights of "Art and Reason (Poetry)"' and thus in the agency of 'the new poet (artist)', was necessary for the gathering of fragments of a spiritual universe and creating a redemptive one.

The colonial superstructural problematic cannot work itself out in the post-colonial epoch by ignoring it or by treating it with half measures. It has to be engaged consciously and persistently. This is an imperative of freedom, sovereignty, of identity and development, the pedagogy of decolonisation.

In LeRoy Clarke's philosophy, the starting point for addressing this imperative: the development of the post-colonial state and society, and especially the development of the state of the post-colonial mind and agency, is the douen. Douen or douendom, is the ontological constructing altar of indignity, epochal generational pain, hurt, marginality and alienation from self. It is the epistemic, psychological knots, chains and slop that suffocate the flow of the invigorating identity-agential nutrients of ancestry, of redemption, of sovereign existentialism. This occidental visibility, the basis for African invisibility, is what Clarke calls douen/ douendom. Douendom thus becomes a philosophical category of invisibility and marginality in Clarke's philosophy of being.

'In Trinidad and Tobago folklore, douens are the spirits of babies who died before religious rites are performed', and, according to David Brizan, 'who linger perennially in a dismal twilight' (Ravello 2003, 22). The Douen thus lacks the capacity to be ancestral in consequence of the state and brevity of his/her life. Therefore, he/she is not part of the pantheon of the ancestors and hence, of that evolving foundation of future generations through connection with previous generations. 'Existentially, this raggedly dressed, faceless creature (in straw hat) with a protuberant belly and feet turned backwards, wanders about the forest on the margins of civilization, eating fruits and water crabs and enticing and haunting children during full moon' (Hutton 2011, 80).

So when some persons say they are not douens in their upset with LeRoy Clarke for allegedly calling them so, they are missing the finer, more intended philosophical point which he has been making: that is, slavery, colonialism and neo-colonialism have dehumanised and marginalised in dystopian dimensions, all Africans, whatever their status or state of consciousness. LeRoy Clarke uses the Douen as a signifier or metaphor to denote the zero of things to which Africans were reduced, or 'the compass-less cape of beginnings' (Clarke 2008,

xxix) that must be navigated by imagination and creativity, by art and reason, by assuming the agency and methodologies of the artist. Hence his charge: '[Y]ou must be brave enough to go behind the zero of things...and invent eyes with which you can see. Because you have to reinvent yourself.'

Douendom then, is that ontological state which Clarke calls 'the zero of things' to which Africans were reduced by the forces of slavery and colonialism, that existential abyss from which Africans must climb by themselves, to selfhood, by re-inventing or re-creating themselves. The cosmological dust from which the recreation of black selfhood is accomplished in LeRoy Clarke's philosophy, are the fragments of a spiritual life, those ontological signatures of ancestral African nations shattered and scattered into obscurity by slave-making and colonialising Europeans who, in their bid to control the resources of the world, principally supported and enacted positions of ontological dominance (white supremacy), a powerful psychological tool of domination, such as the one articulated by the slave-making Frenchman, Hilliard d'Auberteuil:

> Policy and safety require that we crush the race of Blacks by a contempt so great that whoever descends from it even to the sixth generation shall be covered with an indelible stain (qtd. in Rogers 1994, 99).

This indelible stain was manifestly expressed by an African Jamaican woman in 1894:

> I nebber could lub a black little chile same as I do de white. I worship de little massa an' if I lucky, eben I may hab a fair chile one day. Not ob course a real white one, dat asking too much, but still one dat is almost white, an' den I worship it, an' work for it fe true. Dress it nicely too, in clean white clothes, wid shoes an' all, jest like a Buckra baby...I hope I nebber hab a black or dark chile to shame me (Spinner 1894, 52).

One hundred and four years later, another Jamaican, a student, would write a letter to *The Gleaner*, a Jamaican newspaper, stating:

> We should be grateful for slavery...Look at where we are today. Blacks are involved in every line of work; we even have white employees. I say that the best thing that ever happened in the lifetime of my foreparents was being taken across the Middle Passage so their

descendants – us – could make something of ourselves (*The Gleaner*, April 16, 1998).

These vulgarities, signatures of a broken identity, are more often expressed in many refinements today, but their implication for knowing, identity, agency, development, sovereignty and freedom remains hugely problematic.

Jamaica and Trinidad and Tobago are almost six generations removed from slavery, Haiti is over seven generations removed, while the US is five generations removed. This suggests that Hilliard d'Auberteuil was too conservative with the time he gave for the ontological desecration of the black body to recover from that indelible stain because, while the policy of enslaving Africans ended, the contempt to which Europeans subjected Africans has been passed on to their descendants six generations and counting.

During all of this time, including from before d'Auberteuil, Africans have been identifying, naming, theorising, philosophising and developing policies to counteract what d'Auberteuil called 'a contempt so great that whoever descends from it even to the sixth generation shall be covered with an indelible stain.' In the early nineteenth century, Pompée Valentin Vastey, a leader and statesman of the Haitian Revolution and Haitian State, told of persons who were 'Blacks and Mulattoes in their outward complexion alone, but Ex-colonialist in heart and principle' (Vastey 1969, 30 ); while James Lynch, an African American abolitionist, made a speech in May 1865 at a meeting of the Young Men's Literary and Debating Society of Philadelphia, the United States, about 'Colored men standing in the way of their own race,' men 'who set no value on the ability of their race and adopt the opinions respecting them that prejudiced white men hold' (Foner 1972, 316–17).

Meanwhile, in Jamaica, in 1905, Theophilus Scholes described it as 'the unenviable and despicable position of the average Europeanised Ethiopian', who, '[h]aving, from the dawn of consciousness upwards, been taught to associate with the white skin everything possessing superior merit, he ends with the conviction that he himself is but a mass of demerit and inferiority...' (Scholes 1905, 60). Marcus Garvey called this behaviour mental slavery, the worst state of not being free. Hence, his charge: 'Liberate the minds of men and ultimately you will liberate the bodies of men' (Jacques Garvey and Essein-Udom 1987, 57).

How much have post-colonial governments/authorities/political parties/ communities/ agents of socialisation in the grand epoch of independence during the 1960s and beyond, consciously and persistently without the encumbrances of their existential vision of self and development, dealt with this issue? Not nearly enough. In Jamaica, 51 years after independence, timid/tenuous steps are just being taken to teach Garveyism in the Jamaican school, even though an act of the Jamaican Parliament announced/pronounced Marcus Garvey Jamaica's First National Hero, decades ago.

The metaphysical and psychological asset that Garvey is to self-emancipation and development has been obscured by multitudinous webs of subterfuges. 'How long shall they kill our prophets while we stand aside and look?' Bob Marley asks. Implied in his question is another question: 'How long shall we kill our prophets while we stand aside and look?'

So long as persons like Marcus Garvey, who have been recognised by persons of their generation and subsequent generations, as possessing the ability to sense, feel, grasp and summon their seemingly rare gifts of native creative insights to cut and clear, to grasp and to extract, to weave and to fashion, to choreograph and to compose from the ancestral, spiritual, emotional, social and existential corpus of their subjected people, an epic story of their dreams, pain and joy, their hopes for redemption, so long as such persons are kept in pedagogical abeyance, buried in obscurity in the daylight of our existence: we are killing our prophets for now.

LeRoy Clarke has developed such a body of work. It is a body of work denoting a knowledge system of self-liberation, sovereignty and freedom extracted from the epistemological, ontological and psychological consequences of slavery and colonialism. Put another way, it is an epic story of how to imagine, to think, to know and to recreate self out of 'the ruins', the 'mash-upness', 'the shit', the 'fragments of a spiritual', the cathedral of epistemic encumbrances unfurling plagues of mamaguy to kill, cramp and paralyse the creative, imaginative, aesthetic compass of our redemption.

Clarke's works: 'the blessed heights of "Art and Reason!"' are philosophical manifestos – the basis for the architecture of a self, recreated, free and sovereign. His art, his poems, his essays, his conversations, speak in tongues, the 'fragments of a spiritual' gathered and choreographed into a universe of unflinching fidelity to freedom, sovereignty and identity.

Clarke's redemptive (epistemic and ontological) landscape is the creative transformation of fragments of a spiritual consciousness gathered from the obscurity of a memory, a time, a rhythm, voice and sight indelibly stained by a dystopia of extermination, absorption, erasure and silence, to endow an agency of the apotheosis of self.

Selwyn Cudjoe's assessment of LeRoy Clarke and his works and their agential/inspirational impact on him is worth citing at length:

> When I look at the paintings of LeRoy Clarke, meditate upon his writings, or converse with him, I know that I am in the presence of greatness; someone who has laid claim to his space; someone who has left an indelible impression upon his time; and someone who has achieved all of the attributes of royalty. I can testify. LeRoy Clarke is the finest of our generation; the supreme representative of our pains, our sufferings and our strivings; the most inspirational of our prophets; and spiritual architect of our becoming. His work transcends the politics of our every-day life and the precariousness of our narrow existence. At its best, it penetrates into our unconscious and demand (sic) that we explore the meaning of our existence (Cudjoe 2003, 32).

Furthermore, Cudjoe notes:

> His erudition takes me into that part of myself (and my people's history) that has been mired into wretchedness and forgetfulness. When he expresses himself via the visual medium I am uplifted by his spiritual integrity, the nobility of his undertaking and the evanescence of his artistic enterprise. In one sweeping moment, he bids us to return to the redemptive fountain of our being. In his oeuvre lie many signatures of our salvation (32).

Moreover, Cudjoe opines:

> When we see the varied visual forms that he represents; when we see the intricate patterns and lines through which he interprets our beauty; when we see the fantastical arrangement of figures in his composition; when we see the depth of feeling that animates and is generated by his art, they challenge us to dig beneath the surface and discover ourselves anew. When we see the complex movements of a mind that doubles upon itself revealing other layers of intricate beauty; when we see the cannibalistic motifs that transcend (sometimes dissolve into) time and space, we know he is expressing

dimensions of our being for which there is no exact verbal equivalent in the truncated vocabulary of our culture. To me, the algebra of Clarke's genius consists in his ability to capture our spiritual reality through abstract motifs that cannot be gleaned through verbal or even musical experiences and therein lays his uniqueness (32).

Finally, Cudjoe notes:

> If we interrogated that foundational dimension of his work further, we realise he is probing the alluvium of a reality that has lain fallow ever since we left the shores of Africa. His is the task to remove those alluvial layers of our past, step by step, before we discover the complex beauty hidden beneath the noxious odium of our lives. Clarke allows us to discover ourselves in our golden recrudescence and awakens in us a new mode of selfhood (32).

I have taken the liberty to cite Cudjoe at length because he expresses my exact feeling, sentiment and intellectual judgement on LeRoy Clarke's works. Selwyn Cudjoe was, in my assessment and experience in studying and feeling LeRoy Clarke's art, able to feel, sense and to philosophise in caring poetic language, the impact of Clarke's art on his/our metaphysicality and agency. In LeRoy Clarke's art, Cudjoe discerns what I consider to be the spring of unfurling choruses of flocks of distant voices and blurred focus images of dethroned gods and beauty and rituals of our presences unpresented/unrepresented in our daily existence, lurking in the dormant awakening imagination of untended presence; the glimpse of possibilities: recreation, creation and redemption.

Cudjoe thus advances the very reasons why we should value LeRoy Clarke and why we should consciously study and teach about his art in school as well as use his artistic methods as pedagogy. I want to see and to hear children and adults reciting and invocating LeRoy Clarke's poems and wondering into the wondrous, liberating philosophical landscape of his paintings and to feel the feeling of freedom and of possibilities that will incite them to unfurl bridges to the boundless wellspring of their imagination, to 'the redemptive fountain of their being' and shaping their agency.

We can learn profound things not only from LeRoy Clarke's astonishing works of art, but also from how he created this body of works. How does he think and construct meaning? How does he construct art? Put another way, what are his methods of constructing art? My interest in and assessment of Clarke's creative methods, his creative compass, has been published as a book chapter titled 'LeRoy Clarke: Des Yeux Pour Voir Derrière le Zéro des Choses et Apprendre à Reconstruire les Ruines' (Leroy Clarke's Art: Eyes to see Behind the Zero of Things to Reinvent self and Rechart the Ruins), published 2012 in *Art Contemporian de la Caraïbe: Mythes, Croyances, Religions et Imaginaries*. The issue here is what are the possible social, political and economic consequences/implications of learning from LeRoy Clarke's art/reason and his method of constructing art?

In LeRoy Clarke's second solo exhibition, *Fragments of A Spiritual*, shown at the Studio Museum, Harlem in 1972, I note that 'LeRoy Clarke's painting began to become eyes that could aid people to see behind the zero of things, to (re)discover the redemptive ancestral alluvium of their being' (Hutton 2012, 391). This important juncture in the development of Clarke's art signalled a style and a vision of his own, 'evident in the structural formation of his art – composed of bold, sturdy, black outlines and raw colours delineating an assemblage of partially overlapping figures, objects, spaces and ideographic constructs pervading the painted surface like marching masquerade bands on the streets of Port-of-Spain' (391). It is from this emerging style, that the aesthetic grandeur of LeRoy Clarke's art has evolved and developed into a universe of redemptive beauty, freedom and sovereignty which can be articulated in the words of Bob Marley's song *Misty Morning*:

> The power of philosophy
> Floats through my head
> Light like a feather
> Heavy like lead.

Fragments of a spiritual life denote a style of artistic construction and the method of constructing that style, as well as the philosophical structure of the vision to which this art would serve: a cipher to rechart the ruin and 'piece it together in its beginning'. The method of style, as well as the structure of style (aestheticism), and the structure and philosophical vision of Clarke's art were spawned in the crossroads cultural womb of the Civil Rights struggles, Black Power/Black Consciousness, African/Pan Africanism, Pan Caribbeanism and the general progressive movements in Harlem, New York in the late 1960s and 1970s.

To be specific, in this womb in which LeRoy Clarke's art, philosophy and agency were spawned, were the constantly interacting/fermenting presence and or signatures of Jacob Lawrence, Romare Bearden, Afri-COBRA, Tom Feelings, Twin Seven Seven, Elizabeth Catlett, Gordon Parks, James Van De Zee, Ornette Coleman, Randy Weston, Archie Sheppe, Nina Simone, C.L.R. James, Wilson Harris, Aimé Césaire, Frantz Fanon, René Dépestre, Derek Walcott, Wifredo Lam, J.D. Elder, Pablo Neruda, David Siqueiros, Diego Rivera, Aubrey Williams, Jackson Pollock, and the Orishas, Jumbi, Papa Bois, Douen, Soucouyant, La Diablesse, Ligahoo, Mama Dlo, Bad John, Obiya (Obeah) and others.

It is from these sources and more that LeRoy Clarke has entered the beginning of himself, constantly recharting/recreating our existence by gathering and choreographing 'fragments of a spiritual' to create a redemptive universe in which an open-ended adventure of imagination and creation becomes a core expression of freedom and sovereignty. It is to the arts, to imagination and creation and the methods thereof that we should more look to, for the parables and anthems of our intellectual culture and muses for nation building. As Prince Buster, a pioneering icon of Jamaican popular music, puts it in *Creation*, one of his songs: 'It takes creation to build a nation.'

Indeed,

> [f]rom the days of slavery, when Africans ritually repossessed themselves through sacred nocturnal ceremonies, thereby temporarily transforming their commercialised bodies: bodies possessed and desecrated by slave makers into bodies exorcised, (re)created, (re)textured and (re)possessed by ancestral spirits and deities, to post-slavery – Africans' struggles to be(come), were necessarily, modes of reinventing or recreating themselves, requiring the tools and aesthetic compass and agency of the artist (Hutton 2013, 6).

LeRoy Clarke is a supreme agency of this tradition, whose body of work, should we embrace it, could open up vistas to the empowerment of ourselves.

Ten years ago, LeRoy Clarke noted: 'For the past 35 years I have been attempting to make sense of a vision of humanity that dwells in me. Eye have come to understand, after the musings of much labor, only the task of recharting the ruins, particularly of an African soul splayed across a hostile world.' He further notes that 'This journey has taken me through a series of works which amount to an epic moment of self-discovery!' 'For me,' Clarke adds, 'Art is not a thing apart from one's life, but rather the languaging of life itself...It is the "how" of life. That Art, that life, is determined by sustainability of an intense and continuous creation of self where every word is a climb, a perfectioning, an attempt to rarer states of grace.'[1]

Here, we have a clear, precise Clarkesonian (El Tucuchean) philosophy of being and agency, of the building of ontological freedom and agential capacity from fragments of a spiritual and in the process, or as part of the process, talking or 'languaging' the self out of obscurity, out of silence and invisibility, into the sunlight of visibility and presence denied in the historical landscape of occidental visibility. This narrative of self-articulation is taken to be the arrogance of LeRoy Clarke. But could it be a principal tool of his success, of his creativity, of his creative ethos: a psychological tool for talking self out of obscurity into El Tucuchean presence?

For Clarke, we have to invent 'new tools of imagination and assessment' (Clarke 2008, xxix) because '[n]o other people in the history of mankind has endured such an exclusive, imperial system - geared to vanquish all elements of their nature' (xxix). In this long journey out of this dystopia to El Tucuchean selfhood, Clarke notes that

> Deeper wounds are now made on it by re-invented Africans themselves – our black men and black women – who, as painters, musicians, intellectuals et al., ascribe to the propaganda that nothing is pure or can be pure anymore, particularly in their own race (xxix).

Here, Clarke's philosophical conception of pure should not be taken, as some would, to mean the restoration of the African to what he/she was before his/her enslavement. His view of recreation by gathering and choreographing fragments of a spiritual, is a denial of this. The wholesomeness that Clarke wishes to see is not a re-enactment of the past – but the sum total of the gathering, continuously, of the shattered fragments and re-constituting them into an evolving modernist presence. Thus:

> With new tool of imagination and assessment, delve where self is revealed as a conscious work of art created, brought to full centre, accordingly justified as the voice in one's own stories. Which, as self, is centred; not, as with marginalized objects in subordination but, as authors; Pointers, who grasped the structures of Obeah, its parables

as a signification or as a signifier whose textual authority undergoes continuous shifts in self-determined imperatives (xxix).

Here, the El Tucuchean person is revealed by Clarke. El Tucuche, the second highest mountain peak in Trinidad, a natural majestic pyramid shrouded in anthems of mists, becomes the metaphor for the highest expression of free sovereign personhood, the apotheosis of self, where Simon Lee (2003), in reference to Clarke, notes that 'De Poet glimpsed the Godhead and saw his own perfection, saw God in himself and himself in God' (95). Here, God is metaphorically represented by Trinidad's highest peak: Aripo.

In 2013, we mark LeRoy Clarke's 75th birthday anniversary and 45 years of him creating/weaving/wording a majestic body of works; his gift of redemption to us: manifestoes of how to be free, sovereign and royal in the magnificence of obscured beauty and liberating episteme; anthems of imagination never imagined, so shrouded in the ceaseless righteous presence of Occidental hegemonic certainty, covering in subterranean silence a universe of banished ancestry teeming with signatures of elekes, veves, mumpoko...; El Tucuche, a powerful philosophy of decolonisation. Our task, know LeRoy Clarke's works, teach him.

### Note

1. Leroy Clarke, Clarke-Smithsonian Latino Center. www.latino.si.edu/rainbow/pages/Clarke.html. Accessed August 22, 2013.

### References

Clarke, LeRoy. 1981. *Douens: Poems and Drawings by LeRoy Clarke*. New York. KaRaEle.
———. 2008. *Secret Insect of a Bird Deep in me, wanting to Fly: A Collection of Drawings by Master Artist LeRoy Clarke*. Trinidad & Tobago: Paria Publishing Company Limited.
Cudjoe, Selwyn R. 2003. Meditation on (a) Genius. In *LeRoy Clarke: Of Flesh and Salt and Wind and Current: A Compilation of Works by and about LeRoy Clarke, Artist/Author/Poet*, ed. Caroline C. Ravello, 32–33. Port of Spain: The National Museum and Art Gallery of Trinidad and Tobago.
Foner, Philip S., ed.1972. *The Voice of Black America: Major Speeches by Negroes in the United States, 1797-1971*. New York: Simon and Schuster.
Hutton, Clinton. 2011. From Douens to El Tucuche: Becoming and the Meaning of Being in LeRoy Clarke's Art. In *LeRoy at 70: The Art, The Poetry, The Man*, 76–85. Trinidad & Tobago: Trinidad and Tobago National Commission for UNESCO.

———. 2012. LeRoy Clarke: Des Yeux Pour Voir Derrière e Zéro des Choses et Apprendre à Reconstruire les Ruines (Leroy Clarke's Art: Eyes to see Behind the Zero of Things to Reinvent Self and Rechart the Ruins). In *Art Contemporiande la Caraïbe Mythes, Croyances, Religions et Imaginaries*, ed. Renée-Paule Yung-Hing, 323–53 and 391–93. Paris: Hervé Chopin & Région Martinique.

———. 2015. Leonard Howell Announcing God: An Examination of the Permissive Conditions which Gave Birth to Rastafari in Jamaica. In *Leonard Percival Howell and the Genesis of Rastafari*, ed. Clinton Hutton, Michael Barnett, D.A. Dunkley & Jalani Niaah, 9–52. Jamaica, Barbados and Trinidad and Tobago: University of the West Indies Press.

Jacques Garvey, Amy, and E.U. Essien-Udom, eds. 1987. *More Philosophy and Opinions of Marcus Garvey*. Vol.3. London: Frank Cass & Co. Ltd.

Lee, Simon. 2003. Mental Archaeology of the Psyche. In *LeRoy Clarke: Of Flesh and Salt and Wind and Current: A Compilation of Works by and about LeRoy Clarke, Artist/Author/Poet*, ed. Caroline C. Ravello, 94–95. Port of Spain: The National Museum and Art Gallery of Trinidad and Tobago.

Ravello, Caroline C. 2003. Retrospectively Speaking: Clarke – Esteemed Umpire of Taste. In. *LeRoy Clarke: Of Flesh and Salt and Wind and Current: A Compilation of Works by and about LeRoy Clarke, Artist/Author/Poet*, ed. Caroline C. Ravello, 22–24. Port of Spain: The National Museum and Art Gallery of Trinidad and Tobago.

Rogers, J.A. 1994. *Sex and Race: A History of White, Negro and Indian Miscegenation in the Two Americas*. St Petersburg, Florida: Helga M. Rogers.

Spinner, Alice. 1894. *A Study in Colour*. London.

Vastey, Baron de. 1969. *An Essay on the Causes of the Revolution and Civil Wars of Hayti....* Tr. from French by W.H.M.B. 1823. New York: Negro Universities Press.

# 16 | *The Radical Aesthetic of Sistren Theatre Collective, Jamaica**

Nicosia Shakes

**Introduction**

Black artists are integral to radical thought and action in Africa and the African Diaspora. Many theorists, philosophers and activists have emphasised the need to consider art inseparable from economics and politics and to view appreciation of black art as a necessary aspect of black radicalism (See Ford-Smith 1989; Garvey 1937; Hooks 1990; Moten 2003; Tate 2009; Wright 2003). Some scholars have also highlighted the Eurocentric nature of separating the artistic sphere from others in our understandings of activism. For example, in *Black Intellectuals, Black Cognition and a Black Aesthetic*, W.D. Wright (1997) argues that placing the artistic, the political, scientific and intellectual into discrete categories emerges from European systems of cognition.[1] He contends that in contrast to these Eurocentric binaries, African cognitive systems have historically viewed these elements as interconnected parts of a whole. Wright states that this holistic understanding of the world is crucial in developing and acknowledging black aesthetics. Similarly, in her essay, 'Notes Towards a New Aesthetic', Honor Ford-Smith (1990) states:

> The idea of the artist as it has been imported into our societies carries within it a very specific cultural ring. It implies that the arts are somehow...cordoned off from economic and political processes... the task of the cultural worker is an attempt to re-create life so that the realms of thought, feeling and action are no longer kept separate and distinct (27).

In addition to emphasising the interconnectedness of artistic work and other forms of activism, as Ford-Smith and Wright do, it is extremely important to recognise the efficacy of the arts in their own right. Because the arts provide infinite possibilities for sensory, pedagogic, emotional and spiritual expressions, they can give birth to representations that transcend other components of radical movements and initiatives. For instance, black artists have been crucial in challenging patriarchy, elitism and heterosexism *within* black organisations, communities and nations. (See Cooper 1999; Davis 1998; Ferguson 1994; Ford-Smith 2004, Vogel 2009.)

Black woman artists stand firmly within the black radical tradition. These theatre makers, poets, singers, dancers, visual artists and others, have critically tackled the ways in which white supremacy affects black women and men similarly, as well as the gendered aspects of this oppression as manifested in white and black patriarchal systems. Concomitant to their articulations against various forms of oppression, they have been crucial in the valorisation of African/African Diasporic cultures, especially as regards knowledge production and the development of black aesthetics.

This chapter examines the work of Sistren Theatre Collective (STC), Jamaica, viewing Sistren's repertoire as a site of black radical theatre aesthetics. I define radical theatre aesthetics as: theatrical methods and content that aim to challenge and subvert various systems of domination, drawing on the subjectivities of oppressed groups. Sistren's work has been critical in the development of feminism in Jamaica/the Caribbean, particularly in its articulation of working-class black women's realities. Their techniques and frameworks have also been integral in the development of activist theatre and performance in Jamaica. Many scholars have written on Sistren, focusing on different elements of the Collective (Allison 1986; Batra 2011; Booler 1999; Carr 2002; Cooper 1995; Di Cenzo and Bennett 1992; Ford-Smith 1986, 1997; Goodman 1993; Green 2006; Smith 2008, 2011, 2013). However, there has not yet been a comprehensive study of Sistren's aesthetic, in particular, their location within a cohort of progressive theatre artists committed to creating radical Jamaican theatre. I draw on as well as add to the current scholarship by focusing on how these women have innovated theatre techniques that accomplish two aims: First, these techniques valorise popular African/African Diasporic forms of performance and spirituality; and second, they allow Sistren to engage working-class women in discussions about issues on their own terms in ways that transgress official and elite understandings. In both respects, Sistren challenges elite norms of respectability and patriarchy in Jamaica and the rest of the Caribbean. These norms are racial, economic, cultural and gendered.

## Sistren's Formation and the Development of a Radical Theatre Aesthetic

Sistren's aesthetic was born from the unique relationships formed and sustained by the women in the Collective, and the progressive but difficult cultural and political context of the 1970s in which it was founded. The 1970s followed almost a decade of political independence from Britain, in which many Jamaicans were frustrated with the slow pace of transformation in the country. By the middle of the 1960s, Jamaicans began to seek new, more radical ways of thinking about national development than the early post-independence state was prepared to pursue. The 1970s was marked by the relative legitimacy that the state gave to the national movement for change, which found solidarity in international progressive movements. As Sistren's co-founder and former Artistic Director, Honor Ford-Smith states, the period was one of 'democratic opening' in Jamaica:

> This was one of the only times that I've ever seen Jamaica mobilised to overcome its past ...Globally there was the Third World Movement. There was this moment of revolution that was happening in Africa. There was the rise of the anti-Apartheid movement. There were the African liberation struggles. There was the Panthers...It was a moment of great potential locally and globally (Ford-Smith, personal interview).

Sistren was heir to a long Caribbean/Jamaican feminist and gender activist tradition dating back to the colonial era, and the Collective had collaborators and supporters within the upsurge of women's activism in the 1970s, which constituted the second wave of Jamaican/Caribbean feminism. This upsurge included the development of several women's organisations and institutions, and acceleration in the activities of others that were formed in the 1960s. Among the most influential groups and institutions were: the Committee of Women for Progress (CWP), the governing People's National Party (PNP) Women's Movement, and the Women and Development Unit (WAND) at the University of the West Indies, Mona. In the field of culture, the 1970s was also a period of abundant possibilities. This was most clearly visible in popular culture. Reggae music took off internationally, there was a burgeoning dancehall music scene and dub poetry developed as a distinctly Jamaican poetic form. The government, operating under a democratic socialist paradigm, was relatively amenable to activists concerned with cultural development that was rooted in the experiences of the black majority. The Cultural Training Centre (CTC), which was later renamed the Edna Manley College of the Visual and Performing Arts, was established by the government in 1976 to train Jamaicans in the visual arts, dance, and drama. Various community-based arts projects, aimed at using theatre as a tool of social engagement, were linked to different sections of the CTC. Sistren began as one of these special projects, operating under the auspices of the Jamaica School of Drama (JSD).[2] At the time of Sistren's formation, the JSD was developing methods aimed at creating a Jamaican theatre aesthetic. Some of the theatre artists at the drama school who experimented with, and developed different techniques during the 1970s were: Caroll Dawes, one of the founding Directors of Studies; Thom Cross, Dennis Scott, who became Director of the JSD in 1977; Honor Ford-Smith; Brian Heap; Hertencer Lindsay-Sheppard; and Henry Muttoo. They engaged with language, the significance of the actor's body and movement, and popular Jamaican/Afro-Diasporic practices. An example of one of the techniques that emerged from this work was Dennis Scott's Labrish. Taken from the Jamaican word meaning 'to chat, or gossip',[3] the Labrish technique involved the use of random words to construct verbal and non-verbal forms of communication.

Like other cultural activists in the country, the teams at the JSD were engaging in a cultural politics of decolonisation drawing on progressive national and international tendencies, with a core appreciation of the cultural modes practised by the black majority in Jamaica. One of the major legacies of British colonialism and slavery in Jamaica has been the devalorisation of African knowledge systems and culture, including and especially language, religion, art and philosophy. (See Cooper 1995; Nettleford 1972; Thomas 2004.) Black artists in Jamaica and elsewhere have resisted colonial cultural domination through the content and techniques of their art. In the realm of theatre, works produced in the early twentieth century transgressed colonial notions of valuable culture, though sometimes utilising Eurocentric aesthetics. The list includes plays and other dramatic pieces produced by poet, playwright and actor, Louise Bennett; Black Nationalist leader, Marcus Garvey; poet, playwright and journalist, Una Marson; the various artists who worked with the Universal Negro Improvement Association (UNIA) and Edelweiss Park, Kingston;[4] and actor and playwright, Ranny Williams (Bennett and Bennett 2011; Hamilton 1988; Ford-Smith 2004; Sistren 2004). The evolution of the annual pantomime from a distinctly British aesthetic to Jamaican form and content, and the establishment of the National Dance Theatre Company (NDTC) in the 1960s are also important examples of this anti-colonial cultural work. The team at the JSD were influenced by, but also transcended, the work of their precursors by drawing upon the radical socio-political context created by 1960s black radicalism, political decolonisation in Africa and the Caribbean, the spread of leftism in Jamaica and other parts of the Caribbean, the black assertion within Rastafarian aesthetics, and emerging popular forms such as reggae music and dub poetry. Awam Amkpa (2004) offers a useful framework through which to analyse the aims of the JSD team: they were creating methodology and content that represented '*post-colonial desire* – the act of imagining, living and negotiating a social reality based on democracy, cultural pluralism and social justice'(10). Alongside their local and regional influences, many of the theatre artists at the drama school were also trained in international forms that were geared at utilising theatre for social engagement and protest. These international influences included American story theatre, drama-in-education techniques from England, Brechtian[5] epic theatre, and therapeutic theatre techniques, which were applied to a Jamaican context.

Honor Ford-Smith refers to Sistren as the 'feminist manifestation', of the theatrical aesthetic being developed at the drama school in the 1970s (Ford-Smith, personal interview). More specifically, Sistren was a product of the progressive theatrical influence of the JSD as well as the feminist politics of the era. The Collective began in 1977 when a group of women employed to the government's Impact Programme[6] (commonly called the Crash Programme) were asked to develop a skit for a Workers Week concert. Honor Ford-Smith, then a tutor at the JSD, was asked to assist them. After their performance of the play, *Downpression Get a Blow*,[7] at the concert, the women decided to stay together and to continue developing work that dealt with problems that affect women.[8] The name Sistren, one of the pluralised forms of the English word 'sister', was selected because of its resonances in women's movements globally, as well as in Afro-Diasporic culture, as an assertion of fictive kinship among black people. Sistren, like its male equivalent, 'brethren', also has religious and spiritual connotations in Jamaica, particularly in the Afro-Christian religion of Revival as well as in some Christian denominations, where it is used to refer to female members of the congregation. Under the Sistren banner, the women produced four major plays within their first four years, including *Bellywoman Bangarang* (1978), *Bandoloo Version* (1979), *Nana Yah* (1980), and *QPH* (1981). After they were expelled from the auspices of the JSD in 1981 by the newly elected Jamaica Labour Party (JLP) government,[9] they went on to establish their own headquarters and broaden their aesthetic focus.

Sistren was supported by continued relationships with dramatists from the JSD and other theatre artists, their own experimentation, research into Afro-Diasporic ritual performances, and education in emerging international theatre forms. They benefited from the work of the core working-class grassroots members as well as the contributions of middle-class resource persons.[10] By the late 1980s, the Collective had various departments, including the theatre arm, a research section, a screen-printing business, publications unit and filmmaking initiatives. Like many women and grassroots activists who work in theatre, Sistren did not codify and publish dramaturgical pieces on their specific methods.[11] As Joan French states, like other contemporaneous activists, they were too preoccupied with 'doing the work' in order to pay enough attention to recording and publishing everything that they did (Joan French, personal interview). Honor Ford-Smith, the Sistren member who has been most prolific at publishing on the Collective, also stated that it was difficult for the theatre artists during that time, including the group at the JSD, to conduct the work as well as theorise about it and publish books on their methods.[12] A detailed history of Sistren's aesthetic, and by extension, a history of the progressive work done at the JSD in the 1970s, is still yet to be comprehensively documented. However, there are many elements of Sistren's complex methodology that can be singled out and analysed. These include: collective creation, research to performance, mimetic storytelling, therapeutic theatre, Boalian[13] forum theatre, dub poetry, ritual performance and movement, and popular Jamaican music. When considered as a whole, these methods, in complement with the Collective's aims to give voice to Jamaican women, constitute the Sistren aesthetic. I will examine three distinctive aspects of this aesthetic. These are: collective creation, their use of popular Jamaican/Afro-Diasporic forms of orality, and subversive movement. There is a considerable amount of valuable scholarship that focuses on the radical content of Sistren's plays and their book, *Lionheart Gal: Life Stories of Jamaican Women* (1987). I focus on Sistren's methods of composition and performance.

**Collective Creation**

In theatre, collective creation is a process in which plays and other productions are developed by multiple authors. It involves a complex method of community and/or small-group interface, improvisational exercises and research-to-performance methods. This form of theatre composition is exhausting and complex. It involves consistent consultation, improvisational work and hours upon hours of transcription and editing (Ford-Smith, Lindsay-Sheppard, Small, Williams, personal interviews). Sistren utilised various methods and activities during these processes of composition, including ring games, singing, personal testimony and dance. The following is Lana Finikin's description of one of Sistren's early collective creation sessions, which drew on personal testimony:

> We sit and talk about our life experience as women within work space, within home, within community, whatever the space might be and within that space I would talk about my work in the garment factory and I would speak about her role as a child growing up with her grandparents and so on. And then immediately Becky [Knowles] would say, 'Mi chipping into Honor [Ford-Smith],' because it jogs memories of her childhood with her grandparents or whatever it is; my working environment jogs memories of you working in a similar situation. So right across the room everybody's realising that within the space, one or three of us, or four of us have gone through similar experiences. And after we finish all of that, Honor would then say, 'based on all of this that we got, this is what comes out of it and this is one that is emerging as the issue that we will have to improve.'
>
> (Finikin, personal interview).

Finikin's account indicates the two-pronged aim of collective creation within Sistren: a means through which the women are able to share their common experiences within a friendly space, as well as to create a collective medium for disseminating these experiences to the public.

It is therefore a forum through which women who make theatre can vent about their experiences, as well as channel the conversations enabled through this process into a work of art. Among the reasons for Sistren and many other theatre makers' use of this technique are: a need to avoid the authoritarianism that may result from having a single playwright; and the importance of centering the perspectives of people who ordinarily do not get the opportunity to have their voices heard – in this case, working-class Jamaican women.

Collective creation critiques the model of the single playwright, and acknowledges the role of the actors, wider community, researcher and activist in the process of making a story. The emphasis is on the work of the group or community, rather than the talent of one or a few individuals. Individualism has historically supported patriarchy and other hierarchical systems. Canonical figures, usually men, often end up representing entire groups and movements. Thinking more broadly about the organisational work that goes into activism gives exposure to women, poor and working-class people and others who traditionally are not elevated to major leadership positions. Therefore, collective play creation is one example of the ways in which a theatrical aesthetic has developed around questions of political organisation, leadership and social transformation. It is important to note that though collective creation lessens the hierarchies within theatre creation, it never eliminates it. The director ultimately exercises a considerable degree of artistic control over the final product. However, the director and scriptwriter – which in Sistren's case, was normally the same person – function mostly in the capacity of mediator, compiler, curator and/or editor than as the ultimate creator, and though different directors brought their own sense of creation to Sistren's process, the plays maintained a strong focus on the role of the actors and other members of the Collective in composing the story. This collective model extended to Sistren's administrative process. The Sistren Parliament, the general meeting in which every member equally voted on the Collective's major decisions, was based on an interpretation of participatory democracy devised to accommodate a diversity of opinions. There are definitely drawbacks to the collective method of creation as well as the collective structure of organising more broadly. (See Ford-Smith 1997; Goodman 1993.)[14] Yet, because of the advantages that it has offered, Sistren continued to utilise it, and it has been one of the popular techniques used by feminist theatre groups globally. (See Case 2007; Goodman 1993).

**Orality**

Orality refers to a performative and philosophical paradigm in which emphasis is on the spoken word. It does not preclude the use of writing. Rather, writing functions generally as the transcript of what was developed through oral transmission. Orality may seem a bit self-evident in theatre given that plays that involve speaking are necessarily using language as spoken word. However, my emphasis on Sistren and orality is with regard to the process of play creation as well as the function of popular Jamaican oral practices in their creations. There is no seamless separation between the oral and the scribal in Sistren's work, and that of many other performers and artists in Jamaica and globally. Isidore Okpewho (1992) views orality as a form of literature, rather than an antithesis to literature, broadly defined as a creative text. He utilises the term, *oral literature*, meaning, 'literature delivered by word of mouth', as the basis of his analysis (3). The term, oral literature, makes the distinction between literature whose creation involves a one-step process of writing down thoughts, research and ideas, and literature that is essentially the transcript of a work of art that initially was composed orally and maintained through non-scribal means. Carolyn Cooper's (1995) conceptualisation, *oraliterature*, joins together the two descriptors, oral and literature, emphasising orality's location within a continuum composed of the oral and scribal at two poles, with various iterations in between. Both Isidore Okpewho and Cooper's formulations, as well as the general descriptor, *orality*, are useful to understanding Sistren's work and the work of similar artists in other parts of the world. Examples of artistic forms that can be located within the category of orality/oral literature/oraliterature are: mimetic storytelling, chants, riddles, proverbs, ceremonial songs, and performance poetry.

In Sistren's plays, the Jamaican language, (commonly referred to as Patwa), which until recently was not widely standardised as a written language, forms the basis of their use of orality. Speech, singing and poetry are done mostly in Jamaican, and English is normally used for the dialogues delivered by the few middle-class characters. Sistren has extended the use of Jamaican into their publications, including the published play scripts, and their groundbreaking book, *Lionheart Gal: Life Stories of Jamaican Women* (1987), which was also the basis for the play, *Buss Out* (1989). Sistren's members were certainly not the first set of Jamaican artists to emphasise the importance of speaking and writing Jamaican. Other artists like poet and storyteller Louise Bennett, and playwright and actor, Randolph Williams, laid much of this groundwork. Sistren belongs within the cohort of elder artists who emphasised that Jamaican is a language within its own right, and not *broken English*, the pejorative label that many have applied to it. With the work of scholars like Jamaican linguists, Frederick Cassidy[15] and Hubert Devonish, and literary/cultural theorist, Carolyn Cooper, and the recent formation of the Jamieka Langwij Unit (Jamaica Language Unit) at the University of the West Indies, significant progress has been made around legitimising Jamaican. However, Sistren and others were faced with a more hostile environment towards recognising Jamaican as a language during the 1970s and early 1980s. One of the most remarkable aspects of their commitment to the language is that they rarely, or never, Anglicised it in their performances for non-Jamaican audiences. Plays like *Bellywoman Bangarang* (1978), *QPH* (1981) and *Muffet Inna All A Wi* (1986) toured throughout the Caribbean and to places like the US, Canada, Britain and Germany without translations. It is significant that Sistren resisted the pressure to edit their language and context for the benefit of international audiences. For example, Hertencer Lindsay-Sheppard, director of *QPH* (1981) recounted to me that when the topic came up she vehemently refused to translate the dialogue for the play's 1982 international run:

> There was something about, 'should we translate into English so that the audience would understand in England and in Canada?' And I said, no. If you change the women's voices it's a different play. They've got to speak with their own voice, and in the same way that we watch opera in Italian and everybody is prepared to listen to them sing in Italian, and watch French movies, because they're avant-garde... so why should we dilute our thing? And we didn't do it. And it touched everybody (Lindsay-Sheppard, personal interview).

Many artists, especially from developing countries, are often encouraged to change their language, or to be overly explicatory to accommodate audiences in developed countries. This pressure is not as pervasive for artists from developed countries travelling to developing countries. Lindsay-Sheppard's refusal to not change the women's speech in *QPH* is indicative of an intentional anti-imperial and anti-colonial politics within Sistren's work generally, and particularly an acknowledgement of how language figures into this politics.

Sistren's use of orality also included their engagement with oral-centered Jamaican art forms. This includes Jamaican performance poetry, especially dub poetry,[16] contemporary and older music forms, call and response patterns of speech especially to engage with audiences, chants, mimetic storytelling[17] and ring games. The use of different forms of drumming as an accompaniment as well as an onomatopoeic guide for speech is also prevalent throughout the repertoire. Perhaps the play that was most reflective of the emphasis on orality is *Muffet Inna All A Wi* (1986), which brought together many elements of Sistren's oral aesthetic, including collective creation through improvisation, call and response, mimetic storytelling, dub poetry and reggae and dancehall music. *Muffet* (1986) premiered at Zinc Fence, an outdoor venue close to downtown Kingston, which served as the headquarters for the famous Jamaican band, Third World. By staging *Muffet* at a concert venue rather than at a conventional theatre, Sistren underscored the play's grounding within a framework of Jamaican popular culture. The title signifies on the British nursery rhyme, *Little Miss Muffet*, which depicts a spider frightening a girl as she is eating. Sistren drew on this nursery rhyme and created a different story, formatted to a Jamaican context, and in which Muffet is depicted as a brave woman withstanding various odds, as opposed to the easily terrified girl depicted in the nursery rhyme. The spider in the rhyme appears in the play as Ananse, the Akan/Jamaican trickster figure, who is the subject of many mimetic stories. Ananse (alternatively spelt *Anancy*, in the play script) is a central villain/trickster, terrorising the major characters, who are all named Muffet. This kind of subversion of European content into a distinctly Jamaican/Afro-Diasporic aesthetic has been a well-known characteristic of Jamaican theatre since the colonial period. This tendency does not merely display the cultural hybridity characteristic of the Diasporic condition. It also indicates the intentional duplicitous nature of many Jamaican artistic productions. Here, a globally recognised European story is referenced in order to introduce an entirely new narrative derived from the experience of black Jamaicans, and to comment on the utility as well as the inapplicability of European aesthetics in

Jamaica. In this respect, Sistren's *Muffet* is similar to several of the plays staged by the Pantomime Company, especially during the 1950s to 1960s, more recent plays staged in commercial theatres, as well as the work of some dub poets.[18] The play explores the various tribulations faced by Jamaican women, including sexual harassment, economic exploitation, self-identity issues and various forms of violence. Though the nursery rhyme, *Little Miss Muffet* functions strategically as a well-known trope through which to present the story, the play's aesthetic is grounded in mimetic storytelling and reggae music.

*Nana Yah* (1980), directed by Jean Small, was similarly based on Jamaican oral techniques. The play was produced in 1980, in honour of Nanny of the Maroons, who was declared a national hero in 1975. Its title is based on what many assert was her actual honorific Ashanti title, *Nana* (i.e., queen/mother). The play is formatted as a wake[19] that memorialises Nanny. In the prologue, the audience is treated as attendees at the wake, greeted with food and hymn sheets for singing as they arrive and take their seats; and throughout the performance, the cast directly addresses them. The major character is a storyteller who narrates the action for the audience. The involvement of the audience in the action, as well as the constant direct communication with them is an element of call and response, which is prevalent in Jamaican popular theatre and influenced by mimetic storytelling. Where *Muffet* is driven by reggae and dancehall according to the 1986 context in which it is set, *Nana Yah* relies a lot on poetry and chanting with a drum accompaniment. Rastafarian linguistics is a main influence on the play, especially the repetition of the affirmative first person noun, 'I', and 'I and I' in some of the dialogue. Proverbs are also prominently featured.

Sistren also privileged the oral as a means of accommodating members who were non-readers, or who possessed only basic reading skills. Many of the plays were not read by all of the cast members, and some of the smaller productions, including the first play, *Downpression Get a Blow* (1977) were never scripted. Many of the actors featured in these plays learned lines by rote or through improvisation. This is a skill that requires a significant degree of concentration, as well as such an intense understanding of the character that lines can change with each performance if they are forgotten, while maintaining the integrity of the story. There are problems of transfer with this approach. Difficulties can arise when a new actor takes on a role, or when the principal actor has to depend on an understudy.

It can also pose problems for certain performances in which flexibility can be a drawback. For example, as Hertencer Lindsay-Sheppard stated, because *QPH* depended on sacred rituals, which are formatted according to particular conventions, they tried as much as possible to avoid fluidity, so actors had to employ fixed memorisation of the play (Lindsay-Sheppard, personal interview). Despite these limitations, when a script becomes a secondary rather than a primary base for a production, this can allow for some positive degree of experimentation into a range of verbal expressions. It also facilitates the development of non-verbal means of communication, including movement.

**Subversive Movement**

Sistren's repertoire of movement, including dance, still needs to be properly acknowledged in the scholarship on the Collective, but it was an essential element in their work and entailed the same degree of thought and experimentation as the oral and scribal aspects. Movement, in theatre and performance, refers to any use of the actor's body that replaces or emphasises speech, music and other modes of expression. In my analysis, I include all of the methods through which actors transfer messages, including gestures, various ways of walking or running and the relationship between costuming and how actors carry their bodies in a performance. Sistren's use of movement is strongly influenced by Jamaican and other African Diasporic ritual performance practices and recreation. They also reflect modes that can be found in feminist performance globally. I have characterised these movements as subversive for two reasons: First, Sistren's representations of the actors' bodies often transgressed some mainstream understandings of how women should be presented onstage; and second, Sistren utilised Afro-Diasporic ritual movements as a mode of resistance and black self-affirmation.

Perhaps the most obviously controversial aspect of Sistren's aesthetic has been the use of all-woman casts, including in their portrayals of male characters. This, combined with their feminist commitments, earned them the ire of some audiences, especially men, and anti-lesbian and sexist slurs were normally directed at them during the late 1970s and 1980s.[20] Some people's unwillingness to accept women depicting men emerged from their difficulty in reconciling between naturalistic theatre[21] and Sistren's application of non-naturalistic theatre, which depended on minimalism. Minimalist techniques, a main characteristic of Sistren's aesthetic, are reliant on flexible role shifts that sometimes involve actors playing roles that transgress their physical form, including their sex. As Afolashade, a Sistren founding member stated, 'you will have certain individuals feeling uncomfortable about women playing men, because the thing is, for them, theatre, I mean...is reality...So, our style of theatre in a way was a kind of challenge for some individuals' (Afolashade, personal interview).

Though, generally, critics and many audiences lauded Sistren for their portrayals of men, others expressed disdain and surprise, exacerbated by the fact that the actors who played male roles were extremely convincing in their craft, including how they dressed, modified their voices and moved their bodies on stage. Lana Finikin related to me a very telling post-performance encounter that they once had with some male audience members in the late 1970s:

> When we finished the men come back stage asking that they want to see 'di man dem'. And Becky [Knowles], Jasmine [Smith] and [Lorna] Burrell came out. That time dem did tek off di makeup, an seh, 'We were the ones who were playing the male roles.' An dem [the men] seh 'No man, unnu go fi di man dem roun deh weh a play di role, unnu cyaa tell mi nuttn seh a neva some man deh pan stage wid unnu.' And they went back around, put on back the makeup, come back round inna dem costume an come back round to dem an seh, 'Here we are, wha unnu want?' And dem seh, 'How unnu fi up pan stage a talk bout dem tings deh, an ray ray.' And *in front of them* Burrell tek di cotton an wipe di makeup an tek off har top wid har bra. And him seh, 'No star, dis kyaa be real. *You* dawta, up pan stage a behave like man? No man dat cyaa real.' An dem walk away an seh, 'Blertnaat star, no man!' (Finikin, personal interview).

Sistren's members were definitely not the first set of Jamaican theatre performers to cross gender lines. Jamaican popular theatre has a history of performers depicting members of the opposite sex. However, usually it has been male actors depicting women in farcical ways, and/or stereotypical black female, or black queer mannerisms being utilised for comedic effect. The contemporary 'roots' play genre, which has beginnings in popular theatre in the early twentieth century, has been a main site of this gender bending. Sistren was unique in that they formed a repertoire that depended on women's constant depiction of men, and these depictions were not farcical. Though there were elements of comedy in the characterisations, the male characters were usually abusive and uncaring. And perhaps most importantly, the male characters were secondary to the female characters.

Sistren's subversions using the actor's body as a site of non-verbal representation included their depiction of sexual and violent scenarios on stage. One of the best examples of this is the depiction of Marie's rape in Act III, scene 3 of *Bellywoman Bangarang* (1978), a play about early sexual activity, exploitation and teenage pregnancy. The scene, '...made a clear distinction between sex and violence' (Ford-Smith, personal interview). It begins with the actors spreading the terror into the rest of the theatre by wailing, banging on the walls and tearing pieces of paper. Three stocking-faced actors appear as the rapists. Two of them suspend Marie from a beam, with her legs splayed on their shoulders, while the third rapist, takes on the movement of a boxer and makes quick, forceful jabs in the space between her legs. In real time, the scene is very short. In the 2013 redux directed by Carolyn Allen at the JSD, it was less than 30 seconds long, but very jarring. Not all audiences were satisfied with these techniques. At a 1982 performance of *Bellywoman* at Strand Theatre in the city of Montego Bay, Sistren was booed, and the cast and crew had to rush from the venue to escape an angry audience who felt cheated. They had expected that *Bellywoman* would fit the roots play genre of Jamaican theatre – known for its farce, naturalism and often, sexual explicitness.

There is a decidedly gendered reasoning behind audience expectations of a play that deals with sexuality. In Jamaican theatre, like in other theatres and dramatic mediums throughout the world, women's bodies, stereotypical female mannerisms and voices have historically functioned as major elements in entertainment – especially of a comedic nature.[22] Thus, many feminist and women's theatre artists challenge those norms through inventive uses of bodies and voices that counter sexual and gendered tropes. For example: In *Nomzamo* (2013), written and directed by Swazi theatre artist, Gcebile Piliso Dlamini, the constant rape of a young girl is depicted every time the actor runs frantically in circles, reliving the very first time the assault happened. There have also been black woman performers who have utilised their nude bodies in their work as a way of reclaiming sexual agency and making statements about the exploitation of black women's bodies. (See Fleetwood 2011.)

Sistren's repertoire also entails dancing and mime, mostly influenced by Jamaican and other African Diasporic forms. *QPH* (1981), *Nana Yah* (1980), *Bellywoman Bangarang* (1978), *Muffet Inna All A Wi* (1986) and to a lesser extent, *Buss Out* (1989), are examples of what Osita Okagbue (2009) refers to as total theatre. This is a form of theatre in which movement, poetry, music and ritual do not exist on the periphery, supplementing the characters' dialogues. They are all equally essential to the main action. For Okagbue, 'dialogue is not the soul' of many African and Caribbean theatre productions (193). He also argues that, just as African cosmologies are often predicated on the notion of life as an experience of totality, these ways of doing theatre unite various methods of communication into a whole. For example, *Nana Yah* (1980) was broken into 11 movements consisting of singing, chanting, storytelling, monologues and dialogues.

For many of their plays, Sistren relied on research into Jamaican ritual performances found in religious, spiritual and secular practices. The influence of ritual performance was most clearly seen in *QPH* (1981), which is based on the disastrous 1980 fire at the Eventide Home for the Aged in Kingston, in which approximately 153 elderly women perished. Though it was widely suspected that the fire was caused by arson, and though it was a fact that the deplorable and unsafe conditions under which these women lived led to the high death toll, no one was held criminally responsible for the tragedy.[23] *QPH* was a compassionate representation of the lives of these destitute women, who constituted a part of Jamaica's underclass. Hertencer Lindsay-Sheppard, the play's director, was a tutor at the JSD, with training in therapeutic theatre techniques, i.e., the use of theatre to engage individuals and communities dealing with traumatic experiences. Lindsay-Sheppard and the other women who worked on *QPH* combined these techniques with Jamaican ritual practices, including those that centre on healing, ancestral veneration and funeral rites. Sistren undertook extensive field research on Revival, Etu, Nago, and Kumina, and incorporated performatic aspects of these religions and rituals, as well as secular Jamaican practices into the play. These not only drove the action, but also facilitated character development and expression. For instance, different dances guided the movements of the three eponymous characters, Queenie, Pearlie and Hopie.[24] Each had a distinct form of movement according to her physical and psychological traits. For example, Hopie, who was physically challenged, was guided by Dinkimini, a form of dance that involves shuffled feet, axial hip movements and uneven dropping of the knees. Etu, a ritual that venerates the ancestors, was especially influential in *QPH*.[25] It served as the philosophical, movement-oriented, and mnemonic device used to weave the story of the three women. For example, in the prologue, Queenie rises from her hospital bed where she is recovering from the fire, transforms into the Queen of the Etu ritual and resurrects Hopie and Pearlie so that the play may begin. Etu is used from the prologue onwards for scene transitions, role shifts and costume changes, and the play ends with a grand Etu ritual.

Caribbean theatre practitioners have a history of utilising popular performance forms rooted in Afro-Diasporic performance techniques and rituals, in order to make social commentary. Elaine Savory-Fido (2005) refers to this as a 'rehabilitation of popular traditions as anti-imperialist forms' (12). Sistren's uses of movement from within popular Jamaican/Afro-Diasporic ritual performance, their centering of orality and Jamaican oral literature (Okpewho 1992) and oraliterature (Cooper 1995), and focus on collective production of plays functioned within these anti-imperialist paradigms, and added an essential gender component to them.

## Sistren's Aesthetic Legacies and Lessons

In 'The Politics of Black Radical Subjectivity' Bell Hooks states, 'Opposition is not enough. In that vacant space after one has resisted there is still the necessity to become – to make oneself anew' (15). Sistren went beyond opposing problematic norms of race, class and gender. The Collective also developed an aesthetic centred on the everyday experiences of black Jamaican people, particularly working-class women. In her analysis of Sistren, Kanika Batra (2011) draws on the work of Tracy Robinson (2003) to propose the concept of post-colonial sexual citizenship through drama/performance. Robinson (2003) focuses on the ways in which Caribbean constitutions undervalue women, implying in law and practice that marriage and motherhood are 'key sites where women prove they are good citizens or not' (246). Batra states that Sistren's 'unique achievement was to subvert these morally inflected debates by making poor women the subjects of their own discourse on sexuality and citizenship'(48). In agreement with Batra, I argue further that Sistren did this in the content of their plays as well as in their aesthetic as a whole, which has been influential in community-engaged performance as well as in the development of feminist and gender consciousness in Jamaica and the rest of the Caribbean.

Sistren's members and collaborators have emphasised the catalytic role of the organisation in their lives, including the work that many currently do (Afolashade, Lana Finikin, Honor Ford-Smith, Beverly Hanson, Hilary Nicholson, personal interviews). In addition, many women's organisations have benefited from the work of Sistren. For example, several Sistren members and resource persons worked with other women in the formation of Women's Media Watch of Jamaica (WMWJA) and the Caribbean Association for Feminist Research and Action (CAFRA). Sistren has also worked intimately with groups like Development Alternatives for Women of a New Era, Caribbean (DAWN Caribbean), the Bureau of Women's Affairs, Jamaica, and the Association of Women's Organisations of Jamaica (AWOJA).'[26] (Finikin 2014; French, Nicholson, personal interviews).

The Collective's activities have unfortunately decreased considerably since the early 2000s. There are many reasons for this including the end of funding cycles; the death, retirement or migration of members; and organisational issues that were unresolved, including what Afolashade and Hilary Nicholson refer to as the absence of a succession plan (Afolashade, Nicholson, personal interviews). Several scholars have critically analysed Sistren's problems (Ford-Smith 1997; Green 2006; Smith 2008, 2011, 2013).

Founding member, Beverly Hanson, views Sistren's community engagement – an aspect of the Collective that still continues, as its essence:

> ...When we do the workshop pieces, we find that this is the core of Sistren and this is not something you could just put on a back burner...even though we don't have the original members and we might not have our own children involved or our next of kin... there are young people – men and women, who still have that urge, that sense of urgency to say, well ok, we gotta do something about this (Beverly Hanson, personal interview).

Though the major plays have received the most attention, there were several important small productions that Sistren produced through workshops in collaboration with other groups. Some of these plays were scripted. Examples include, *The Case of Iris Armstrong* (1984) about the economic and social hardships faced by women in Jamaica's sugar belt,[27] and *Tribute to Gloria who Overcame Death* (1982), developed from research on the lives of women in urban communities. More recently, Sistren's workshop processes have been utilised in their involvement with the Citizens Security and Justice Programme (CSJP), initiated by the Jamaica Ministry of National Security.[28] Through the CSJP and other projects, the Collective's methods have been transferred to various community cultural groups, and in particular, to the Hannah Town Cultural Group (HTCG) and the Rockfort Cultural Group (RCG), which Sistren formed in 2006.

The Hannah Town Cultural Group[29] and Sistren produced the pro-choice play, *A Slice of Reality* in 2009 as their submission to the government on the debates around amending Jamaica's anti-abortion laws. They made history by being the first group of activists to perform a play in the Jamaican Houses of Parliament. Collectively created through ethnographic research on actual women's experiences, *Slice* is a 15-minute example of total theatre (Okagbue 2009), applied to political activism utilising dialogue, dub poetry, dancing and singing. It builds on and adds another angle to Sistren's radical aesthetic – a direct confrontation with state officials in the space in which decisions are made. *Slice* disrupted the tone of the debates around amending Jamaica's anti-abortion laws[30] by centering the subjectivities of working-class Jamaican women in a process dominated by the middle-class elite.[31] (See Heron, Toppin and Finikin 2009.) This consistent challenge to Jamaican elitist norms of behaviour and aesthetic tastes is the core of Sistren's legacy.

There is still a need for comprehensive studies of theatrical radicalism in Jamaica, in particular, how these methods and content constitute an important element of black radicalism in the country. For example, how do we assess Tribe Sankofa's *Black Bodies* (2015) or Karl Williams's *The Black That I Am* (2005), within the history of Jamaicans' development of theatre that engages with questions of race, class and gender, contemporary modes of imperialism, and the legacies of Jamaica's colonial past? In many ways, the repertoire of Sistren Theatre

Collective is the most enduring manifestation of the efforts to develop a distinctly Jamaican theatre aesthetic, which coalesced at the Jamaica School of Drama in the 1970s, drawing on aesthetic traditions within Jamaica, the rest of the Caribbean and elsewhere. Sistren's repertoire is also an excellent example of the ways in which black women have developed aesthetics that theorise and transgress the combined effects of racial, class-based and gendered oppression.

*This research was supported by a dissertation research fellowship from the Inter-American Foundation (IAF) Grassroots Development Program and a grant from the Pembroke Center for Teaching and Research on Women, Brown University.*

## Notes

1. Specifically, this compartmentalisation derives in part from Cartesian dualisms, disseminated throughout the world under European colonialism. It also emerges generally from European Enlightenment ideals, which have been globally influential in social organisation, especially at the level of governance. For gendered critiques of this compartmentalist way of thinking, see also Eudine Barriteau (1998), Liz Stanley and Sue Wise (1993) and Carole Pateman (1998).
2. Some other cultural programmes also assigned to the Jamaica School of Drama were The Cultural Therapy Program at the Bellevue Psychiatric Hospital (Bellevue Theatre) and The Gun Court Cultural Movement, aimed at using theatre in the rehabilitation of young men convicted of gun-related crimes. Later on, the Graduate Theatre Company was established by graduates of the JSD in 1981 and operated for many years using drama for education and community engagement (see Bennett and Bennett 2011; Hickling 2004).
3. This English translation of 'labrish' does not truly reflect its emphatic and performative importance in Jamaican culture.
4. Edelweiss Park, Kingston served as the international headquarters of the Universal Negro Improvement Association and African Communities League (UNIA/ACL) from 1929 to 1935. The Edelweiss Amusement Company was formed in 1931 to oversee the cultural activities there. For many years, Edelweiss Park was a significant fixture in Jamaican cultural life and nurtured the talent of many black Jamaican artists, including famous actor and playwright, Randolph Williams. Though Edelweiss stopped being the UNIA's international headquarters after Garvey moved to England in 1935, it continued to be a major cultural venue for several years. Garvey himself was a prolific poet, songwriter and playwright.
5. German Marxist director, Bertolt Brecht (1898–1956) was very influential in the work of many radical theatre artists globally. He created epic theatre drawing on influences from Chinese theatre and the work of fellow German, Erwin Piscator, and others. Epic theatre centres the lesson offered in the play

over the emotional connection that an audience may develop for the character. In Brecht's dramaturgy, the audience is supposed to engage in critical self-reflection and leave the theatre motivated to change the particular social crisis that was represented in the play.
6. The Impact Programme provided temporary work for unemployed people, mostly women. The women who would later form Sistren worked as teachers' aides and street cleaners for a while under this programme.
7. *Downpression* was about a strike organised by women employed in a garment factory. The word, 'downpression' illustrates Sistren's tendency to draw on Jamaican linguistics – in this case, Rastafarian subversion of the English word, 'oppression'.
8. The co-founding core members were: Lorna Burrell-Haslam, Pauline Crawford (now Afolashade), Beverly Elliott, Lillian Foster, Lana Finikin, Barbara Gayle, Beverly Hanson, Rebecca Knowles, Vivette Lewis, Jasmine Smith, Cerene Stephenson and Jerline Todd. Honor Ford-Smith is Sistren's founding Artistic Director (See Ford-Smith 1997).
9. Sistren was widely regarded as a People's National Party-affiliated organisation, partly because the core members had been employed in the Impact Programme (Crash Programme), which was commonly seen as a programme that awarded PNP supporters with jobs. In actuality, the women held different political perspectives (Afolashade, Lana Finikin, Ford-Smith, Hertencer Lindsay-Sheppard, personal interviews).
10. There is generally a distinction made between the working-class women who formed the core of the organisation and part-time resource persons who worked with the women on different projects. This distinction centres the working class women's formation of the Collective, and their grounding within a grassroots-oriented framework. However, a few middle-class women became members of Sistren and/or worked with the Collective for long periods. For example, Honor Ford-Smith, the founding Artistic Director, and Hilary Nicholson, who performed several duties, including fundraising, are Sistren members.
11. As a discipline, theatre and performance studies in the Western hemisphere continue to have mostly white men as its canonical figures, including Bertolt Brecht, Antonin Artaud, Jersy Grotowski and Augusto Boal. Racial and gender privilege, as well as the logocentricity within the field partly account for this imbalance. Women theatre makers, especially women of colour, have not been as prolific in publishing books on methods that they develop. One of the reasons for this is that woman theatre activists, like grassroots activists (and by extension woman academics) are usually more overworked and underpaid than their male peers.
12. Ford-Smith's essay, 'Notes towards a New Aesthetic' (1989), quoted at the beginning of this chapter, is partly a manifesto on the dramaturgical methods that were developed at the JSD, by Sistren and by other initiatives. It is one of the few writings produced on theatre method in Jamaica. The essay is not specifically about Sistren's work.
13. This globally practised technique includes audience participation in the action. It was conceptualised by Augusto Boal (1931–2009), the progressive

Brazilian theatre artist and activist, as an element in his theatre-of-the-oppressed dramaturgy. See Boal 1985.

14. In Sistren's case, there were tensions around whether the collective structure was one of the reasons that they were not able to bring enough new members into the organisation to ensure its sustenance. In her study of feminist theatre collectives in Britain, Goodman (1993) notes that sometimes the concern with having everybody contribute to the creation process ended up weakening the artistic structure of the plays.
15. The system developed by Cassidy in the 1960s forms the basis of the system currently utilised by the Jamieka Langwij Unit.
16. This is a form of performance poetry that emerged in the 1970s, influenced by toasting – i.e., a deejay chanting over the dub (instrumental) side of a record. Oku Onuora, one of Jamaica's pioneer dub poets, coined the term. Women like Anita Stewart aka Anilia Soyinka, and Jean Binta Breeze were integral to the development of dub poetry in the 1970s to 1980s.
17. This is a form of storytelling in which the storyteller is both the narrator and the cast, taking on the roles of all the characters.
18. There are numerous examples of this from the Pantomime Company, including Louise Bennett's *Anancy and Pandora* (1955) and Louise Bennett and Randolph Williams's *Quashie Lady* (1958), a Jamaican retelling of the American musical, *My Fair Lady*, adapted from George Bernard Shaw's *Pygmalion*. More recently, Jambiz International staged *Cindy-Relisha and the DJ Prince* (2005), by Patrick Brown, loosely based on *Cinderella*, the European folk tale. In dub poetry, *Muffet inna All a Wi* calls to mind Mutabaruka's *Nursery Rhyme Lament*, and one of the lines in Mikey Smith's *Mi Cyaa Believe It/I Can't Believe It*: 'one likkle bwai come blow im horn, an mi luk pan im wid scorn.' (from the British nursery rhyme, *Little Boy Blue*).
19. I use the term 'wake' here, because that is the term used in the play script. But this is not the same as a wake in the US or British understanding. The format of the play is more along the lines of a 'nine-night', a Jamaican ceremony/gathering for a recently departed person. Nine-nights were traditionally held for nine nights after the death of the person, but now normally exist as one-night events.
20. Sistren members were often verbally abused with the anti-lesbian Jamaican titles, *man royal, sodomite* and *batty woman* (Finikin, Ford-Smith, Nicholson, personal interviews).
21. This refers to the genre mostly seen in Jamaican commercial theatre today. It consists of acting, set design, costuming and special effects that are as close as possible to how they appear in the real world.
22. These characterisations are complex. For example, the tropes of the strong working-class woman character, or male character playing a woman, or male character with stereotypical female mannerisms have also been integral to voicing the often muted opinions of poor black Jamaican women and homosexual men. However, when not handled carefully, this character can enforce stereotypes.
23. Generally, people suspected that arson was behind the fire, and there were different rumors around who was responsible for it. There had been several police reports about gunmen harassing the staff and residents of the home in

the months leading up to the fire, including one incident in which two staff members were injured (Robinson 2011). According to Robert Carr (2002), it was commonly believed that the Eventide fire was a JLP reprisal for the Orange Street fire of 1980, allegedly set by a gang associated with the PNP. In this fire, 11 people died, including two babies and five children (215). There are also allegations that the Central Intelligence Agency (CIA) played a role in the fire in their effort to undermine the ruling PNP government and its democratic socialist policies. See *Jamaica CIA: Eventide Fire Who Cares? 153 Dead Old Women 5/20/80*. https://www.youtube.com/watch?v=Vf2MQC4v9ts (accessed May 1, 2016). Though Sistren did not speak to the allegations of political motivation behind the fire, they were often harassed during the play's Jamaican run. They also had to cancel one performance because of a death threat (Ford-Smith, Lindsay-Sheppard, personal interviews).

24. The three characters were based loosely on elderly women who lived at Eventide (Allison 1986, Lindsay-Sheppard, personal interviews, Sistren 2001).
25. Etu is an African-based ritual/ceremony mainly practised in Western Jamaica.
26. According to Joan French, former Workshop Coordinator with Sistren, and co-founder of CAFRA, 'It is Sistren who went down into these islands and did the skits and the workshop work with community women and got a lot of that going that actually spurred the energy that could allow for the formation a of a CAFRA' (French, personal interview).
27. This workshop was the subject of the documentary, *Sweet Sugar Rage* (1986), produced by Sistren and the affiliated company, Video for Change founded by Sistren member, Hilary Nicholson, and Cynthia Wilmot.
28. The CSJP aimed at mobilising residents of volatile communities through various strategies by encouraging greater collaboration with the police and finding avenues for youth to express themselves creatively.
29. HTCG is comprised of ten women and three men. They are: Tony Allen, Althea Blackwood, Pauline Blake-Palmer, Sonia Britton, Karlene Campbell, Cinderella Green, Kadian Jones, Sandra Hanson, Patricia McCrae, Adrian Raphael, Patricia Riley, Joan Stewart, Marlon Thompson. Only the women performed *A Slice of Reality*.
30. Jamaica has retained the archaic anti-abortion provisions of sections 72–73 of the Offences Against the Persons Act (OAPA), which was introduced under British colonialism in 1864. Under the act, abortions are illegal, though common law precedent has made exceptions in cases where the mother's health is threatened. In February 2007, the government's Abortion Policy Review Group (APRG) identified abortion as a serious public health issue and the government was urged to repeal the OAPA and replace it with a civil law titled, the Termination of Pregnancy Act, legalising abortion in most cases and providing government-staffed health centres that provide abortion services. From 2007 to 2009, Parliament collected submissions on the legalisation of abortion from different groups. Since then, nothing has been done to amend the law, because powerful conservative Christian lobby groups and conservative Parliamentarians have held up the process.
31. The submission from the Coalition of Lawyers for Defence of the Unborn was particularly classist in its references to the sex lives of mostly poor urban Jamaican women and the prevalence of black women in abortion statistics in the US (CLDU 2008).

## References

Afolashade. 2014. Interview with Author. October 30.
Allison, Helen. 1986. *Sistren Song: Popular Theatre in Jamaica*. London: War on Want.
Aston, Elaine, and Sue-Ellen Case, eds. 2007. *Staging International Feminisms*. Basingstoke and New York: Palgrave Macmillan, 2007.
Barriteau, Eudine. 1998. Theorizing Gender Systems and the Project of Modernity in the Twentieth-Century Caribbean. *Feminist Review*, no. 59 (Summer): 186–210.
Batra, Kanika. 2011. *Feminist Visions and Queer Futures in Postcolonial Drama: Community, Kinship, Citizenship*. New York: Routledge.
Bennett, Wycliffe, and Hazel Bennett. 2011. *The Jamaican Theatre: Highlights of the Performing Arts in the Twentieth Century*. Kingston, Jamaica: University of the West Indies Press.
Bhabha, Homi K. 2004. *The Location of Culture*. London: Routledge.
Boal, Augusto. 1985. *Theatre of the Oppressed*. Transl. Charles A. McBride. New York: Theatre Communications Group.
Booler, Deborah. 1999. 'Getting to the Core of Reality': The Sistren Theatre Collective: Performing for Change. MA dissertation, International Cultural Studies, UK: Nottingham Trent University.
Boyce Davies, Carole, and Elaine Savory Fido, eds. 1990. *Out of the Kumbla: Caribbean Women and Literature*. Trenton, NJ: Africa World Press.
Carr, Robert. 2002. A Politics of Change: Sistren, Subalternity, and the Social Pact in the War for Democratic Socialism. In *Black Nationalism in the New World: Reading the African-American and West Indian Experience*, 201–44. Durham, NC: Duke University Press.
———. 2002. Black Nationalism in the New World: Reading the African-American and West Indian Experience. Durham, N.C.: Duke University Press.
CLDU. 2008. Submission of the Coalition of Lawyers for the Defence of the Unborn to the Joint Select Committee of Parliament Considering Abortion. Kingston.
Cooper, Afua, ed. 1999. *Utterances and Incantations: Women, Poetry and Dub*. Toronto: Sister Vision Press.
Cooper, Carolyn. 1995. *Noises in the Blood: Orality, Gender and the 'Vulgar' Body of Jamaican Popular Culture*. Durham: Duke University Press.
Davis, Angela. 2004. *Women, Race and Class*. New York: Seal Press.
Davis, Angela Y. 1998. *Blues Legacies and Black Feminism: Gertrude 'Ma' Rainey, Bessie Smith, and Billie Holiday*. New York: Pantheon Books.
Di Cenzo, Maria, and Susan Bennett. 1992. Women, Popular Theatre and Social Action: Interviews with Cynthia Grant and Sistren Theatre Collective. *ARIEL: A Review of International English Literature* 23, no. 1 (January): 73–96.
Ferguson, Roderick A. 2004. *Aberrations in Black: Toward a Queer of Color Critique*. Minneapolis: University of Minnesota Press.
Finikin, Lana. 2015. Interview with Author. January 9.
Finikin, Lana, and Honor Ford-Smith. 2014. Interview with Author. August 16.
Ford-Smith, Honor. 1995. An Experiment in Popular Theatre and Women's History: 'Ida Revolt Inna Jonkunoo Stylee'. 1995. In *Subversive Women: Women's Movements in Africa, Asia, Latin America and the Caribbean*, ed. Saskia Weiringa, 147–64. London: Zed Books.
———. 1997. Ring Ding in a Tight Corner: Sistren, Collective Democracy and the Organisation of Cultural Production. In *Feminist Genealogies, Colonial Legacies,*

*Democratic Futures*, ed. M. Jacqui Alexander and Chandra Talpade Monanty, 213–58. New York and London: Routledge.

———. 1986. Sistren: Exploring Women's Problems through Drama. *Jamaica Journal* 19, no. 1:2–12.

Garvey, Marcus. 1987. Lesson 16 of the School of African Philosophy: Propaganda [1937]. In *Marcus Garvey, Life and Lessons: A Centennial Companion to the Marcus Garvey and Universal Negro Improvement Association Papers*, ed. Robert A. Hill and Barbara Bair, 289–95. Berkeley: University of California Press.

Goodman, Lizbeth. 1993. *Contemporary Feminist Theatres: To Each Her Own*. London: Routledge.

Green, Sharon L. 2006. On a Knife Edge: Sistren Theatre Collective, Grassroots Theatre and Globalization. *Small Axe* 11, no. 1: 105–108.

Hanson, Beverly. 2015. Interview with Author. August 27.

Hickling, Frederick. 2004. From Explanitations and Madnificent Irations to De Culcha Clash: Popular Theatre as Psychotherapy Interventions. *International Journal of Post-Colonial Studies* 6, no. 1:45–66.

Hooks, Bell. 1990. *Yearning: Race, Gender, and Cultural Politics*. Boston: South End Press.

Kleymeyer, Charles David. 1994. Women's Theater in Jamaica: Sistren Theatre Collective. In *Cultural Expression and Grassroots Development: Cases from Latin America and the Caribbean*, ed. Charles David Kleymeyer, 71–82. Boulder, CO: L. Reiner.

Levine, Lawrence W. 1978. *Black Culture and Black Consciousness: Afro-American Folk Thought from Slavery to Freedom*. Oxford: Oxford University Press.

Moten, Fred. 2003. *In the Break: The Aesthetics of the Black Radical Tradition*. Minneapolis: University of Minnesota Press.

Nettleford, Rex M. 1972. *Mirror Mirror: Identity, Race, and Protest in Jamaica*. New York: Morrow.

Okagbue, Osita A. 2009. *Culture and Identity in African and Caribbean Theatre*. 1st ed. London: Adonis & Abbey Publishers Ltd.

Okpewho, Isidore. 1992. *African Oral Literature: Backgrounds, Character, and Continuity*. Bloomington: Indiana University Press.

Pateman, Carole. 1988. The Sexual Contract. Stanford, CA : Stanford University Press.

Robinson, Corey. 2011. Eventide Fire Remembered: Torrington Park Marks Anniversary with Demand for an End to Political Rivalry. The *Jamaica Observer*, May 23. http://www.jamaicaobserver.com/news/Eventide-fire-remembered_8844433. Accessed May 1, 2016.

Robinson, Tracy. 2003. Beyond the Bill of Rights: Sexing the Citizen. In *Confronting Power, Theorizing Gender: Interdisciplinary Perspectives from the Caribbean*, ed. V. Eudine Barriteau, 231–61. Kingston: University of the West Indies Press.

Simmonds, Orville. 2006. Lady Chance and the Butterfly Dance. Unpublished play script.

Sistren. 1980. Nana Yah. Unpublished play script.

———. 1984. The Case of Iris Armstrong. Unpublished play script.

———. 1986. Muffet Inna All a Wi. Unpublished play script.

———. 1998. Buss Out. Unpublished play script.

———. 2001. Bellywoman Bangarang. In *Contemporary Drama of the Caribbean*, ed. Erika J. Waters and David Edgecombe, 77–131. Kingshill, St Croix: University of the Virgin Islands.

———. 2001. QPH. In *Postcolonial Plays: An Anthology*, ed. Helen Gilbert, 153–78. New York and London: Routledge.

———. 2004. *The Drums Keep Sounding: Based on the Life of Miss Lou*. Sistren Theatre Collective and Video for Change. DVD.

Sistren, and Honor Ford-Smith, eds. 1987. *Lionheart Gal: Life Stories of Jamaican Women*. Toronto: Sister Vision.

Small, Jean. 2015. Interview with Author. May 13.

Smith, Karina. 2005. Invoking the Spirit of the Warrior Woman: Sistren's 'Nana Yah'. MäComere 7:77–92.

———. 2008. Narratives of Success, Narratives of Failure: The Creation and Collapse of Sistren's 'Aesthetic Space'. *Modern Drama* 51, no. 2:234–58.

———. 2011. Struggling to Cross the Race and Class Divide: Sistren's Theatrical and Organizational Model of Collectivity. *Theatre Research International* 36, no. 1 (March): 64–78.

———. 2013. From Politics to Therapy: Sistren Theatre Collective's Theatre and Outreach Work in Jamaica. *New Theatre Quarterly* 29, no. 1 (February): 87–97.

Stanley, Liz, and Sue Wise. 1993. *Breaking out Again: Feminist Ontology and Epistemology*. London: New York, 1993.

Tate, Shirley Anne. 2009. *Black Beauty: Aesthetics, Stylization, Politics*. Farnham, Surrey, England: Ashgate.

Thomas, Deborah A. 2004. *Modern Blackness: Nationalism, Globalization and the Politics of Culture in Jamaica*. Durham: Duke University Press.

# Contributors

**Anthony Bogues**
Anthony Bogues teaches at Brown University where he is the Asa Messer Professor of Humanities and Critical Theory and the inaugural director of the Center for the Study of Slavery and Justice. His forthcoming books include an edited volume on black political thought, *From Slave Petitions to Black Lives Matter* and a volume on Sylvia Wynter and radical Caribbean thought. He is the co-convener of the Global Curatorial Project on Slavery.

**Mark Figueroa**
Mark Figueroa has, since 1974, pursued an academic career at UWI, Mona, where he has researched the development of Caribbean ideas and policy, giving special attention to Arthur Lewis. He is also known for his work on the garrison phenomenon in Jamaica and socio-economic outcomes.

**Paget Henry**
Paget Henry is professor of Sociology and Africana Studies at Brown University. He is the author of *Peripheral Capitalism and Underdevelopment in Antigua*, *Caliban's Reason: Introducing Afro-Caribbean Philosophy*, then, *Shouldering Antigua and Barbuda: The Life of V.C. Bird*, and most recently, *The Art of Mali Olatunji*. He is the editor of the *CLR James Journal*, and the *Antigua and Barbuda Review of Books*, and has been a strong contributor to the discussions on Antigua and Barbuda's development.

**Clinton A. Hutton**
Clinton A. Hutton is a Professor at The University of the West Indies specialising in Caribbean Political Philosophy, Culture and Aesthetics. He has published numerous book chapters and journal articles on the Haitian Revolution, the culture of enslaved Africans, the Morant Bay uprising, Caribbean Art and Aesthetics, Rastafari, Revival and Jamaican

popular music. His most recent book is *Colour for Colour Skin for Skin: Marching with the Ancestral Spirits into War Oh at Morant Bay* (2015). He is lead editor and author of *Leonard Percival Howell and the Genesis of Rastafari* (2015). Hutton is a noted painter and photographer.

**F.S. J. Ledgister**

F.S.J. Ledgister teaches political science at Clark Atlanta University in Georgia, US. He is the author of *Class Alliances and the Liberal Authoritarian State: The Roots of Post-Colonial Democracy in Jamaica, Trinidad and Tobago, and Suriname* (1998); *Only West Indians: Creole Nationalism in the British West Indies* (2010); and *Michael Manley and Jamaican Democracy, 1972–1980: The Word is Love* (2014).

**Rupert Lewis**

Dr Rupert Lewis is Professor Emeritus of Political Thought in the Department of Government at the University of the West Indies, Mona, Jamaica. He has published widely on Marcus Garvey and the Garvey movement, Pan-Africanism and Caribbean radicalism. He is author of *Walter Rodney's Intellectual and Political Thought*, and recently completed a short biography of Marcus Garvey.

**Mawuena Logan**

Mawuena Logan is an associate professor in The Department of Pan-African Studies at the University of Louisville, Kentucky, where he teaches African and African Diaspora Literature and Critical Race Theory. His publications include *Narrating Africa* (1999), 'Postmodern Identity: Blackness and the Making of President Obama' (2012) and 'Legba in the House: African Cosmology in Their Eyes were Watching God' (2013)

**Jermaine McCalpin**

Jermaine McCalpin is Assistant Professor and Director of the African and African-American Studies program at New Jersey City University. He specializes in transitional justice, genocides and truth commissions, and has written on reparations for African enslavement, the Armenian genocide and the South African, Haitian and Grenadian truth commissions.

## Charles W. Mills
Charles W. Mills is a Distinguished Professor of Philosophy at the CUNY Graduate Center. He works in the general area of oppositional political theory and is the author of six books, the most recent being *Black Rights/White Wrongs: The Critique of Racial Liberalism*.

## Ken Post
Emeritus Professor Ken Post died on March 12, 2017, aged 82. After lecturing at the University of the West Indies, Mona, Jamaica, Post joined the Centre of West African Studies at the University of Birmingham and in 1969 the Institute of Social Studies in The Hague where he worked as Professor of Political Science until his retirement in 1990. A prolific Marxist author and a phenomenal scholar, he published books on Nigeria, Jamaica, Vietnam and modern Europe.

## Nicosia Shakes
Nicosia Shakes is Assistant Professor in the Department of Africana Studies at The College of Wooster, Ohio, specializing in gender and sexuality studies, theatre, performance and activism. Her current research is on the work of Sistren Theatre Collective, Jamaica and The Mothertongue Project, South Africa. She holds a PhD in Africana Studies from Brown University.

## Linda Sturtz
Linda Sturtz is Chair of the History Department at Macalester College, Saint Paul, Minnesota. Linda Sturtz is researching connections among history, public performance and collective memory. Her publications include articles on loyalists during the American Revolution and masquerade in Montserrat along with the book *'Within Her Power': Propertied Women in Colonial Virginia*.

## Maziki Thame
Maziki Thame teaches political science at Clark Atlanta University. Her research interests and publications focus on the postcolonial Caribbean, the place of race, violence, radicalism, identity and gender in political life.

**Linnette Vassell**
Linnette Vassell, a consultant on gender and development, has combined activism in communities and women's movements from the 1970s with academic engagements to advance the empowerment of women and communities in Jamaica and the Caribbean. Her discussion on Elean Thomas's life and contribution as a revolutionary is rooted in their friendship and her understanding of Elean's personal and political life journey.

# Index

Abeng, viii, ix, x, 24, 25, 26, 27, 28, 29, 30, 31, 32–33, 34, 57–58, 83, 84, 94, 137, 139, 143, 148, 149, 159, 253, 254
academic and professional honours, 265
acts of decolonization, 93
Addis Ababa, 168
Afolashade, 324, 328
Africa, x, 2, 9, 10, 11, 13, 19, 29, 41–43, 45, 49–50, 57, 59, 64, 68, 72, 74, 78, 80, 84, 84, 87, 90, 91, 92, 94, 98, 111, 139, 142, 144, 145, 147, 162, 163, 165, 168, 169, 172, 179, 239–41, 242, 243, 244, 247, 251, 252, 260, 263, 264, 265, 266, 267, 268, 298, 305, 311, 313, 315
African history, 13, 46, 49, 111, 142
African intellectuals, 241
African Liberation movements, 58
African Nationalism, 42, 43
African Nationalist Union (ANU), 43
African Philosophy, 297
African Socialism, 43, 146–47, 156
African Studies Association of the West Indies (ASAWI), 49
African-Chinese, 168
African-Jamaican population, 43
Afri-COBRA, 307
Afro-Caribbean identities, 144
Afro-Caribbean socialism, 149
Afro-Caribbean subaltern, 93
Afro-Cuban, 73, 92, 93
Afro-Jamaicanism, 87–88
Akan concept, x

Akan, x, 155, 239, 321
Alleyne, Mervyn, 49
all-woman casts, 323
alternative symbolic order, 87
American Liberian, 242
Anglo-Saxon prejudices, 241
Angola, 74, 244
Anguilla, 33
antebellum US, 209
anti-colonial black mobilization, 39
anti-colonial movements, 65
Antigua and Barbuda, 57, 133, 138, 158, 167
anti-occidental forces, 196
Aripo, 309
armoured cars, 15, 17
artistic agency, 218
Asia, 72, 162–64, 169, 170, 265
Asian Infrastructural Bank (AIB), 170
autocratic styles of rule, 149
axiology, 182

Bad Friday, 44
Bad John, 307
Bamboo Club, 14
Bandung conference, 163, 164, 169
banned books, 21
Barbados, 57, 75, 133, 134, 164, 167, 269
Baudrillard, Jean, 208, 209
Bauxite, 5, 27
bauxite industry, 5
Beckford, George (G Beck), 5, 14–15, 22, 24, 27, 46, 53, 57, 89, 253
Belgian rule, 243
Belize, 166, 167

Bennett, Louise, 314, 320
Berlin Conference, 244
Bertram, Arnold, 48, 52, 58
Best, Lloyd, 24, 81, 89, 142, 254
Bishop, Maurice, ix, 70, 116, 151, 285, 286
black aesthetics, 311, 312
black art, 311
   blackconsciousness, 10, 13, 20, 21, 27, 33, 44, 45, 49, 109, 306
Black Enterprise Board of Economists, 264
black liberalism, 172
black nationalism, viii–ix, 40, 41, 42, 65, 66, 84, 87, 88, 108, 172
black poverty, 48
black power militants, 11, 22
black power movement, 12, 39, 51, 57–59, 67, 68, 270
black radical consciousness, 174
black radicalism, 45, 46, 91, 172, 311, 315, 329
Blackburn, Robin, 35, 192, 199
Blue Gang, 8
Bogues, Anthony, xii, 83
Bongo-man, 30, 31, 57
Brathwaite, Edward Kamau, 49
British High Commission, 33
British Labour Party, 33, 255, 276
Buck-Morss, Susan, 192, 195, 199
Burnham, Forbes, 74, 167
Bustamante Industrial Trade Union (BITU), 5, 15, 52
Bustamante, Alexander, 5, 39, 99
Buster, Prince, 12, 25, 50, 307

Canada, 129, 167, 297, 320
capital accumulation, 138
capitalism, ix, 6, 44, 59, 65, 66, 71, 72, 73, 78, 108, 138, 143, 144, 145, 151, 152, 155, 157, 159, 162
Caribbean Basin Initiative (CBI), 132
Caribbean Development Bank (CDB), 264

Caribbean Free Trade Association (CARIFTA), 264
Caribbean political thought, x, xii, 84, 141
Caribbean socialism, ix, 137, 141, 143, 149, 150
CARICOM Reparations Commission, 78
Castro, Fidel, 11, 45, 50, 73, 106, 112
Cesiare, Aime, 90, 154, 239, 242, 307
Chinese riots, 109
Christophe, Henri, 201
Chronixx, 73
civil rights, 42, 164, 183–84, 306
Clarke, LeRoy, xi, 297–300, 303, 304, 305, 306, 307, 308
Coard, Bernard, 70
colonial constitutions, 269
Colonial Development Corporation (CDC), 259
colonial legacies, 39, 41, 43
Committee of Women for Progress (CWP), 291, 313
communitarianism, 172, 175
Community Work Brigade (CWB), 123
Congo, 242–27
Council for Peace and Civil Liberties, 255
creole slaves, 193, 194
Cuba, 11, 24, 49, 54, 69, 73–75, 77, 92–93, 106, 134–35, 149, 164, 169
Cuban Revolution, viii, 69, 76
Cubism, 92
Cudjoe, Selwyn, 305
Cugoano, Quobna Ottobah, x, 151, 172–73, 178–88
culture, xi, 16, 19, 35, 69, 88, 90, 91, 93, 102, 107, 108, 111, 112, 121, 127, 141, 150, 154, 191–93, 197, 198, 199, 211, 212, 247, 251, 254, 265, 272, 293, 298, 305, 307, 313, 314, 315, 321

d'Auberteuil, Hilliard, 302
DBurns, 282, 292, 293
democratic centralism, 128, 290
democratic socialist, 71, 143, 151–53, 155, 158, 159–60, 269, 285, 314
dependent relationship, 131
deportation, 20–22, 141
Dessalines, Jean-Jacques, xi, 64, 191, 195–96, 198, 201–204
development economist, 251, 268
dictatorship, 69–70, 75, 102, 119
diplomatic relations, 164, 167
Dizzy, Ras, 10, 12, 13, 20, 50
dogmatism, 143, 149, 150
Domingo, W.A., 40, 142
Dominica, 132–33, 167,
double consciousness, 173
Douen (douendom), 300, 301, 307
Dubois, W.E.B, 42
Duncan, D.K., 51, 58

East Kingston, 44, 50
Eastern Europe, 71, 129, 146, 149
education, 16, 48, 59, 68, 75, 77–79, 101, 119, 121–22, 124, 126, 154, 159, 216, 254, 264, 272, 282, 293, 315, 316
egalitarian democracy, 103
El Salvador, 135, 136
El Tucuche, 298, 309
Engels, Frederick, 84, 144
entrepreneurial dependence, 160
epistemic rupture, 93
epistemological, 191–93, 195, 198, 199, 201, 204, 292, 303
Equiano, Olaudah, 240
Ethiopian, 43, 109, 302
Etu ritual, 327
Europeanised, 298, 302
external threat, 71, 131

Fabian Colonial Bureau Advisory Committee, 260
Fabian groups, 255

Fabian socialism, 103, 157
Fanon, Frantz, 143
Fedon, 126
feminist, xi, 175, 313, 315, 319, 323, 325, 328
France, 192, 194, 195, 199, 244
French restoration of slavery, 203

Garvey, Marcus, viii, xii, 12, 19, 25, 29, 41, 46, 49, 83, 93, 98, 107, 108, 111, 112, 139, 140, 207, 239, 245, 254, 297, 302, 303, 314
Garvey Jr., Marcus, 29, 43, 57, 59
Garvey movement, 39, 42, 65, 78
Garveyite, 10
gender equality, 77
Germany, 192, 320
Girvan, Norman, 5, 14, 18, 22, 24, 27, 89, 142, 265
Glissant, Édouard, 90
Gonsalves, Ralph, 3, 14, 15, 51, 54
Great Depression, 137
Green Bottom, 46
Grenada, ix, 5, 58, 70, 75, 116–17, 120, 123, 128–32, 134, 135, 139, 148, 150, 156, 167, 178, 285–86, 288, 294
Grenada Revolution, ix, 58, 128, 130, 132, 285, 288
Guatemala, 135
Guyana, 18, 24, 54, 141, 142, 164, 167

Haiti, 90, 92, 191, 192, 197, 198, 199, 202, 203, 291, 299, 302
Haitian Revolution, xi, 64, 73, 74, 191–204, 302
Hannah Town Cultural Group, 329
Hill, Robert 'Bobby', 51, 57, 253
Hispaniola, 212
Historian, Ras, 50
Hopie, 326–27
Howell, Leonard, 44, 109
Hulme Evening Centre, 262

human rights, 10, 12, 22, 26, 41, 49, 50, 165, 170, 274, 292
Hutton, Clinton, vii, xi, 191, 198, 199, 201, 203, 204, 209, 280, 297, 300, 306, 307

Impact, x, 57, 83, 140
ID, Ras, 50
imperialism, x, 12, 48, 73, 103, 118, 128–34, 179, 271, 329
Indo-Caribbean identities, 144
Indonesia, 163, 164, 165
infrastructure, 117, 166
institutionalised poverty, 133
International African Friends of Ethiopia (IAFE), 255, 275
International African Service Bureau (ISAB), 255, 272
international communism, 23
International Foundation for Education and Self-Help, 264
International Monetary Fund (IMF), 133–34, 151, 152, 166
International Peacemakers Association, 46
international solidarity, 130, 131, 162

Jacques Garvey, Amy, viii, 40, 42, 49, 84
Jamaica Broadcasting Corporation (JBC), 48
Jamaica College, 48
Jamaica Constabulary, 14
Jamaica Defence Force (JDF), 15, 16, 55
Jamaica School of Agriculture, 28
Jamaican Chinese, 167, 169
Jamaican government, 1, 24, 53
Jamaican Young Socialists, 24
JAMAL, 103
James, C.L.R., 19, 85, 86, 142, 154, 173, 192, 199, 200, 255, 276, 307
Joint Policy Committee (JPC), 16
Jumbi, 307

Katanga, 245
Kelly, Sharon, 280
Kenyatta, Jomo, 98, 255
Khama, Sereste, 259
King George VI Memorial Park, 15
King Jr., Martin Luther, 41, 56, 110
King Leopold, 244
King, Audvil, 86
Kinte, Kunta, 243
Kongo, 246

L'Ouverture, Toussaint, 64, 74, 151, 193, 195, 196, 198–201, 203,
Latin America, 116, 162, 163, 164, 265
leftist activity, 23
Legislative Council, 98–100
Lenin, Vladimir, 139, 144
Leninism, 91
Lewis, Arthur, x, 157, 250, 251, 253, 256, 265, 276
Lewis, Rupert, vii–xi, 1, 3, 12, 19, 22, 25, 39, 57, 64, 81, 83–86, 89, 91, 93, 94, 116, 137, 139, 162, 253, 280, 285, 286, 288
Lewisian phase, 157
Liberty Hall, xii, 65, 93, 140, 150
local political elites, 138
Locke, John, 172, 178, 179
Lockean worldview, 172
looting, 8, 15, 53

M'Neel, Thomas, 214
Mace, 55
Maceo, Antonio, 73
Macpherson, C.B., 176
Makonnen, Ras, 255
Malcolm X, 42
Mali, 244
Mama Dlo, 307
Manchester, 1, 20, 21–22, 34–35, 53, 258, 259, 260, 261, 262–63

# INDEX

Manchester Council for African Affairs, 263
Manley, Michael, ix, 58–59, 74, 99, 102, 106, 108, 110, 148, 164, 285
Manley, Norman, 5, 22, 28, 100, 106
Marley, Bob, 20, 74, 173, 267, 297, 303
Maroons, 24, 57, 92, 224, 322
Mars, Jean Price, 90
Marshall, Bernard, 48
Marson, Una, 78, 256, 276, 314
Marti, Jose, 73
Marx, Karl, 144
Marxist, viii–ix, 3, 7, 18, 20, 24, 27, 29–32, 65–66, 67, 142, 144, 148, 151, 154, 156, 175, 253, 255, 286, 288
mass incarceration, 152
materialist radicalism, 73
Maternity Leave Law, 120, 291
Matisse, Henri, 92
mento, 9
Middle East, 170
Ministry of Home Affairs, 15
mixed economy, 116, 151, 157–58
modernity, xi, 173, 174, 178, 180, 191–93, 196
Moko, 57
Morant Bay Rebellion, 64, 140
Morgan, Poco, 48
Moss Side Community House Social Centre, 262
Moyne Commission, 251, 252, 276
multiple messages, 224–25
Munroe, Trevor, 27, 30, 32, 57, 139, 140, 253
music, 9, 12, 19, 44, 45, 47, 58, 72, 102, 169, 211–13, 219, 220, 222, 251, 273, 307, 313, 315, 316, 321, 322, 323, 326

Nanjing University, 157
Nanny, 64, 293, 322

Nanny Children's Workshop, 293
National Association for the Advancement of Colored People (NAACP), 42, 264
National Commercial Bank (NBC)
national democratic path, 116, 118
National Heroes Park, 42, 108
National Home Guard, 105
National Women's Organisation, 123
National Workers Union (NWU), 5
National Youth Organisation, 123
National Youth Service, 105
native elite, 91
Native Liberians, 242
Natural rights tradition, 183
Navahos, 155
Negritude, x, 87, 90, 146, 239, 241, 243, 246
Negus, Ras, 9, 28, 44, 50
Neruda, Pablo, 307
Nettleford, Rex, 11, 16, 41, 85–86, 314
Neville, Bongo, 26, 50
New International Economic Order, 152, 165
New Jewel Movement, 70, 116, 123, 285
New Negro, 242
New World Group, 18, 24, 145
newspapers, x, 58, 83, 125, 263
Newton, Huey, 29
Nicaragua, 132, 134–35, 291
Nicholson, Hilary, 260, 328
Nkrumah, Kwame, 42, 43, 147, 263
noisy aggression, 219
Nora, Pierre, 240
Northern Rhodesia (Zambia), 244, 259, 261
Nugent, Maria, 214–15
Nyasaland (Malawi), 259
Nyerere, Julius, 43, 145, 146, 173

OAU Liberation Committee, 50
Obiya (Obeah), 307

345

occidental cultural values, 200
occidental socialization, 194
Ogun, Omo, 25, 29
Oil Nut, 293
Oilfield Workers Trade Union (OWTU), 86
Ojo-Ade, Femi, 243, 245, 247
Okpewho, Isidore, 319, 327
ontological, 191–92, 193, 195, 198, 199, 200, 201, 203, 204, 297, 298, 300, 301, 302, 303, 304, 308
OPEC, 129
orality, xii, 317, 319, 321, 327
Ossie, Count, 50
Outlet, 57

Padmore, George, 19, 42, 142, 154, 255
Palisadoes Airport, 10, 13
Pan-Africanism, x, xi, 42, 64
Panama Canal, 3, 65, 166, 167
Papa Bois, 307
parochial Jamaican nationalism, 99
party gangs, 7
Patterson, Orlando, 49
Patterson, P.J., 74
Pearlie, 326–27
People's National Movement (PNM), 164
People's National Party (PNP), 5–7, 11, 22, 28, 32, 40, 50, 53, 55, 57, 58–59, 76, 97, 98, 102, 103, 104, 106, 112, 139, 167, 284, 285, 289, 291, 313
People's Revolutionary Government (PRG), 70, 75–76, 116
petit bourgeoisie, 143, 144, 148, 150, 158
Phillips, Peter, 48–49
Picasso, Pablo, 92
pioneering role, xi, 192, 265
Pivot, 57
Planno, Mortimo/Ras Planno, 10, 27, 44, 50

plural societies, 267
plural solutions, 267
pluralism, 267, 315
police violence, 40
Pollock, Jackson, 307
Post, Ken, viii, 1, 20, 21
postcolonial sexual citizenship, 327
Poupeye, Veerle, 92
Prince Buster's Record Shack, 26
public utilities, 117

Queenie, 326, 327

race and class, ix, 3, 41, 111, 112, 142, 148, 153
race relations, 110, 139, 263, 267, 269
raceless society, 264, 267
racial dimension, 169
racial hierarchy, 110
racial stereotypes, 162, 168
radicalisation of politics, 3
radicalism, 4, 45, 46, 58, 66, 68, 71, 73, 74–75, 78, 83, 84, 91, 151, 172, 181, 187, 311, 315, 329
rape, 325
Rasta (Rastafari/Rastafarians), viii, 8–12, 13, 20, 27, 28, 29, 39, 43–45, 47, 48, 50, 51, 52, 55, 57, 67, 72, 84, 93, 107, 109, 139, 142, 143, 164, 173, 281, 294, 297
Ratoon, 57
Reddock, Rhoda, 78
repatriation, 11, 41–43, 45, 50, 59, 67, 108
restorationist, 193, 194, 195
restrictions on voting rights, 152
resurgent Africanism, 199
Revivalism, 65
rock steady, 9, 12, 28
Rodney riots, 66
Rodney, Pat, 52
Rodney, Walter, viii, 13, 17, 19, 29, 39, 43, 46, 48, 49, 67, 68, 76, 84,

87, 104, 108, 109, 110, 140, 141, 173, 174
Roots, 243
Royal Africa Company, 179
rude boys, 8–9, 12, 13
Running African, 293
rural-urban migration, 47
Russian Revolution, 65

Saint Domingue, 191, 192, 195, 196, 197, 198, 199, 202, 203
Sangster, Donald, 102
School of Oriental and African Studies (SOAS), 49, 142
Scientific Socialism, 146, 147
Seaga, Edward, ix, 18, 19, 22, 59, 97–98, 100–13
Selassie, Emperor Haile, 9, 10, 41, 43, 45, 46, 49, 107, 109, 110
self-reliance, 46, 132, 145, 165
Seminoles, 155
Senghor, Leopold Sedar, 146
separatist tendencies, 252
Sett Girls, xi, 207, 210–14, 216, 218–21, 225–26
Shearer, Hugh, 17, 18, 22, 23, 40, 46, 51, 53–55, 56, 59, 102, 109
Sherlock, Sir Phillip, 16, 18
Simone, Nina, 307
Singapore, 166, 263
Single, Ras, 50
Sistren Theatre Collective (STC), xi, 311, 312
Sixth Pan African Congress, 147
ska, 8, 9, 19
slavery, xi, 2, 13, 76, 78–80, 93, 154, 177–80, 181–83, 185–86, 193–94, 196, 198, 199, 202, 203, 208, 209, 213, 221, 226, 239, 240, 241, 247, 268, 269, 297, 300, 30–303, 307, 314
slaves, 2, 10, 24, 35, 45, 79, 151, 178, 179, 182, 187, 193, 194, 196, 208, 210, 217, 220, 221, 223, 241

Sloly, Dennis, 26, 27
Small, Hugh, 22
Small, Jerry, 48, 50
Smith, M.G., 11, 99, 100, 111
social democrat, 269
socialism, 71, 76, 102, 103–104, 110, 113, 137, 141, 143–51, 155, 156, 157, 159, 165
socialist regimes, 146
Sorbonne students, 12
Soucouyant, 307
South Africa, 80, 165, 244
Southern Rhodesia (Rhodesia/ Zimbabwe), 16, 25, 244, 259, 260
Soviet Union, 91, 146, 164, 245
Special Branch, 46, 49, 51, 54, 56, 109
squatter settlements, 47
St Kitts, 33, 166, 215
St Lucia, 11, 132, 133, 167, 255
St Vincent and the Grenadines, 54, 57, 133, 167
state intimidation, 51
steel band, 273
Stone, Carl, 47
Student Christian Movement (SCM), 255
subversive fashionability, 218
subversive messages, 210
sugar belt, 329
Suriname, 132, 169
systems of domination, 208, 312

Tacky, 64
Tafari, Ras, 43–44
Taiwan, 167
Tanzania, 13, 142, 145–47, 173
Teacher Education Programme, 122
The Blackman, 43, 58, 253
The Crusader, 32
The Jungle, 92–93
The Keys, 256, 257
The New Jewel, 70, 116, 123, 125
Tignor, Robert, 250, 257–58, 263, 271

Tivoli Gardens, 8, 19
Torchlight, 125
Trade Union Recognition Law (TURL), 123
transatlantic slave trade, 39
Trinidad and Tobago, 164, 167, 298, 299, 300, 302
Trouillot, Michel Rolph, 203
Tse-tung, Mao, 157
Turkey, 165
Twelve Tribes, 59
Twin Seven Seven, 307

Ujamaa socialism, 145–46
Uncle Natty, 281
Unemployed Workers' Council, 23
African Communities League (ACL), 42
Universal Negro Improvement Association (UNIA), 10, 242, 297, 315
universalist principles, 195–97, 201
uprising, 30, 65, 138, 139, 224
utilitarian social welfare, 184

Van De Zee, James, 307
Vassell, Linnette, ix
Vastey, Pompee Valentin (Baron de Vastey), 192, 302
Vice Chancellor of UWI, 265
Vietnam, 149
Vodou, 200, 204
voluntary community work, 123

wa Thiong'o, Ngugi, 85
Walcott, Derek, 149, 307
West Africa, 13, 65, 251, 260, 266, 267, 268
West Indian, 2, 28, 58, 65, 88, 125, 211, 252, 254, 261, 262, 264, 265, 266, 269, 272, 273
West Indian Manhood Project, 88
West Indies Guild of University Teachers (WIGUT), 17

Western Kingston, 98
Western Marxism, 154
Wilberforce, William, 211
Williams, Eric, 78, 142, 164
worker participation, 105
Workers' Party of Jamaica, 31, 76, 112
world capitalist crisis, 128, 131
Wright, Richard, 154, 169
Wynter, Hector, 88
Wynter, Sylvia, x, 78, 86–88, 89–93, 143, 153, 154, 155

Xiaoping, Deng, 74, 157

Yoruba, 25, 155

Zand, Nicole, 243

www.ingramcontent.com/pod-product-compliance
Lightning Source LLC
Chambersburg PA
CBHW030218170426
43201CB00006B/124